Page deliberately left blank

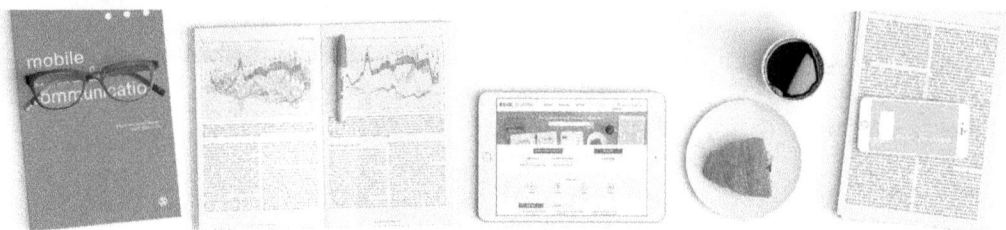

# Sign up for FREE updates about the latest research!

journals.sagepub.com/action/registration

Register online at SAGE Journals and start receiving...

## New Content Alerts

- Receive table of contents alerts when a new issue is published.

- Receive alerts when forthcoming articles are published online before they are scheduled to appear in print (OnlineFirst articles).

## Announcements

- Receive need-to-know information about a journal such as calls for papers, special issue notices, and events.

## Search Alerts

- Create custom search alerts based on recent search keywords or terms.

journals.sagepub.com

**⑤SAGE** journals

# THE
# ANNALS
## of the American Academy of
## Political and Social Science

VOLUME 691 | SEPTEMBER 2020

## The Rise of the Regulatory Welfare State:
## The Use and Abuse of Social Regulation

SPECIAL EDITORS:

**David Levi-Faur**

*Hebrew University of Jerusalem*

**Avishai Benish**

*Hebrew University of Jerusalem*

# ⑨SAGE

Los Angeles | London | New Delhi
Singapore | Washington DC | Melbourne

# The American Academy of Political and Social Science

202 S. 36th Street, Annenberg School for Communication, University of Pennsylvania,
Philadelphia, PA 19104-3806; (215) 746-6500; (215) 573-2667 (fax); www.aapss.org

---

**Origin and Purpose.** The Academy was organized December 14, 1889, to promote the progress of political and social science, especially through publications and meetings. The Academy does not take sides in controverted questions, but seeks to gather and present reliable information to assist the public in forming an intelligent and accurate judgment.

**Meetings.** The Academy occasionally holds a meeting in the spring extending over two days.

**Publications.** THE ANNALS of The American Academy of Political and Social Science is the bimonthly publication of the Academy. Each issue contains articles on some prominent social or political problem, written at the invitation of the editors. These volumes constitute important reference works on the topics with which they deal, and they are extensively cited by authorities throughout the United States and abroad.

**Subscriptions.** THE ANNALS of The American Academy of Political and Social Science (ISSN 0002-7162) (J295) is published bimonthly—in January, March, May, July, September, and November—by SAGE Publishing, 2455 Teller Road, Thousand Oaks, CA 91320. Periodicals postage paid at Thousand Oaks, California, and at additional mailing offices. POSTMASTER: Send address changes to The Annals of The American Academy of Political and Social Science, c/o SAGE Publishing, 2455 Teller Road, Thousand Oaks, CA 91320. Institutions may subscribe to THE ANNALS at the annual rate: $1257 (clothbound, $1419). Individuals may subscribe to the ANNALS at the annual rate: $134 (clothbound, $197). Single issues of THE ANNALS may be obtained by individuals for $41 each (clothbound, $58). Single issues of THE ANNALS have proven to be excellent supplementary texts for classroom use. Direct inquiries regarding adoptions to THE ANNALS c/o SAGE Publishing (address below).

All correspondence concerning membership in the Academy, dues renewals, inquiries about membership status, and/or purchase of single issues of THE ANNALS should be sent to THE ANNALS c/o SAGE Publishing, 2455 Teller Road, Thousand Oaks, CA 91320. Telephone: (800) 818-SAGE (7243) and (805) 499-0721; Fax/Order line: (805) 375-1700; e-mail: journals@sagepub.com. *Please note that orders under $30 must be prepaid.* For all customers outside the Americas, please visit http://www.sagepub.co.uk/customerCare.nav for information.

# THE ANNALS

Editorial Office: 202 S. 36th Street, Philadelphia, PA 19104-3806
For information about individual and institutional subscriptions address:
SAGE Publishing
2455 Teller Road
Thousand Oaks, CA 91320

For SAGE Publishing: Peter Geraghty (Production)

From India and South Asia, write to:
SAGE PUBLICATIONS INDIA Pvt Ltd
B-42 Panchsheel Enclave, P.O. Box 4109
New Delhi 110 017
INDIA

From Europe, the Middle East, and Africa, write to:
SAGE PUBLICATIONS LTD
1 Oliver's Yard, 55 City Road
London EC1Y 1SP
UNITED KINGDOM

International Standard Serial Number ISSN 0002-7162
ISBN 978-1-0718-4071-9 (Vol. 691, 2020) paper
ISBN 978-1-0718-4073-3 (Vol. 691, 2020) cloth
First printing, September 2020

Information about membership rates, institutional subscriptions, and back issue prices may be found on the facing page.

**Advertising.** Current rates and specifications may be obtained by writing to The Annals Advertising and Promotion Manager at the Thousand Oaks office (address above). Acceptance of advertising in this journal in no way implies endorsement of the advertised product or service by SAGE or the journal's affiliated society(ies) or the journal editor(s). No endorsement is intended or implied. SAGE reserves the right to reject any advertising it deems as inappropriate for this journal.

**Claims.** Claims for undelivered copies must be made no later than six months following month of publication. The publisher will supply replacement issues when losses have been sustained in transit and when the reserve stock will permit.

**Change of Address.** Six weeks' advance notice must be given when notifying of change of address. Please send the old address label along with the new address to the SAGE office address above to ensure proper identification. Please specify the name of the journal.

# THE
# ANNALS
## of the American Academy of
## Political and Social Science

VOLUME 691 | SEPTEMBER 2020

IN THIS ISSUE:

*The Rise of the Regulatory Welfare State:*
*The Use and Abuse of Social Regulation*

Special Editors: DAVID LEVI-FAUR and AVISHAI BENISH

# FORTHCOMING

*Toward a Better Approach to Preventing, Identifying, and Addressing Child Maltreatment*
Special Editors: LAWRENCE M. BERGER and KRISTEN S. SLACK

*The Dynamics of Homelessness: Research and Policy*
Special Editors: BARRETT A. LEE, MARYBETH SHINN, and DENNIS P. CULHANE

The preface presents the main themes of this special issue. It starts by presenting the argument that the welfare state and the regulatory state are not dichotomies, arguing that both regulation and fiscal transfers for social purposes are increasing, particularly after the financial crisis of 2007, the climate crisis, and the COVID-19 crisis. Then it moves to introduce the articles that compose this special issue, their arguments, and their theoretical and empirical contributions.

# The Reassertion of the Regulatory Welfare State: A Preface

By
AVISHAI BENISH
and
DAVID LEVI-FAUR

*Keywords:* welfare state; regulation; governance; social services; social benefits; fiscal transfers; social rights

This special issue explores the expansion of regulation in the welfare state and in the social policy arena. Regulation and fiscal transfer by governments for social purposes have always been intertwined, before, during, and after the heyday of the welfare state after the Second World War. Both continue to grow, although regulation is growing faster and perhaps further than fiscal transfer. As the articles in this special issue demonstrate, they reassert

*Avishai Benish is an assistant professor (tenured) at the Paul Baerwald School of Social Work and Social Welfare at the Hebrew University of Jerusalem. His fields of expertise are social law and administration, and his main research is on regulation and governance reforms in welfare states.*

*David Levi-Faur is a professor of regulation and policy in the Department of Political Science and the Federmann School of Public Policy at the Hebrew University of Jerusalem. He is a founding editor of* Regulation & Governance, *a journal that serves as the leading platform for the study of regulation and governance in the social sciences.*

NOTE: We would like to thank the Israeli Science Foundation for their Research Grant (1029/15) and Workshops Grant (2223/18). This is also the opportunity to thank our research assistants, Yuval Peleg, Daniel Hirsch, and Tslil Landau.

Correspondence: levifaur@mail.huji.ac.il

DOI: 10.1177/0002716220949216

themselves in day-to-day policies, in grand designs, and in the structure and expansion of the state itself—even as private actors and jurisdictions beyond the state (global and regional) are growing (Levi-Faur 2012).

With the financial crisis of 2007, the climate crisis, and the COVID-19 crisis, the regulatory welfare state (RWS) is reasserting itself. Legitimacy and effectiveness of social benefits and services are again assumed and expected by the mainstream political parties. To a varying extent they are indeed provided by states and not only, or not primarily, by markets or civil society. In this special issue, we challenge the long-established suggestion that regulation replaces the locus of redistribution in the welfare institutions that were built after the Great Depression and the postwar era (1945–1975).

We argue that regulation for social purposes is actually *increasing*. This was especially the case after the post-2008 politics of austerity, and this also seems to be the case today amid the global COVID-19 pandemic and its expected aftermath. The welfare state, with its poor laws origin (in Tudor's England and elsewhere), was always regulatory. What was different, then and now, were the laws' purpose, the subjects, the techniques, and the administrative mechanisms in which regulation was used to constitute, distribute, and redistribute welfare and society.

Still, and as suggested in this special issue most explicitly by John Braithwaite's paper, the COVID-19 pandemic is a dramatic, current illustration of how crises—financial crises, climate crises, health crises—have economic, social, health, and political implications. Our world seems to move toward a larger RWS and a more formidably regulatory form of capitalism. If we had doubts about the growth of the state, the current COVID-19 and economic crises should serve to remind us of its centrality. At the same time, it should reinforce it as a political institution that grows significantly out of social and popular demands in times of crisis.

The opening article of the special issue, by Benish and Levi-Faur, provides an historical and theoretical account for the concept of regulatory welfare. It outlines the concept of the RWS, showing that regulatory welfare is an emerging but still greatly understudied field in contemporary research. By transcending the "welfare state" versus "regulatory state" dichotomy, we analyze the interplay between these concepts in an age of rapid expansion of regulation through liberalization, privatization, and the new public management of social services. We then provide a multifaceted explanation of the RWS by presenting analytical frameworks of the concept in three central dimensions: the normative, the institutional, and the individual.

John Braithwaite's article, "Meta Governance of Path Dependencies: Regulation, Welfare, and Markets," asserts that regulation, welfare, and markets grow interdependently, often shaping, reinforcing, and supporting each other. Regulation-welfare-market interdependence is conceived as a path-dependent governance ensemble. Crises often drive those path dependencies. Path dependencies of co-expansion from one institutional arena reach into opportunities opened up by path dependence for expansion in other institutional arenas. Markets allow the expansion of welfare states. Welfare states create demand for regulatory state services that help to solve perceived welfare problems. New crises create opportunities for new path dependencies for growth of market, regulatory, and welfare institutions. Then, mutually reinforcing tendencies of one institutional arena to seize opportunities for expansion in other arenas engender a capitalism of expanding markets, expanding welfare, and expanding regulation. The particular character of crises that challenge capitalist institutions creates demand for expansion of the welfare state. Crises grow problem-solving innovation in markets (e.g., carbon markets) and expand regulation. There is enormous path-dependent momentum toward interdependent risk of ecological crises, economic crises, and security crises. Yet regulatory-welfare-market path dependencies might be mustered to counter it. Perhaps only path dependence can muster the momentum to govern path dependence? Meta governance can steer path-dependent regulation, welfare, and markets for the governance of path-dependent crises. In such a game, policy-makers do not directly pull levers as much as harness path dependencies. More and less successful responses to the COVID-19 pandemic illustrate these policy dynamics.

Hanan Haber's article, "The Political Economy of Regulating for Welfare: Regulation Preventing Loss of Access to Basic Services in the UK, Sweden, the EU, and Israel," raises two questions. First, what does the state do to prevent consumers from losing access to basic services in the market due to financial hardship? Second, how and under what conditions will loss of access to basic services occur? To answer these questions, Haber brings the literature on regulatory governance together with that on the welfare state. The evidence is discussed in a comparative analysis of eleven regimes for preventing loss of access: in the electricity and housing credit sectors in the UK, Sweden, Israel, and the EU, with additional comparisons made to the water sector in the three national cases, from the early 1990s to the 2010s. Regulation addressing this issue was introduced in all but the Swedish cases, in which regulation preventing the loss of services is either absent or provided by social services. This leads Haber to suggest that the institutions of the welfare state set the context within which regulation at the sectoral level will develop. A comprehensive welfare state, as in Sweden, mitigates the social risks that lead to debt, arrears, and service termination, thus reducing the demand for regulation at the sectoral level. The opposite is true in residual welfare states. Alternative explanations, such as Right-Left partisanship and the role of social need and focusing events, do not seem to play a similarly significant role. Haber's findings highlight how the RWS developed in the context of, and as a complement to, the national welfare states, as well as the significance of regulation for the future study of the welfare state.

Miriam Hartlapp's article, "Measuring and Comparing the Regulatory Welfare State: Social Objectives in Public Procurement," asserts that social regulation has the potential to create more solidarity, equality, social cohesion, and justice not only within the welfare state, but also in other policy areas. She constructs an index to capture the strength of social objectives in the economy. The index draws on theories of economic regulation and the welfare state literature to develop a general understanding of social objectives. It combines three analytically distinct dimensions of regulation: the substance of provisions, as well as their outcomes in the dimensions of potential impact and enforcement. Thus, the index covers a larger proportion of the policy cycle than regulatory output only, and it goes beyond a formal view to include potential impact and enforcement. The application of the index is illustrated for public procurement regulation in France and Germany. It shows an overall increase in the strength of social objectives that point toward a growing potential for public procurement to achieve wider societal benefits. The index also brings to the fore that in the regulation of the economy, different social objectives are prioritized in France and Germany. While regulation in Germany is particularly strong with relation to individual social rights that support employers who find themselves as the weaker party in a market relationship, French regulation is oriented toward collective goals of social solidarity and equality in markets. These differences underline country-specific relationships between the welfare state and social objectives that suggests a close conceptual link. Consequently, future analysis interested in causal explanations of the RWS beyond social policy should not be limited to theories of economic regulation. Rather, they would benefit from drawing more explicitly on the complex explanations offered in the welfare state literature.

Caroline de la Porte, Trine P. Larsen, and Dorota Szelewa's article, "A Gender Equalizing Regulatory Welfare State? Enacting the EU's Work-Life Balance Directive in Denmark and Poland," analyzes whether the EU could be emerging as a gender equalizing RWS. Specifically, it examines the tensions that have arisen in Denmark and Poland due to EU regulations of paid parental leave. Drawing on the Europeanization, feminist, and RWS literatures, the authors develop three analytical concepts to capture tensions that arise from regulatory decisions at a higher level of governance but that require implementation and funding at lower levels of governance. The concepts, which could be relevant for future RWS analyses, are EU-national subsidiarity, state-family subsidiarity, and fiscal constraint. Their findings show that the tensions shape the positions of the actors both before and after the adoption of the directive. In both countries, there are similar parental leave schemes ex-ante, and similar positions of the major actors' initial stance on parental leave, favoring stagnation. Yet the plans of implementation show how the actor positions changed, and the likely result is double expansion and degenderization of parental leave. Although in two different institutional settings, the similar outcome suggests that these changes are due to the EU being an emerging RWS, which influences member states in terms of regulatory instruments with fiscal elements.

Philipp Trein's article, "Bossing or Protecting? The Integration of Social Regulation into the Welfare State," empirically analyzes how social regulation is integrated into the welfare state, comparing integration within health, migration, and unemployment policy. He uses an original dataset measuring policy change events that integrate social regulation and welfare in Australia, Austria, Canada, Belgium, France, Germany, Italy, the Netherlands, New Zealand, Sweden, Switzerland, the UK, and the U.S. from 1980 to 2014. His results show that governments have pursued such reforms, in the three policy fields, in all countries. Nevertheless, in migration and unemployment policy, regulation and welfare are more tightly coupled, and welfare services have a higher potential to be conditional upon compliance with regulations. Furthermore, countries differ regarding how reforms integrating regulation and welfare are complemented with cash transfers. Trein argues that such reforms can pursue a double goal, as they serve to control and "boss" citizens but are also an instrument to protect them from new social risks. The integration of regulation and welfare can provide better protection from risks, such as unemployment and bad health, but it can also mean that the state has new capacities to drive individuals to take up any job and send back migrants and refugees due to minor offences and social noncompliance. Trein concludes the article by pointing to two different approaches in social policy to the integration of regulation and welfare. The first is a "regulation first approach," in which the government uses primarily social regulations to improve welfare and transfer measures have a complementary role. The second is a "transfer first approach," which contains the primary use of transfers and in which social regulations play a secondary role.

Wei Li and Bao Yang's article, "Politics, Markets and Modes of Contract Governance: Regulating Social Services in Shanghai and Chongqing, China," affirms that the concept of the RWS captures the recent expansion of expenditure on and regulation of social service contracts by the Chinese government. The article identifies four primary modes of governance in regulating contracting processes and contract implementation: market-based, hierarchical, professional, and relational. Each mode represents a form of regulatory welfare that advances different values and uses different accountability mechanisms. Trade-offs and overlaps among the four modes pose both challenges and opportunities for effective regulation. Based on a comparative analysis of contract governance modes in Shanghai and Chongqing, the study finds that governments in two localities prioritize and integrate the hierarchical and relational modes, relying less on the market-based and professional modes. The emphasis on the hierarchical-relational mode advances the values and mechanisms of trust, adaptation, and alignment with top-down priorities, but may hinder public and legal accountability. The dominance of this hybrid mode is atypical in democratic welfare states and reflects China's authoritarian and transitional context. The study posits that dynamics between political context and market conditions affect the formation and effectiveness of hybrid modes of contract governance. Regulators in different countries are advised to factor in such dynamics when designing contract governance modes in regulating social services.

Tanja Klenk's paper, "Views from Below: Inspectors Coping with Hybrid Accountabilities," explores hybrid accountabilities in the regulation of long-term care service provision. Tanja Klenk asks how inspectors who are responsible for the implementation of regulations handle the uncertainties arising from hybrid accountabilities. In the case of long-term care provision, hybrid accountabilities result from blurring boundaries between market, bureaucracy, and professionalism. Actors, values, and mechanisms from different accountability regimes are mixed and integrated into a new hybrid accountability regime. While the prevailing interpretation in the literature is that hybridity creates tensions that have a negative impact on the quality of regulation, she demonstrates that different accountabilities can also reinforce each other. However, situations in which

inspectors can develop a positive stance toward hybridity and integrate competing logics are rare. Hybrid professionalism requires training, education, and
resources, as well as a joint regulatory culture with inspectees—preconditions
that are hardly present in recent institutional settings of long-term care regulation. The results of the study have implications for policy: first, working conditions of quality care inspectors are crucial for the design of more effective
accountability relations. Decent work seems to be a necessary, although not sufficient, condition for enabling inspectors to integrate competing logics in a meaningful way. Second, the empirical results also indicate that welfare markets with
fierce competition result in inspector-inspectee relationships that hamper the
establishment of a joint regulatory culture.

Lihi Lahat's article, "Changing Expectations? The Change in the Role of the
Welfare Ministry in the Regulation of Personal Social Services," suggests that
many welfare states have increased their regulatory role, but research has given
little attention to historical changes in the regulatory role of ministries. Her study
embraces a mezzo perspective and explores the regulatory role of the Welfare
Ministry of Israel in the field of personal social services, asking the following
questions: 1) What are the changes in regulatory expectations versus practices
over the last five decades? 2) How can we explain these changes and their outcomes? Methodologically, it is a qualitative analysis and data sources include
mainly the Israeli State Comptroller Reports and other resources. The findings
reveal a growing gap between society's expectations of the Ministry as a regulator
versus its capacities. The study makes a theoretical contribution by identifying
the different intensities of the expectations-abilities gaps, which create a variety
of regulatory spaces in a RWS. The Israeli case is relevant for other countries that
have experienced processes of outsourcing and privatization in the welfare state
and whose ministries had to change their practices to encompass a more profound regulatory role.

Renate Reiter's article, "Is Service Quality a Driver of the Regulatory Welfare
State? Policies for Health Services in Germany and France," empirically analyzes
which factors shape the design and development of the RWS in the field of social
services. It argues that the discovery of the issue of service quality in the 1990s had
the potential to accelerate RWS's development. Using the example of the health
sector in Germany and France, two countries that represent a similar type of welfare state but also exhibit striking differences in their national regulatory styles,
Reiter examines the interplay of long-term institutional factors and short-term
political factors in the establishment and development of the RWS. Using qualitative comparative analysis, she shows that in Germany, characterized by a corporatist state tradition and a cooperative regulatory style, the political debate on quality
(either as a parameter of competition or as a concept for the professional consolidation of service production) had a greater influence on the design of the national
quality regulation system (goals, instruments, processes, institutions) than in
France, which is characterized by a state-centered Napoleonic tradition and a
directive regulatory style.

Lilach Litor, Gila Menahem, and Hadara Bar-Mor's article, "The Rise of the
Regulatory Constitutional Welfare State, Publicization, and Constitutional Social

Rights: The Case of Israel and Britain," deals with the role that courts play in shaping changes in the way governments provide social services in recent years, done primarily by applying publicization to private bodies. They suggest that publicization of private entities supplying social services is one mode of interaction between regulatory and welfare regimes. More specifically they suggest publicization, as one of a range of interactions between goals and tools, may shape a space for the two regimes' coexistence. Their study investigates publicization, applied by the courts to "transform" private social service suppliers into hybrid entities. Such declarations allow private service suppliers to be subjected to dual systems of law—private and public. Hence, courts, by recognizing private entities as hybrid bodies, preserve the continuity of welfare norms in privatized welfare arenas. Courts nevertheless differ in their use of organic (focusing on the type of connection maintained with the public authority) versus functional (stressing the task performed) tests in the application of public law norms to private entities. Based on the different patterns of publicization employed, the authors identify two variants of regulatory regimes: the *regulatory constitutional welfare state* and the *regulatory constitutional neoliberal welfare state*. To examine the fruitfulness of this distinction, they then examine the welfare services domain in two jurisprudences—that of Israel and that of the UK. An analysis of these systems shows that differences in their rulings have shaped important aspects of each variant of the regulatory state. Their analysis contributes to the development of the theory of the polymorphic state, where the state can extend its various roles simultaneously. Their contribution focuses on the role of courts in the formation of the variants identified.

Linda Voigt and Reimut Zohlnhöfer's article, "Quiet Politics of Employment Protection Legislation? Partisan Politics, Electoral Competition, and the Regulatory Welfare State," discusses the role of political parties and party competition in explaining the expansion and retrenchment of the RWS. Voigt and Zohlnhöfer examine the claim that the RWS is driven by "quiet politics" beyond partisan differences and electoral competition and analyze that argument both theoretically and empirically for employment protection legislation (EPL). EPL is a mature and often politically salient instrument of the RWS. It aims to protect vulnerable groups, essentially by making dismissals more difficult. While the program thus shields certain groups from the risk of unemployment, employers experience substantial interventions in their managerial prerogatives and economists have claimed that EPL might affect the labor market negatively. Consequently, EPL has experienced substantial retrenchment since the mid-1980s. Given the substantially different preferences of employers and workers and the potential tradeoffs between social protection and employment growth, EPL is a most-likely-case for the applicability of theoretical approaches regarding partisan politics developed for the study of the spending welfare state. Voigt and Zohlnhöfer test three prominent mechanisms for how electoral competition conditions partisan effects from that literature: the composition of Left parties' electorates, the strength of pro-EPL parties, and the emphasis put on social justice by pro-EPL parties. Analyzing EPL in twenty-one established democracies since 1985, they find that the partisan politics of EPL is conditioned by electoral competition only under very specific circumstances. The emphasis put on social justice in election manifestos by Left parties has different effects on the EPL policies of governing Christian democrats depending on whether the Left is in opposition to or in a governing coalition with Christian democrats. Moreover, these effects are only statistically significant for employment protection for regular employment.

Işık D. Özel and Salvador Parrado's article focuses on the "Varieties of Regulatory Welfare Regimes in Middle-Income Countries: A Comparative Analysis of Brazil, Mexico, and Turkey." They suggest that the expansion of social welfare regimes has become a global phenomenon in a number of middle-income countries (MICs) and involves the adoption of robust social assistance programs. Aiming to alleviate poverty and diminish inequalities, most of these programs entail noncontributory, means-tested conditional cash transfers (CCTs). Examining the regulatory governance of the CCTs, the authors focus on the processes of selection and recertification of beneficiaries. They state that the ways in which those processes are regulated may either create ample room or minimize the space for political discretion. Based on a comparative analysis of three MICs, they identify a variety of social assistance regulatory regimes, namely "loose decentralism" in Brazil, "strict centralism" in Mexico, and "subcontracted *dirigisme*" in Turkey. They illustrate that the regulatory design is key to understanding how the newly flourishing welfare regimes in these countries can control political manipulation.

There are several important implications of this article. Where such manipulation occurs, social assistance programs may deviate from their initial objectives and partially fail to reach the poor. Targeting errors and recertification failures may cause contestations of the concerning programs and trigger fairness concerns which, in turn, may impede their sustainability, endangering the welfare of the poor. Moreover, potential misallocation of public funds might lower trust in the government and political institutions. Where they work in line with their objectives, eschewing political discretion, regulatory welfare states in social assistance may enhance trust in and legitimacy of political institutions. A centrally regulated social assistance governance nurtured by local knowledge should be a key element to avoid political manipulation and attaining the objective of alleviating poverty, a major issue in the MICs.

John Lapidus's article, "Indirect and Invisible Regulations Set in Stone: A Driving Force behind the Rise of Private Health Insurance in Sweden," suggests that the Swedish welfare model is gradually losing its characteristics, noticed not least by the extensive privatization of provision and the emerging privatization of funding, primarily through new and half-private services in healthcare, education, and elderly care. The clearest example is the rapid rise of private health insurance, which is now signed by every tenth person of working age. This article points out the different types of regulations that have provoked the rise of private health insurance, especially the extensive privatization of provision, and it discusses those types of regulations that could potentially slow it down. Regulations fomenting private health insurance are indirect and sometimes hidden or even invisible, while regulations that would interfere and slow down the progress are perceived as very ambitious and far-reaching. The article goes on to analyze three official welfare investigations and their reports published from 2016 to 2019. The investigations avoid discussing the decisive regulations they are supposed to discuss, and sometimes they go against their own directives to do so. The article demonstrates that regulations for private health insurance have occurred without much debate, while every potential regulation against private health insurance is very much disputed. The rapid rise of private health insurance forms part of a development of increasing inequality in general, with income as a strong example. This article argues that private health insurance is one of many steps away from the traditional Swedish welfare model and that it challenges the first paragraph of the Swedish Healthcare Act, stating that healthcare shall be given due to needs and on equal terms for all citizens.

Sora Lee and Valerie Braithwaite's article, "Missing in Action: Bridging Capital and Cross-Boundary Discourse," uses two specific welfare-to-work programs, one in Korea and one in Australia, to illustrate the institutional interconnections that are in play within the RWS, and then proceeds to argue that in situ, individuals are lacking discursive infrastructure and the will to discover a new language and a new way of thinking about governance in the RWS. At the implementation coalface, people are steeped in messiness and are looking to authorities to make sense of what is happening and work with them to solve the problems on the ground. Authorities, on the other hand, appear blind to intelligence from beyond their power base. They are blinded by old institutional categories that pit market mentalities against welfare mentalities with regulation as an ideological tool, rather than an integral part of the solution in successfully interconnecting institutional forms. Genuine transparency and cross-boundary listening are necessary to create the bridging capital to reconnect democratic governments with their citizens. At the heart of the problem is lack of trust, a problem that becomes particularly acute as the COVID-19 crises, financial crises, and environmental crises accelerate and demand effective responses from democratically elected governments. Governments need to be embedded in the best intelligence to earn trust through competence: it may be timely to revisit the benefits of street-level bureaucrats to answer the question, what's happening on the ground? Politicians need to hone their skills of listening and seeking wise counsel to answer community needs, another element of earning trust. And finally, leaders must be capable of assimilating and explaining the best intelligence and advice and acting decisively, yet humbly, in the face of complexity and uncertainty.

Tobias Schulze-Cleven's article, "Organizing Competition: Regulatory Welfare States in Higher Education," takes us to the field of higher education. Governments around the world have turned to higher education to sustain economic development and social welfare. This article uses the concept of the RWS to examine how state authorities in the United States and Germany have sought to spur structural changes in the education sector. Schulze-Cleven argues that policy-makers have combined fiscal and regulatory policies to organize competition among universities by sharpening the market principles of self-reliance, rivalry, and decentralized decision-making. The analysis, moreover, contends that understanding the variability of institutional transformations cross-nationally requires putting evolving national regimes of state-university relations into historical perspective. A historical institutionalist approach to regulatory welfare states in higher education illuminates states' shifting governance strategies as important drivers of the sector's contemporary reimagination and clarifies the ongoing recomposition of broader public infrastructures. It also helps to identify negative side effects of regulation-induced change that raise questions about the quality and scope of the welfare being promoted.

Finally, Avishai Benish's article, "The Logics of Hybrid Accountability: When the State, the Market and Professionalism Interact," suggests that although the delivery of public services increasingly operates under multiple and hybrid public, market, and professional accountability regimes, we have much still to learn about how these accountability regimes mingle and relate to each other. The article develops an analytical framework for systematically analyzing hybrids of public, market, and professional accountability and their respective underlying logics. The level of compatibility among these regimes is assessed by the compatibility of their goals, values, and principles, as well as the compatibility of their steering mechanisms. The analysis is informed and illustrated by empirical studies on accountability in welfare state services, a field that offers a wealth of empirical evidence on hybrid accountability arrangements. The article concludes by discussing the interplay between accountability regimes and the conditions under which they undermine or reinforce each other. It stresses that compatibility between regimes significantly depends on the content of accountability rather than on accountability mechanisms, which are usually emphasized in the literature; and it highlights the importance of trust between the parties entering into accountability relations and the proximity of their institutional logics.

# Reference

Levi-Faur, David. 2012. From "big government" to "big governance." *The Oxford handbook of governance*, ed. David Levi-Faur, 3–18. New York, NY: Oxford University Press.

# The Expansion of Regulation in Welfare Governance

By
AVISHAI BENISH
and
DAVID LEVI-FAUR

This article provides an historical and theoretical account of the emerging regulatory welfare state, which is greatly understudied in contemporary regulatory and welfare research. We analyze the interplay between the *welfare state* and the *regulatory state* in an age in which regulation is expanding through liberalization, privatization, and the new public management of social services. We then provide a multi faceted framework for understanding the regulatory welfare state and discuss its implications in terms of 1) the normative social goals of the state; 2) the ways in which social policy is delivered through institutions; and 3) the implications of the framework for individuals' rights and duties.

*Keywords:*   welfare state; regulation; governance; social services; social benefits; privatization; social rights

O ver the last four decades we have witnessed a rapid growth of regulation within and outside welfare and social arenas, such as the regulation of private old-age pension funds and the regulation of non–state actors providing welfare-to-work services. This growth has

*Avishai Benish is an assistant professor (tenured) at the Paul Baerwald School of Social Work and Social Welfare at the Hebrew University of Jerusalem. His fields of expertise are social law and administration, and his main research is on regulation and governance reforms in welfare states.*

*David Levi-Faur is professor of regulation and policy in the Department of Political Science and the Federmann School of Public Policy at the Hebrew University of Jerusalem. He is a founding editor of* Regulation & Governance, *a top journal that serves as the leading platform for the study of regulation and governance in the social sciences.*

NOTE: We would like to thank the Israeli Science Foundation for their Research Grant (1029/15) and Workshops Grant (2223/18). This is also the opportunity to thank our research assistants Yuval Peleg, Daniel Hirsch, and Tslil Landau.

Correspondence: levifaur@mail.huji.ac.il

DOI: 10.1177/0002716220949230

been driven by different processes, causes, and actors, including changes in governments and public welfare preferences; a growing capacity to regulate beneficiaries of welfare programs; a growing emphasis on quality of services; new, potential conflicts of interests; and the search for more cost-effective welfare governance. The expansion of regulation is not unique to welfare; it is a part of a larger regulatory expansion that affects—negatively as well as positively—the wider environment of our governing institutions. Regulation comes from global, regional, and national actors and institutions. It affects all regulatory regimes, and it has distributive, redistributive, and constitutive processes and outcomes. Privatization, marketization, and commodification processes are critically important in the growth of regulation. Freer markets mean more rules, and this holds true for welfare markets. More rules are needed to constitute and promote welfare markets (such as in the field of pensions) and to secure competition among private providers. In addition, policy-makers and policy advocates increasingly turn to regulatory instruments for promoting welfare norms and outcomes in privatized and liberalized markets. Likewise, with the widespread outsourcing of social services, regulation is increasingly used for steering services and protecting users' rights vis-à-vis non-state service providers. Social regulation is also dominant at the supranational level, such as in the EU (e.g., the EU's work-life balance directive) and in nongovernmental initiatives (e.g., the International Organization for Standardization's social responsibility standards). Thus, regulation, which was somewhat a "hidden side" of social policy, has become much more visible in these new forms of welfare state governance, redefining policies and state roles in society and in the economy.

Welfare governance and regulation and their relations have impacts also on the "theory of the state." This means that the state, as *the* meta-organization of our political, economic, and social life, is taken seriously, and that we need to think about the relations between regulations and welfare as well as the relations between the regulatory state and the welfare state. Two approaches are visible and influential. According to one approach, regulation and the regulatory state replace and transform the postwar welfare state (e.g., Majone 1997). An alternative approach, however, suggests that the regulatory state and the welfare state largely coexist and co-expand, that the state is polymorphic, and that in welfare governance it is useful—theoretically and empirically—to focus on the "regulatory welfare state" (RWS) (Levi-Faur 2013, 2014; Benish, Haber, and Eliahou 2017).

The theoretical work around the RWS is slowly growing, but it is still largely understudied in contemporary regulatory and welfare research. The goal of this article is therefore to attract more attention to the interaction and co-dynamics of regulation and welfare, social and economic regulation, and the regulatory and welfare state. This work reflects the ongoing collaboration between an international group of scholars working on this concept via conference meetings and workshops in the last three years. We believe it will be of broad interest to policy-makers and scholars across a wide range of disciplines. In this article, we provide a historical and theoretical account of the concept of regulatory welfare. Transcending the *welfare state* versus *regulatory state* dichotomy, we analyze the interplay between these concepts and provide analytical frameworks for understanding the meaning of regulatory welfare at normative, institutional, and individual levels.

# The Relations between the Welfare State and the Regulatory State

There is no single definition or common agreement for what the welfare state is. Generally speaking, the term refers to the extent to which states pursue social goals in the effort to uphold values of equality, solidarity, fairness, and social justice (the normative dimension) and the institutions that implement these goals (the institutional dimension) (Leisering 2011). Most scholars see the welfare state as a relatively new, innovative, and social-democratic postwar institution, while others see it as a much older institution and expect it to have an effect and a presence well beyond social democratic values and ideologies. Despite these differences and debates, we assert that at the minimum the welfare state attempts to decommodify some social and economic needs (in domains such as health, education, and living standards) and secure them to each individual as a citizenship-based social right, irrespective of their position in the market as workers or consumers. The scope of this commitment varies, with their minimal decommodification in conservative welfare states, which tend to be concerned with maintaining status, and more provisions in social democratic welfare states, which take a more universal and generous approach to benefits and services (Esping-Andersen 1990). However, despite the noble goals of caring and support, the welfare state also has paternalistic features toward individuals, and is often criticized as a social control mechanism for "regulating the poor" in a disciplinary, paternalistic, and sometimes punitive manner (Piven and Cloward 2012). Most efforts to "measure" the welfare state focus on fiscal transfer, assuming—and at the same time reinforcing—the idea that decommodification is done mainly through fiscal transfer rather than through the institutionalization of rights.

The dominant interpretation suggests that the welfare state emerged after, and as a response to, the night-watchman state of the nineteenth century with its radical economic liberalism of *laissez-faire* capitalism. In that period, civil society systems (such as households and communities' charitable or religious organizations) were the source of welfare. But these systems failed to mitigate the excessive levels of poverty and social segregation produced by laissez-faire capitalism. The welfare state extended its reach in Western capitalist democracies during the first decades of the twentieth century as a political response to the realities of laissez-faire systems, with its high-water mark in the postwar period from the 1950s to the 1970s. States took over much of the responsibility for welfare by delivering services in fields such as education, health, social care, and income maintenance. Policy-makers perceived these services as being different and separate from market delivery (Gilbert 2005), aimed to protect market flaws and serve as a form of politics of states *against* markets (Leisering 2012, 141).

However, since the 1970s, a combination of forces—the ascendancy of neoliberal ideology, economic globalization, and intensive social and demographic changes—have led to an ongoing crisis of welfare states all over the world (Dean 2015; Pierson 1998; Taylor-Gooby 2013). Neoliberalism has played a central role in challenging the welfare state on both its normative and institutional foundations. Those who ascribed to neoliberalism harshly criticized the welfare state for its intense intervention in economic and social life and for undermining personal responsibility and work incentives while encouraging economic dependence, passivity, and poverty traps. In addition, they also criticized social welfare institutions for being inefficient, unresponsive, cumbersome, paternalistic, self-serving and fiscally irresponsible. This criticism was accompanied by a call for rolling back the state from its welfare role and delegating welfare responsibilities back to civil society and to individuals and markets.

The process of privatization (i.e., the rollback of the state from state-owned enterprises and public services), mainly in the economic sphere, is the context in which the discussion about the rise of the regulatory state made its first impact. Majone (1994), in his highly influential work on the rise of the regulatory state, identified this period as an era of transition from the positive (welfare) state to the regulatory state. He observed that since the 1970s, Western governments have shifted from direct intervention in the economy to achieve social, political, and economic goals to the regulation of privatized and liberalized markets with the aim of correcting market failures and promoting economic efficiency. This transition was reflected, for instance, in the increasing economic integration through rulemaking within the EU and in large-scale privatization of state-owned enterprises and utilities (Obinger, Schmitt, and Zohlnhöfer 2014). It was also reflected in a host of public administrative reforms—under titles such as "New Public Management" (NPM) (Hood 1991) and "entrepreneurial government" (Osborn and Gaebler 1992)—which sought to infuse market and private sector culture into the management of public services.

Majone's conceptualization of the regulatory state has imprinted the notion that the welfare state and the regulatory state are opposing and competing forms of state organization. According to his theorization, the rise of regulation signifies the decline of redistribution through the fiscal tools of taxing (or borrowing) and spending. In this regard, scholars perceived Majone's conceptualization of the regulatory state as neoliberal in essence, with limited government concentrated first and foremost through competition-led economic and administrative efficiency, while keeping the welfare state's politics of equality and social justice out. Levi-Faur (2013, 2014) rejects this antagonistic and monomorphic conceptualization of the relations between the welfare state and the regulatory state. According to Levi-Faur, regulatory and fiscal tools are not trade-offs; the rise of one is not necessarily the decline of the other. Regulations are not confined to procedural aspects; they can carry substantive values and outcomes. Therefore, the regulatory state is not necessarily a neoliberal state; it may pursue different goals, including the provision of welfare. Thus, in principle, the regulatory state and the welfare state can coexist and even strengthen each other. This is a notion that was demonstrated in both the UK Labour Party's policy of "welfare ends *through* market means" (Taylor-Gooby, Larsen, and Kananen 2004; see also Gilbert's [2005] *enabling state* model) and even more so in the extension of rights—human, workers' citizenship, social, political and economic—via mainly regulatory means.

And indeed, detailed examination of the relations between the regulatory state and the welfare state's roles as funder and provider of social services shows that the rise of regulation and the rise of the regulatory state is not simply a shift back to laissez-faire capitalism (Gamble and Thomas 2010). Instead, it reflects the polymorphic character of capitalism. Despite the strong neoliberal rhetoric against redistribution and for the dismantling of welfare state services, Paul Pierson and others have shown that the expenditure for state-funded social benefits and services is relatively stable (see, e.g., Pierson 2001). Although this argument can be contested, especially in periods of austerity, the point is that it should not be a priori assumed that the rise of the regulatory state means that public funding for social goals is in retrenchment, and definitely not across all the social arenas, nor at the rate or in the scope to which neoliberal recipes aspire. Moreover, there are clear indications of social policy expansion and expanded welfare commitments in "rising powers," such as in Brazil, China, India, and South Africa (Tillin and Duckett 2017).

Moving the discussion from funding or social expenditure to the role of the welfare state as a provider, we identify much slower progress with plans for the wholesale transfer of health, education, and social insurance to the private sector when compared to the privatization of state-owned enterprises and utilities (Gamble and Thomas 2010). Only a small number of social arenas, such as pensions, were straightforwardly moved to private finance and administration (Leisering and Mabbeth 2011). In most other social arenas, the privatization energy was channeled to NPM reforms focused on the "restructuring" and "modernization" of public services through contracting out and market-like management. These arrangements profoundly change the ways that social services are organized and managed, and they clearly reduce the role of the state as the direct provider of social policy. But still, as the purchaser of services, the state maintains a major role in planning and funding these services.

This is a good point in the discussion to turn to another important role of the welfare state: its role as regulator. As mentioned, regulation was always embedded in the welfare state, mainly through social regulation in areas such as health and safety, environment, and labor protection (Mabbett 2010). However, a detailed examination of this role in recent decades suggests that regulation is increasing in number and scope, reaching much deeper into the heart of the welfare state (Windholz and Hodge 2012; Levi-Faur 2014). This is part of the wider trend of "regulatory capitalism" as characterized by privatization and regulatory growth (Levi-Faur 2005). But here we want to emphasize two major paths of regulatory expansion in the welfare state. The first is the mounting role of the state as the purchaser of social services through tendering, contracting, and monitoring providers. These practices make the task of managing public services much more regulatory in nature, signifying the "entry of the regulatory state into the welfare state" (Mabbet 2010, 217). In addition, these practices of indirect delivery often lead to the proliferation of regulatory bodies inside government, and to the inclusion of audit-oriented requirements into spheres that were formerly administered and self-regulated by professionals (Power 1997; Benish, Halevy, and Spiro 2018).

The second avenue for regulatory expansion within the welfare state is the expansion of social regulation in the privatized and liberalized sectors. Such expansion was documented by Haber (2011, 2017), for instance, in privatized public utilities (such as electricity and water), in which, as he shows, regulation is used in a variety of ways for social purposes. Social regulation is also extending in markets for social goods and services that were created due to the state's retreat from some domains, such as pensions. As Leisering and Mabbett demonstrate, after privatization and liberalization, state regulation increased, and, somewhat paradoxically, pension markets became much more socially regulated. These regulations now go beyond customer protection and the correction of market failures to promote social goals, such as alleviating poverty and addressing inequality (Mabbett 2010; Leisering 2011; see also Benish, Haber, and Eliahou 2017). In this context, it is important to note that the scope and reach of regulation in the welfare state is increasing not only due to state regulation but also due to the rise of global and private forms of regulatory governance. In this regard, privatized social services are more publicly, privately, and globally regulated. Moreover, as we show here, regulatory tools have become much more diverse than in postwar positive states, and often these new regulatory instruments—such as "nudging"—are intended to regulate not only the service providers but also the services users.

In sum, we believe that the relations between the welfare state and the regulatory state, and more generally between regulation and other policy instruments, are much more complex than the trade-off relations that Majone has suggested. We argue that the rise of the regulatory state is not necessarily a return to the night-watchman state in which the responsibility for welfare was in the realm of civil society; but at the same time, it does not allow the custodians of the "old" welfare state to keep ignoring markets. As a result, the rise of the regulatory state opens the possibility for a variety of new types of "division of labor" among the state, the market, and civil society in taking responsibility for steering, funding, and delivering social welfare. The challenge of understanding how this actually works is at the core of the intersection of the fields of regulation, welfare, and governance.

# A Regulatory Welfare State

The concept of the RWS thus deals with the role of the state in society, politics, and the economy, and in the various ways in which the state may use both regulatory and fiscal tools, as well as other tools, to pursue social goals. It rests on institutional and historical approaches for understanding what the welfare state is, what the regulatory state is, and what the interaction between them tells us about the dynamics of the de/re/commodification of society and citizenship. As such, it opens a space for a multifaceted and nuanced study of how fiscal and regulatory tools are combined and used. In this section, we develop this theoretical

TABLE 1
The Polymorphic Welfare State

|  |  | Effects of the state's social regulation | |
|  |  | Commodification | Decommodification |
| **Effects of the state's social spending (fiscal expenditures)** | **Commodification** | Neoliberal regulatory welfare state | Liberal regulatory welfare state |
|  | **Decommodification** | Paternalistic regulatory welfare state | Social Democratic regulatory welfare state |

SOURCE: Levi-Faur (2014).

framework, discussing it in terms of 1) the normative social goals of the state; 2) the ways in which social policy is delivered through institutions; and 3) how it bears on the implications for individuals' rights and duties.

## The normative dimension

What are the goals of the state in the social domains (Levi-Faur 2014)? The theoretical framework of the RWS is based on the assumption that both regulatory tools and fiscal tools can be used for expansion, stagnation, and retrenchment of social goals; policy-makers can use them to commodify, *de*commodify and *re*commodify, and they may have progressive or regressive results at the same time. Moreover, both regulation and social expenditures can function as disciplinary and repressive measures to achieve the goals of social control.

Based on these assumptions, it is useful to distinguish between different types of RWS in terms of their normative dimension (see Table 1). Along the lines of regulatory and fiscal commodification and decommodification, four ideal types of RWS can be identified. The first is the *neoliberal regulatory welfare state*, a state that uses both regulation and social expenditures with the aim of commodification. The provision of welfare in this type of state is conditional on the participation in the labor market. Thus, social rights are offered via instruments such as tax expenditures, corporate pensions, corporate health insurance, and corporate programs for parental leave. This type of state is closely related to Jessop's "workfare state" (Jessop 1993).

The second model is the *liberal regulatory welfare state*. This model uses regulation to decommodify while keeping fiscal transfers for commodification purposes by encouraging, for example, home ownership. In this type of welfare state, fiscal transfers are mainly directed toward nurturing the labor and investment markets, while regulation can be used to moderate and balance the effects of commodification.

TABLE 2
The Interactions between Different Social Spending vs. Social Regulation Goals

|  |  | Social regulation goals | | |
|---|---|---|---|---|
|  |  | Retrenchment | Stagnation | Expansion |
| Social spending (fiscal expenditures) | Retrenchment | **Double retrenchment** | Mixed dynamics | Regulation-led expansion |
|  | Stagnation | Mixed dynamics | **Double stagnation** | Regulation-led expansion |
|  | Expansion | Fiscal transfers-led expansion | Fiscal transfers-led expansion | **Double expansion** |

SOURCE: Levi-Faur (2014)

The third model is the *social democratic regulatory welfare state*. Under this model, both fiscal transfers and social regulation are used mainly to decommodify labor and social relations. Here, for example, both regulation (e.g., rent control) and housing subsidies (e.g., for social housing) are used to promote decommodified housing services.

And finally, the fourth model is the *paternalistic regulatory welfare state*, in which fiscal transfers are the main instrument for decommodification, whereas social regulation is used for commodification. The inherent logic of this arrangement is to provide popular goods (subsidies) directly and visibly while using fewer visible tools such as regulation to commodify. Money is visible while regulations are not, thus subsidies will be used to shape social life and to create (or reflect) a clientelistic network. Thus, we can expect, for example, housing benefits and subsidies in the form of transfers but not, for example, as rent control.

Moreover, acknowledging the redistributive aspect of regulation and the regulatory aspects of the redistributive process provides an analytical space for understanding situations in which social regulation and social expenditures are entwined in the same policy framework (see Table 2). The state can retrench, stagnate, and expand with the retrenchment, stagnation, and expansion of each of these instruments independently. Policy-makers may choose either or both. In this regard, retrenchment, stagnation, and expansion are the three "states of the world" that characterize the dynamics of social regulation and social fiscal transfers independently of one another (see Levi-Faur 2014).

*The institutional dimension*

How is social policy, in its various normative forms, delivered? As mentioned, the delivery function of the welfare state has undergone significant transformation due to privatization and NPM reforms. In fact, social services were one of the chief realms of change under such regulation and governance reforms. Braithwaite (2000) observes that this "new regulatory state" (in contrast with the

TABLE 3
Varieties of Regulatory Welfare States: The Institutional Dimension

| | | Steering tools | |
| --- | --- | --- | --- |
| | | Fiscal tools | Regulatory tools |
| **Type of delivery** | **Public actors** | *Provider state* (public benefits and services) | *Public option* (State-run, but not funded, services operation within the market) |
| | **Private actors** | *Quasi-markets* (Contracting out and voucher arrangements) | *Regulated market provision* (Caps on prices, prevention of service disconnection, products defined by regulation) |

SOURCE: Benish, Haber, and Eliahou (2017)

"old" command-and-control state of the postwar era) uses a mixed array of new tools—such as incentive systems, conventions, standards, targets, best practices, benchmarking, certification, and voluntary codes, forms of negotiated soft law, and other collaborative and responsive techniques—which substitute for direct command and control.

These transformations of social policy delivery—the use of both public and private actors and both regulatory and fiscal means—create an analytical structure for variations of how social policy is delivered under the RWS (see Table 3). This analytical framework, created from the intersections between these delivery methods, adds three additional delivery strategies to the traditional provider-state model of state funding and delivery.

The first strategy is *quasi-markets*, whereby the state funds the services delivered by the market through competitive contracting or vouchers (Le Grand 1991). This model is usually used in the delivery of in-kind social services. The funding of these arrangements remains basically public, but regulatory and market-mimicking approaches are adopted to steer these services (see Benish 2010, 2014; Benish and Maron 2016). In such instances, the decoupling of public funding and state delivery creates a model of service delivery in which the state funds services that are delivered through voluntary and market actors.

The second strategy is *regulated market provision*, whereby regulatory rule making is used to ensure that individuals and families have access to certain goods and services in the market with no direct public financing (see Haber 2011, 2017). These instances of provision of services through regulated markets demonstrate how non-fiscal tools can be used in the market for social welfare purposes, even though they usually aim at a low level of decommodification, such as poverty relief.

The third strategy is *public option*, in which services are provided by a public entity without public financing. In this respect, the public provision of services is offered *within* the market alongside private options. This strategy allows the state to play an active role in addressing social problems and promoting social goals, but the services operate within a competitive market environment and need to survive financially without public funding. The state sets standards for price and quality, not through direct social regulation but by offering customers an option to choose a socially driven product or service (for example, by offering low-fee pensions to low-wage pension savers; see Benish, Haber, and Eliahou 2017).

Under these additional strategies for welfare provision, the state does more steering than rowing (Osborne and Gaebler 1992; Braithwaite 2000). It relies on nonstate, voluntary, and commercial actors for the delivery of social welfare (a model also known as welfare pluralism). But it is important to note that the commercialization of social welfare involves not only a massive entry of nonstate providers into the social arena, but also an infusion of the logic of the market into the culture of social provision (Gilbert 2005). It also involves opening up social sectors to competition and to pressure from the global market, thus breaking the hold of professional groups and trade unions, and introducing new forms of accountability (Gamble and Thomas 2010; Benish 2014).

## The individual dimension

How do the normative and institutional dimensions of the RWS bear on individuals' rights and duties? Here, there are two basic assumptions: first, that the state can protect, promote, and secure social rights using a variety of means, and not only by providing services directly but by financing and/or regulating services delivered by nonstate providers (Dean 2015); second, that the choice of policy instruments or tools reflects the values of the policy-makers and the norms of their institutional environment. This choice reflects alternative conceptualizations of citizenship. We therefore add the new dimension of "regulatory citizenship" to Marshall's notion of social citizenship (Benish, Haber, and Eliahou 2017): an alternative path for decommodification that establishes social rights without direct state funding and/or state provision. Moreover, the marketization of social services provides citizen-consumers with a wider array of tools of choice and voice (Stirton and Lodge 2001). This empowers them to shape and to enforce their social rights (Le Grand 1991) and gives a stronger focus on users' involvement in service delivery.

However, the shift to regulation may affect the nature and meaning of social rights. Braithwaite, Makkai, and Braithwaite (2007), for instance, found that in aged care homes in the United States, the UK, and Australia, the elderly have the right to buy their own provision from a plurality of residential and nonresidential providers. Moreover, the rights of the aged to privacy, to participation in care planning, to a homelike environment, to freedom of movement, to political participation, and to lodge formal complaints have also expanded in all three nations. However, these rights do not necessarily promote decommodification; they actually look more like consumer rights than citizenship-based social rights. Similarly, in what they term as the "civilization" of social rights, Leisering and Mabbett (2011) found that in the context of privatized pensions, conventional social rights give way to civil rights set in a social context. Here again, the pension savers' rights were more about regulating access to the market and about procedural fairness than

TABLE 4

Socializing and Desocializing the Costs of Fiscal and Regulatory Policies

| | | Burden of regulatory costs | |
| --- | --- | --- | --- |
| Burden of fiscal costs | | Public | Individuals |
| | **Public** | Social democratic regulatory welfare states | Paternalistic regulatory welfare states |
| | **Individuals** | Liberal regulatory welfare states | Neoliberal regulatory welfare states |

being concerned with welfare outcomes and redistribution. Furthermore, when the regulatory state intersected with the agenda of activation and responsibilization, as many recent social reform programs do (Gilbert 2005; Mann 2005), the meaning of social rights may take the form of recommodification, demanding that people "participate in markets, including 'quasi-markets' within the public sector" (Dean 2015, 13).

The RWS also comes with new regulatory ways of steering individuals' behavior within it. In addition to influencing individuals' behavior in the traditional way of using economic incentives, legal duties, and public information campaigns, there are also new methods of influence, such as nudging people to change their behavior or setting default options that individuals will need to change actively (Thaler and Sunstein 2008). These forms of intervention—sometimes labeled as "libertarian paternalism"—try to influence the individual's choice without taking away his or her choice, but rather trying to "push" them in a direction that seems preferable to the policy-makers (Greve 2015).

These distinctions are reflected in how the burden of increasing regulatory expansion is shared between the public and individuals (see Table 4). We assert first that the burden of regulatory (compliance) and fiscal (revenue) costs are most often socialized in social democratic regulatory welfare states and are most often transferred to the individual in neoliberal regulatory regimes. Second, we also assert that the extent to which these costs are punitive depends on different conceptions of the state of its citizens and on the values that guide policies and policy-makers. Some efforts are directed at responsibilization (Shamir 2008), others at empowerment (Rappaport 2002). We now look at how different types of regulatory welfare states are dividing the costs between the public and the individual. We distinguish first between neoliberal states that individualize both the fiscal and regulatory costs and social democratic states that socialize them. Two hybrid situations—or varieties of regulatory welfare states—reflect paternalistic attitudes when the individual carries the costs of regulation but not the costs of fiscal expenses and policies. Finally, in liberal regulatory welfare states the costs or regulation are socialized, but the costs of welfare provision are carried by the individual. What makes neoliberalism different from liberalism is therefore also the degree to which the costs of regulation are socialized.

# Conclusion

We have argued that the theory of the RWS, connected to wider shifts in capitalism, expands our ability to grasp the polymorphic meanings of contemporary statehood. Transcending the simple ideas of a trade-off between welfare and regulation offers a more nuanced theoretical framework for understanding exactly how welfare is governed today. As such, the concept of the regulatory welfare state expands the scope of scholarship for both regulation and the welfare state. It allows us to make sense of the various combinations of responsibility and delivery among state, civil society, markets, and individuals. However, at the same time, it also highlights how complex the analyst's task is in times of constant moving, shifting, and blurring of the boundaries among these realms. Challenges, such as the COVID-19 outbreak—which is going on as these lines are being written—as well as other economic and social challenges to come, will require an ongoing scholarly effort to update and refine these analytical frameworks.

# References

Benish, Avishai. 2010. Re-bureaucratizing welfare administration. *Social Service Review* 84 (1): 77–101.

Benish, Avishai. 2014. Outsourcing, discretion, and administrative justice: Exploring the acceptability of privatized decision making. *Law & Policy* 36 (2): 113–33.

Benish, Avishai, and Asa Maron. 2016. Infusing public law into privatized welfare: Lawyers, Economists, and the competing logics of administrative reform. *Law & Society Review* 50 (4): 953–84.

Benish, Avishai, Hanan Haber, and Rotem Eliahou. 2017. The regulatory welfare state in pension markets: Mitigating high charges for low-income savers in the United Kingdom and Israel. *Journal of Social Policy* 46 (2): 313–30.

Benish, Avishai, Dana Halevy, and Shimon Spiro. 2018. Regulating social welfare services: Between compliance and learning. *International Journal of Social Welfare* 27 (3): 226–35.

Braithwaite, John. 2000. The new regulatory state and the transformation of criminology. *British Journal of Criminology* 40 (2): 222–38.

Braithwaite, John, Tony Makkai, and Valerie Braithwaite. 2007. *Regulating aged care: Ritualism and the new pyramid*. New York, NY: Edward Elgar Publishing.

Dean, Hartley. 2015. *Social rights and human welfare*. New York, NY: Routledge.

Esping-Andersen, Gosta. 1990. *The three worlds of welfare capitalism*. Princeton, NJ: Princeton University Press.

Gamble, Andrew, and Robert Thomas. 2010. The changing context of governance: Implications for administration and justice. In Administrative justice in context, ed. Michael Adler, 3–24. Oxford: Hart Publishing.

Gilbert, Neil. 2005. The "Enabling State?" From public to private responsibility for social protection. OECD Social, Employment and Migration Working Papers, Working Paper No. 26, OECD, Geneva.

Greve, Bent. 2015. *Welfare and the welfare state: Present and future*. New York, NY: Routledge.

Haber, Hanan. 2011. Regulating-*for*-welfare: A comparative study of "regulatory welfare regimes" in the Israeli, British, and Swedish Electricity Sectors. *Law & Policy* 33 (1): 116–48.

Haber, Hanan. 2017. Rise of the regulatory welfare state? Social regulation in utilities in Israel. *Social Policy & Administration* 51 (3): 442–63.

Hood, Christopher. 1991. A public management for all seasons? *Public Administration* 69 (1): 3–19.

Jessop, Bob. 1993. Towards a Schumpeterian workfare state? Preliminary remarks on post-Fordist political economy. *Studies in Political Economy* 40 (1): 7–39.

Le Grand, Julian. 1991. Quasi-markets and social policy. *The Economic Journal* 101 (408): 1256–1267.

Leisering, Lutz. 2011. Transformations of the state: Comparing the new regulatory state to the post-war provider state. In *The New Regulatory State*, ed. L. Leisering, 254–74 New York, NY: Palgrave Macmillan.

Leisering, Lutz. 2012. Pension privatization in a welfare state environment: Socializing private pensions in Germany and the United Kingdom. *Journal of Comparative Social Welfare* 28 (2): 139–51.

Leisering, Lutz, and Deborah Mabbett. 2011. Introduction: Towards a new regulatory state in old-age security? Exploring the issues. In *The New Regulatory State*, ed. L. Leisering. 1-28 New York, NY: Palgrave Macmillan.

Levi-Faur, David. 2005. The global diffusion of regulatory capitalism. *The ANNALS of the American Academy of Political and Social Science* 598 (1): 12–32.

Levi-Faur, David. 2013. The odyssey of the regulatory state: From a "thin" monomorphic concept to a "thick" and polymorphic concept. *Law & Policy* 35 (1–2): 29–50.

Levi-Faur, David. 2014. The welfare state: A regulatory perspective. *Public Administration* 92 (3): 599–614.

Mabbett, Deborah. 2010. The regulatory rescue of the welfare state. In *Handbook of the politics of regulation*, ed. D. Levi-Faur, 215-226 Cheltenham: Edward Elgar Publishing Limited.

Majone, Giandomenico. 1994. The rise of the regulatory state in Europe. *West European Politics* 17 (3): 77–101.

Majone, Giandomenico. 1997. From the positive to the regulatory state: Causes and consequences of changes in the mode of governance. *Journal of Public Policy* 17 (2): 139–67.

Mann, Kirk. 2005. Three steps to heaven? Tensions in the management of welfare: Retirement pensions and active consumers. *Journal of Social Policy* 39 (1): 77–96.

Obinger, Herbert, Carina Schmitt, and Reimut Zohlnhöfer. 2014. Partisan politics and privatization in OECD countries. *Comparative Political Studies* 47 (9): 1294–1323.

Osborne, David, and Ted Gaebler. 1992. *Reinventing government: How the entrepreneurial spirit is transforming the public sector*. New York, NY: Addison-Wesley Publishing Company, Inc.

Pierson, Paul. 1998. Irresistible forces, immovable objects: Post-industrial welfare states confront permanent austerity. *Journal of European Public Policy* 5 (4): 539–60.

Pierson, Paul, ed. 2001. Post-industrial pressures on the mature welfare states. In *The new politics of the welfare state*, 1st ed, 80–105. Oxford: Oxford University Press.

Piven, Fox Frances, and Richard Cloward. 2012. *Regulating the poor: The functions of public welfare*. New York, NY: Vintage.

Power, Michael. 1997. *The audit society: Rituals of verification*. Oxford: Oxford University Press.

Rappaport, Julian. 2002. In praise of paradox: A social policy of empowerment over prevention. In *A quarter century of community psychology*, 121–45. Springer, Boston, MA.

Shamir, Ronen. 2008. The age of responsibilization: On market-embedded morality. *Economy and Society* 37 (1): 1–19.

Stirton, Lindsay, and Martin Lodge. 2001. Transparency mechanisms: Building publicness into public services. *Journal of Law and Society* 28 (4): 471–89.

Taylor-Gooby, Peter. 2013. The double crisis of the welfare state. In *The double crisis of the welfare state and what we can do about it*, 1–25. London: Palgrave.

Taylor-Gooby, Peter, Trine Larsen, and Johannes Kananen. 2004. Market means and welfare ends: The UK welfare state experiment. *Journal of Social Policy* 33 (4): 573–92.

Thaler, Richard H., and Cass R. Sunstein. 2008. *Nudge: Improving decisions about health, wealth, and happiness*. New York, NY: Penguin.

Tillin, Louise, and Jane Duckett. 2017. The politics of social policy: Welfare expansion in Brazil, China, India and South Africa in comparative perspective. *Commonwealth & Comparative Politics* 55 (3): 253–77.

Windholz, Eric, and Graeme A. Hodge. 2012. Conceptualising social and economic regulation: Implications and economic regulation: Implications for modern regulators and regulatory activity. *Monash University Law Review* 38:212–39.

# Meta Governance of Path Dependencies: Regulation, Welfare, and Markets

By
JOHN BRAITHWAITE

Regulation, welfare, and markets grow interdependently, shaping, reinforcing, and supporting each other: markets allow for the expansion of welfare states, and welfare states create demand for regulatory state services that help to solve perceived welfare problems. Crises can drive this path dependency because they create opportunities for growth in markets, regulation, and welfare institutions. The momentum toward interdependent risk of ecological crises, economic crises, and security crises is formidable, but regulatory-welfare-market path dependencies might be mustered to counter it. This article proposes a meta governance of path dependence, emphasizing multiple interactions in the regulation-welfare-market system and suggesting that meta governance can steer path-dependent regulation, welfare, and markets in the governance of crises. I discuss whether patterns of path dependence explain why regulation, welfare, and markets interdependently persist and grow.

*Keywords:* regulatory capitalism; welfare; markets; COVID-19

Regulation-welfare-market interdependence is a path-dependent governance ensemble. Crises often drive that path dependence. Path dependencies of co-expansion from one institutional arena reach into opportunities opened up by path dependence for expansion in other institutional arenas. Markets allow the expansion of welfare states. Welfare states create demand for regulatory state services that help to

*John Braithwaite is an emeritus professor in the School of Regulation and Global Governance (RegNet), which he founded with Valerie Braithwaite and where he cofounded the journal,* Regulation & Governance, *under the leadership of David Levi-Faur. Braithwaite is best known for work on restorative justice, responsive regulation, peacebuilding, crime, and globalization of regulation.*

NOTE: Thanks to Gale Burford, Valerie Braithwaite, Yan Zhang, the editors, referees, and all conference participants for helpful comments on this work.

Correspondence: John.Braithwaite@anu.edu.au

DOI: 10.1177/0002716220949193

repair disintegration of welfare state institutions. New crises create opportunities for new path dependencies for growth of market, regulatory, and welfare institutions. Then, mutually reinforcing tendencies of one institutional arena to seize opportunities for expansion in other arenas engender a capitalism of expanding markets, expanding welfare, and expanding regulation in the *longue durée*. The particular character of crises that challenge capitalist institutions creates demand for expansion of the welfare state. Crises grow problem-solving innovation in markets (e.g., carbon markets) and expand regulation in response to path-dependent momentum toward interdependent crisis risks. Perhaps only path dependence can muster the momentum to govern path dependence? Meta governance can steer path-dependent regulation, welfare, and markets for the governance of path-dependent crises. In such a world, perhaps strategic policy-makers do not directly pull levers as much as harness path dependencies. More and less successful responses to the COVID-19 pandemic illustrate these policy dynamics.

## Levi-Faur on Markets-Welfare-Regulation

My starting point is David Levi-Faur's (2013, 2014) interpretation of capitalism that argues that it emerges, institutionalizes, and develops polymorphically. The specific polymorphy of interest to Levi-Faur is the rise of mutually reinforcing institutions of the market, welfare, and regulation. These are three important morphs, or structural facets, of what I call *regulatory welfare capitalism*. The objective of this article is to attempt to provide a little extra insight into Levi-Faur's polymorphous capitalism by challenging it with the idea of meta governance of path dependence. Unlike other accounts of the path dependence of capitalism, I emphasize multiple interactions in the regulation-welfare-market interdependence of path dependencies. I discuss whether patterns of path dependence explain why regulation, welfare, and markets interdependently persist and grow. These patterns are conceived as partly driven by the emergence and invention of crises. Market, welfare, and regulatory institutions intermittently strengthen in response to crises. When states, businesses, charities, and other institutions respond effectively to crises, this can bolster their legitimacy. We consider this with the way some states and civil societies responded early and well to the COVID-19 virus by strengthening welfare and regulation, even to the point of one regime winning an election to implement a "Korean New Deal" during the pandemic. This included regulation to help markets bounce back post-crisis. Lost legitimacy for weak crisis management in the past has induced regime change. It will be intriguing to observe which regimes lose or build legitimacy after COVID-19.

This article uses the terms *regulatory state* and *welfare state*. While these are statist terms, their appeal here is as elements of regulatory welfare capitalism. Regulatory welfare capitalism exists in societies where institutions of the market, welfare, and regulation are resilient and grow stronger. I find Levi-Faur and Jordana (2005) and Braithwaite (2000, 2008) more attractive when they theorize regulatory capitalism than when they analyze the regulatory state, which risks a myopically statist discourse to describe dynamics that reach beyond the state. Regulatory welfare capitalism sometimes expands in ways that are as much or more about markets and civil society than about the state. For example, this article argues that the sharpest growth of the "regulatory state" in the decade after September 11, 2001, was in homeland security. Much of that was in private security contracts to private airport corporations around the world, for instance to scan bags, bodies, and filter access by digital checks on facial features. The sharpest regulatory state expansion of the next decade (up to 2020) was cyber security; yet most of this regulatory work was and is done by IT employees in private corporations who prevent, detect, diagnose, and disable cyberattacks.

Libertarians tend to perceive a hydraulics where the rise of regulatory institutions drives down market institutions. Leftists are inclined to believe that neoliberal markets drive down regulation and welfare. I argue that none of these kinds of hydraulics have happened at the macro level in the longue durée of capitalism, even though they frequently occur at the micro level in short-run see sawing of policy dynamics. My theoretical contribution is to suggest that this is so because the rise of regulation creates new path dependencies for growth that sit beside pre-existing path dependencies of markets and welfare. Path dependence is the dependence of outcomes on the paths of previous routines, processes, and outcomes. In the next section, I explain the logic of path dependence toward growth when one institutional arena of path-dependent growth discovering opportunities to reinforce that growth inside old path dependencies of other institutions. I find much mutual reinforcement of path dependencies in Levi-Faur's polymorphous market-welfare-regulatory capitalism. This is assisted by citizen demand and market demand to solve perceived and real crises.

The next section also explains more fully Levi-Faur's view of the emergence of polymorphous capitalism. It considers five hypotheses on the role of path dependence and crises. In the section that follows, I identify regulatory and welfare trajectories of the longue durée that make these crisis and path-dependence hypotheses plausible. The fourth section argues that a fundamental weakness of governance scholarship in the Asian Century is that it still focuses most scholarly attention on Western states. I use the COVID-19 pandemic to illustrate the importance of crises and the power of regulatory-welfare-market path dependencies in the fifth section. Legitimacy threats from this crisis wrenched the gaze of Western policy-makers away from the West and toward East Asia, where the most instructive governance action took place. The conclusion is that crises and path dependencies ultimately channel Western and Eastern governance to the regulatory and welfare conditions for problem-solving capitalism to flourish. Strategic meta governance of path dependencies is central to this project.

## Polymorphous Capitalism

David Levi-Faur (2013, 2014) argues that the rise of the regulatory state does not necessarily imply welfare state decline. The welfare state became a regulatory welfare state as it became more polymorphous. His earlier work on the idea of regulatory capitalism contends that stronger regulation has not produced weaker markets (Levi-Faur 2005). Regulation is actually and potentially widely deployed to strengthen markets and strengthen welfare provision on old as well as new concerns and social needs (Levi-Faur 2014). We see this in contingent ways in a contemporary crisis like COVID-19. States dispense "corporate welfare" to airlines and their employees with an eye on ensuring that in a postcrisis airline industry, it is not only the strongest that survive and then monopolize markets. States want second competitors to survive in domestic aviation markets to sustain future price competition. In an infrastructural sense, competition law and contract law are forms of legal regulation that constitute and nurture the very existence of markets. Here Levi-Faur is inspired by Polanyi and other institutionalist thinkers about capitalism.

This special issue suggests that regulation for welfare purposes is increasing. Regulatory capitalism is conceived as one morph of a polymorphous capitalism that helps to constitute other morphs such as the welfare state. Levi-Faur critiques Majone's (1994, 1997) sequencing as monomorphic because Majone argues for a period of history of the liberal Nightwatchman state where market institutions were dominant, followed by another Keynesian period when the institutions of the welfare state become dominant, followed by a third era of the regulatory state that has been in place since 1980.

In this thinking about historical sequences in the character of capitalism, regulatory scholars (this one included [Braithwaite 2000]) think too hydraulically: perceiving something new, we assumed it pushed down something old. This lent drama to the character of global changes depicted in our models. The rise of regulatory institutions did not shut down the path dependencies along which market institutions and welfare institutions continued to expand. Commonly, the logic of new institutions is to create new path dependencies that sustain their own future growth paths, with this bearing no strong connection to shutting down old path dependencies.

To clarify the concept of path dependence, consider research on drugs to treat cancer. Sometimes the regulatory state seeks to steer state research and development (R&D) investment away from certain drugs for a particular cancer onto higher priority cancers or nondrug therapies. Such attempts to suppress the welfare state by the regulatory state might not deliver great change. Universities have powerful professors who dedicate their lives to a particular cancer and their approach to treating it. They recruit new scholars to work on it; they use their power in science decision-making to support grants for their established research network. Pharmaceutical companies build on their extant marketing networks for the drugs produced by the research of those professors. Indeed they "disease monger" to widen claims for their drugs. They lobby to expand the welfare state and the regulatory state by lengthening the duration of patents. They continue to capture physicians with conferences at resorts and baubles to continue prescribing their product (Braithwaite 1984; Dukes, Braithwaite, and Moloney 2014). They capture politicians to sustain welfare funding for their cures.

These examples illustrate that many expansions of the welfare state and the regulatory state are regressive rather than progressive, serving corporate interests rather than sick people. Some regulatory and welfare expansions are disciplinary and oppressive, and others are emancipatory. One example of how marketing to expand the welfare state can be oppressive is big pharma pitches to aged care homes to multiply chemical restraint of the frail elderly that crushes their freedom. Likewise, crises can have disastrous impacts on societies, even on extinction of species, or can be opportunities for emancipatory transformation. Because meta governance of institutional path dependencies and crises can be a dangerous game, players must be careful and mindful of the normative theory that informs their moves. That topic receives no systematic attention in this article, but it has elsewhere (Braithwaite 2008).

Meanwhile, institutions of the regulatory state are stretched to the limit in evaluating the safety and efficacy of new drugs, leaving limited resources for reassessing old evaluations of the benefit-cost of established drugs. Most societies have many pharmaceuticals that were approved for marketing in the 1930s or earlier that are still used, even though 1930s regulation was perfunctory for testing safety and efficacy. Not only do regulatory institutions fail to steer the welfare state downward in this respect; the systematic bias is high barriers for the new but low barriers to keeping the old. Grandfathered state funding of drugs tested inadequately under older, weaker regulatory regimes is an example of a path dependency to welfare accumulation. These various examples illustrate how regulatory institutions and market institutions tend to reinforce path dependencies of welfare spending. The regulatory-market influences used here to illustrate dynamics of welfare growth included grandfathering, disease mongering, capture of regulation by professors with a vested interest in a program of research, corruption of physicians and health ministers by big pharma, and global lobbying to blow out the health budget by lengthening patent monopolies.

All these path dependencies persist during crises as grave as COVID-19 concern over crumbling welfare and markets and deficit blowouts. Efforts of the World Health Organization to push for open source biotechnology so that all scientists can share their breakthroughs have widely failed, as they did with the SARS and HIV-AIDS crises (Drahos 2010); corporate champions were backed by their states to defend patent walls around their innovations, making therapies unaffordable to poor people in poor countries. Even tests for the presence of the COVID-19 virus were unaffordable in poor countries as demand peaked. As always, regulatory enforcement was needed against widely distributed fraudulent test kits that did not work and/or kits that were counterfeits of tests that did work (U.S. Food and Drug Administration 2020). This is a problem when the pandemic might spread among the planet's poor to return to afflict the West in future waves. Bribery and capture by corporate power are implicated in these dynamics (Braithwaite 1984; Dukes, Braithwaite, and Moloney 2014). Disease mongering persists as major corporations that lose in the tournament for the life saving breakthrough opt for the second-best strategy of disease mongering. That means their public relations machines push the idea that COVID-19 can be treated by one of its products patented to cure a completely different disease. Sometimes this disease mongering will be right; perhaps an antimalarial drug might have an antiviral impact on COVID-19. At the same time, we know that commercial interests that drive disease mongering systematically produce fraudulent effectiveness claims (Dukes, Braithwaite, and Moloney 2014). The point here is not about adjudicating when disease mongering saves lives and when it kills. It is the simpler point that there is path dependence toward disease mongering, as with all the pharmaceutical paths discussed.

Consider another dynamic in the growth of polymorphous capitalism. University researchers invent a new technology for managing a rare variation of a welfare state problem such as cancer or a new drug, device, or treatment; or a powerful research group at a university promotes disease mongering because it believes that the drug they work on can become more important. R&D is not profitable because the market is small for rare variants of diseases. If my mother is about to die from that rare cancer, however, I might find 40 other families in the same situation. Big pharma funds me to organize them because I argue for subsidies from the welfare budget to make their unprofitable drug profitable. With support from the company's public relations machine, I argue that if 40 passengers disappear on a flight or 40 are trapped underground, we spare no resources. This is not a story of a new mini crisis that arises for the welfare state. These 40 savable lives were always there; saving them was simply not recognized as a policy option. The new technological possibility created by medical markets creates a mini crisis of a need for new welfare funding that is actually a crisis of neglect across all previous history.

Genuinely new crises are the more important generators of new path dependencies for regulatory, market, and welfare institutions. The 9/11 Al Qaeda attack on the United States was a spike in such an emergent crisis. A result was that the biggest expansion of regulatory states in the first decade of this century was homeland security (Braithwaite 2008). Markets in private security also grew; for example, corporations that manufactured better scanning technologies at airports, other corporations that staffed those machines, firms that manufactured drones, and security cameras and artificial intelligence to diagnose risk from billions of images. The military-industrial complex was renewed by resultant wars in Afghanistan, Iraq, Pakistan, the Philippines, Syria, Libya, and across Africa. This was more than just growth in the state and in markets for weapon systems; there was growth in private military corporations like Blackwater, service providers to militaries like Halliburton, and mercenary armies such as Russia's Wagner Group. The 9/11 crisis fueled further welfare state growth. War spikes demand for trauma services. Nearly twenty years after the initial crisis, not all of these have closed because crises cascaded to other crises, cascading new demands upon the welfare state. In the case of 9/11, the cascade to new foreign wars drove demand for counseling services. Cases of veteran suicide spiked. Recent Australian research shows that the more important welfare effects of war are on the families of war veterans, especially daughters of veterans, in terms of suicide attempts, alcohol and drug abuse, smoking, post-traumatic stress disorder symptoms, and even rape victimization (O'Toole et al. 2018). Welfare demand from daughters of veterans are larger, longer-lasting welfare drivers than those from veterans themselves. Hence intergenerational trauma spikes from deadly violence spur new welfare demands that states have no choice but to meet, even if only from hospital admissions associated with them.

As illustrated in Özel and Parado (2020) and Lee and Braithwaite (2020), the invention of cybermarkets created new opportunities for markets to penetrate the welfare state. Likewise, markets infiltrate national security states in destabilizing ways, creating new risks of accidental nuclear war, for example (Ellsberg 2017; Beebe 2019). Penetration of cybermarkets into welfare path dependencies and national security path dependencies puts new demands on regulatory institutions. Cybermarkets are regulated by novel forms of choke point regulation (Tusikov 2017). This is overwhelmingly private policing by firms like Facebook, Google, and TikTok. The cybersecurity sector is estimated to have created 6 million new regulatory jobs, with chief information security officers (CISOs) ubiquitous in the private and public sectors alike (Button 2020). New hotlines or regulatory assurances are needed when a cyberattack intended to harm a commercial competitor is accidentally perceived as an attempt to compromise missile defense systems (Beebe 2019). Cybermarkets were always going to give rise to cyber welfare, cyber crime, and cyber warfare.

Braithwaite (2019) has argued that economic crises tend to cascade into security crises and ecological crises and vice versa, so that these three kinds of crises tend to be mutually reinforcing. Pandemics reveal a somewhat different pattern. COVID-19 certainly has cascaded into an economic crisis and a crisis-ridden welfare safety net with gaping holes that demands historic hikes in welfare spending. In this case, however, the economic shutdown was so extreme as to make some contribution to reducing pollution. For example, the virus reduced emissions by shutting down factories, air traffic routes, and diminishing car travel. At the time of writing, civil unrest has been modest from COVID-19, but growing.

To summarize this reinterpretation of Levi-Faur's take on polymorphous capitalism:

1. Institutions of the market, welfare, and regulation ebb and flow, but in patterned path dependencies toward expansion.
2. These path dependencies are mutually reinforcing. Path dependencies of growth in one institutional arena reach into opportunities opened up by path dependencies for growth in other institutional arenas. For example, the welfare state creates demand for regulatory state services that help to solve perceived welfare problems.
3. New crises, real and manufactured, create new path dependencies for growth of market, regulatory, and welfare institutions. Then, mutually reinforcing tendencies see one institutional arena rush into opportunities for growth in others.
4. Path dependencies of the regulatory state therefore drive into new markets, and they drive into new welfare initiatives. Likewise marketization path dependencies drive into renewed regulatory institutions. Carbon trading is an example of marketization driving into regulation. Hence we might see the regulatory welfare state as regulatory path dependencies driving into

      the welfare state and welfare state path dependencies driving into regula-
      tory institutions.
5. The particular character of macro crises that cascade into one another cre-
      ates demand for expansion of the welfare state to expand problem-solving
      innovation in markets (e.g., carbon markets) and to expand regulation.

Nothing I have discussed denies the growth of neoliberal ideologies alongside
burgeoning markets within polymorphous capitalism (Braithwaite 2000, 2008).
My analysis does not deny that neoliberal ideologies have delivered some potent
retrenchments of the welfare state and the regulatory state. I argue that welfare
and regulatory path dependencies also have power and crises have power in
explaining the shape of polymorphous capitalism. The next section identifies an
empirical background of regulatory and welfare trajectories of the longue durée
that make these five hypotheses plausible. I do not test the theory in any systematic way. This is a theoretical contribution where empirics are employed only to
illustrate the sense and plausibility of abstractions.

    Valerie Braithwaite's critical comment on this article is that path dependence
is intrinsic to institutions as enduring ensembles of norms and structures that
reproduce themselves. Should we therefore reframe the second point above:
institutionalization in one arena reaches into opportunities opened up by institutionalization in other arenas? That would have the virtue of parsimony. On the
other hand, it might make an already abstract theory overly abstract. I see merit
in the specificity of path dependence and crises as mechanisms that insinuate
resilience *and change* into institutions, thereby constituting polymorphous
capitalism.

# The Longue Durée of Welfare and Regulation

The golden decades of welfare state expansion had passed by the final decades of
the twentieth century. An era of expanded influence of markets had arrived.
Every state has a different history of incursions of neoliberal ideologies that
trimmed welfare and regulatory states and risked disintegration. Despite these
histories, considerable empirical research emphasizes longer-run tendencies for
regulatory state growth (Vogel 1996; Levi-Faur 2005; Braithwaite 2008) and welfare state growth (Aspalter 2017) compared to the early capitalism that emerged
from the eighteenth to the mid-twentieth century, and limited evidence for
medium-term shrinkage since 1980 (Castles 2004), especially if account is taken
of growth in state health spending, homeland security regulation, cybersecurity,
and regulatory and welfare state growth for the majority of the world's population
in Asia. On the other hand, some forms of welfare contraction, such as in public
housing, have been widespread in Western societies, and the welfare state has
come under pressure everywhere from regressive reduction in income and corporate taxation of the wealthy since 1980. Diverse micro welfare and regulatory
state contractions occurred in the medium term, but macro expansion of

regulation and welfare is evident in the longue durée of capitalism. I conclude this is insufficient expansion, however, to respond adequately to crises associated with the financialization of capitalism, the climate crisis, markets in weapon systems, and the globalization of disease. Hence, further expansion across these institutional arenas is more than possible.

Even for the least likely case (the most "neoliberal" case), for an association between long-run welfare state growth that is real and that drives GDP growth, the United States, this association exists (Garfinkel and Smeeding 2015). Empirically, the growth of regulatory capitalism, market capabilities, and steering capabilities that grow in harness have also existed across U.S. history since the New Deal (Braithwaite 2008). The logic of market institutions and of welfare growth as imperative for keeping markets ticking is buttressed by evidence that societies that hold down levels of poverty secure higher levels of growth (Breunig and Majeed 2019). These empirical associations are background empirics for the plausibility of the five hypotheses.

One general factor that has driven long-run welfare state and regulatory state expansion since the nineteenth century is conservative political leaders joining arms with social democrats to promote this growth when their regime stared down risks of being outflanked from the Left. We see this at least from Bismarck's late–nineteenth century promotion of the German welfare state for fear of rising Communism. The same was true of liberals like Lloyd George who promoted these trends as part of their resistance to a pink Labour Party and a red communist party. One might retort that social democratic parties are no longer pink and reds are no longer under the beds of Western states. Yet Bismarck still resonated with Donald Trump who feared that his authoritarian populism could be outflanked by Left populism of a competitor in the Bernie Sanders mold. Hence Trump has selectively appropriated pro-regulatory Left causes such as opposition to the North American Free Trade Agreement and the Trans-Pacific Partnership. Trump's moments of support for the welfare state have been more exceptional, with the COVID-19 crisis one big exception. Yet Trump has been the most aggressive recent presidential advocate of the infrastructure state. The reds that Trump fears are in charge of the state that is a more expansive infrastructure state than the United States. More of the world's Right populisms are regulatory welfare populisms than meet the eye of analysts who misspecify Right populism as neoliberalism.

Small authoritarian capitalist states like Singapore, Qatar, and the UAE; medium-sized ones like Vietnam and Cambodia; and large ones like China, Bangladesh, and Indonesia have outperformed the growth of liberal capitalist economies by a wide margin since the 2007 global financial crisis. This is a different pattern of growth from that observed during the twentieth century when liberal Western economies became progressively more dominant as the gap widened between their wealth and that of authoritarian societies. Among the reasons for this growth have been the superior regulatory capabilities of many of these authoritarian states for containing two crises that the West was episodically incapable of managing in the late twentieth and twenty-first centuries: first, sustaining adequate demand and savings to avert economic crises in an era of the financialization of capitalism (Braithwaite 2019),[1] and second, containing ecological crisis. Managing a pandemic is emerging as a third example of this. Lower-growth twenty-first-century Western economies have so far proved incapable of steering a safe course between these crises. What paralyzed them was fear that if they went too far in responding to the climate crisis, they would become less competitive in what they misperceived as the "neoliberal" global economy. The paradox is that this analysis paralysis handed the game to China. China very recently emerged as the leader in renewable energy technologies like solar panels (Fialka 2016), electric cars, and much more. On the other hand, this conjuncture has left Chinese banks and party leaders overconfident and under-transparent, especially in relation to heavy indebtedness through off-balance-sheet investment vehicles. China is, therefore, overdue for the financial crashes it avoided in 2007 and 1998. COVID-19 revealed how important China's transparency weaknesses can be. It is fascinating that one-party-state Vietnam discerned lack of transparency as China's weakness in COVID-19 management, and a strength of Singapore's one-party-state. So Vietnam's brilliantly effective community-led pandemic management was highly transparent (Nguyen 2020).

## Welfare and Regulation in the Asian Century

The empirical work that informed the rise of the regulatory welfare state was mostly North Atlantic, with significant Latin American data contributions. Yet China is where the power of markets has risen most dramatically since 1980 in harness with formidable lifts in state regulatory capabilities, and this in a society that had been impoverished and chaotic during the Cultural Revolution. The last decade saw a massive shift from consumption of consumer durables to services consumption, including welfare services. Evidence of this is discussed in an earlier iteration of this article (available from the author; Braithwaite 2019). It also discussed how Japan's recent investment in innovation to confront climate change rivals Europe's combined contribution. While ideologues such as President Trump play to their base with promises to cut "green tape," the reality of recent decades has been increased environmental regulatory stringency across the Organisation for Economic Co-operation and Development (which excludes China, the state with the highest regulatory growth and industrial growth); and that stronger national investment in "green tape" increases long-run economic growth (Feng et al. 2019; Yang 2020).

Here I concentrate only on the Chinese regulatory state's contribution to slow the climate crisis. China has far more electric cars on its roads than any country (Pressman 2017), increasing its proportion of the world's electric car sales from zero in 2012, to a sixth in 2014, and more than half by 2017 (Busch 2018; Niu 2018). Its domination in electric buses and electric two-wheel vehicles is now 99 percent of the world's production (DiChristopher 2018). While it grew its economy faster, China worked out how to produce the most successful renewable energy alternative (solar panels) at a fifth of the cost managed in the West. China became the largest generator of solar power; the largest manufacturer of solar panels; the top producer of wind energy (OECD 2019); leader in batteries and smart grids; and the largest domestic and outbound investor across all forms of renewable energy (Jaeger, Joffe, and Song 2017). By 2017 China accounted for 45 percent of global renewable energy investment, which was delivering a steeply increasing proportion of renewable energy patents (29 percent by 2016). Other countries will eventually narrow the green technological gap with China. They might find that some fast pathways follow aspects of the tracks of China's regulatory welfare capitalism. Despite this, no nation contributes anywhere near as much carbon to the climate crisis as China. China is still building coal fired power plants where demand peaks; plants grew five-fold between 2000 and 2018 (Carbon Brief 2019). Yet China is also closing the worst plants, and its pipeline of new and planned plants has shrunk by 70 percent since 2016 (Carbon Brief 2019).

For all that, Peter Drahos (forthcoming) could be right that China is the best hope for leadership to avert catastrophe by combining its regulatory welfare capitalism bargain with pulling strong state levers to decarbonize through new energy paradigms, just as it is in this moment the best hope for supplying personal protective equipment (PPE), ventilators, and personnel to help societies overwhelmed by COVID-19. China's environmental accomplishments are enabled by experimental cities designed from scratch that include hydrogen cities, circular cities, and smart cities that connect information technologies and artificial intelligence to the green challenge; forest cities of buildings that suck carbon dioxide with horizontal trees and vertical gardens; and sponge cities (that are designed to capture all run-off water and recycle). If too many fail, of course, they can threaten the Chinese economy. That is one possible tragic end to this story. The scale of China's green experimentalist construction of completely new cities is unprecedented. They amount to the largest suite of technological experiments at scale in human history. There are 285 new ecocities planned (Shepard 2017). If only half are built, they could come to house populations approaching the current population of the EU or the United States. Some former ghost cities that until recently were standard fare for derision of Chinese state planning by Western journalists became decarbonizing boomtowns.

Drahos might also be right that Western thinking places too much emphasis on putting a higher price on carbon because at times of immediately impending crisis the price mechanism delivers change too slowly compared to state research and development investment in energy paradigm shifts or perhaps state-funded greenfield ecocities as fulcrums of transformation. Best, Bourke, and Jotzo's (2020) comparison of 142 countries with and without carbon pricing finds that carbon pricing works, but only reduces the growth rate in $CO_2$ emissions by two percentage points. Drahos seems right that this crisis has cascaded to the point where earth systems are shifting to new equilibria at a pace that overwhelms the top speed at which market equilibria can shift. Markets can be particularly slow when media empires and commercial interests that fund democratic political parties are ossified around extant paradigms and sunk investment in them (while green start-ups are short of funds to buy politicians). On the other hand, China is mostly a prudent state investor in steering strategies that hedge its bets by also steeply increasing the price of carbon through lifting taxes on petroleum and elevating various other environmental taxes on industry and experimenting with regional environmental trading that is evolving into a national emissions trading scheme.

China has moved in the direction of regulatory welfare capitalism (Li and Yang 2020). One reason China could become more hegemonic, in short, is that it is grasping a more-welfare-more-regulation reconfiguration of its market economy. The West is more timid about grasping this option than is China because of its fear of a neoliberal chimera created in the backward-looking political imaginations of Westerners. That timid analysis prioritizes an imperative to cut welfare and regulation to be competitive in the face of what Westerners see as the unassailability of neoliberal policy settings. In their attitudes to welfare and regulation, these neoliberal and neoconservative analysts may not be the realists. The realists may be authoritarian regimes that thrive through their sovereign wealth funds and their state-owned and private bank investments in Western economies. Western economies have subsidized authoritarianism by shifting wealth from Western workers to the profit share of national incomes. That profit share is then appropriated by the national income of their authoritarian competitor societies through purchase of shares by banks and sovereign funds from authoritarian states. Then these realist authoritarian states use that Western wealth to buy off their own populations with expanded welfare benefits and by steering state and private investment into infrastructure (a visible example being the superior airports of thriving authoritarian states compared to U.S. airports). China also uses that Western wealth to subsidize technologies it can sell to the West to ameliorate the climate crisis. Of course it also sells surveillance technologies to authoritarian national security states. In his new book, Drahos (forthcoming) develops in a brilliant way the applicability of this analysis to China.

The era when the West could easily hold off the threat from China by superior information technology has begun to pass, a shift signaled by Western trade barriers against Huawei's technological superiority over Western firms. One way the West clings to geopolitical dominance is by stepping up taxpayer investment in their national security states to sell new military technologies to each other, as well as to allies in the Middle East and Global South. This is a rather partial solution because China, while it accomplishes only a sixth of the arms exports of the United States (SIPRI 2018), has been dramatically, secretly, growing its share.

Schulze-Cleven (2020) shows that the character of regulatory welfare capitalism for universities is "competition-sustaining and market-making reregulation." A state that runs up debt by investing in expanded higher education and R&D systems is akin to an investor who borrows to buy real estate that returns a higher capital gain than interest on the debt. States for decades have been able to borrow at interest rates less than one-third of the return to GDP of increased investment in secondary or higher education (Psacharopoulos and Patrinos 2018). So why do many states not do that? They fail to when they are captured by neoliberal fundamentalism about the evils of state debt. China is massively scaling up investment in higher education; this drives an expanding number of Chinese institutions up university rankings (O'Malley 2017). Put another way, China sees that it needs to exercise its regulatory capabilities through state intervention to increase the size and excellence of its university system. It prioritizes accelerated welfare state spending needed to support educational opportunities, especially for talented students from poor families. In the end game, this will strengthen the Chinese economy in R&D markets; it increasingly sells enrollments in its universities to international students who are attracted to their excellence, especially in engineering, accounting, biotechnology, robotics, and artificial intelligence. This will increase Chinese soft power, just as the eras of British domination of university excellence, then German university leadership, then U.S. domination, increased their soft power in the nineteenth and twentieth centuries.

## East Asian Path Dependencies and COVID-19

It is too early to evaluate which states and cities steered more and less effective responses to COVID-19. Ultimately, there will be decades of analysis of a stupendous database. Which cities introduced which regulatory and welfare responses at which times, with what effects on control of COVID-19 infections and deaths? This research will not only be a resource for epidemiology; it will also inform regulation and governance scholarship. One plausible set of hypotheses will go to the regulatory capitalism literature. It will assess a paradox of COVID-19 management: states that mobilized early with large regulatory infrastructures may do better at keeping their markets strong. They might do better at averting excesses of long and repeated lockdowns that devastate markets, and shutdowns of education and of face-to-face civil society. New York, London, Milan, and Madrid may come to be seen as experiencing less decisive early regulatory escalation than East Asia, but also more total and widespread deprivation of freedom of movement and other liberties such as access to education than East Asia. East Asia has experienced no countrywide full lockdowns (Pardo et al 2020). Where the infrastructure of regulation and welfare were strong, perhaps the data will come to show that markets and freedom remained stronger in the medium term. While that seems plausible for first waves of the pandemic, it remains to be seen what happens in second and third waves. Will societies that survived their first wave well fare more poorly in second and third waves because they have created little immunity in their population? Will a vaccine take years during which treatment improves to the point where the health costs of mass unemployment begin to exceed the health benefits of disease containment? Will the latter be even more true in societies like India, where national lockdowns caused mass migrations and mass hunger for the precariat? Only a decade of patient data collection will provide answers.

East Asian societies, even though they were much more densely connected to the original site of the outbreak (Wuhan) than the West, and include the two most transited ports in the world (Hong Kong and Singapore), may be seen to have suppressed COVID-19 more successfully. This seems to have been the case, even though Wuhan authorities disgracefully covered up for three weeks as they started quarantine and contact tracing. At least Wuhan's population of 11 million was quickly sealed off from the rest of China in a way that at the time of writing has prevented major epidemics in any other Chinese metropolis. Infection and death rates outside of Hubei Province are far below the Western average at the time of writing. London and New York were not quickly sealed off in this way and catastrophic epidemics did spread to other major cities like Manchester, New Orleans, and Miami.

It has not been just one-party East Asian states that have performed better than the West; it is *all* East Asian states so far. Taiwan is an example of a Wuhan near neighbor with an effective first wave response. Taiwan has many direct flights to Wuhan, strong business interconnections, 850,000 citizens living and 400,000 working in China, and more mainland China visitors per capita than other countries (Wang, Chun, and Brook 2020). Internally, Shanghai is even more densely connected to Wuhan as the great financial hub connected to the industrial hub of Wuhan. Shanghai and Taipei have a larger combined population than New York and London; yet while New York City has had 23,000 reported deaths and London 6,000, Shanghai and Taipei have each reported 7.[2] While all four cities had problems with under-counting, the general magnitude of the difference is massive, visible to independent observers and uncontestable. Xi Lin (2020) has contrasted the infrastructural power of the Chinese state for delivering autonomy and safety from the virus in Shanghai compared to the British state in London. Japan has also had a much lower death rate than the West even though it indulged in early politics of denial as it sought to persuade other countries to commit to the 2020 Tokyo Olympics, and like South Korea, it suffered a severe early infection shock upon its large aged demographic. Other nearby East Asian societies that kept the death rate and economic disruption even lower so far have included Vietnam (Nguyen 2020), Singapore, Thailand, South Korea, and Hong Kong. Shenzhen, just across the water from Hong Kong, may prove more impressive than Hong Kong when all postcrisis mortality data are tabulated (with only 3 deaths in a population of 13 million by July 14, 2020). One of the most spectacular welfare state enhancements came early in Wuhan with the building of two massive hospitals for COVID-19 quarantine from the ground up in days rather than weeks, an infrastructural capability for rapid scaling up that has been less visible in Western states since World War II.

East Asian authoritarianism and paternalistic Confucian deference to the state were popular tropes in Western media chatter to explain this. Regional social scientists see no evidence to support a Confucian cultural interpretation "as implausible as the argument that Europe's and the United States' failures stem from their Christian roots" (Pardo et al 2020). A month into their COVID-19 crisis, Australian policy-makers asked if they were mistaken in their normal pattern of following North Atlantic leads for diffusion of policy ideas. Australia, with its huge population of Chinese citizens and visitors, decided that North Atlantic societies were squandering their advantage in lead time to prepare for the pandemic. Australia moved to the idea that short, sharp, early East Asian regulation was the way to defend both welfare and markets in the long term. Early Australian nodes of infection in Sydney and Melbourne where most international travelers enter were sealed from other states and territories. As of July, 14, 2020, Australia has suffered only 108 deaths by following the lead of their East Asian neighbors, though in this it has not done as well as New Zealand, with 22 deaths and 73 days without any community transmission at the time of writing.

Doubtless, much more was involved than willingness to shift early to short regulatory state escalations. The United States actually shut schools more quickly and for much longer than East Asian societies that fared better, at least with the initial wave of the crisis. During that protracted period when Singaporean and Taiwanese schools were open and U.S schools were closed, every child arriving at those East Asian schools was having their temperature checked and hands sanitized on arrival. School days were punctuated with 20 second disciplined handwashing and education about why this was important. In Australian schools when mandated handwashing did finally commence, social distancing was farcical initially as children jostled and splashed one another during perfunctory hand washing, and soap ran out in unprepared schools.

Most regional scholars think East Asian preparation and planfulness about how schools should respond to the crisis were more important than Confucian authoritarianism. Why might this be so? East Asia had learned particularly from the SARS epidemic, but also the swine flu and MERS epidemics, that next time their education system, their welfare state, and their state and civil society regulatory institutions would be ready for rapid escalation, but situated rather than universal escalation. Market responsiveness was readied to scale up PPE and personnel. This preparedness was crystallized in East Asian regulatory institutions whose task was rapid coordination of all institutions of the society for epidemic response from January 2020. It was not totally state institutions, but hybrids; professional institutions from civil society and community volunteerism were prominent. Chinese responses were locally highly variegated in response to local urban geography interpreted by party members who led highly localized residents' committees. Taiwan was prepared with an action plan of 124 discrete measures overseen by its National Health Command Centre (established as a SARS lesson learned) and by local preparedness teams (Wang, Chun, and Brook 2020). We might conceive these through a Foucauldian lens as 124 oppressive capillaries of power. Regulatory scholars are more likely to see them as a long list of situated and responsive micro regulatory measures that previous experience with epidemics had proven helpful. For the regulatory theorist, the lesson of greater interest might be that no grand theory of how to regulate worked (like Boris Johnstone's early infatuation with herd immunity as a solution). Rather, outcomes may flow from as large a number of capillaries of regulation as 124. The people of Australia were pleasantly surprised when its government followed evidence-based lessons from East Asia rather than the early politics of denial that prevailed in the West. They were surprised to learn that at least two of Australia's prime ministers of the past decade had attended a one-day pandemic crisis response scenario training.

Regulatory theorists are interested in the infrastructure of meta-regulatory mobilization that could deliver as many capillaries as 124. East Asia faced the bigger, more immediate surprise than the West, but they were better prepared with plans to minimize disruption to markets, to maximize welfare mobilization (especially in the health and education sectors), and for bigger, faster escalations of contextually attuned regulation. The intercontinental divergence was not just about preparedness. China and East Asia generally were more evidence-based than Europe and the Americas. An example was mask wearing, especially with aged-care work where preventable Western deaths were massive and under-counted. Western hemisphere regulatory policy-makers sentenced thousands of their citizens to death through this policy failure on masks in a way that was reminiscent of their protracted resistance to mandating the wearing of seat belts, then air bags, in cars. East Asia was also more attentive than the West to learning lessons from how a small number of impoverished African societies did such a brilliant job of extinguishing the more deadly Ebola virus. These were lessons about contact tracing, sealing off, and welfare support for geographical nodes of infection. China coordinated its vast society for surge capacity to apply these African lessons to hot spots that hit the peak of the infection curve earlier, a capability late in arriving to Western societies.

Regulatory studies might therefore learn from East Asia (and Africa) about rapid capabilities for scaling up regulatory infrastructure, strategic redundancy of multiple capillaries of regulation, selection strategies for adding new capillaries as new learning comes in, and learning about coordination to shift regulatory and treatment capabilities from one part of the state to another, as well as one part of the planet to another (with coordination from WHO, civil society mobilization by organizations like Médecins Sans Frontières, to sequentially surge medical capabilities into global pandemic hot spots). This means a global gift economy where gifts are given to pandemic peak economies by pre-peak and post-peak economies, gifts of knowledge from open source research architectures, and gifts of medical equipment and personnel. Meta regulation of states by the WHO, of national macroeconomic policies by the G-20, of education systems and private firms by states, strategic dedication to finding ways to regulate the problem without shutting down markets might be guided by centralized and decentralized learning from other places about options for selecting and sequencing regulation. All these are commended topics for regulation and governance research.

Perhaps when all the data are in, my suggestions will prove totally wrong. Perhaps these incipient patterns of path dependencies for capillaries of preparedness will prove exaggerated. All I have shown is that regulatory welfare capitalism supplies evocative, not totally implausible, hypotheses to guide future evaluations of pandemic responses. A key hypothesis is that the paths East Asia learned to take in response to the SARS epidemic created a virtuous path dependency of regulatory preparedness, welfare preparedness, and market preparedness for epidemic responsiveness. More than that, this path dependency was institutionalized through nodes of evidence-based governance like Taiwan's National Health Command Centre. The COVID-19 crisis shows that all societies, West and East, were forced by a crisis to think in radically new ways about strengthening regulation, expanding welfare, and strengthening measures to preserve jobs and markets. President Moon won an April 2020 election with a pandemic-induced "Korean New Deal" for a fairer regulatory welfare state (Kim 2020). In the moment of crisis, those who thought they were neoliberals or communists found themselves to be practitioners of regulatory welfare capitalism.

Against all of this, it must be said that some exaggerated analyses flourish about how fundamental the changes ushered in by the COVID-19 crisis might be. An example is COVID-19 causing a transformational rupture to globalization. This will not be totally wrong. Yet we might consider that just as new path dependencies laid down from SARS to COVID-19 might have explanatory power, extant institutions of the market, regulation, and welfare have their own path dependencies. These are independent of epidemics and doubtless more powerful than epidemic path dependencies. Yes, new path dependencies are created by crises. But they generally do not shut down path dependencies that resume their growth logics once subsided crises allow them to grow again.

## Conclusion: Meta Governance of Path Dependencies

COVID-19 is just a dramatic current illustration of how a crisis can demand a larger welfare state and a more formidably regulatory form of capitalism. It highlights imperatives to get better at putting markets, regulation, and welfare more strategically in harness for crisis management. Consider the more profound new risks of accidental nuclear war posed by cyber warfare and cyber crime capabilities that can disconcert satellites that control doomsday machines (Ellsberg 2017; Beebe 2019). These risks demand stronger investments in nuclear nonproliferation regimes and regulation of cyber crime. Descriptively, the most massive growth in regulation during the past decade has been regulation of cyber threats. This is mostly private sector regulation by IT personnel, though state regulation is also burgeoning.

It is hard to imagine an economy that averts a climate catastrophe without shifting the shape of the economy (Denniss 2017) to one with fewer factory jobs, reduced consumption of consumer durables, and increased consumption of services, including welfare services and regulatory services (Burford, Braithwaite, and Braithwaite 2019). If this is right, we might think of regulatory welfare capitalism as not only a descriptively accurate tendency in the trajectory of capitalism, but normatively as one that societies must accelerate in directions that are helpful to surviving existential threats.

Sadly, the path dependencies that sustain markets in carbon and markets in destabilizing new weapons systems that threaten mass destruction (Ellsberg 2017) have their own resilient path dependencies. Hence, for regulation and governance scholars, the steering of path dependencies toward more and better regulation and more and better welfare might be the most central of meta-regulatory topics.

Neoliberal ideologies have certainly shifted the shape of welfare states. Yet I hypothesize that crises and path dependencies mean that, at the macro level, welfare states have resisted these ideological pressures with expansion effects that probably exceed contraction effects. Many of these, such as aged care crises associated with population aging, are beyond the scope of this article. Likewise with welfare states, responses to COVID-19 illustrate why regulatory welfare capitalism might not disappear any time soon.

Our responsibility is to understand the dynamics of regulatory welfare states and how to diagnose their meta governance (Sørensen and Torfing 2016; Parker 2002). Societies might then learn to steer interdependent threats that include the globalization of disease, economic crises, ecosystem collapse, proliferation of weapons of mass destruction, and other existentially dangerous path dependencies. It may be that these path dependencies are cascading so relentlessly toward catastrophe that confronting them with creative meta regulation of the power of regulatory-welfare-market path dependencies is as good a hope as we have.

Maybe not: crises ultimately move all species from path dependencies of survival to extinction paths. In the era of COVID-19, the new equilibrium we hope we are heading for is an unfolding mystery. It can make sense to grapple for meta governance strategies that might "flatten the curve" for somewhat improved conditions of catastrophe when no cure is yet in sight. War and financial crises are well studied examples of catastrophes that are hard to predict, hard to end, and that tend to cascade into each other. United Nations peacekeeping repeatedly fails to end wars. Yet the evidence is strong that when peacekeeping is multidimensional in helping to nurse many different kinds of institutions back to health, it can flatten the curve of cascades of killing, and this in turn helps economies to resume growth path dependencies (Braithwaite and D'Costa 2018, 494–97). The World Health Organization and the United Nations Department of Political and Peacebuilding Affairs are nodes of meta governance that matter when they partner with local nodes of meta governance to steer path dependencies of epidemics of disease or violence. This meta governance is a messy business. Path dependencies recurrently slip out of any policy-maker's control. That does not make the meta governance of cascading path dependencies less worthy of policy learning.

## Note

1. Hilferding's definition of financialization is the increasing political and economic power of banks and the rentier class (rentiers are those who live off income from investments in property or securities rather than from producing anything). Financial profits as a share of total profits have increased steeply since the 1950s. Financialization is a particularly strong trend in command economies. In the Forbes 2000 list of the most powerful corporations in the world for 2018, first, second, fifth, ninth, and tenth places are occupied by Communist Chinese banks that are mostly state-owned (Braithwaite 2019).

2. All these data are up to the date of final revisions of this article, July, 14, 2020.

## References

Aspalter, Christian, eds. 2017. *The Routledge handbook to welfare state systems*. New York, NY: Routledge.
Beebe, George S. 2019. *The Russia trap: How our shadow war with Russia could spiral into nuclear catastrophe*. New York, NY: Thomas Dunne.

Best, Rohan, Paul J. Burke, and Frank Jotzo. 2020. Carbon pricing efficacy: Cross-country evidence. *Environmental and Resource Economics*. doi: 10.1007/s10640-020-00436-x.

Braithwaite, John. 1984. *Corporate crime in the pharmaceutical industry*. London: Routledge.

Braithwaite, John. 2008. *Regulatory capitalism: How it works, ideas for making it work better*. Cheltenham: Edward Elgar.

Braithwaite, John. 2000. The new regulatory state and the transformation of criminology. *British Journal of Criminology* 40 (2): 222–38.

Braithwaite, John. 2019. Tempered power, variegated capitalism, law and society. *Buffalo Law Review* 67 (3): 527–94.

Braithwaite, John, and Bina D'Costa. 2018. *Cascades of violence*. Canberra: ANU Press.

Breunig, Robert, and Omer Majeed. 2019. Inequality, poverty and economic growth. *International Economics* 161:83–99.

Burford, Gale, John Braithwaite, and Valerie Braithwaite, eds. 2019. *Restorative and responsive human services*. New York, NY: Routledge.

Busch, Chris. 3 May 2018. China's all in on electric vehicles: Here's how that will accelerate sales in other nations. *Forbes*.

Button, Mark. 26 February 2020. Vigilantes and private security are policing the internet where governments have failed. *Global Policy*.

Carbon Brief. 26 March 2019. Mapped: The world's carbon power plants. Available from https://www.carbonbrief.org/mapped-worlds-coal-power-plants

Castles, Francis G. 2004. *The future of the welfare state: Crisis myths and realities*. Oxford: Oxford University Press.

Denniss, Richard. 2017. *Curing affluenza: How to buy less stuff and save the world*. Carlton: Black Inc.

DiChristopher, Tom. 2018. Electric vehicles will grow from 3 million to 125 million by 2030, International Energy Agency forecasts. *CBBC*. Available from https://www.cnbc.com.

Drahos, Peter. 2010. *The global governance of knowledge: Patent offices and their clients*. Cambridge: Cambridge University Press.

Drahos, Peter. Forthcoming. *Survival governance: Energy and climate in the Chinese century*. Oxford: Oxford University Press.

Dukes, Graham, John Braithwaite, and James P. Moloney. 2014. *Pharmaceuticals, corporate crime and public health*. Cheltenham: Edward Elgar.

Ellsberg, Daniel. 2017. *The doomsday machine: Confessions of a nuclear war planner*. London: Bloomsbury.

Feng, Guahua, Keith McLaren, Ou Yang, Xiaohui Zhang, and Xueyan Zhao. 2019. The impact of environmental stringency on industrial productivity growth: A semi-parametric study of OECD countries. Melbourne Institute Working Paper 16/19.

Fialka, John. 19 December 2016. Why China is dominating the solar industry. *E&E NEWS*. Available from https://www.scientificamerican.com/article/why-china-is-dominating-the-solar-industry/.

Garfinkel, Irwin, and Timothy Smeeding. 2015. Welfare state myths and measurement. *Capitalism and Society* 10 (1): 3–26.

Jaeger, Joel, Paul Joffe, and Ranping Song. 6 January 2017. China is leaving the U.S. behind on clean energy investment. *World Resources Institute*. Available from https://www.wri.org/blog/2017/01/china-leaving-us-behind-clean-energy-investment.

Kim, Hyung-A. 11 June 2020. South Korea's digital quarantine success. *East Asia Forum*.

Lee, Sora, and Valerie Braithwaite. 2020. Contested values in the regulatory welfare state in Australia and South Korea. *The ANNALS of the American Academy of Political and Social Science* (this volume).

Levi-Faur, David. 2005. The global diffusion of regulatory capitalism. *The ANNALS of the American Academy of Political and Social Science* 598 (1): 12–32.

Levi-Faur, David. 2013. The odyssey of the regulatory state: From a "thin" monomorphic concept to a "thick" and polymorphic concept. *Law & Policy* 35 (1–2): 29–50.

Levi-Faur, David. 2014. The welfare state: A regulatory perspective. *Public Administration* 92 (3): 599–614.

Levi-Faur, David, and Jacint Jordana. 2005. Regulatory capitalism: Policy irritants and convergent divergence. *The ANNALS of the American Academy of Political and Social Science* 598 (1): 191–97.

Li, Wei, and Bao Yang. 2020. Mapping hybridity in regulating and managing the new welfare service contracting regime in China. *The ANNALS of the American Academy of Political and Social Science* (this volume).

Majone, Giandomenico. 1994. The rise of the regulatory state in Europe. *West European Politics* 1 (3): 77–101.

Majone, Giandomenico. 1997. From the positive to the regulatory state: Causes and consequences of changes in the mode of governance. *Journal of public policy* 17 (2): 139–67.

Niu, Isabelle. 2018. Your next car could be electric—and Chinese. Available from https://qz.com/1463563/your-next-car-could-be-electric-and-chinese/%0A%0A.

Nguyen, Trang (Mae). 4 June 2020. Vietnam's astonishing success at curbing COVID-19 outbreaks. *The Regulatory Review*.

OECD. 2019. Renewable energy (indicator). doi: 10.1787/aac7c3f1-en.

O'Malley, Brendan. 5 September 2017. Chinese universities hit new heights in global ranking. *University World News*.

O'Toole, Brian, Mark Dadds, Sue Outram, and Stanley Catts. 2018. The mental health of sons and daughters of Australian Vietnam veterans. *International Journal of Epidemiology* 47 (4): 1051–1059.

Özel, Isik, and Salvador Parado. 2020. Regulating social welfare regimes in the Global South. *The ANNALS of the American Academy of Political and Social Science* (this volume).

Pardo, Ramon, Mauricio Avendano-Pabon, Xuechen Chen, Bo-jiun Jing, Takuya Matsuda, Jeong-ho Lee, Joshua Ting, and Kaho Yu. 27 May 2020. Learning and remembering: How East Asia prepared for COVID-19 over the years. *Global Policy*. Available from https://www.globalpolicyjournal.com/blog/27/05/2020/learning-and-remembering-how-east-asia-prepared-covid-19-over-years.

Parker, Christine. 2002. *The open corporation: Effective self-regulation and democracy*. Cambridge: Cambridge University Press.

Pressman, Matt. 19 August 2017. Top electric car countries. Available from https://cleantechnica.com/2017/08/19/top-electric-car-countries-charts/.

Psacharopoulos, George, and Harry A. Patrinos. 2018. Returns to investment in education: A decennial review of the global literature. *Education Economics* 26 (5): 445–58.

Schulze-Cleven, Tobias. 2020. Disruption through regulation: Transforming higher education in the United States and Germany. *The ANNALS of the American Academy of Political and Social Science* (this volume).

Shepard, Wade. 1 September 2017. No joke: China is building 285 ecto-cities, here's why. *Forbes*. Available from https://www.forbes.com.

SIPRI. 2018. *Stockholm International Peace Research Institute Yearbook 2018 Summary*. Oxford: Oxford University Press. Available from https://www.sipri.org/sites/default/files/2018-06/yb_18_summary_en_0.pdf.

Sørensen, Eva, and Jacob Torfing, eds. 2016. *Theories of democratic network governance*. New York, NY: Springer.

Tusikov, Natasha. 2017. *Chokepoints: Global private regulation on the internet*. San Francisco, CA: University of California Press.

U.S. Food and Drug Administration. 2020. Beware fraudulent coronavirus test, vaccines and treatments. Available from https://www.fda.gov/consumers/consumer-updates/beware-fraudulent-coronavirus-tests-vaccines-and-treatments/.

Vogel, Steven. 1996. *Freer markets, more rules: Regulatory reform in advanced industrial countries*. Ithaca, NY: Cornell University Press.

Wang, Jason, Chun Y. Ng, and Robert H. Brook. 2020. Response to COVID-19 in Taiwan: Bid data analytics, new technology, and proactive testing. *Journal of the American Medical Association* 323 (14): 1341–42. doi:10.1001/jama.2020.3151.

Xi, Lin. 26 March 2020. Letter from Shanghai. Global Policy.

Yang, Ou. 10 July 2020. Actually, Mr. Trump, it's stronger environmental regulation that makes economic winners. *The Conversation*.

# The Political Economy of Regulating for Welfare: Regulation Preventing Loss of Access to Basic Services in the UK, Sweden, the EU, and Israel

By
HANAN HABER

What does the state do to prevent consumers from losing access to basic services in the market due to financial hardship, and under what conditions will this occur? Bringing together the literature on regulatory governance and the welfare state, this article compares regulatory regimes that prevent loss of access to services in the UK, Sweden, and Israel in housing credit, electricity, and water, as well as to the electricity and housing credit sectors in the EU, from the early 1990s to the 2010s. The article finds that regulation to address this issue was introduced in all but the Swedish cases. This highlights the significance of the welfare state context in addressing these issues through regulation, as more residual welfare regimes are associated with more social protection through regulation.

Keywords:  regulation; welfare; housing; electricity; water; utilities; social policy

What does the state do when consumers cannot or do not pay their bills? How are people protected from losing access to crucial services, such as electricity, water, or mortgaged housing, once they face debt and arrears? These questions have far-reaching social, political, and economic impacts, as could be seen, for example, in the 2008 global financial and housing crisis, or following the economic hardship resulting from the COVID-19 health crisis. They also pose a theoretical challenge to the literature on the modern capitalist state: the literature on social protection and on regulation of economic reform has generally overlooked these questions or offered an expectation of little or no policy to address such issues.

Hanan Haber is a lecturer in public management (regulation) at King's Business School, King's College London, and a research associate at the Centre for Analysis of Risk and Regulation (CARR) at the London School of Economics.

NOTE: The author would like to acknowledge the support of the British Academy for this research, as part of a British Academy postdoctoral fellowship, pf170149.

Correspondence: Hanan.haber@kcl.ac.uk

DOI: 10.1177/0002716220954399

ANNALS, AAPSS, 691, September 2020

Scholarship on regulation has described a shift from state involvement in the economy through state ownership to regulation of liberalized markets, occurring in Europe and elsewhere since the late 1970s. This has been dubbed the transition from the positive state to the regulatory state (Majone 1997, 2011). In this view, the regulation of markets is aimed at enhancing economic efficiency, while questions of social protection and distribution, previously addressed politically or administratively under a state ownership regime, are now framed out of the design of regulation and regulatory agencies. This view suggests a normative, as well as an empirical, expectation for regulation to focus on addressing market failures, not economic hardship.

A similar expectation for little regulation addressing these types of issues arises from the literature on the welfare state. While regulation has always been part of social protection (e.g., through the regulation of the labor market), it has not been as central as social spending and insurance in the study of the varieties of welfare capitalism and the discussion of welfare state retrenchment and austerity (Esping-Andersen 1990; for an overview see Arts and Gelissen 2002; Danforth 2014; Pierson 1994; Jensen, Wenzelburger, and Zohlnhöfer 2019; Pierson 2001). When regulation is discussed in the context of social provision, it usually focuses on regulating the provision of public and privatized social services, such as education or health, rather than on the social aspect of market services, such as utilities.

What is lacking from these common understandings of the role and limits of regulation is the study of the social aspects of regulating market services. This goes beyond the welfare state's focus on decommodification in the labor market, toward at least partial decommodification of access to services or goods in markets. It also goes beyond the well-established role of regulation in consumer protection, toward protection of those who cannot afford to be consumers. This is regulation not of market failure, but of a failure in the ability to participate in markets.

The study of regulatory welfare has increased in recent years, including the study of such areas as electricity, water, housing credit, rail, pension fees, public procurement, and immigration. Research has detailed the manner in which regulation is being used for social purposes in economic sectors (Haber 2011, 2015, 2018; Leisering and Mabbett 2011; Mabbett 2013; Levi-Faur 2014; Pflieger 2014; Benish, Haber, and Eliahou 2016; Haber, Kosti, and Levi-Faur 2018; Eckert 2017; Hartlapp 2020; Trein 2020). However, we still require a comprehensive view on how regulatory regimes in different countries and sectors address these issues, as well as the drivers of these types of policies.

To address the question of how such regimes of regulating-for-welfare (Haber 2011) develop, this article compares the regulatory regimes for social protection in the electricity sector and in housing credit in the UK, Israel, and Sweden from the 1990s to the 2010s, with additional comparisons made to the residential water sector in these countries, and to the electricity sector and housing credit at the European Union (EU) level. The article argues that existing institutions and policy context are driving (or inhibiting) the development of regulatory welfare policies. The development of regulatory welfare was an addition to existing social and economic settings, and specifically to existing policies and institutions of the welfare state. The development of regulatory welfare is thus dependent on, but also contributes to, how citizens are already protected from social risks.

The research design is a compound, comparative medium-N design (Levi-Faur 2006), allowing for comparisons across several different dimensions of interest: across the same sector in different countries, between different sectors in the same country, and across different sectors in different countries.

The case choice represents an effort to maximize relevant dimensions of both similarity and difference of both regulatory and social policy. In the case of electricity, reform occurred in the mid 1990s, including the liberalization of the sector, the creation of independent regulatory agencies, and efforts toward marketization of national providers. In the housing credit sector, the similarities lie in high rates of homeownership and a prominent role for the state in encouraging private homeownership as the dominant form of tenure. At the same time, the cases represent different models of welfare states, from a Social Democratic model (Sweden), to a Liberal model (UK), to a hybrid model (Israel), to no welfare state (EU). This can also be seen as a distinction between an institutionalized model of the welfare state, as in Sweden, to a more residual model, as in the UK and Israel.[1]

The findings show that the most consistent variation between the cases is at the country, rather than the sector, level. Regulatory welfare, or regulation and other types of policy addressing service termination, developed in Israel, the UK, and the EU, but not in Sweden. This finding supports the claim that national-level context matters for the development of regulatory welfare, as more residual welfare regimes are associated with more social protection through regulation. The findings do not seem to offer similar support for alternative explanations, such as a left-right partisan divide, social need and focusing events, interest groups, or the power of ideas.

## Explanatory Framework

This article asks how consumers are protected from losing access to basic services such as electricity, water, and repossession of mortgaged housing due to economic hardship, debt, and arrears across different national contexts.

However, the literature and practice of creating regulatory regimes as part of the "rise of the regulatory state" do not support an expectation for a regulatory response to social hardship. This is because of the focus of regulatory agencies on the correction of market failures, and on structuring these regimes and the regulatory agencies that oversee them as autonomous from political actors and pressures (Majone 1994, 1997, 2011).

In such regulatory regimes, we expect little scope for addressing social issues. Indeed, we might even expect regulation to formally bar social considerations from setting tariffs or providing services, as was the case, for example, when the electricity sector in Israel was initially reformed (Haber 2011). At the same time, the formal independence of regulators means that even if political pressure to address social needs might develop, there would again be little recourse for addressing these issues within these regulated sectors, as regulators were intentionally placed at arm's length from their political principals.

The focus on market failures should not be seen just in terms of their formal effect on legislation or market structure, but also as a normative reference point for regulators and other actors in the sector. The principles of welfare economics and Pareto efficiency might be expected to inform, in this view, not just the actions but the worldviews of those involved in regulation, informing what *is* through a shared understanding of what ought to be.[2] The question is, then, despite these expectations, why might regulation still develop to address such issues? Below, several different types of explanations or possible answers to this question are briefly discussed.

## Social needs and focusing events

First, the more severe social issues or needs are, the more likely it is that regulators and policy-makers may be prompted to react. This type of answer to the question of why such regulation develops sees policy-making as a more or less rational process of problem-solving, following from a functionalist view of social policy-making (Midgley 1986). This view can be seen as dating back to Karl Polanyi's "double movement," as economic liberalization is followed by a demand for social protection from the effects of liberalization (Polanyi 1946). In this view, we might expect more severe social issues to be more likely to be met with a policy response.

What might draw policy-makers' attention to social needs are focusing events, such as economic crises or natural disasters. Such events not only highlight policy problems to policy-makers, but also mobilize those affected or those who aim to represent them, also opening opportunities for policy change (Birkland 1998).

## Party politics and political actors

Even given the existence of social problems within a sector, we might expect party politics to play a role in the extent and type of regulation and policy put in place, either through the political policy-making agenda or through pressure or influence on delegated rule-making by independent regulators. Broadly, a partisan view expects social policy to be expanded by the political Left, in line with the interests of these parties' voter base. As the power resource approach argues, the relative strength of organized labor and the political Left is the leading determinant of the extent of social policy (Korpi 1983; Schmidt 1996).

## Ideas and policy diffusion

A perspective focused on the role of ideas (Béland 2009; Blyth 2013) would argue that ideas about the appropriate use of regulation—in this case, market failure rationales of regulation, as well as perceptions of acting in the public interest through maximizing economic welfare in aggregate (pursuing Pareto efficiency), rather than addressing the specific needs of one group or another (Majone 1997, 2011)—are found not only in regulation text books, but also in the manner in which regulators and economic reformers perceive their role. These perceptions can be expected to hinder regulation, which impedes efficiency or addresses the needs of a specific social group, for example by cross subsidy in prices.

Conversely, as the use of regulation as a form of social protection occurs, the manner in which it has been implemented in one sector may then play a role in introducing similar ideas about policy problems and policy solutions to other sectors, nationally and internationally. As regulation and policy regarding social hardship develops in one sector, we can expect it to be adopted elsewhere as well, offering a practical counterargument to the market failure perspective.

## Interest groups

An additional explanatory perspective is one in which regulators and political actors respond to pressures from organized groups, particularly from industry. This could be because such groups pose a threat to regulatory organizations' reputations (Carpenter 2002), or because they provide valuable resources to policy-makers, such as information and compliance.

In the context of service termination or housing eviction, a useful tool for determining the expected type of politics is the extent to which costs and benefits of regulation are allocated. In this case, one might argue that the concentration of costs to service providers, and the relatively dispersed benefits to a large number of economically vulnerable consumers, situates this type of policy under what Wilson called "entrepreneurial politics," in which we can expect policy "heroes" to emerge and champion for a disorganized and unrepresented public interest (Wilson 1980).

## Existing institutions and policy context

This perspective focuses on policies themselves: existing policies, both within and beyond the regulatory and social realms, and how these relate to the emergence of and solutions for social hardship. Existing policy is not only self-reinforcing, but it also sets the context within which new policies are made, intentionally or not. Research has argued that this constrains future policy-making, leading sectors and countries down ever increasingly self-reinforcing paths (Pierson 2000; Thelen 2003).

Thus, existing welfare policies for unemployment, pensions, and health set the backdrop within which policies regarding service disconnection or housing evictions are made. Adequate unemployment benefits may prevent service termination or repossession at an earlier stage, before this problem ever reaches regulators or service providers. This means that the welfare state impacts the way social problems develop, as well as sets the context within which further regulatory policy is decided upon.

# Findings: How Does the State Address Service Termination?

Regulation and policy either preventing, delaying, or compensating for service termination due to debt and arrears exist in different forms in both electricity and housing credit in Israel and in the UK, as well as in the EU electricity and housing credit directives. Conversely, in Sweden, service disconnection due to debt and arrears may be dealt with by social services (in electricity) or not at all (housing credit) (Haber 2011, 2015). A similar picture arises when the regulation of service termination in residential water supply is compared among the three national cases.

In the electricity sector in Israel, the state-owned electricity provider is required to offer a cross subsidized discount to specific groups of vulnerable consumers, such as pensioners receiving income support and people with disabilities (Haber 2016). Some of these groups are now also partially or completely protected from service disconnection (Electricity Authority 2017).[3]

In the UK, the regulator, service providers, and the state are all involved in protecting vulnerable consumers, such as pensioners and people with disabilities or chronic illness, in the electricity sector. This includes social discounts, a disconnection ban during winter for specific groups, (e.g., pensioners), and a pledge by some energy suppliers "to never knowingly disconnect a vulnerable customer at any time of year" (Haber 2011; OFGEM 2020).

The EU increasingly included issues related to vulnerable consumers and "energy poverty" over time, from its first (1996) to its third (2009) directive. These changes included suggesting that Member States ban disconnection of vulnerable consumers during "critical times," and protect vulnerable consumers through electricity-related measures or through the national social security system (Haber 2018).

Conversely, in Sweden, the protection of vulnerable consumers is left primarily to social services, rather than to the regulator or service provider. In practice, this means that social services would be notified in the case of consumer default, and may then choose to pay the debt (Haber 2011). Even after the 2009 EU electricity directive required Member States to act on behalf of vulnerable consumers and energy poverty, the regime in Sweden continued to rely primarily on social services for protecting vulnerable consumers.

Table 1 summarizes how consumers are protected from service termination in the electricity sector in Israel, the UK, and Sweden, as well as the 2009 EU electricity sector directive, focusing on disconnection bans and on social discounts or schemes to prevent or compensate for service termination.

This picture is similar when compared to service disconnection in the residential water sector. In Israel, service termination due to nonpayment is forbidden, unless approved by a committee and only once the consumer's debt has reached a certain level. This directive comes alongside a social discount for vulnerable groups, similar to those receiving discounts in the electricity sector (Haber 2016). In the UK, service termination of water at a consumer's residence due to

TABLE 1
Social Protection in the Electricity Sector in Four Countries

|  | Disconnection ban? | Social discounts or schemes |
|---|---|---|
| **Israel** | Yes, for specific groups | Yes |
| **UK** | Yes, during winter, for specific groups | Yes |
| **EU** | Yes, suggested for vulnerable groups and critical times | Yes |
| **Sweden** | No | No |

SOURCE: Haber 2011, 2016, 2018; OFGEM 2020.

nonpayment is forbidden. Several schemes also exist to lower the cost of service or have the water bill paid directly from government benefits; these are again targeted at vulnerable consumers (OFWAT 2020). In Sweden, service termination due to nonpayment is permitted, unless this will result in serious harm to consumers. Service providers may reduce the flow of water, allowing for enough water for essential needs. There are no social tariffs (EurEaU 2016). Table 2 summarizes the differences.

In the housing credit sector in the UK, the process of housing repossession due to debt and arrears on housing credit is regulated by a financial regulator and through a "pre-action" protocol to be followed by lenders before repossession. This process aims to ensure fair treatment of borrowers. There are also different kinds of government benefits and schemes to support mortgage borrowers, including those struggling to meet their housing credit payments. Several such "mortgage rescue" schemes, aimed at borrowers facing the prospect of repossession, were introduced following the 2008 global financial crisis; they aim to delay or prevent housing repossession. Such schemes included a variety of measures, such as loans and deferment of interest payments (Haber 2015; for current schemes see Money Advice Service 2020).[4]

In Israel, legislation historically protected mortgage borrowers facing repossession, making them protected tenants of the lender, or requiring lenders to supply them with alternative housing. However, these protections were eroded over time, as clauses requiring borrowers to waive these protections commonly became part of the mortgage agreement. However, in the mid-2000s, reforms to the writ of execution law again strengthened the protection of mortgage borrowers: the first (in 2004), regulating the repossession process, prevents lenders from demanding full and immediate repayment upon default, which would result in significant losses to the borrower. The second (in 2008) requires lenders to provide a year and a half of alternative housing for borrowers facing repossession, and makes this protection one that cannot be waived (Lerner 2011).

Conversely, in Sweden, the regulation of the repossession process is relatively lighter than in the UK or Israel. The repossession process is similar to other types of property attachment (Haber 2015). It is managed by the national enforcement authority (KFM), which states that it aims to avoid repossessing one's home, but

TABLE 2
Social Protection in the Water Sector in Three Countries

|  | Disconnection ban? | Social discounts or schemes |
|---|---|---|
| **Israel** | Yes | Yes |
| **UK** | Yes[a] | Yes |
| **Sweden** | No | No |

a. "In Northern Ireland, domestic customers do not receive water bills as the service is funded from general taxation" (EurEaU 2016, 44)
SOURCE: Haber 2016, OFWAT 2020, EurEaU 2016.

that in some cases it has "no choice, even if the debt is small." KFM sells the home in auction, providing some conditions are met, such as ensuring the sale of the property generates a surplus after the costs of the sale (KFM, n.d.).

A similar approach is reflected in the regulatory response in Sweden to the 2008 housing crisis, after which the financial regulator aimed to prevent excessively risky mortgage lending (for example, by limiting the maximum loan-to-value ratio), rather than preventing repossession once debt and arrears have already occurred (Haber 2015).

Thus, in the housing sector, in the UK and in Israel the state devotes more effort to mitigating the consequences of mortgage default and repossession than in Sweden. Table 3 provides typical examples of regulatory social protection in each country.

At the EU level, one reaction to the financial crisis has been to strengthen mortgage market regulation (Kenna 2018). This included the 2014 mortgage credit directive (2014/17/EU),[5] which requires Member States to "encourage creditors to exercise reasonable forbearance before foreclosure proceedings are initiated" (article 28). This directive was followed by guidance from the European Banking Authority on such forbearance, suggesting lenders might implement such measures as a change in the interest rate or a payment holiday (European Banking Authority 2015; for a full overview see Kenna 2018).

Summarizing the main differences between these cases, regulation and policy preventing service termination appears to vary considerably by country: while regulation addressing or even banning service termination is found in different forms in the electricity, water, and housing credit sectors in the UK and Israel, as well as in EU electricity and housing credit sectors, it is uncommon in Sweden, in which social issues in these sectors are either unaddressed or addressed by social services.

# What Explains the Development of Regulatory Welfare?

Thus far, I have discussed several theoretical explanations for the drivers of regulation and social protection related to service termination. The evidence in

TABLE 3

Social Protection in the Housing Credit Sector in Three Countries

| | Typical examples of protection against repossession |
|---|---|
| **Israel** | Alternate housing arranged by lenders |
| **UK** | Pre-action protocol before repossession; mortgage rescue schemes |
| **Sweden** | Regulation reducing risky lending |

SOURCE: Haber 2015; Lerner 2011.

support of each perspective is discussed in this section, which first highlights the role of existing institutions and policy context in explaining the differences among the national cases.

### Existing institutions and policy context: The role of the welfare state

This explanation highlights the role of existing policy, which sets the context within which new policy is formed. Existing institutions impact the way social problems develop and set the context within which further regulatory policy is made. The consistent difference found at the country level, between Sweden and the other cases, implies that the explanation for this difference may also be found at the country level. One such common country-level contextual factor is the existing policies of the welfare state. A common factor in the UK and Israel is a residual welfare regime, which offers limited protection against the types of social risks (such as unemployment or retirement) that raise the likelihood of financial hardship that results in debt, arrears, and loss of access to market services. Conversely, the institutionalized welfare context in Sweden offers better protection against the social risks that would have otherwise resulted in consumers facing service termination.

Thus, the existing context of the welfare state in this case impacts the social problems that policy-makers face, which, in turn, impacts the extent to which they are likely to introduce regulation for social purposes, as the demand for such regulation will differ accordingly. At the same time, it also shapes the contexts within which the other explanatory factors posited above operate, such as social need, partisanship, or ideas.

That is, social need and focusing events can be expected to affect different welfare state contexts differently in how severely such social issues affect citizens, but also in terms of what is perceived as a social problem requiring public intervention and how social and economic problems should be addressed.

For example (and as I discuss further next), even while electricity prices and mortgage repossessions rose in both the UK and in Sweden, policy responses differed in the two countries. This difference may be due to how the welfare state cushioned the impact of these risks on citizens. Similarly, while ideas regarding the use of regulation strictly for efficiency purposes existed in the regulation of electricity in Sweden, Israel, the UK, and at the EU level, this principle was only fully upheld in Sweden, while policy-makers in other contexts were willing to introduce policy that did not fully follow this principle. That is, ideas about Pareto efficiency are easier to uphold when the social risks involved are already being addressed through the welfare state.

This perspective can be further demonstrated in the Swedish case, in how the EU electricity sector directives required Sweden, alongside other Member States, to take action regarding vulnerable consumers in the electricity sector. This included, for example, requiring Member States to define vulnerable consumers and take action to protect such consumers through, for example, drafting national action plans and considering bans on disconnection for vulnerable consumers during critical times. Swedish regulators were asked to transplant an existing conception of the policy problem of energy poverty, which originated in the UK policy context, through binding EU regulation (Haber 2018), even when this was not necessarily previously perceived as a policy problem in the Swedish context. However, even when this occurred, it did not necessarily change the underlying principles of the Swedish regime.

Following the directive, the electricity regulator in Sweden defines vulnerable consumers and estimates how many such consumers exist. Legislation on electricity and heating now requires service providers to follow a procedure before service can be terminated, and again stresses the obligation of providers to notify social services. However, the regulator states that vulnerable consumers are protected by social legislation that provides for their "right to receive financial assistance to cover their electricity and natural gas needs" (EI 2017). Thus, the income support benefit includes a basic national rate and "reasonable costs for other common needs such as housing and household electricity" (Socialstyrelsen, n.d.).

That is to say, even after the Swedish regulator was required to address the issue of vulnerable consumers, the regime continued to rely on social services and on the support of the welfare state as the main way of protecting consumers and funding their access to electricity. This example demonstrates the direct relation between the protection of the welfare state and social protection within the electricity sector in Sweden.

These examples demonstrate how the existing institutions of social policy impact regulation in sectors beyond the welfare state. This can occur in different ways: through reducing the impact of social risks that lead to service termination, through offering existing solutions to policy problems that occur within such sectors, or by impacting how social issues and appropriate solutions are framed and understood. As a result, countries with residual welfare states are more likely to develop regulatory welfare, while this is less likely in countries with institutionalized welfare states.

## Social Need and Focusing Events

Both in the electricity and housing sectors, regulatory measures may be related to social issues and focusing events that highlighted or exacerbated them. In the UK, the death of a couple of London pensioners in 2003 after their heating was disconnected due to debt on their gas bill was cited by the UK energy regulator (OFGEM) as the cause of a later review of service providers' conduct on disconnection, and related to a voluntary ban on disconnections during winter, which was later also mandated by regulation (OFGEM 2004). Similarly, rises in the number of housing evictions and repossessions after the 2008 financial crisis were followed by regulation and social "mortgage rescue" schemes in the UK (Haber 2015).

However, while focusing events may have prompted a regulatory response, in some cases similar policy initiatives predate the occurrence of such events.[6] For example, the UK financial regulator's provisions on fair treatment of consumers in housing credit debt and arrears date back to 2004, and programs supporting mortgage interest payments date back to the 1990s, similarly predating the 2008 crisis. Thus, social regulation does not only follow from focusing events.

Second, the comparison with the Swedish case shows that focusing events, such as the financial crisis, may or may not elicit the same policy response. Both Sweden and the UK used macro-prudential regulation to limit risky borrowing after the crisis. But even after the number of repossessions in Sweden doubled (Haber 2015) the issues of those already facing repossession were addressed only in the UK.

A similar argument can be made about regulating in response to longer term changes in social needs in the absence of a focusing event. In the electricity sector, again, prices rose in a similar manner in the 2000s in both Sweden and the UK (Haber 2011), yet this elicited a response in the UK, but not in Sweden. At the same time, a recent example from the Israeli housing credit sector makes an opposite point: a recent piece of legislation requires banks to offer borrowers who face a sudden change in circumstances a deferral of payments for a limited time without cost. However, this measure was created despite the protests from the Israeli central bank, who claimed that repossession hardly occurs, putting the number of repossessions in the two preceding years at roughly 65 annually (Economic Committee 2017).

The connection between social needs and regulatory welfare seems, then, to be tenuous. While regulation may react to both long-term social needs and more sudden focusing events, this type of reaction does not necessarily occur, nor is such regulation necessarily a response to a clear case of social needs.

## Politics and Political Partisanship

The cases above demonstrate no clear connection between the Right-Left political divide and the development (or lack thereof) in regulation for social issues. That is, the Left but also the Right enacted this type of policy, as did single-issue parties, such as religious and immigrant parties in Israel (Haber 2016). Even in the UK, where the introduction of much of these types of measures occurred under New Labour, similar measures were later introduced by conservative governments as well.

The social and economic traits of these policies do not seem to vary by partisan or ideological leaning. This type of regulation is primarily residual, similarly targeted at vulnerable groups across the different sectors in which it is has been enacted, focusing on low-income groups, such as low-income pensioners, but also groups of people with other types of vulnerabilities, such as low-income Holocaust survivors and people with specific medical conditions (Haber 2016).

Similarly, in terms of the economic efficiency of these types of policies, it is difficult to argue that parties on the Right aim only to enact policy in line with the market failure perspective: Members of Knesset (MKs) from the Likud were instrumental in mandating that social discounts be funded through electricity tariffs, rather than through the state budget. More recently, a conservative-coalition government in the UK enacted regulations that require large service providers to fund a rebate of £140 for low-income pensioners and other vulnerable groups during winter. Entitled the "warm home" discount, this measure, which has subsequently extended under conservative rule, is funded through consumers' energy bills and has been estimated to cost each one an annual £13. The government has even set an annual "spending objective" for energy companies to meet in this scheme (Department of Business, Energy and Industrial Strategy 2018). Thus, neither the partisan affiliation of those who enact these types of regulations, nor how these types of programs are targeted or funded, seem to conform to a simple Right-Left partisan hypothesis.

However, political actors did play an important role in the enactment of these policies, often in opposition to bureaucratic and regulatory actors, as evidence shows from the Israeli and the EU cases, in which MKs and members of the European Parliament (MEPs) were instrumental in bringing issues regarding vulnerable consumers to the policy agenda (Haber 2016, 2018). This may hint at Wilson's (1980) "entrepreneurial politics" and the role of policy entrepreneurs in advocating for this type of regulation.

# The Power of Ideas

My findings show that ideas on the appropriate role of regulation, arising from a market failure perspective, and the appropriate division of labor between market regulation and social services and the welfare state play a role in preventing the use of regulation for social purposes. This is especially clear in the Israeli case, as bureaucrats, primarily from the treasury, the electricity regulator, and even from the Israeli electricity corporation all highlighted how the idea of cross subsidizing prices for vulnerable consumers from the prices paid by other consumers is detrimental to efficiency, as well as often in contradiction to existing statutes. As a representative of the service provider put it in a Knesset committee meeting: "I, as an economist, am telling you that this is wrong, it is wrong for the electricity rates to subsidize the entire country" (Haber 2011, 126).

Similarly, a recurring debate among regulators is about the manner in which social issues should be dealt with—by social services, or through the welfare state via the public purse. A recent example of this is how a representative of the Bank of Israel objected to introducing a mandatory deferral of payments for housing credit borrowers who are out of work: "We are saying that if the state wants to take care of the unemployed, it should do this directly" (Economic Committee 2017). Or as a Swedish regulator explained:

> "[W]e have no arrangements for people with low income. . . . We have no social tariffs in Sweden, not at all. If you cannot pay your electricity bill—if you are a poor family and need milk for your children, you cannot ask the store for a price reduction because of being poor. If you are poor, you should rely on the social welfare system, not the electric- ity market." (Rubinstein Reiss 2009, 121, quoted in Haber 2011, 126)

However, the strength of such arguments was, in practice, limited, as regula- tion was enacted in some cases even when such arguments were raised, as can be seen in the Israeli and EU electricity sectors. However, those countering this argument often used examples from other policy sectors in which such policy has been implemented, either internationally or in other sectors in the same country.

For example, in Israel, in the discussion (already mentioned) of deferring interest payments for out-of-work mortgage borrowers, regulation of electric- ity and water disconnection was raised by both the representative of the banks and political actors (Economic Committee 2017). Similar exchanges occurred during the discussion of social regulation in the electricity sector, as the head of the Knesset economic committee asked "What [did] the economists at the water authority know that those at the electricity regulator did not?" (Haber 2016, 450).

## Power of Interests

The evidence regarding the role of powerful interests and industry in the devel- opment of regulation preventing service termination is mixed. On one hand, while providers often objected to the social regulation of sectors, such regulation was enacted, if often in a modified form, after a process of negotiation. For exam- ple, in Israel, a final version of legislation, stipulating banks must provide alterna- tive housing to evicted borrowers, placed the required period of alternative housing at 18 rather than 36 months, following the banks' objections (Duanis 2008; Farkash Barouch 2009). Additionally, in the UK housing credit sector, some of the schemes protecting consumers were entered in by lenders after they received government incentives. For example, lenders agreed not to repossess mortgages of the recipients of the Support for Mortgage Interest benefit in the UK after the government agreed to pay the benefit directly to lenders (Mabbett 2011; Haber 2015).

Similarly, regulation sometimes mirrors policy already in place as commercial practice: for example, before water disconnection in Israel was banned, some providers had already ceased this practice out of commercial considerations

(Haber 2016). Thus, even if industry often objected to the introduction of regulation in the first place, the policies put in place were often agreed to, similar to policies they already followed, or even favorable to the industry. Thus, industry may not dictate whether regulation occurs, but it seems to play an important role in the shape regulation takes.

# Conclusion

This article asks how and why the state addresses the question of individual-level service terminations, based on evidence from a compound, comparative study of several policy sectors in different polities. These questions have significant social implications for households facing debt and arrears in these services, such as losing their homes or access to vital services. These questions also matter for markets, as losing access to such services impacts people's ability to participate in economic life, in turn impacting service providers, lenders, and the economy more generally, as we saw following the 2008 economic crisis and the systemic impact of mortgage default. These questions also matter theoretically, for the scholarship on the regulatory state, which often assumes that regulation of economic sectors focuses on economic efficiency, and they matter for the study of the welfare state, which has typically focused on social spending.

The current study's findings show that contrary to these expectations, in many cases, regulation was introduced to reduce and even prevent the occurrence of services termination, as well as to compensate for the social impacts of services being withdrawn due to economic hardship. The most consistent variation in the development of this type of regulation is at the national level, as it developed in Israel, the UK, and the EU, but not in Sweden. This implies that explanations based on policy context, and specifically that of differences in existing welfare policies, shape the development of regulation addressing termination and repossession due to economic hardship. This implies a substitutive relationship between welfare policy through spending to social policy pursued through regulation. Institutionalized welfare states are characterized by less regulation addressing social issues in consumer markets, while residual welfare states use more regulatory measures in this regard.

The welfare state impacts how regulation for welfare will develop within economic sectors. When compared to the residual welfare states in the study, the Swedish case demonstrates how an institutionalized welfare state mitigates social risks before they impact consumers' ability to pay for electric power, water, or housing. The welfare state also allows regulators to rely on existing cash benefits, rather than introduce new and often less than efficient forms of regulation. At the same time, an institutionalized welfare state may also constrain the introduction of sector-level regulation through limiting what is perceived as an appropriate form and target of social policy.

What further strengthens this argument is the study's compound research design, which highlights both within-country similarities between the different sectors, and the between-country differences, especially between the UK and

Israel on one hand, and Sweden on the other. At the same time, the study shows differences between the same policy sector in different countries. These similarities and differences taken together imply that drivers of regulatory welfare should be sought out at the national level.

The current study is limited in the number of national cases, as well as by the lack of additional types of welfare states, namely conservative cases. If welfare states matter for how regulatory welfare develops, then it would be important to know how a conservative welfare state affects the development of such regulation as well as how differences between such welfare states (such as Germany or France) impact a state's development.

The interaction between EU-level directives of the kind discussed here and subsequent regulation at the Member State–level is another driver of regulatory welfare requiring further study. Studying the impact of EU regulation on different types of Member States may also offer insight into the development of regulatory welfare and how it develops in the context of different welfare states and state traditions.

Finally, the question of fairness and efficacy of this type of social protection requires further study. The social impacts of regulatory welfare require attention, both at the individual sector level and at the national level, and beyond. How does taking regulatory welfare into account across multiple sectors impact people's welfare, and how does it change our overall understanding of welfare efforts between different countries (Haber 2016; Howard 2007)?

This research demonstrates growth in the use of regulation for the protection of vulnerable people in markets for crucial goods and services. While theoretically unexpected and often opposed by regulators and service providers, it may be seen as part of how regulatory regimes and social protections are developing, at least in the context of residual welfare states. The study of regulation for welfare purposes matters, then, for the study of regulation of markets, showing how regulation addresses issues beyond the economic, and how it may support the functioning of markets (Haber 2011, 2018). At the same time, studying how regulation ensures access to crucial market services is important for our understanding of the welfare state and how it is changing.

## Notes

1. In a Liberal welfare state, "state provision of welfare is minimal, benefits are modest and often attract strict entitlement criteria, and recipients are usually means-tested and stigmatised, " while in a Social Democratic welfare state, "Welfare provision is characterised by universal and comparatively generous benefits, a commitment to full employment and income protection, and a strongly interventionist state used to promote equality through a redistributive social security system" (Bambra 2007, 1098). The Israeli welfare state has been characterized in different ways, such as a hybrid model, combining elements of different welfare state types (Gal 2004), a liberal model, or in a transition toward becoming a Liberal welfare state (Haber 2011). A similar distinction between types of welfare states is that between an institutional, or comprehensive and highly redistributive welfare state as in Sweden, and a more residual welfare state, in which the level of benefits and redistribution is lower (Sainsbury 1991), as in the UK and in Israel.

2. Majone describes these concepts in the following way: "the fundamental theory of welfare econom-ics . . . states that, under some assumptions, competitive markets lead to an efficient allocation of resources, that is, to a situation where there is no rearrangement of resources . . . such that someone can be made better off without, at the same time, making someone else worse off. Such a situation is said to be Pareto efficient (or Pareto-optimal)" (Majone 1996, 28).

3. The regulation requires that most vulnerable consumers in arrears be moved to a prepayment meter instead of being disconnected, while a small number of consumers, those requiring life-saving medical equipment and Holocaust survivors receiving a social discount, cannot be disconnected (Electricity Authority 2017).

4. Mortgage rescue schemes are no longer active in England (Money Advice Service 2020).

5. Directive on credit agreements for consumers relating to residential immovable property.

6. See, for example, the UK's Warm Homes and Energy Conservation Act of 2000, aiming to reduce fuel poverty.

# References

Arts, Wil, and John Gelissen. 2002. Three worlds of welfare capitalism or more? A state-of-the-art report. *Journal of European Social Policy* 12 (2): 137–58.

Bambra, Clare. 2007. Going beyond the three worlds of welfare capitalism: regime theory and public health research. *Journal of Epidemiology and Community Health* 61 (12): 1098–1102.

Béland, Daniel. 2009. Ideas, institutions, and policy change. *Journal of European Public Policy* 16 (5): 701–18. https://doi.org/10.1080/13501760902983382.

Benish, Avishai, Hanan Haber, and Rotem Eliahou. 2016. The regulatory welfare state in pension markets: Mitigating high charges for low income savers in the United Kingdom and Israel. *Journal of Social Policy*. DOI: https://doi.org/10.1017/S0047279416000593.

Birkland, Thomas A. 1998. Focusing events, mobilization, and agenda setting. *Journal of Public Policy* 18 (1): 53–74.

Blyth, Mark. 2013. Paradigms and paradox: The politics of economic ideas in two moments of crisis. *Governance* 26 (2): 197–215. https://doi.org/10.1111/gove.12010.

Carpenter, Daniel. 2002. Groups the media agency waiting costs and fda drug approval. *American Journal of Political Science* 46 (2).

Danforth, Benjamin. 2014. Worlds of welfare in time: A historical reassessment of the three-world typol-ogy. *Journal of European Social Policy* 24 (2): 164–82. https://doi.org/10.1177/0958928713517919.

Department of Business, Energy and Industrial Strategy. 2018. *Warm home discount scheme 2018/19*. Available from https://beisgovuk.citizenspace.com/home-local-energy/warm-home-discount-2018/.

Duanis, Nati. 2008. The Union of Banks in the Committee for Constitution Legislation and Law: "We are concerned about a revolution in the writ of execution law." Available from http://www.economist.co.il/?CategoryID=1312&ArticleID=1692.

Eckert, Sandra. 2017. Two spheres of regulation: Balancing social and economic goals. *Regulation & Governance*. https://doi.org/10.1111/rego.12137.

Economic Committee. 2017. Protocol No. 600, Economic Committee Meeting. Available from https://oknesset.org/meetings/2/0/2021244.html.

EI. 2017. The Swedish Electricity and Gas Market 2016. Available from https://www.ei.se/PageFiles/310277/Ei_R2017_06.pdf.

Electricity Authority. 2017. Regulating the collection of consumption bills of residential consumers. Available from https://www.gov.il/BlobFolder/policy/52501d/he/Files_Hachlatot_nisp1_01525.pdf.

Esping-Andersen, G. 1990. *The three worlds of welfare capitalism*. New York, NY: Polity Press.

EurEaU. 2016. *Access to water and measures in case of non-payment*. Available from http://www.eureau.org/resources/position-papers/137-access-to-water-and-measures-in-case-of-non-payment-august2016/file.

European Banking Authority. 2015. Final report: Guidelines on arrears and foreclosure. Available from https://eba.europa.eu.

Farkash Barouch, Rimona. 28 July 2009. The amendment meant to prevent the eviction of debtors out into the street. Calcalist. Available from https://www.calcalist.co.il/money/articles/0,7340,L-3335322,00 .html.

Gal, Jon. 2004. Decommodification and beyond: A comparative analysis of work-injury programmes. *Journal of European Social Policy* 14 (1): 55–69.

Haber, Hanan. 2011. Regulating-for-welfare: A comparative study of "regulatory welfare regimes" in the Israeli, British, and Swedish Electricity Sectors. *Law & Policy* 33 (1): 116–48.

Haber, Hanan. 2015. Regulation as social policy: Home evictions and repossessions in the UK and Sweden. *Public Administration.* https://doi.org/10.1111/padm.12171.

Haber, Hanan. 2016. Rise of the regulatory welfare state? Social regulation in utilities in Israel. *Social Policy & Administration.* http://onlinelibrary.wiley.com/doi/10.1111/spol.12194/pdf.

Haber, Hanan. 2018. Liberalizing markets, liberalizing welfare? Economic reform and social regulation in the EU's electricity regime. *Journal of European Public Policy* 25 (3):307–26. https://doi.org/10.1080/13501763.2016.1249012.

Haber, Hanan, Nir Kosti, and David Levi-Faur. 2018. Welfare through regulatory means: Eviction and repossession policies in Singapore. *Housing Studies* 34 (3): 1–18. https://doi.org/10.1080/02673037.2018.1447095.

Hartlapp, Miriam. 2020. Measuring the strength of social objectives in the economy? A regulatory output index. *The ANNALS of the American Academy of Political and Social Science* (this volume).

Howard, C. 2007. *The welfare state nobody knows: Debunking myths about US social policy.* Princeton, NJ: Princeton University Press.

Jensen, Carsten, Georg Wenzelburger, and Reimut Zohlnhöfer. 2019. Dismantling the welfare state? After twenty-five years: what have we learned and what should we learn? *Journal of European Social Policy.* https://doi.org/10.1177/0958928719877363.

Kenna, Padraic. 2018. Mortgage law developments in the European Union. *Journal of Law, Property, and Society* 4:45–80.

KFM. n.d. Attachment. Kronofogdemyndigheten. Available from https://www.kronofogden.se/en-GB/Utmatning2.html.

Korpi, Walter. 1983. *The Democratic class struggle.* New York, NY: Routledge & Kegan Paul Books.

Leisering, Lutz, and Deborah Mabbett. 2011. Introduction: Towards a new regulatory state in old age security? Exploring the issues. In *The new regulatory state. Regulating private pensions in Germany and the UK*, ed. Lutz Leisering. New York, NY: Palgrave.

Lerner, Pablo. 2011. Alternative housing in the case of repossession of a dwelling: Discussion following rulings and the reform in the writ of execution law. *Hapraklit* 51 (1): 51–104.

Levi-Faur, David. 2006. Varieties of regulatory capitalism: Getting the most out of the comparative method. *Governance* 19 (3): 367–82.

Levi-Faur, David. 2014. The welfare state: A regulatory perspective. *Public Administration.* https://doi.org/10.1111/padm.12063.

Mabbett, Deborah. 2011. Disfunctional equivalence: Financial regulation and social policy. 23rd Annual Meeting of the Society for the Advancement of Socio-Economics Autonomous University of Madrid, June 23–25.

Mabbett, Deborah. 2013. Polanyi in Brussels or Luxembourg? Social rights and market regulation in European insurance. *Regulation & Governance* 8 (2): 186–202.

Majone, Giandomenico. 1994. The rise of the regulatory state in Europe. In *The state in Western Europe: Retreat or redefinition*, eds. Wolfgang C. Müller and Vincent Wright, 77–101. Essex, UK: Frank Cass & Co.

Majone, Giandomenico. 1996. Theories of regulation. In *Regulating Europe*, ed. Giandomenico Majone, 28–46. London: Routledge.

Majone, Giandomenico. 1997. From the positive to the regulatory state: Causes and consequences of changes in the mode of governance. *Journal of Public Policy* 17 (2): 139–67.

Majone, Giandomenico. 2011. The transformations of the regulatory state. In *The new regulatory state. Regulating private pensions in Germany and the UK*, ed. Lutz Leisering. New York, NY: Palgrave.

Midgley, James. 1986. Industrialization and welfare: The case of the four little tigers. *Social Policy & Administration* 20 (3): 225–38. https://doi.org/10.1111/j.1467-9515.1986.tb00253.x.

Money Advice Service. 2020. Government help if you can't pay your mortgage. Available from https://www.moneyadviceservice.org.uk/en/articles/government-help-if-you-cant-pay-your-mortgage.

OFGEM. 2020. Energy supply disconnection and prepayment meter rules. Available from https://www.ofgem.gov.uk/consumers/household-gas-and-electricity-guide/who-contact-if-its-difficult-paying-energy-bills/energy-supply-disconnection-and-prepayment-meter-rules.

OFWAT. 2020. Customer Assistance. Available from https://www.ofwat.gov.uk/households/customer-assistance/.

Pflieger, Géraldine. 2014. What "regulatory state"? Explaining the stability of public spending and redistribution functions after regulatory reforms of electricity and rail services in the United Kingdom and Germany. *Law & Policy* 36 (2): 195–221. https://doi.org/10.1111/lapo.12018.

Pierson, Paul. 1994. *Dismantling the welfare state? Reagan, Thatcher, and the politics of retrenchment*. Cambridge: Cambridge University Press.

Pierson, Paul. 2000. Increasing returns, path dependence, and the study of politics. *The American Political Science Review* 94 (2): 251–67.

Pierson, Paul. 2001. *The new politics of the welfare state*. Oxford: Oxford University Press.

Polanyi, Karl. 1946. *Origins of our time, great transformation*. Rev. ed. London: V.Golancz.

Rubinstein Reiss, D. 2009. Agency accountability strategies after liberalization: Universal service in the United Kingdom, France, and Sweden. *Law & Policy* 31 (1): 111–41.

Sainsbury, Diana. 1991. Analysing welfare state variations: The merits and limitations of models based on the residual–institutional distinction. *Scandinavian Political Studies* 14 (1): 1–30.

Schmidt, Manfred G. 1996. When parties matter: A review of the possibilities and limits of partisan influence on public policy. *European Journal of Political Research* 30 (2): 155–83. https://doi.org/10.1111/j.1475-6765.1996.tb00673.x.

Socialstyrelsen. n.d. Social Assistance. Available from https://web.archive.org/web/20190331161115/http://www.socialstyrelsen.se/socialassistance.

Thelen, K. 2003. How institutions evolve: Insights from comparative historical analysis. In *Comparative historical analysis in the social sciences*, eds. James Mahoney and Dietrich Rueschemeyer, 208–40. Cambridge: Cambridge University Press.

Trein, Philipp. 2020. Bossing or protecting? The integration of social regulation into the welfare state. *The ANNALS of the American Academy of Political and Social Science* (this volume).

Wilson, James Q. 1980. *The politics of regulation*. New York, NY: Basic Books.

# Measuring and Comparing the Regulatory Welfare State: Social Objectives in Public Procurement

This article constructs an index that translates the substance of policy documents into numeric values across three dimensions of regulation—a qualitative assessment of policy substance, its potential impact, and enforcement of regulation—which aims to capture the strength of social objectives in the economy. It draws on theories of economic regulation and literature on the welfare state to develop a general understanding of social objectives. The use of the index is illustrated through public procurement regulation in two European countries (France and Germany) and shows an overall increase in the strength of social objectives. It also highlights systematic differences in country priorities in the regulation of their economy. The index demonstrates that social regulation can be measured and compared in a meaningful way within and across countries.

*Keywords:* public procurement; regulation; social goals

*By*
MIRIAM HARTLAPP

Freer markets come with more rules (Vogel 1998), but the rules do not relate exclusively to competition and price efficiency. Free market rules can promote other objectives, such as welfare norms and social ends. Such rules ensure that services offered in hospitals meet standards of maximum working hours or that mortgage credits offer old age security. The literature on the regulatory welfare state (RWS) provides analytical leverage in studying

*Miriam Hartlapp is a professor of comparative politics (Germany and France) at the Freie Universität Berlin. She teaches and researches European integration and comparative politics, in particular questions of power, contestation, and conflict in the EU Multilevel System; the intersection of economic and social integration; as well as implementation and compliance.*

NOTE: An earlier version of this article was presented at the workshop "Regulation & Welfare" at Jerusalem University, May 2019. I wish to thank all participants for the discussion, Konstantin Schönfelder and Léonore Stangherlin for valuable research assistance, and the two anonymous reviewers as well as the editors of this special issue for their excellent comments.

Correspondence: Miriam.hartlapp@fu-berlin.de

DOI: 10.1177/0002716220952060

these developments (Windholz and Hodge 2013; Levi-Faur 2014; Benish and Levi-Faur, this volume). Yet scholars interested in the RWS have mostly focused on social policies, and there are few analyses that study how regulation addresses social objectives in other policy fields, such as the provision of utilities or financial products (Haber 2018; Eckert 2018; Schwartz 2009; Hartlapp and Rauh 2013). This is unfortunate, because regulation has the potential to create more solidarity and equality among different groups of market participants, create social cohesion in societies, and promote justice in access or consumption of goods and services that link directly to economic policy. One example is that of public procurement: regulation can create more solidarity by requiring that the footballs used in public schools and produced in the Global South have been sewed by adults rather than children. It can create social cohesion by requiring the bidder to ensure payment of collective wages in its production chain and promote justice by setting aside a certain percentage of jobs in public construction sites to groups of citizens discriminated against in the labor market. Furthermore, existing studies focus on single instruments or country cases, and are limited in the time period that they cover.

This article develops an index of regulation for social purposes that works toward systematizing our knowledge of the RWS, and potentially yielding comparative insights. I go on to illustrate use of the index for public procurement, a topic that lends itself to the study of regulation for social purposes beyond the field of social policy. Public procurement regulation aims to support and promote competition and flexibility in public contracting. It targets private enterprises, intermediaries, and supply chains, and regulates production as well as products. Public procurement regulation applies to anything from purchasing food for public schools to large-scale infrastructure construction. In terms of scale, public procurement is an economically significant policy area, with about 14 percent of GDP spent on public contracts across the European Union (EU) (European Commission 2016) and an estimated \$1.5 trillion annually in the United States (Conway 2012, 143).

Public procurement is an interesting subject for study in social regulation not just because of the volume of government spending that is channeled into the economy. Two other reasons are material to my arguments in this article. First, in a narrow sense, public procurement regulation has the potential to render a market more social for equal levels of spending. When purchasing workwear for \$ 1,000, a public enterprise can go to a sweatshop or buy fair trade labels. Thus, for equal spending levels, a state can decide whether to spend money on the basis of a pure cost-benefit analysis, or whether to also include social goals (McCrudden 2004; Wiesbrock 2015). Critics argue that social criteria in public procurement distort the market, create unnecessary complexity, and increase prices (e.g., Sánchez-Graells 2015; for an overview see Conway 2012, 146). Therefore, some public procurement regimes prohibit their use. Where contracts are awarded to bidders offering lower prices, enterprises are unlikely to respect collective agreements or will discriminate against less advantaged groups in the labor market. Similarly, without social criteria, products offered at a lower price are likely to be purchased without regard, for example, for unfair working conditions. Social goals in public procurement therefore steer the behavior of market participants away from simple price efficiency. They do so directly, via contracts, and indirectly, when a large number of competing bidders change their behavior to conform to award criteria that include social goals. At least some of these bidders are then likely to align their future behavior with these social objectives, too. Thus, social objectives in market regulation are interesting because they affect outcomes of markets.

My second interest in this article is public procurement as a case of regulation that increases welfare beyond the state. If social goals and norms are not limited to the welfare state, this opens up questions on the similarities and differences of the process and driving factors supporting these goals and norms in the welfare state and other areas of the state, as well as—regarding outcomes—their substitutive or supplementary nature. This analysis can thus provide insights for the study of boundaries of the regulatory welfare state and has the potential to travel to other cases, for example, para-state agencies or service delivery (Reiter, this volume; Klenk, this volume).

To aid in my study of the points above, I propose a measure for regulation for social purposes that can be applied to a broad range of regulatory topics. To construct this measure, I draw on different understandings of social objectives in theories of regulation and the welfare state literature. Theories of economic regulation summarize social objectives under a general public interest in functioning markets, but they do not differentiate *social* from other market-enabling objectives. The welfare state literature, on the other hand, is specifically interested in public (and increasingly private) policies that provide individuals with social rights or protect them against social risks. This article borrows from this literature with the aim of discussing what social objectives are and how they can be identified in the economy.

Against this background, and building on advances in macro-qualitative policy analysis (Steinebach and Knill 2017; Deakin, Lele, and Siems 2007; Caughey and Warshaw 2016; Kholodilin et al. 2019), I develop an index that translates the substance of policy documents into numeric values across three dimensions of regulation: a qualitative assessment of policy substance, its potential impact, and enforcement of regulation. Extending the policy-cycle in this manner allows us to move beyond the focus on formal regulatory output prevalent in existing studies (Guidi, Guardiancich, and Levi-Faur 2020, 8), and to work toward practical relevance for a society.

The main aim of the article is exploratory. Yet measuring and comparing regulation for social purposes promises to provide insights that could be helpful for advancing broader debates on the RWS (Benish and Levi-Faur, this volume). First, existing scholarship differs in response to the question whether the regulatory state grows instead of (Majone 1997), within, or alongside the welfare state (Trein, this volume). This differentiation is important for understanding the potential of regulation to condition (growing) markets, as well as possible trade-offs with welfare state policies. For example, Schwartz (2009) has shown how mortgage credit regulation operates as a substitute for broad public pension instruments in the United States. Second, and closely related, is the question whether we should conceive of the RWS as an independent concept or whether regulation is simply another tool in the box of the welfare state. While answering this question is beyond the scope of this article, the index can help to identify regulatory regimes or time periods that are particularly promising for a more in-depth analysis of the nexus of welfare state institutions (Rothstein, Paul, and Demeritt 2020, 24) or state traditions (Guidi, Guardiancich, and Levi-Faur 2020, 15) and regulatory output.

The remainder of the article is in four parts. The first part provides a conceptualization of the two core concepts of the argument: regulation and social objective. Next, the article turns to the question of how to distill large quantities of information on policies into only a few numbers, and to this aim suggests a three-dimensional index. The third part illustrates the application of the index to public procurement as an important area of economic regulation in Germany and France. The final part then discusses the potential of the index to capture and analyze regulation across countries and over time, and explores the meaning of the findings in terms of the RWS.

# Conceptualizing Social Objectives in Regulation of the Economy

Neither in economic nor in political science scholarship is there a fixed definition of the term *regulation*. For the purpose of this article, I define regulation in such a way that it covers legislative acts as well as rules negotiated by actors outside the legislative process, such as administrations, agencies, or private actors. This goes against the delineation of legislative politics and regulation commonly put forward in the literature. Legislation, by definition, originates in the legislator. Regulation, meanwhile, involves a potentially greater range of rule-makers. It is frequently associated with the rise of network agencies, bureaucratic actors, and other arm's length bodies, such as public corporations (Jordana, Fernández-i-Marín, and Bianculli 2018). To this can be added private actors who self-regulate (cf. Eberlein et al. 2013). However, for a comparative analysis of social objectives in regulation, a focus on either one of the rule-makers risks the introduction of bias. Depending on the set-up of their political system, countries are likely to differ in the relative weight given to administrative and legislative rule making. What is more, countries also differ in the influence they grant to market and civil actors in regulation (Levi-Faur 2011, 8). A good example are corporatist countries in which social partners independently negotiate collective agreements, while in other countries statutory working time and wage standards exist. Excluding either one of the rule-makers might thus distort our assessment across countries. What is more, regulation goes beyond what is "in the books" to include potential impact and enforcement. I therefore side with the classical definition that Selznick (1985, 363) gives that "regulation refers to sustained and focused control exercised by a public agency over activities that are valued by a community." Thus, regulation does not stop with rule making because rules still have to be monitored, assessed, sanctioned, or enforced by other means. Ultimately, and with reference to the definition of regulation I just provided, we therefore broaden public enforcement to also include cooperation with market or civil actors. With this understanding of regulation in mind, we now turn to a clarification of *social objectives*.

## Social objectives in regulation theory

My focus on regulation of the economy makes economic theories of regulation a natural point of departure for understanding regulation's objectives and their drivers. Yet theories of regulation give little guidance on social objectives. To define social objectives, these theories will need to be combined with insights from welfare state research. Somewhat simplifying economic theories of regulation, they may be divided into public interest theories and private interest theories (Ogus 1994). Public interest theories assume that regulators hold sufficient information and enforcement powers to pursue public interests in case of market failures. They may regulate for social objectives where a market price does not reflect the true costs for a society. Typical examples are objectives related to health, safety, consumer protection, and the environment. Yet in these theories, it is not possible to differentiate social objectives from other market enabling conditions. What is considered good for society is anything that allows individual utilities to be aggregated in a market (Windholz and Hodge 2013, 22). Beyond this, the general public interest remains underspecified (Prosser 2007, 243). Private interest theories, in turn, assume that regulators lack information and enforcement powers vis à vis private interests (Stigler 1971). Here, private demands explain regulation, and social objectives will be pursued only where they coincide with private interests. These two strands of traditional regulation theory differ in their assumptions and consequently in their explanations for regulation. But for both, market efficiency is key. Meanwhile, social regulation theorists work against this focus on market efficiency and explicitly include social objectives as noneconomic factors in their regulation theory.

For Prosser (2006), such social objectives include (individual) rights and the maintenance of social solidarity. Ogus (1994, 46) defines distributional justice, paternalism, and community value as wider social objectives.[1] Regulation can seek these objectives directly, where it is "primarily designed to pursue redistribution goals" (Ogus 1994, 48), or indirectly, where the objective is different but its distributional consequences are considered. And yet, social regulation theory mainly understands social objectives in negative terms, as the exclusion of market efficiency. We therefore turn to the welfare state literature for a positive conceptualization of social objectives.

## Social objectives seen from the welfare state

Welfare state theories make two suggestions on how to define social objectives: individual rights and collective protection. For social objectives as individual rights, Thomas H. Marshall's (1950) work provides a classic starting point. For him, social objectives range from "a modicum of welfare and security to the right to share to the full in the social heritage and to live the life of a civilized being according to the standards prevailing in society" ( 81). In contrast, collective protection is built around the objectives of distributional justice, social solidarity, and equity when addressing social risks. Historically, the range of identified social risks grew with the development of welfare states: sickness was covered first under Bismarck (Germany, 1881), followed by work injuries and pension.

Today, all welfare states pursue these goals to some degree, but the relative importance of specific objectives has been linked to particular configurations of ideas, interests, and institutions. According to Esping-Andersen (1990), liberal welfare states pursue individual rights via market solutions. Here, egalitarian protection is limited to residual public welfare. In contrast, universal social protection as a social objective is more fully developed in social democratic welfare states. For Esping-Andersen (1990), such variation in the social objectives must be attributed to mobilization of the working class and cross-class alignments. These result in particular institutions that shape developments along historical paths of liberal, social democratic, and conservative worlds of welfare state capitalism.

While this is not the place to discuss the merits of Esping-Andersen's argument or to highlight alternative explanations, it illustrates a phenomenon that is important for our argument. That is, in contrast to economic theories of regulation, many welfare state scholars focus on broader output patterns or entire regimes, rather than single instruments. Further, while theories of economic regulation center industry interests or "the state" as causes for regulation, the welfare state literature typically offers more complex explanations that link ideas, interests, and institutions across historical trajectories.

Scholarship on the RWS has taken inspiration from the welfare state literature to describe and explain differences between regulatory regimes. These regulatory regimes, including their social objectives, are shaped by a range of different factors: the polity (political institutions and administrative and legal system), and the economy (sector and coordination) (Guidi, Guardiancich, and Levi-Faur 2020, 9), as well as "welfare provision and wider norms and traditions of state action" (Rothstein, Paul, and Demeritt 2020, 21). Following this line of reasoning, we expect that regulation, which increases welfare beyond the state, should be driven by similar factors as the welfare state. We can further expect such regulation to include strong social objectives, particularly in countries and during time periods where welfare provisions are well-developed, and where polity and economy show characteristics of social democratic welfare states. While such a causal link seems theoretically plausible, the actual link between social objectives and regulatory regimes remains open to empirical investigation. And while a descriptive index will not be able to answer this question, the patterns emerging from the index could render such a link more plausible. Further, comparison could help to identify regulatory regimes or time periods that are particularly promising for in-depth analysis.

# Index Building

Regulatory indices are typically built on broad topic categories such as housing (Kholodilin et al. 2019), data protection (Mizrahi-Borohovich and Levi-Faur 2020), or financial services (Hartlapp and Rauh 2013). Within each topic, a number of goals and strategies can be identified to address an existing policy problem. In the words of Mizrahi-Borohovich and Levi-Faur (2020, 113), these strategies create sub-regimes. For example, in housing we can differentiate sub-regimes for rent control, tenant protection, and the rationing of rental housing (Kholodilin et al. 2019). Following our research interest, we have selected those sub-regimes for analysis that follow a social objective, as conceptualized here.[2] We propose that the strength of social objectives is affected by three analytically distinct dimensions of regulation: substance, potential impact, and enforcement.

*Substance* refers to the content and meaning of the standards and provisions that form a policy. In terms of their substance, sub-regimes may cover social objectives more or less broadly. In a first step, a list of the possible standards catering to a social objective is drawn up for each sub-regime. This is achieved by a thorough reading of the existing regulation, on the basis of which we inductively generate a list of possible standards. Our sources include legislation; national, European, or international soft law instruments, such as guidelines; as well as reports; webpages; and newspaper articles. Next, the standards identified in a concrete case are compared to this list of possible standards by dividing the number of concrete standards found by the number of possible standards. We are aware that we cannot assume the same standards to be applicable across all countries. However, the list of possible standards may serve as a benchmark against which to measure the efforts for social regulation in different countries and time periods (for a similar approach see Kholodilin et al. 2019; Mizrahi-Borohovich and Levi-Faur 2020, 114). For each sub-regime, the measure will amount to a value between 1 and 0. Where a country regulates a large number of the possible standards on the list, it will score closer to 1.

The *potential impact* of a sub-regime is captured by considering its relevance for a society. We acknowledge that any measure of actual impact would require systematic evaluation studies. However, this stands in tension with our aim to develop an index that allows us to compare broadly over time and across countries. The index, therefore, focuses on potential impact. Standards differ in their potential societal relevance, which is operationalized as the scope of beneficiaries. Regulatory sub-regimes differ in such scope, for example where they apply to specific groups, such as pensioners, or sectors, such as agriculture. Scope is affected by level of regulation, with subnational levels scoring lower, and exemptions, such as thresholds. For most standards we can assume that societal benefits grow in relation to their scope. As we want to avoid the impression that we can measure potential impact in all its detail, we operate with three broad categories. A multiplier of 1 applies where the entire population is (potentially) affected; a multiplier of 0.6 is applied where a large subgroup of society is covered, such as a specific age group or entire sectors; and a multiplier of 0.3 is applied where the objective applies to a small group only.[3]

Finally, sub-regimes differ along the dimension of *enforcement*. Existing accounts frequently use court cases as an indicator of such variation. According to the above conceptualization, it would be misleading to limit enforcement to courts. Typically, judicial enforcement is open to legislative instruments only, and excludes (soft) regulation (Hartlapp and Hofmann 2020). Consequently, we suggest a twofold measure that has the potential to contribute to a better understanding of enforcement, mainly by making hindrances in the legal provision and systematic noncompliance visible. First, we ask: is a sub-regime legally binding? Rules that are nonbinding are less likely to be followed. However, under specific circumstances, financial or other compliance incentives integrated into the rule can act as a functional equivalent to formally binding rules. Second, we ask: are enforcement measures reasonable or deficient? Enforcement covers a broad range of measures that are enacted by administrations, such as labor inspectorates, or jointly, by public and private actors (Hartlapp 2014). Reasonable enforcement is objective-specific (specific monitoring and sanctioning measures such as setting up supervisory bodies; empowering an agency with more money, staff, and competences; or providing proactive information), as well as systemic (sanctioning capacity as visible in the severity of punishment and judicial authority) (Hartlapp 2014). As in the case of potential impact, we want to avoid the impression that we can measure enforcement in all its detail and operate again with three broad categories. Sub-regimes characterized as nonbinding are multiplied by 0.3. Binding rules with deficient enforcement are counted with a multiplier of 0.6.

To calculate the strength of social objectives within a sub-regime, the scores for substance, potential impact, and enforcement are multiplied. Meanwhile, to answer many of the questions raised in the introduction to this article, we should look at a specific sub-regime. Frequently, they allow us to differentiate who (in terms of socioeconomic group) benefits from a social objective. Finally, for a measure of the overall strength of social objectives, the scores of different sub-regimes are aggregated. A higher score tells us that, rather than exclusively catering to price efficiency, regulation conditions the market to focus either on wider societal goals of distributional justice, on (individual) rights, or on the maintenance of social solidarity and equity.

Although ours is certainly not the first attempt to measure regulation for social purposes, the index we propose is unique in two ways. First, unlike indices that are developed for a specific policy problem (housing, see Kholodilin et al. 2019; consumer credit, see Mizrahi-Borohovich and Levi-Faur 2020), our index is grounded in general reasoning on social objectives. It can therefore travel widely to be applied to a broad range of regulatory topics beyond the area of social policy. Second, the index goes beyond regulatory output, allowing us to anticipate actual outcomes by including potential impact and enforcement as dimensions of regulation. While the index does not aim to measure or even explain outcomes in terms of more or less social markets, as these are affected by many other economic and social variables, it is constructed in such a way that it provides insights into a longer stretch of the policy cycle than already existing indices.

There are also limitations to the index. Most importantly, the index has to square the circle of offering a sufficiently valid measure of social objectives while remaining extensive enough to cover functionally equivalent standards and formulations across topics, countries, and time. This means it risks sacrificing one for the other. In a way, this risk is the flip side of what is also the index's greatest strength, namely that it is general rather than policy-specific. Another limitation concerns the relative impact of the different dimensions. Far-reaching substantial changes could be easily levelled out by potential impact and enforcement. This means that regulatory changes are likely to be underestimated where they are not accompanied by changes in scope and enforcement measures. This can potentially diminish the value of the index for dynamic causal analysis that looks, for example, for the effect of government change on social objectives in regulation.

## Putting the Index to Work: Public Procurement

This section applies the index to the cases of France and Germany, which have been chosen pragmatically on the basis of availability of data. In both countries, a roughly similar share of public expenditure goes to public procurement,[4] and EU public procurement regulation suggests a common regulatory frame, one that does not include social goals. Differences in social goals are thus expected to stem from specific national ideas, interests, and institutions. In the two cases the index reveals interesting differences, both between sub-regimes and over time. This suggests a potential for the index to bring out meaningful patterns for a wider range of cases. In the final part of this section, we explore a link to causal analysis by discussing scope and dynamics of the scores in light of German and French conceptualizations of the welfare state.

### Public procurement

At the national level, social criteria in public procurement have a long history, dating back to the nineteenth century in the United States, when President Van Buren issued an executive order on a "Ten Hour Work Day" in public works (31 March 1849). With privatization of public production and outsourcing of formerly public services, procurement has gained importance over the last decades. To identify the strength of social objectives in public procurement regulation we proceed in three steps: first, we identify sub-regimes seeking social objectives on the basis of secondary literature; second, we identify the universe of possible standards in these sub-regimes on the basis of primary sources; and third, we calculate and compare the standards in France and Germany.

First step: for public procurement the literature focuses on three sub-regimes that seek social objectives. They are discussed largely independently from one another, and different labels are used by different authors. Writing from a comparative politics perspective, scholars interested in public procurement emphasize (national) "production conditions." Geographically these studies focus on continental Europe (e.g., Sack and Sarter 2018). A second strand in the public procurement literature is interested in "products" that are sustainable in their provision of services and/or the (transnational) supply chain (e.g. Martin-Ortega and Methven O'Brien 2019; Hassel and Helmerich 2016). Finally, "insertion" is highlighted as a sub-regime mostly by U.S. scholars, typically focusing on race as a group characteristic (Noon 2009; Conway 2012).

Second step: we then gather possible standards in the three sub-regimes through an analysis of primary documents. Each standard may manifest in nuanced ways. Appendix Table A1 online provides a list of the standards that have been identified as possible standards seeking social objectives and describes a range of measures that allow for the identification of a standard in different countries with specific regulatory traditions and institutions.

1) The *production* sub-regime regulates the conditions under which goods and services are produced for the state. Three standards contribute to the production regime: 1.1) working conditions, such as maximum work and rest hours, or health and safety standards; 1.2) wage regulation, such as minimum wages, living wages, reference to statutory wages, and/or collective agreements; and 1.3) gender equality measures, such as antidiscrimination rules in recruitment and during employment.

2) The *insertion* sub-regime aims to correct injustices in employment, such as discrimination in hiring, promotion, or compensation against certain groups, and to create solidarity (Conway 2012, 146, 154). Standards provide five socially and economically disadvantaged groups with access to the labor market: 2.1) apprentices, 2.2) the disabled, 2.3) the unemployed, 2.4) veterans and war widows/widowers, and 2.5) minority businesses. Percentage goals, set-asides, and mandatory purchasing for one or all of these groups serve as instruments through which the standard can be put into practice.

3) The *product* sub-regime regulates goods and services for a more just and solidary society. Three possible standards can be identified: 3.1) barrier-free infrastructure; 3.2) sustainable public services and products; and 3.3) the application of ILO core labor standards when supplying, producing, assembling, or handling products in other countries and down the supply chain.

In public procurement the *potential impact* of a standard depends on its scope. Sometimes, waivers and *de minimis* rules are applied to public contracts. Production standards are frequently regulated at the level of industries that are particularly relevant for public procurement, such as public works. The scope of insertion standards is influenced by the size of the benefitting groups in a given country. For product standards the potential impact is likely to be high where infrastructures and services are provided for the entire society.

In many countries binding law is complemented by nonbinding standards and soft law, such as administrative manuals and guidelines. A lack of information about the legal hierarchy of different (soft and hard) rules can hamper *enforcement*.

FIGURE 1
Social Objectives in Different Sub-Regimes of Public Procurement (2000–2018)

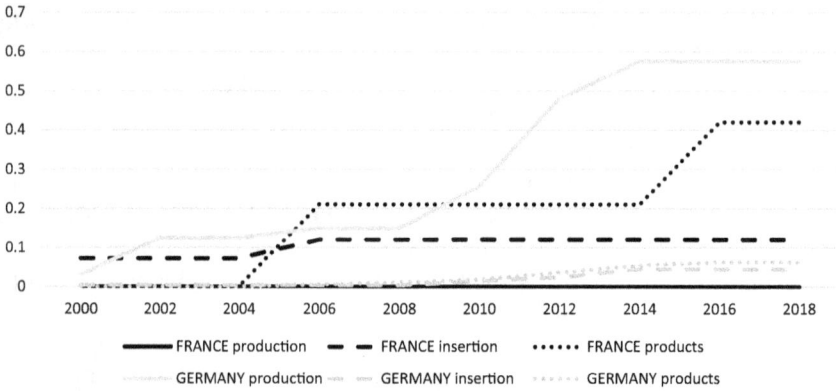

SOURCE: Data compiled by author (cf. online appendix A2).

Uncertainty might prevail, for example, regarding which groups are subsumed under a specific call or contract. Where great amounts of public money are spent, award criteria may serve as incentives to follow even nonbinding rules. Enforcement measures are carried out by labor inspectorates and customs authorities, while in some countries social partners are involved, too.

Third step: the strength of social objectives is measured by comparing the social standards in a concrete case against possible standards, while taking into account their potential impact as well as enforcement. This third step is illustrated through the cases of Germany and France. For Germany, assessment is based on the legislation of the sixteen federal states who (apart from Saxony) all exhibit social criteria in public procurement as well as soft law measures adopted by other actors (e.g. Deutscher Städtetag et al. 2010).[5] In France, hard and soft instruments by different actors (legislator, administration, local entities) are considered (e.g., Alliance Villes Emploi 2011). Figure 1 depicts the index for the three sub-regimes: production, insertion, and product for the period of 2000 to 2018. A detailed description of sub-regimes, their standards, potential impact, and enforcement is provided in online Appendix A2, and transformed into social regulation scores that are visualized in Figure 1.

The index clearly shows that, during the period under investigation, both countries have increased their social objectives in public procurement regulation over time. In Germany, the index highlights a pronounced focus on production standards (solid line). Here, regulation of remuneration is the most important standard. Many federal states require firms to remunerate in accordance with collective agreements, for example, when employing workers on public construction sites. More recently, minimum wages have replaced collective agreements as the primary reference point in a number of federal states. This is related to legal uncertainty due to discrepancies in EU and national legislation and related case law of the European Court of Justice (*Rüffert C-346/06* and *PostRegio C-115/14*) (Hartlapp and Hofmann 2020). Increased scores since 2010 can be attributed to newly introduced standards on gender equality. The two sub-regimes of insertion (dashed line) and social production (dotted line) have both become part of public procurement more recently and thus remain weaker. The insertion sub-regime is focused on apprentices, and standards can be identified early on; however, their scope is limited to four federal states. Integration of disabled people into the labor market is a measure pursued by only two federal states. Production standards are also limited in their potential scope, but the number of federal states in which purchased products should obey ILO core labor standards has grown to eleven over the last decade. In both sub-regimes, lower scores on the index can be attributed to the enforcement dimension, as standards here remain nonbinding.

For France, the index highlights that public procurement turned "social" later than in Germany and remains more contained overall. Here, groups disadvantaged in the labor market (dashed line) and products (dotted line) are the most important areas of regulation that render public procurement social. The insertion regime comprises standards that aim at the integration of unemployed and disabled people into the labor market. For the unemployed, measures typically take the form of administrative decrees and swing in accordance with the economic situation. Yet they are formulated and enforced rather ambiguously. The disabled are a second group of people that gain enhanced access to the labor market via public procurement regulations. This standard is responsible for the rise in the score in 2006. At this point, enforcement turned much more stringent via set-asides for sheltered work centers and incentives to award contracts to firms employing a majority of disabled people. Scores also rose in 2006 for the product sub-regime, because public infrastructure is now required to be barrier-free on a conditionally binding basis (*"chaque fois que possible"*). The product sub-regime was further strengthened in 2014 by the introduction of new standards on sustainability of public goods and services. Strikingly, production standards that target working conditions of those employed in public works or in the provision of public goods play no role at all.

Comparing developments between countries, the index clearly shows a greater strength of social objectives in Germany than in France. More importantly, it brings out differences in sub-regimes. For Germany, the index highlights a strong focus on individual social rights to strengthen the weaker party in an employment relationship. In France, the regulation of the economy seems to be geared toward social solidarity and equity over individual social rights. This difference brings out specific national patterns in *how* markets regulate for social objectives. Another clear merit of the index is that it captures variation across the three dimensions of regulation and makes this variation comparable across countries. In Germany, changes in the number of federal states applying a standard account for much of the dynamism via the potential impact dimension. Lower scores in France are by and large due to many nonbinding standards and thus are influenced more strongly by the enforcement dimension. Such explanations for country-specific dynamics would have remained obscured in a more classical assessment of law that considers substance of standards independent of their scope or enforcement. In sum, applying the index to public procurement regulation shows how the index can capture variation across sub-regimes and across the three dimensions of regulation, as well as how it makes this variation comparable between countries.

## Summary and Outlook

Where freer markets come with more rules, questions arise around whether and how such rules can render markets more social. Therefore, this article has asked how to best assess regulation for social purposes in the economy. Scholarship on economic regulation has considered social objectives at a general level. By drawing on conceptualizations of social objectives in the welfare state literature, this article identified two broad sets of social goals: individual rights that aim to strengthen the weaker party in a market relationship, and objectives of distributional justice, social solidarity, and equity that fill the notion of a public interest with specific meaning. I then used these objectives to identify and measure the strength of social objectives through a three-dimensional index. The index covers a larger proportion of the policy-cycle than regulatory output only and goes beyond a formal view to include potential impact and enforcement.

The illustration of the use of the index for public procurement regulation in France and Germany shows an overall increase in the strength of social objectives which, in turn, point toward a growing potential for public procurement to achieve wider societal benefits. The index has also brought to the fore that in the regulation of the economy, France and Germany prioritize different social objectives. While regulation in Germany is particularly strong with relation to individual social rights that support employers who find themselves as the weaker party in a market relationship, French regulation is oriented toward collective goals of social solidarity and equality in markets. Other differences between the two countries exist: for many of the standards, potential impact in Germany is limited by unequal application across federal states. In France, enforcement is hindered by nonbinding standards. These regulatory output patterns are specific to the cases at hand. Yet they demonstrate that differences in social regulation can be measured and compared in a meaningful way within and across countries. We, therefore, suggest applying the index to a wider range of topics in future research, for example, financial services, housing, tax, or energy policy. This would bring out systematic differences in *how* countries regulate the economy for social goals by measuring the strength and type of social objectives they seek. In turn, by including the three dimensions, we can identify trade-offs among standards, potential impact for different groups of people in a market, and enforcement across the policy cycle.

While this article is exploratory in nature, the findings contribute to wider debates on the RWS. Comparing regulatory scores in France and Germany provides us with preliminary insights into the link between social regulation of the economy and welfare state development. Patterns in the sub-regimes suggest that this relationship is country specific. In Germany, it is best described as complementary. In all three sub-regimes, procurement regulation reflects existing welfare state standards. This is most evident with respect to wage clauses, whereby public procurement ensures that collective agreements are followed under public contracts. Similarly, gender equality regulation in production and insertion regulation for apprentices refer to welfare state regulation. Meanwhile in France, the relationship seems to be compensatory. A guaranteed legal minimum wage (SMIC - *salaire minimum interprofessionnel de croissance* since 1946) renders wage clauses in procurement superfluous. Similarly, women are not explicitly featured among groups covered in the insertion sub-regime, as the *Code du Travail* specifies far-reaching equal treatment standards that apply to public contracts. Certainly, this argument needs more empirical support and theoretical development.

And yet the stylized comparison suggests that RWS and the regulation of social objectives in the economy are not fully independent from one another. Consequently, future analyses interested in causal explanations of RWS beyond social policy should not confine themselves to theories of economic regulation. Rather, they would benefit from drawing more explicitly on the complex explanations offered in the welfare state literature. Here, the index could help to identify sub-regimes and periods that lend themselves to the study of causal relationships through in-depth analysis.

## Notes

1. Paternalistic goals come close to "public interest" as regulation seeks to avoid costs for society, for example, through addressing drug and alcohol abuse. Community values are understood as objectives that people "want for the community as a whole," such as theatre or the protection of endangered species (Ogus 1994, 54).

2. Frequently, a sub-regime will seek social objectives alongside other objectives.

3. For sub-regimes regulated at federal state level, more fine-grained scores can easily be calculated by taking the share of federal entities into account that implement a specific standard.

4. Percentages change from year to year and were situated at 26 percent (France) and 35 percent (Germany) of public spending in 2019; see http://www.oecd.org/gov/govatglance.htm.

5. The score for potential impact takes into account the number of federal states that have adopted standards in the respective regulatory regime.

## References

Alliance Villes Emploi. 2011. Guide de la Clause sociale. Deuxième édition - décembre 2011: Guide en direction de l'ensemble des acteurs du dispositif, Paris. Available from http://www.ville-emploi.asso.fr/wp-content/uploads/docs/GClauses2010.pdf.

Benish, Avishai, and David Levi-Faur. 2020. The expansion of regulation in welfare governance. *The ANNALS of the American Academy of Political and Social Sciences* (this volume).

Caughey, Devin, and Christopher Warshaw. 2016. The dynamics of state policy liberalism, 1936–2014. *American Journal of Political Science* 60 (4): 899–913.

Conway, Danielle M. 2012. *State and local government procurement*. Chicago, IL: American Bar Association Publishing.

Deakin, Simon, Priya Lele, and Mathias Siems. 2007. The evolution of labour law: Calibrating and comparing regulatory regimes. *International Labour Review* 146 (3–4): 133–62.

Deutscher Städtetag, Bundesministerium für Arbeit und Soziales, and Bundesministerium für wirtschaftliche Zusammenarbeit und Entwicklung. 2010. Die Berücksichtigung sozialer Belange im Vergaberecht. Hinweise für die kommunale Praxis, Bonn.

Eberlein, Burkard, Kenneth W. Abbott, Julia Black, Errol Meidinger, and Stepan Wood. 2013. Transnational business governance interactions: Conceptualization and framework for analysis. *Regulation & Governance*.

Eckert, Sandra. 2018. Two spheres of regulation: Balancing social and economic goals. *Regulation & Governance* 12 (2): 177–191.

Esping-Andersen, Gøsta. 1990. *The three worlds of welfare capitalism*. Cambridge: Cambridge University Press.

European Commission. 2016. Stock-taking of administrative capacity, systems and practices across the EU to ensure the compliance and quality of public procurement involving European Structural and Investment (ESI) Funds, Brussels.

Guidi, Mattia, Igor Guardiancich, and David Levi-Faur. 2020. Modes of regulatory governance: A political economy perspective. *Governance* 33 (1).

Haber, Hanan. 2018. Liberalizing markets, liberalizing welfare? Economic reform and social regulation in the EU's electricity regime. *Journal of European Public Policy* (25): 307–26.

Hartlapp, Miriam. 2014. Enforcing Social Europe through Labour Inspectorates: Changes in Capacity and Cooperation across Europe. *West European Politics. Special Issue: Implementing Social Europe in Times of Crises* 37 (4): 805–24.

Hartlapp, Miriam, and Andreas Hofmann. 2020. The use of EU soft law by national courts and bureaucrats: how relation to hard law and policy maturity matter. *West European Politics*. Online first.

Hartlapp, Miriam, and Christian Rauh. 2013. The Commission's Internal Conditions for Social Re-Regulation. Market efficiency and wider social goals in setting the rules for financial services in Europe. *European Journal of Government and Economics* 2 (1): 25–40.

Hassel, Anke, and Nicole Helmerich. 2016. Institutional change in transnational labor governance: implementing social standards in public procurement and export credit guarantees. In *Global Justice and International Labour Rights*, eds. Yossi Dahan, Hanna Lerner, and FainaEditors Milman-Sivan, 237–38. Cambridge: Cambridge University Press.

Jordana, Jacint, Xavier Fernández-i-Marín, and Andrea C. Bianculli. 2018. Agency proliferation and the globalization of the regulatory state: Introducing a data set on the institutional features of regulatory agencies. *Regulation & Governance* 12 (4): 524–40.

Kholodilin, Konstantin A., Sebastian Kohl, Yulia Prozorova, and Julien Licheron. 2019. Social policy or crowding-out? Tenant protection in comparative long-run perspective. DIW Discussion Papers 1778.

Klenk, Tanja. 2020. Hybrid organizations in the regulatory welfare state: The case of the German medical review board. *The ANNALS of the American Academy of Political and Social Sciences* (this volume).

Levi-Faur, David. 2014. The welfare state: a regulatory perspective. *Public Administration* 92 (3): 599–614.

Levi-Faur, David, ed. 2011. *Handbook on the politics of regulation*. Cheltenham: Edward Elgar Publishing.

Majone, Giandomenico. 1997. From the positive to the regulatory state: Causes and consequences of changes in the mode of governance. *Journal of Public Policy* 17 (2): 139–67.

Marshall, Thomas H. 1950. *Citizenship and social class and other essays*. Cambridge: Cambridge University Press.

Martin-Ortega, Olga, and Claire Methven O'Brien. 2019. *Public procurement and human rights*. Cheltenham: Edward Elgar Publishing.

McCrudden, Christopher. 2004. Using public procurement to achieve social outcomes. *Natural Resources Forum* 28 (4): 257–67.

Mizrahi-Borohovich, Inbar, and David Levi-Faur. 2020. Varieties of consumer credit data regimes: A regulatory governance approach. *Governance* 33 (1): 109–34.

Noon, Christopher R. 2009. The use of racial references in public procurement for social stability. *Public Contract Law Journal* 38 (3): 611–32.

Ogus, Anthony I. 1994. *Regulation. Legal form and economic theory*. Oxford: Clarendon Press.

Prosser, Tony. 2007. Regulation, markets, and legitimacy. In *The changing constitution*, eds. Jeffrey L. Jowell, 237–60. Oxford: Oxford University Press.

Prosser, Tony. 2006. Regulation and social solidarity. *Journal of Law and Society* 33 (3): 364–87.

Reiter, Renate. 2020. The quest for service quality as a driver of the regulatory welfare state: Exploring the case of hospital quality policy in Germany and France. *The ANNALS of the American Academy of Political and Social Sciences* (this volume).

Rothstein, Henry, Regine Paul, and David Demeritt. 2020. The boundary conditions for regulation: Welfare systems, state traditions, and the varied governance of work safety in Europe. *Governance* 33 (1): 21–39.

Sack, Detlef, and E. K. Sarter. 2018. Collective bargaining, minimum wages and public procurement in Germany: Regulatory adjustments to the neoliberal drift of a coordinated market economy. *Journal of Industrial Relations* 60 (5): 669–90.

Sánchez-Graells, Albert. 2015. *Public procurement and the EU competition rules*. London: Bloomsbury Publishing. Available from http://gbv.eblib.com/patron/FullRecord.aspx?p=2059934.

Schwartz, Herman. 2009. Varieties of residential capitalism in the international political economy: Old welfare states and the new politics of housing. In *The politics of housing booms and busts*, eds. Herman Schwartz and Leonhard Seabrooke, 1–27. New York, NY: Palgrave.

Selznick, Philip. 1985. Focusing organizational research on regulation. In *Regulatory policy and the social sciences*, eds. Roger G. Noll. Berkeley, CA: University of California Press.

Steinebach, Yves, and Christoph Knill. 2017. Social policies during economic crises: An analysis of cross-national variation in coping strategies from 1980 to 2013. *Journal of European Public Policy* 1–23.

Stigler, George J. 1971. The theory of economic regulation. *The Bell Journal of Economics and Management Science* 2 (1): 3–21.

Trein, Philipp. 2020. Bossing or protecting? The integration of social regulation into the welfare state. *The ANNALS of the American Academy of Political and Social Sciences*.

Vogel, Steven K. 1998. *Freer markets, more rules. regulatory reform in advanced industrial countries*. Ithaca, NY: Cornell University Press.

Wiesbrock, Anja. 2015. Socially responsible public procurement: European value or national choice? In *Sustainable public procurement under EU law new perspectives on the state as stakeholder*, eds. Beate Sjafjell and Anja Wiesbrock, 75–98. Cambridge: Cambridge University Press.

Windholz, Eric, and Graeme A. Hodge. 2013. Conceptualising social and economic regulation: Implications for modern regulators and regulatory activity. Jerusalem Papers in Regulation & Governance. Working Paper No. 49 (February 2013).

# A Gender Equalizing Regulatory Welfare State? Enacting the EU's Work-Life Balance Directive in Denmark and Poland

By
CAROLINE DE LA PORTE,
TRINE P. LARSEN,
and
DOROTA SZELEWA

This article examines the implementation of the European Union's (EU) work-life balance directive in Denmark and Poland through examining the earmarking of paid parental leave. This enables us to assess whether the EU could be emerging as a gender equalizing regulatory welfare state (RWS). Our analysis points to tensions arising when regulatory decisions are made at a higher level of governance but require implementation and funding at lower levels of governance. In both countries, there are similar parental leave schemes ex-ante, and major actors had similar initial stances on parental leave, favoring stagnation. Yet the plans to implement show how the actors' positions changed, and the likely result is extended parental leave, with payment (known as double expansion) and more gender-equal participation (degenderization) in parental leave. Although in two different institutional settings, the similar outcome suggests that these changes are due to the European Union acting as an emerging RWS, which influences Member States' regulatory instruments with fiscal elements.

*Keywords:* work-life balance; gender equality; EU social policy; parental leave; Denmark; Poland; regulatory welfare state

Distinct models of welfare states and labor markets in the European Union (EU) coexist in "legitimate diversity" (Scharpf 2002), and therefore, the EU cannot develop as a full-fledged "regulatory welfare state" (RWS) involving regulation and expenditure in core redistributive areas (Levi-Faur 2014). Yet since the EU is a semi-federalized entity, the main means to shape welfare policies is regulation (Obinger, Leibfried, and Castles 2005). The EU

Caroline de la Porte is a professor of comparative and European welfare policy in the Department of International Economics, Government and Business at Copenhagen Business School. Her research focuses on comparative welfare state reform, the Nordic welfare model, and the Europeanization of welfare states.

Correspondence: cdlp.egb@cbs.dk

DOI: 10.1177/0002716220956910

has a regulatory impact in areas that are adjacent to the welfare state, such as anti-discrimination and labor laws, especially where decision-making is made through qualified majority vote (QMV) (Falkner et al. 2005). Regulation in EU social policy must respect the principle of subsidiarity, that is, the EU must be the most relevant level of governance, and the EU's initiatives cannot involve an unreasonable financial burden on Member States.

The ambition of EU leaders, in the aftermath of the Great Recession that followed the 2008 financial crisis, has been to enhance social rights of citizens. To mark this ambition, EU institutions adopted the "European Pillar of Social Rights" (EPSR) in 2017 to improve social rights for EU citizens. The EPSR, embodying high symbolic political value, consists of twenty principles that update existing policy and regulatory initiatives in the welfare state–labor market nexus (de la Porte 2019). While the EPSR does not present any entirely new initiatives, reflecting the pattern during the last decade (Graziano and Hartlapp 2019), the revised regulatory initiatives can have a significant impact on welfare states from a gender, regulatory, and fiscal perspective.

The work-life balance directive (WLBD), one of the initiatives in the EPSR, is central from the perspective of a gender equalizing RWS, that is, a welfare state that creates new regulations to promote gender equality. The WLBD introduces an important tool for balancing gender division of care within the family, with the EU as the regulator. The WLBD is a revision and renaming of the parental leave directive from 2010 (2010/18/EU), and its purpose is to underline the EU's aims of gender equalizing policies and increasing labor market participation (European Commission 2017). The WLBD aims to be degenderizing to enable equal participation of men and women in care in the private sphere. A central provision of the WLBD is earmarking two months of parental leave, which is an extension of the requirement in the 2010 directive, in which only one month was earmarked to each parent. Yet what is distinct in the 2019 directive is the combination of the regulatory requirement of two months earmarked leave, with payment. In addition, while Member States decide the level of payment, it should "facilitate the take-up of parental leave by both parents" (article 5[2], OJEU 2019). Although not leading to a fully fledged RWS, the parental leave provision of the WLBD could have regulatory, gender equalizing, and even fiscal implications for Member States. These consequences can be considerable because, in most EU countries, statutory paid

*Trine P. Larsen is an associate professor at the Employment Relations Research Centre (FAOS), Department of Sociology, University of Copenhagen. Her main research interests are industrial relations, work-life balance, atypical employment, and segmented labor markets in Denmark and in an international comparative perspective.*

*Dorota Szelewa is an assistant professor in social justice at the University College Dublin. Her research interests center on comparative research on gender and social policy, social investment, and the impact of populist governments on welfare reforms. She is the editor in chief of the* Journal of Family Studies.

NOTE: We would like to thank two anonymous reviewers on very useful comments on a previous version of this article. Also, a special thanks to Sonja Bekker for constructive input on an earlier draft of this article, and to Hanna Kviske, student assistant, for collecting and coding data on the positions of Danish actors in the analytical vignette.

parental leave is associated with low or nonexistent compensation, and consequently, the take-up of parental leave among fathers is low (van Belle 2016).

Following Benish and Levi-Faur (this volume), we are "transcending the welfare state vs. regulatory state" dichotomy, bridging it with the gender perspective on childcare. In our analysis, we use the RWS perspective—capturing regulatory initiatives at a higher level of governance, with regulatory and fiscal implications for lower levels of governance—with key concepts from Europeanization and feminist literature. The former highlights the tensions between EU policy and regulatory rights of actors in Member States, while the latter highlights that the design of parental leave, together with the level of pay, shapes the take-up of leave among fathers. The RWS perspective applied to the WLBD captures the regulatory component (required earmarking of parental leave), along with the fiscal component (level of pay).

The article is organized as follows. The next section summarizes the development of EU parental leave regulation. Then comes the literature review, the analytical framework, and the methodology, including the case selection. The next section comprises the case studies of Denmark and Poland. Each includes a presentation of the regulatory landscape for earmarked parental leave regulation, and the regulatory responses to the WLBD according to the key concepts of our analytical framework: EU-national subsidiarity (the extent to which actors perceive the EU intervening in areas of their regulatory rights), family-state subsidiarity (the extent to which state regulation causes a tension about the state deciding on issues that could be considered as belonging to the private family sphere), and the costs (fiscal challenges arising from new regulation). The article ends with a comparative discussion and conclusion.

Based on our two case studies, our findings are that the European Union is inducing gender equalizing policies in parental leave, through regulation, and with generous financial compensation during leave. If it is implemented in this way in all Member States, the WLBD could lead to more gender equality among parents in the private sphere, which could have positive effects on the labor market. On the other hand, if the provisions are implemented with little or no pay, then gender equalization is not likely to materialize. The lesson for policy-makers is that generous parental leave schemes, in terms of regulation and compensation, are important to maintain a healthy work-life balance.

## EU Regulation of Parental Leave

The EU first attempted to earmark parental leave—three months of unpaid nontransferable leave—in 1983 in a proposed directive on parental leave. However, Member States found the directive contentious because of EU-national and state-family subsidiarity tensions. It was impossible to reach unanimity, which was required to adopt the directive (Falkner et al. 2002; Rubery et al. 1998). In the 1990s, the political climate changed, with more support for leave schemes, which Member States saw as supporting high labor market participation among men and women (de la Porte 2019).

FIGURE 1
Evolution of Parental Leave Regulation at the EU Level, 1996–2019

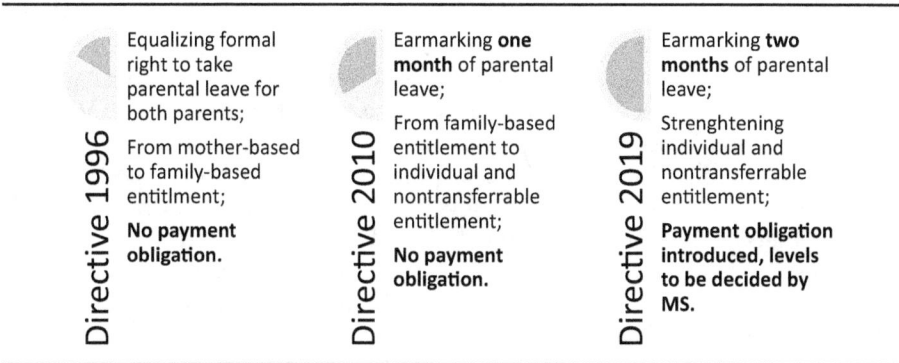

**Directive 1996**
Equalizing formal right to take parental leave for both parents;

From mother-based to family-based entitlment;

**No payment obligation.**

**Directive 2010**
Earmarking **one month** of parental leave;

From family-based entitlement to individual and nontransferrable entitlement;

**No payment obligation.**

**Directive 2019**
Earmarking **two months** of parental leave;

Strenghtening individual and nontransferrable entitlement;

**Payment obligation introduced, levels to be decided by MS.**

SOURCE: Authors' construction on the basis of the directive texts.

The maternity leave directive in 1992, agreed on the basis of a Commission proposal in the Council, involved a fiscal component: the requirement to provide compensation for 14 weeks (European Council 1992). The parental leave directive from 1996, based on a framework agreement among social partners, introduced the possibility for mothers and for fathers to take three months leave, yet leave was not earmarked and pay was optional (Rees 2003). Thus, there was no intrusion on the EU-national, state-family subsidiarity, or pay dimensions. The effect of this directive has been minimal from a gender perspective, since it is often the mother who takes the leave, especially if it is unpaid (van Belle 2016). In 2010, the parental leave directive was revised through the EU level tripartite process. The 2010 revised parental leave directive expanded each parents' leave rights to four months and introduced one month of earmarked leave per parent. However, the earmarked leave did not involve an obligation of payment (European Council 2010). In the absence of a requirement for Member States to provide payment, take-up among fathers remained scarce (van Belle 2016). The directive represents a regulatory change, due to statutory earmarking of leave for the first time.

In 2019, the EU adopted the work-life balance directive, repealing the previous parental leave directive. In doing so, the potential for EU-led regulation of parental leave was enhanced, as it now involved regulation and pay (even if decided in Member States) (OJEU 2019). The timeframe for implementing the directive has been extended from two to three years, as Member States have deemed it complex to implement due to the involvement of a variety of regulatory actors (Ministry of Employment 2018).

## Toward a Degenderizing EU Regulatory Welfare State?

### Literature review and analytical framework

From each relevant body of literature—Europeanization, feminist, and RWS—we draw out concepts that are integrated into our RWS analytical framework for discussing the parental leave regulation of the WLBD.

First, the literature on Europeanization of social policy focuses on the EU legislation in gender equality and antidiscrimination, as well as various areas of labor law, such as working time, and health and safety. The EU has various directives that involve social regulation and, in some cases, a fiscal component. The fine-grained literature on EU social policy shows that political culture and fit-misfit with the EU regulatory system are crucial factors that shape Member States' policy implementation patterns (Falkner et al. 2005; Falkner and Leiber 2004). Some scholars find that EU social policy has been integrated with existing institutions in national contexts, with few substantive changes (Busby and James 2015). Others underscore that although the EU has limited redistributive competencies, its regulatory policies have a redistributive impact, even involving costs carried by Member States when implementing EU policies (Haber 2017; Martinsen 2007). Some authors highlight that EU regulation has led to changes in areas where there has been a stalemate at the national context (Falkner et al. 2002). In their work on the EU's parental leave regulation from 2010, Falkner and Leiber (2004) highlight the clash between labor law regulation in Member States—which could be governed by social partners and/or the state—and EU regulation. Following this direction, we seek to capture the potential tensions between EU regulation and the institutional context in Member States. Thus, we conceptualize EU-national subsidiarity as EU regulation that can impinge upon national modes of policy-making at the welfare state–labor market nexus.

Second, the feminist literature examines the gendered implications of work-life balance policies, including parental leave policies, which seek to engage parents in caring for children close to the time of childbirth (Ciccia and Bleijenbergh 2014; OJEU 2019). Following the WLBD, parental leave is "leave from work for parents on the grounds of the birth or adoption of a child to take care of that child" (OJEU 2019). Relevant concepts from the feminist literature are "genderizing" policies that maintain traditional gender roles: female-carer and male bread winner in child-rearing, while "degenderizing" policies aim to equalize participation of *both* parents in child-rearing (Saxonberg 2013; Fraser 1994). When parental leave involves individual, nontransferrable entitlements, together with a high level of pay (full salary or high replacement rate of salary), then care practices have the potential to become more gender equalizing (Saxonberg 2013). The empirical evidence from countries with such schemes, such as Sweden, shows that take-up among fathers is comparatively high (Lundqvist 2017). Furthermore, countries with such schemes often have lower gender inequality on the labor market because men and women share leave in conjunction with childbirth more equally. When parental leave schemes involve only optional rather than earmarked leave, then leave is primarily taken by mothers, making such schemes implicitly "genderizing" (Saxonberg 2013). The EU's 2010 parental leave directive has had—even if requiring parental leave to be earmarked for one month—very little degenderizing effect, because in most countries, leave is unpaid or compensated at a very low level (van Belle 2016).

The feminist literature also highlights the political and societal tensions that arise with introducing provisions in work-life balance targeted at fathers. This is because it involves (earmarking) parental leave through regulation, which could

be considered a violation of families' right to choose. This is particularly prominent in countries where parental leave is a *family*, rather than individual, entitlement, enabling families to choose how they utilize parental leave (Rogg Korsvi and
Warat 2016; Borschort 2006). The EU's WLBD compels each Member State to
reserve at least two months for each parent, with the obligation to secure payment
during the period of the leave at a level that should, in theory, facilitate take-up of
parental leave by both parents (OJEU 2019). Therefore, our second concept is
state-family subsidiarity, which captures the tension that can arise when states
regulate areas that are identified as belonging to the private (family) sphere.

Third, the RWS perspective is particularly useful regarding parental leave
because it captures the tensions between multiple levels of governance—EU and
national—and merges social regulation with social spending. Furthermore, the
RWS literature also highlights the tensions between regulation at a higher level
of governance and hidden costs for the lower level of governance, at which policy
is implemented (Levi-Faur 2014; Haber 2017; Benish, Haber, and Eliahou
2017). Our third concept is fiscal constraint, which captures the tension arising
from a cost, to be covered at the lower level of governance, without distribution
from the higher level of governance. This cost could be carried by the (welfare)
state, employers-employees (in collective agreements), or social insurance
schemes (Falkner and Leiber 2004; Obinger, Leibfried, and Castles 2005). In
cases where the level of pay accompanying the earmarked leave is very low or
nonexistent, then the cost would be borne by the family, which is implicitly genderizing. In cases where the level of pay to accompany leave is high (or full-wage
compensation), then the scheme would be degenderizing (Saxonberg 2013).

These three tensions shape the positions of various policy-makers and will
ultimately lead to different kinds of regulatory outcomes. Following Levi-Faur
(2014), social regulation and fiscal means applied to parental leave could expand,
stagnate (leave unchanged), or retrench parents' leave rights, and thus may promote or hamper policy developments related to fathers' leave rights. In practice,
and applied to the WLBD, social regulation can lead to different policy outputs
with distinct implications for the degree of degenderization, depending on the
starting point of a Member State and on how a state implements the provision.
In countries where there is already at least two months of statutory earmarked
leave at a relatively high level of compensation, the WLBD would not lead to any
change; that is, there would be *stagnation* in terms of regulation, financial compensation, and gender equality (A in Figure 2). Another possibility is *regulation-
led expansion* (B in Figure 2): when EU regulation expands (earmarked leave)
but where the fiscal component stagnates. Due to the absence of financial compensation, this would probably not lead fathers to increase their take-up of leave
and would thus be implicitly gendered. The third possibility is *cost-led expansion*
(C in Figure 2), which entails the fiscal component being expanded, often from
unpaid or low levels of compensation to more generous payment. However, if the
leave is not earmarked, then it could be genderizing; if the leave is already earmarked, it could be degenderizing if the level of pay is high. The fourth possibility is *double expansion* (D in Figure 2), which involves introducing two months
of earmarked leave (regulation) and ensuring a high level of payment, to

FIGURE 2
Analytical Framework: "EU (degenderizing) Regulatory Welfare State"

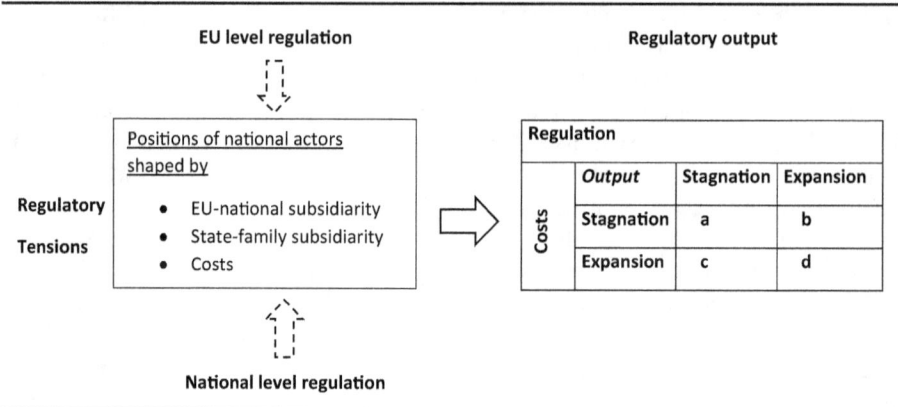

SOURCE: Authors' construction; Regulatory welfare state output adapted from Levi-Faur (2014)

encourage both parents to take leave. In countries where it does not already exist, it would entail a shift from family-based to individual and nontransferrable entitlements, and thus add an additional two months of parental leave to existing parental leave schemes, together with a high level of financial compensation, provided by social partners or the state. This regulatory output would de facto encourage fathers to take parental leave at a higher rate, and thus lead to degenderization in care practices.

Taking into account the three tensions, we apply the adapted version of the RWS to our analysis. In the earmarking of leave in the WLBD, the EU as the regulatory state specifies the regulatory standards—individualizing the right to paid parental leave and requests the level of compensation to encourage the take-up of leave among mothers and fathers—but leaves the level of payment to Member States. As we have explained and illustrated in Figure 2, the directive can lead to different regulatory outcomes, depending on how states implement the regulatory and fiscal provisions on parental leave from the WLBD (Levi-Faur 2014, 605).

### Methodology and case selection

Our country case selection strategy is based on the "most different systems design," but it focuses on similarities (Levi-Faur 2006). Denmark and Poland differ on a number of parameters, including on policies influencing female economic autonomy, such as childcare (see Table 2). However, both countries have similar statutory provisions for parental leave, whereby the potential for a change due to European regulation is comparable. In Denmark, there is dual regulation of parental leave. Social partners regulate parental leave for those covered by collective agreements (83 percent of the labor force), while statutory leave covers

TABLE 1
Case Selection for Parental Leave Regulation

| | | Regulation of parental leave | |
| --- | --- | --- | --- |
| | | State | Social partners |
| Costs of parental leave | State | **Denmark** (flat rate, at level of unemployment benefit); **Poland** (flat rate for uninsured) | |
| | Labor market/ social insurance | **Poland** (60-80% wage compensation) | **Denmark** (100% wage compensation for part of the leave) |

SOURCE: Authors' construction.

workers not covered by collective agreements. Earmarked parental leave covered by collective agreements involves full-wage compensation for parts of the leave period, while longer leave is covered by statutory pay only, which is lower (at the level of unemployment benefits). The second case, Poland, is a case of statutory regulation with limited involvement of social partners in the regulatory process. The pay is provided through social insurance, and is thus dependent on employer and employee contributions for mothers and fathers who are active in the labor market. There is a scheme with a flat-rate monthly payment (for 12 months) for those who are not insured, and thus de facto coverage is achieved for all citizens.

Thus, if the response to regulatory pressure from the EU is similar in these two EU countries, then the results would be applicable for countries with similar regulatory features, that is, the first group of countries characterized by dual regulation with social partner autonomy and statutory rules and the second group of countries characterized by only statutory regulation of parental leave policy. Table 1 summarizes our case selection process and criteria, according to labor market regulation and financing of parental leave schemes.

Prior to the implementation of WLBD, both countries had 32 weeks of paid parental leave, but they only had one month of unpaid earmarked statutory parental leave. Yet there are different regulatory dilemmas. In Denmark, all parents have the right to (non-earmarked) statutory paid leave (at the level of unemployment benefits). Most Danish parents, however, are also covered by collective agreements, giving them the entitlement for full-wage compensation for part of the parental leave period. In Poland, parental leave is regulated at the state level, and the compensation rate for the total period is between 60 percent and 80 percent of the parents' wage. Despite the regulatory differences and distinct levels of compensation in Denmark and Poland, mothers continue to take most of the leave in both countries, thus the leave schemes are implicitly gendered. Yet the broader work-life balance policy differs in the two countries, as Denmark has publicly subsidized and made childcare widely available for children under three. In Denmark, 66 percent of children are enrolled in childcare, while in Poland it is only about 10 percent (see Table 2).

TABLE 2
Denmark and Poland: Parental Leave and Childcare for Newborns–2 year olds

|  | Denmark | Poland |
|---|---|---|
| **Parental leave** | 32 weeks of paid leave, transferrable (family-based) entitlement. Statutory pay (flat-rate, at level of unemployment benefit) but full-wage compensation for up to 18 weeks in collective agreements.° | 32 weeks of paid leave, transferrable (family-based) entitlement. 60 percent or 80 percent wage replacement. Additional scheme of flat-rate payments for uninsured. |
| **Childcare arrangements** | 66 percent of children under three enrolled in childcare. High subsidization and public provision (delivered at municipal level). Guaranteed child care for all. | 10.2 percent of children under three enrolled in childcare. Government program of subsidies is based on open calls. Allocation of subsidies is discretionary and there is no child care guarantee. |

SOURCE: Data on parental leave: the international network on leave policies (leavenetwork. org, data for April 2019); data on childcare enrolment: Eurostat (2019).
°Parents' rights to full-wage compensation varies depending on the collective agreement.

Methodologically, we carried out structured focused analyses using the case study method (George and Bennett 2005). All our data are analyzed on the basis of the conceptual distinctions pertaining to gender equalization and the RWS, especially EU-national subsidiarity, state-family subsidiarity, and costs. Our data include eleven interviews, primary documents (document analysis), and an analytical vignette[1] (as background information) to locate the position of key actors who influence or are involved in the policy-making process. Since the directive has not yet been implemented, we trace the changes in positions of the actors over time, with a focus on how these actors respond to regulatory pressures from the EU. This enables us to assess whether changes could be due to EU regulatory pressure. We use process-tracing as a way to assess the extent to which changes are due to the EU or other factors.

# Political and Regulatory Responses in Denmark and Poland

## Denmark

*The regulatory landscape for parental leave.* Parental leave in Denmark is shaped by dual regulation (see Table 1). The collectively agreed-upon rights are developed in the Danish industrial relations model, where social partners self-regulate issues pertaining to the labor market. The union density—63 percent in 2018—and the collective agreement coverage—84 percent in 2017—are high

(OECD 2017). Wage and working conditions, including parental leave, sometimes earmarked and sometimes with full pay, are primarily regulated through collective agreements at the sectoral and company levels (Due and Madsen 2008). Most collective agreements have more extensive parental leave rights than the legislation in terms of earmarking and pay (Larsen and Navrbjerg 2018). For workers not covered by collective agreements, there is a statutory parental leave scheme (with no earmarking) but pay is rather low (unemployment benefits level).

*Subsidiarity: EU-national level.* Proposals for EU directives hardly ever make it to the public agenda. The WLBD, however, was one of the most publicly debated directives ever due to strong opposition among most political parties and stakeholders,[2] mainly arising from a combination of EU-national and state-family subsidiarity tensions. By tension, we mean a lack of clarity of where the regulatory and financial responsibility lie. Political parties, including the major parties in the center-Left and center-Right, have been skeptical. During the negotiation of the directive, the conservative-liberal government (2015–2019) was openly hostile to the directive. In the Council, Denmark opposed the directive. In the EP, Danish MEPs from the Left and Right opposed (with a few exceptions: social liberals [Radikale Venstre] and the socialist party [SF]). Since then, the Left-leaning minority social-democratic government (2019–present) has followed in these footsteps. In particular, the newly appointed Minister of Equality announced publicly in 2019 that Denmark would ask for an exemption to implementing the directive, which he later retracted. One of the main reasons for his initial statement was a fear about the EU making decisions in an area that social partners typically regulate; that is, EU-national subsidiarity has been a long-standing Danish position toward EU-regulation (Kristiansen 2015). There is also a fear that the European Court of Justice would play a role in interpreting the provisions of the directive, as it has done in past rulings regarding the labor market (Larsen and Andersen 2007). The only parties that supported the directive both before and after its adoption were smaller parties on the Left: the social liberals, the alternative, and the socialist party.

It remains unclear how the Danish government will proceed with transposing the directive into Danish labor law. It is likely that implementation will be closely coordinated with social partners, as have other directives in labor law (Kristiansen 2015). The Ministry of Employment has indicated that Denmark cannot present a yellow card to the Commission (the right of a member state to question a legislative initiative on the basis of the principle of subsidiarity), because the WLBD was a revision to an existing directive, rather than a new directive. Thus, there was no legally justified case to be made for the EU encroaching on Member State competency (Ministry of Employment 2018).

During the negotiation of the directive, social partners—that is, trade unions and employers' organizations—were mostly skeptical; they feared that the EU would force the Danish state to legislate more on parental leave and thereby undermine the authority of social partners in parental leave.[3] The main trade union confederation FH—especially its blue-collar member organizations Danish Metal and 3F (The United Federation of Danish Workers)—initially opposed parts of the directive on the grounds that it undermines the Danish labor market model and that there are uncertainties about who would carry the financial costs associated with implementation.[4] However, these unions have, following the adoption of the directive, extended their earmarking of paid leave for fathers, in line with the directive. Thus, they have attempted to minimize state intervention in their bargaining of parental leave.

After the adoption of the directive, other private sector social partners have also changed their stances. In February 2020, social partners within manufacturing extended their paid parental leave for fathers from five to eight weeks with full-wage compensation. Subsequently, most other private sector social partners followed suit and agreed to earmark eight weeks of parental leave for fathers with full-wage compensation. Social partners in manufacturing usually conclude their sectoral agreement first, which then inspires agreements in other sectors (Due and Madsen 2008). In a few sectors, the requirement of earmarking of paid leave was already implemented prior to the WLBD. In these sectors, such as banking, social partners aim to keep the status quo, since they already offer twelve weeks of fully compensated parental leave per parent (The Danish Employers' Association for the Financial Sector [FA] and The Financial Services Union [Finansforbundet] 2020). The recent regulatory changes agreed upon by social partners were adopted prior to state involvement, which suggests that the EU is an emerging RWS, resulting in expansion in both the regulatory and fiscal arenas in Denmark.

*Subsidiarity: State-family.* The political parties and unions that oppose paid earmarked leave argue that earmarking parts of the parental leave intervenes with families' rights to organize their leave arrangements according to their individual needs (Borchorst 2003; Rostgaard 2002). Such an argument is implicitly gendered. Earmarked parental leave has also been controversial in Denmark on the state-family subsidiarity dimension, prior to the WLBD. The Helle-Thorning government (2011–2015) pledged to introduce earmarked parental leave, especially to encourage fathers to take leave. However, due to disagreement in the parliament, they did not adopt the proposed earmarking (Larsen and Navrbjerg 2018). In the negotiations prior to the EU adopting the WLBD, some unions under the Danish Trade Union Confederation (LO, now FH) feared that fathers would not use their earmarked leave, and provided that it could not be transferred to the mother, it would result in less parental time with children (LO 2017).[5] On the other hand, union confederations, such as The Confederation of Professionals in Denmark (FTF) and The Danish Confederation of Professional Associations (AC), have—similar to the socialist party, the socialist liberals, and the alternative—welcomed the directive. They argue that improved rights for fathers could promote gender equality in the Danish labor market (The Employee Committee 2017).

With the WLBD adopted, some employers have changed their positions. The Confederation of Danish Industries (DI)—the largest employers association and often a first mover among the employers in the private sector—announced that they no longer opposed statutory earmarking, but were instead in favor of such arrangements.[6] They also agreed with the unions to earmark eight weeks paid leave for fathers in their collective agreements. However, their motivation may be driven by concerns about keeping politicians, specifically EU politicians, at arm's length, rather than a genuine interest in promoting gender equality. Danish employers have an historical opposition to earmarked leave for fathers (Borchorst 2003).[7] After DI changed its position, another major umbrella organization for Danish employers, the Danish Chamber of Commerce (Dansk Erhverv), also changed its position on paternal leave. It had previously been very skeptical but changed positions to be more in line with DI, mainly due to retaining regulatory powers, even if a double expansion would entail additional costs on business (Dansk Erhverv 2020).[8] Double expansion refers to new rules, and with their implementation, new costs are incurred.

*Costs.* Social partners are under no obligation to provide payment for earmarked parental leave. However, in Denmark the associated costs for paid parental leave are divided: the state covers statutory paid leave at the level of unemployment benefits, while social partners, through collective agreements, top up parts of the parental leave so employees receive full-wage compensation. The additional costs, up to full-wage compensation, are borne by the employers with distinct collectively agreed-upon and statutory funds (barselsfonde), compelling all employers to contribute to these funds and thus spread the associated leave costs across male- and female-dominated businesses. The Danish social partners in the private sector have agreed that the two months of earmarked parental leave for fathers required by the directive should be paid with full-wage compensation. This means (de facto) that the cost of parental leave will fall partly on the employer in areas of the labor market that collective agreements cover, because they need to top up the flat rate that the state provides. Statutory earmarked leave is likely to be given at the level of unemployment benefits. Furthermore, this would ensure at least minimum coverage for parents who are not covered by collective agreements. This would, in turn, ensure that the Court of Justice of the European Union would not be able to intervene on this aspect, because the new EU regulation on work-life balance would be fully implemented.

The EU's directive has offered leeway for some key stakeholders to change their positions on paternal leave, to overcome political stalemate, and to push through parental leave reforms and thereby avoid government intervention (at the EU and national levels). Thus far, social partners in the country have adopted measures that are altering the Danish parental leave landscape. The earmarking of parental leave will benefit fathers (with full-wage compensation) covered under collective agreements, while mothers will be less penalized on the labor market during child-rearing years. For fathers not covered by collective agreements, the level of pay for earmarked leave is not yet settled. The directive seems to be leading to double expansion of parental leave—regulatory and fiscal—which we consider a degendering policy.

## Poland

*The regulatory landscape before adopting the directive.* The regulation of family-related leave schemes in Poland is rooted in the state-socialist past, where mothers had the right to 16 weeks of maternity leave with full-wage compensation and an optional leave for childcare (unpaid or means-tested flat-rate monthly allowance for 24 months at the maximum). Since the 1980s, fathers have had access to the scheme for extraordinary circumstances, such as the mother's death or chronic illness of a child. At that time, *parental* leave, as such, did not exist in Polish legislation. In preparation for EU membership, Poland adopted regulation in equal treatment in 1996, whereby the government amended the labor code to introduce the equal right for fathers to use the childcare scheme. It was a family-based entitlement, rather than an individual right for each parent.

These schemes remained unaltered until the 2010 directive, when one of 36 months of the unpaid (or flat-rate) childcare leave was earmarked. The most significant change in parental leave arrangements took place in 2013, when the center-Right (liberal) Civil Platform–led government introduced 26 weeks of paid *parental* leave, which was later extended to 32 weeks. Together with extended maternity leave, the leave is now 52 weeks. In parallel to this leave scheme, a flat-rate parental benefit is available for uninsured parents for up to 12 months.

Unlike in Denmark, social partners are not involved in the design and implementation of various social policies. The union density is 12 percent, while the collective bargaining coverage is low, at 17.2 percent (OECD 2017). Thus, welfare reforms are highly politicized, with the political parties as the main actors, hidden from the public debate in a technocratic environment.

*Subsidiarity principle: EU vs. nation state.* The right-wing populist Law and Justice government(s), which has been in power since 2015, has dominated recent debates and decisions on family policy and aims to promote traditional family values. This included a universal childcare allowance to encourage families to have children. It has opposed earmarked paid leave and has been against the EU having any role in this policy area. Poland voted against the first version of the directive in the Council in June 2018 and abstained in 2019. When the directive was announced in 2017, the then-minister of family, labor and social policy argued that "what the directive suggests is interfering too much in our national law" (GP 2017). In contrast to Denmark, the minister in Poland wanted to initiate a yellow card procedure (GP 2017; EurWORK 2020). If approved, then the European Commission would have to remove its legislative proposal. The parliament in Poland issued a special resolution in 2017, arguing that the EU was breaching the principle of subsidiarity, although the resolution recognized the need to support individual entitlements for parental leave for both parents (Sejm 2017). The Law and Justice Party opposed the directive in multiple policy arenas, including in the European Parliament. According to Joanna Wiśniewska, Law and Justice MEP, the directive violated the principles of subsidiarity and proportionality at the same time (Wiśniewska 2017). Yet because it is a revision of an existing directive, Poland was not able to launch a yellow card procedure.

In contrast to the government, the major trade union organization—NSZZ Solidarność (2017)—expressed its support for the directive, while other organizations—OPZZ, All-Poland Alliance of Trade Unions (OPZZ 1)—tacitly supported the EU's initiative. They stressed the EU's role in enhancing social policy standards and positioned themselves against the government and the Parliament.[9] While Law and Justice leaders emphasized the magnitude of changes relating to parental leave, trade union representatives underlined (both before and after the directive) that the regulation fills a gap in family policy provisions[10] and represents one of the most important initiatives of the EPSR.[11] Trade union representatives stressed the importance of EU regulatory power against the weakness of social dialogue in Poland.[12] In contrast to most Danish trade unions, the unions in Poland would like to see more EU regulatory activity in welfare issues, as it is also a way to enhance their own legitimacy. Finally, employers' organizations accept the general goals set by the EU; although, like most employer organizations across the EU, they do not want regulation to hamper business activity.[13]

As one of the deputy ministers of family commented, the fact that Member States could decide on the level of the benefit granted during earmarked leave was a positive (Żebrowski 2019a). The minister also mentioned that the Council for Social Dialogue (an official tripartite body) should be engaged in implementing the directive (Żebrowski 2019b.) Thus far, the ministry has not called for any meetings or consultations.[14]

*Family-state subsidiarity.* The government interpreted earmarking leave as "violating family's autonomy," while also "threatening children's well-being," especially if a mother does not have access to leave and the leave goes unused by fathers (Janos 2017). This mirrors the debate among skeptical actors in Denmark. Employers also argued from a state-family subsidiarity perspective that "taking the two months away from mothers . . . may harm the children" (Janos 2017).

The two major trade union confederations differ in their support for earmarking based on family-state subsidiarity. In contrast to NSZZ Solidarność, OPZZ did not issue any official statement in support of the directive because there was lack of agreement among the unions within the federation on earmarking leave. Some unions considered it to interfere with family decisions, and thus it was difficult for the confederations to issue a statement in support of it.[15] Likewise, NSZZ Solidarność, although very positive of the directive itself, did not explicitly support earmarking leave, which may imply skeptical voices among their member organizations. Nevertheless, Solidarność in general supports solutions that would strengthen fathers' entitlements and support women's participation in the labor market.[16] This is surprising, since the political links between Solidarność and Law and Justice are usually strong.

Proponents for EU regulation stressed that it is important for enhancing gender equality. The biggest opposition party, Civic Platform—a center-Right, liberal, and pro-EU party previously in office (2007–2015) with Donald Tusk as a prime minister (2007–2014)—supported the directive in the European Parliament. A Polish MEP, Agnieszka Kozłowska-Rajewicz, was a rapporteur for the directive representing the Committee on Women's Rights and Gender Equality (FEMM). As a former head of the national gender equality machinery (during Civic Platform's term in office), Kozłowska-Rajewicz advocated for adopting the directive to achieve genuine gender equality at home. By doing so she positioned herself in support of degenderization, and against arguments about how the directive might interfere with internal family issues and violate the freedom of choice (Kozłowska-Rajewicz 2018).

*Costs and fiscal consequences of regulating parental leave and benefit.* Parental leave benefits are paid by the National Insurance Fund and financed through employee contributions to the "sickness and maternity" fund. If there is a deficit in the fund, the state budget may provide subsidies or a loan to be paid later. Therefore, *direct* costs of two additional months of benefit would not be carried directly by the employers but by the National Insurance Fund (with employer and employee contributions), possibly supplemented by the state budget. Therefore, there is a chance that regulation of earmarked parental leave, decided at the EU level, could have fiscal consequences for the state budget. This could materialize, because the sickness and maternity fund has the biggest deficit among all funds in the National Insurance Fund. Contributions cover 60 percent of the costs, while the state covers 40 percent (ZUS 2016).

In terms of *indirect* costs, if the government decides to extend the existing leave by two months, this would mean longer breaks from employment, which would burden employers. Thus, employer organizations prefer that two months should be earmarked out of the current six months, rather than adding two additional months.[17] However, since the cash transfers are paid from the Central Insurance Institution, cost is not of major concern. More recently, the Responsible Business Forum (an employers' association) declared an explicit support for the directive; it researched Poles' attitudes toward earmarking and found that there is moderate but clear societal support for these solutions among both women and men (FOB 2020).

Although there was initially strong resistance in Poland against adopting the directive, the attitude in government has changed after its adoption. However, because the government wants to present itself as family-friendly, it may decide to add two months on top of the existing scheme. Overall, business organizations and unions support the directive, but they are not involved in the process yet.

## Discussion and Conclusion

We have analyzed the regulatory responses to the WLBD in two different cases, but with similar ex-ante parental leave policies. Our adaptation of the RWS perspective captures how regulation—together with a requirement of fiscal commitment—at a higher level of governance could lead to change at a lower level of governance. Drawing on Europeanization and feminist literature, we have added three new concepts to cover tensions related to implementation of EU regulation.

EU-national subsidiarity captures the extent to which actors in national contexts perceive EU activity as encroaching on their regulatory rights. State-family subsidiarity refers to the extent to which state regulation causes a tension about the state deciding on issues that could be considered to belong in the private sphere. Costs refers to the fiscal implications of regulatory policy—in this case, the implementation of earmarked leave—through statutory means or through employers and/or employee contributions in social insurance or collective agreements.

Although the EU does not have exclusive regulatory power in the welfare state, it has progressively extended its regulatory reach in parental leave. We have argued that the EU, through the WLBD, could have a degenderizing effect by individualizing the right to paid parental leave. Our case studies reveal that the main policy-makers in Denmark and Poland were skeptical about the WLBD prior to its adoption mainly due to the EU-national and state-family subsidiarity tensions. After the adoption of the WLBD, policy-makers in Denmark and Poland changed their positions on the directive because it was clear that they had to implement the earmarked leave. In Denmark, social partners in the private sector have embraced earmarked leave and extended existing collectively agreed-upon leave schemes, together with extending the number of leave weeks with full pay. The proactive regulatory engagement of social partners with earmarked leave helps them to maintain their legitimacy among their constituents and limit regulatory intervention by the state. For those without collective agreement coverage, the directive is also likely to lead to degendered regulatory expansion, but at the level of unemployment benefits, to keep costs neutral. In Poland, the government is silent and most likely pushing the decision until the last moment; however, it is no longer openly criticizing the directive.

In Poland, the cost component is a major concern, as the government may not want to burden the National Insurance Fund, which is already under pressure; however, the government also wants to be perceived as family-friendly, so extending paid parental leave is likely. Both countries have moved from supporting no change and implicit genderization toward double expansion, with plans to individualize leave through earmarking. Furthermore, in both countries, the level of pay envisaged is in line with the aims of the directive; that is, pay will be at a comparatively high level, which makes the schemes degenderizing. Although in two different settings, the similar process taken by policy-makers in the two countries we studied allows us to attribute the causal change to the WLBD. Thus, the European Union is inducing degenderizing change as a RWS, combining regulation with fiscal elements.

Based on our cases, we draw tentative conclusions on the likely implementation of the directive across different welfare states. First, we do not foresee the earmarking of leave to be a major challenge, as it is a relatively small extension of what already existed in the 2010 directive—from one to two months of earmarked parental leave. We expect differentiation across Member States on pay, which may have major consequences for the impact of the WLBD, because a high level of pay during parental leave is crucial for the take-up of leave. We expect those countries that already have a long (albeit gendered) parental leave, with generous compensation, to be able to earmark two months of leave for fathers. The likely outcome of this is that fathers would increasingly take parental leave, leading to more degenderizing care practices. Thus, the long-term effect could be upwards social convergence—take-up of parental leave among men and women—despite different models of labor market regulation and different sources of compensation (related to state and social insurance). Future research could focus on the impact of earmarking leave for fathers in countries where there is currently unpaid leave.

There are other regulatory initiatives in the EPSR in the pipeline, including an initiative for an EU minimum wage. The EU minimum wage—especially if mandatory and adopted through regulation—will be in tension with the EU-national subsidiarity and costs. With the EU-national subsidiarity, which actors would be involved in regulatory implementation may arise, and the issue of costs may also arise; although, it seems costs would be borne by employers. The state-family subsidiarity is not, at first sight, present in the issue of wages, although there is an implicit issue of gender, considering the predominance of women in low-wage service sector jobs. Our findings indicate that tensions can be captured with our supplementary concepts to the RWS framework. Thus, researchers could use an adapted RWS framework for future research on the RWS, especially in federations and in the EU context.

# Notes

1. We made an analytical vignette (collected according to the EU-national, state-family, and costs dimensions) for each relevant policy actor.

2. Interview: Danish Ministry of Employment, 2019.

3. Interview: T he Danish Employers Association (DA), 2019; Interview: The Danish Trade Union Confederation (FH), 2019; Interview: The Central Organization of Industrial Employees in Denmark (CO-industri), 2019; Interview: Trade Danish Metal Union, (Dansk Metal), 2017; Interview: Danish Trade Union 3F, 2017; Interview: Danish Industry (Dansk Industri), 2017.

4. Interview: CO-industri, 2019.

5. Interview: The Danish Trade Union Confederation [FH], 2019; Interview: CO-industri, 2019.

6. Interview: The Confederation of Danish Employers (DA), 2019.

7. Interview: DA, 2019.

8. Interview: DA, December 2019.

9. Interviews: NSZZ Solidarność, 2020a; OPZZ, February 2020; with an anonymous trade union expert, TUEx, 2020.

10. TUEx, 2020.

11. Solidarność, 2020a.

12. Solidarność, 2020a; Solidarność, 2020b; OPZZ, 2020.

13. Leviatan, 2019.

14. Interviews: Leviatan, 2019; OPZZ, 2020; Solidarność, 2020; TUEx, 2020.

15. OPZZ, 2020.

16. Solidarność, 2020a.

17. Leviatan, 2019.

# References

Benish, Avishai, Hanen Haber, and Rotem Eliahou. 2017. The regulatory welfare state in pension markets. *Journal of Social Policy* 46 (2): 313–30.

Benish, Avishai, and David Levi-Faur. 2020. The expansion of regulation in welfare governance. *The ANNALS of the American Academy of Political and Social Science* (this volume).

Borchorst, Anette. 2003. *Køn, magt og beslutninger- Politiske forhandlinger om barselsorlov 1901–2002*. Århus: Magtudredningen.

Borschort, Anette, 2006. The public-private split rearticulated: Abolishment of the Danish daddy leave. In *Politicising parenthood in Scandinavia: Gender relations in welfare states*, eds., Anne Lise Ellingsætter and Leira Arnlaug, 101–21. New York, NY: Polity Press.

Busby, Nicole, and Grace James. 2015. Regulating working families in the European Union: A history of disjointed strategies. *Journal of Social Welfare and Family Law* 37 (3): 295–308.

Ciccia, Rossella, and Inge Bleijenbergh. 2014. After the male breadwinner model? Childcare services and the division of labor in European countries. *Social Politics* 21 (1): 50–79.

DA. 2019. Øremærket forældreorlov indføres trods dansk modstand, Pressemeddelse 24. januar 2019. Copenhagen: DA.

Dansk Erhverv. 2020. *Dansk Erhverv støtter Øremærket Barsel*. 3 feb. 2020, Copenhagen: Børsen.

de la Porte, Caroline. 2019. *The European Pillar of Social Rights meets the Nordic Model*, Policy Analysis. Stockholm: Swedish Institute for European Policy Studies (SIEPS). Available from http://www.sieps.se/en/publications/2019/the-european-pillar-of-social-rights-meets-the-nordic-model2/

DI and CO-industri. 2020. *Protokollater for OK20*. Copenhagen: CO-industri.

Due, Jesper, and Jørgen Steen Madsen. 2008. The Danish model of industrial relations: Erosion or renewal? *Journal of Industrial Relations* 50 (3): 513–29.

Employee Committee. 2017. *Forslag til Europa-Parlamentets og rådets diretiv om balance mellem arbejdsliv og privatliv for forældre og omsorgspersoner og om ophævelse af Rådets diretive 2010/18/EU*, Copenhagen: The Danish Parliament.

European Council. 1992. Maternity leave directive 92/85/EEC.

European Council. 2010. Parental leave Directive 2010/18EC: § 4 and 5.

European Commission. 2017. Proposal for a directive of the European Parliament and of the Council on work-life balance for parents and carers and repealing Council Directive 2010/18/EU, COM(2017) 253 final.

EurWORK. 2020. Yellow card procedure. Brussels: European observatory for working life. Available from https://www.eurofound.europa.eu/observatories/eurwork/industrial-relations-dictionary/yellow-card-procedure (accessed 11 August 2020).

FA and Finansforbundet. 2020. *OK-2020 aftale på plads*, Copenhagen: Finansforbundet.

Falkner, Gerda, Miriam Hartlapp, Simone Leiber, and Oliver Treib. 2002. Transforming social policy in Europe? The EC's parental leave directive and misfit in the 15 member states. MPIfG Working Paper 02/11.

Falkner, Gerda, Olivier Treib, Miriam Hartlapp, and Simone Leiber. 2005. *Complying with Europe: EU Harmonisation and Soft Law in the Member States*. Cambridge: Cambridge University Press.

Falkner, Gerda, and Simone Leiber. 2004. Europeanization of social partnership in smaller European Democracies? *European Journal of Industrial Relations* 10 (3): 245–66.

Fraser, Nancy. 1994. After the family wage: Gender equity and the welfare state. *Political Theory* 22 (4): 591–618.

George, Alexander L., and Andrew Bennett. 2005. *Case studies and theory development in the social sciences*. Cambridge, MA: MIT.

Graziano, Paolo, and Miriam Hartlapp. 2019. The end of social Europe? Understanding EU social policy change. *Journal of European Public Policy* 26 (10): 1384–1501.

GP. 2017. Rafalska o projekcie dyrektywy UE ws. urlopów: To nadmierna ingerencja w nasze życie. *Gazeta Prawna*. Available from https://praca.gazetaprawna.pl/artykuly/1066628,rafalska-o-projekcie-dyrektywy-ue-ws-urlopow.html (accessed 12 February 2020).

Haber, Hanan. 2017. The European Union as a social actor. Working Paper 143/15. The Hebrew University of Jerusalem, Jerusalem.

Janos, Krzysztof. 2017. *Rafalska w obronie polskich matek przed dyrektywą UE. Bruksela za skróceniem urlopów*. Available from https://finanse.wp.pl/rafalska-w-obronie-polskich-matek-przed-dyrektywa-ue-bruksela-za-skroceniem-urlopow-6157598976641153a?nil= (accessed 12 February 2020).

Kozłowska-Rajewicz, Agnieszka. 2018. Opinion on the proposal for a directive of the European Parliament and of the Council on work-life balance for parents and carers and repealing Council Directive 2010/18/EU. European Parliament. Available from https://www.europarl.europa.eu/doceo/document/FEMM-AD-618327_EN.pdf?redirect (accessed 15 january 2020).

Kristiansen, Jens. ed. 2015. *Europe and the Nordic collective bargaining model*. TemaNord. Copenhagen: Nordic Councils of Ministers.

Larsen, Trine P, and Søren K. Andersen. 2007. A new mode of European Regulation? *European Journal of Industrial Relations* 13 (2): 181–98.

Larsen, Trine P., and Steen E. Navrbjerg. 2018. Bargaining for equal pay and work–life balance in Danish companies – Does gender matter? *Journal of Industrial Relations* 60 (2): 176–200.

Levi-Faur, David. 2006. A question of size? In *Innovative comparative methods for policy analysis*, eds. Benoit Rihoux and Heike Grimm, 43–66. Boston, MA: Springer.

Levi-Faur, David. 2014. The welfare state: a regulatory perspective. *Public Administration* 92 (3): 599–614.

LO. 2017. LO's bemærkninger til Europa Parlamentets og Rådes direktiv om balance mellem arbejdsliv og privatliv for forældre og omsorgspersoner om ophævelse af Rådets direktiv 2010/18/EU, Copenhagen: LO.

Lundqvist, Åsa. 2017. *Transforming gender and family relations. How active labour market policies shaped the dual earner model*. Cheltenham: Edward Elgar.

Martinsen, Dorte. 2007. The Europeanisation of gender equality: Who controls the scope of non-discrimination? *Journal of European Public Policy* 14 (4): 544–62.

Ministry of Employment. 2018. *Samlet notat om EPSCO-rådsmødet den 21 juni 2018*. Copenhagen: Ministry of Employment.

Obinger, H., S. Leibfried, and F. G. Castles. 2005. Bypasses to a social Europe? Lessons from federal experience. *Journal of European Public Policy* 12 (3): 1–27.

OECD. 2017. *Trade unions and collective bargaining*. Available from https://stats.oecd.org/Index.aspx?DataSetCode=TUD (accessed 24 February 2020).

OJEU. 2019. Directive (EU) 2019/1158 of the European Parliament and of the Council of 20 June 2019 on work-life balance for parents and carers and repealing Council Directive 2010/18/EU. *Official Journal of European Union* 188 (79): 79–93.

FOB. 2020. *Odwaga i równowaga, czyli work-life balance po polsku*. Warszawa: Forum Odpowiedzialnego Biznesu.

Rees, Linda. 2003. Parental leave and gender equality: Lessons from the European Union. *Review of Policy Research* 20 (1): 89–114.

Rogg Korsvi, Trine, and Marta Warat. 2016. Framing leave for fathers in Norway and Poland: Just a matter of gender equality? *NORA - Nordic Journal of Feminist and Gender Research* 24 (2): 110–25.

Rostgaard, Tine. 2002. Setting time aside for the father: Father's leave in Scandinavia. *Community, Work & Family* 5 (3): 343–64.

Rubery, Jill, Mark Smith, Collette Fagan, and Damian Grimshaw, eds. 1998. *Women and European employment*. Basingstoke: Routledge.

Saxonberg, Steven. 2013. From defamilialization to degenderization: Toward a New Welfare Typology. *Social Policy & Administration* 47 (1): 26–49.

Scharpf, Fritz. 2002. The European social model: Coping with the challenges of diversity. *Journal of Common Market Studies* 40 (4): 645–70.

Sejm. 2017. Uchwała Sejmu Rzeczypospolitej Polskiej z dnia 22 czerwca 2017 r. w sprawie uznania projektu dyrektywy Parlamentu Europejskiego i Rady w sprawie równowagi między życiem zawodowym a prywatnym rodziców i opiekunów oraz uchylającej dyrektywę Rady 2010/18/UE za niezgodny z zasadą pomocniczości.

Solidarność. 2017. Decyzja Prezydium KK nr 50/17 ws. opinii o projekcie Dyrektywy Parlamentu Europejskiego i Rady w sprawie równowagi między życiem zawodowym a prywatnym rodziców i opiekunów oraz uchylającej dyrektywę Rady 2010/18/UE.

van Belle, Janna. 2016. Paternity and parental leave policies across the European Union. Policy Brief. Rand Europe. DOI: https://doi.org/10.7249/RR1666.

Wiśniewska, Jadwiga. 2017. A question for written answer (rule 130), Available from https://www.jad wigawisniewska.pl/dzialalnosc/szczegoly/jadwiga-wisniewska-pyta-komisje-europejska-o-dyrektywe-w-sprawie-rownowagi-miedzy-zyciem-zawodowym-a-prywatnym-rodzicow-i-opiekunow (accessed 12 February 2020).

ZUS. 2016. *Prognoza wpływów i wydatków funduszu emerytalnego do 2060 roku.* Warsaw: Zaklad Ubezpieczen Spolecznych.

Żebrowski, Paweł. 2019a. Dodatkowe pięć dni płatnego urlopu? Jeśli tak, to kto za to zapłaci? Avaiable from https://www.prawo.pl/kadry/dodatkowe-piec-dni-platnego-urlopu-jesli-tak-to-kto-za-to-za-placi,376743.html (accessed 12 February 2020).

Żebrowski, Paweł. 2019b. Jest kompromis ws. unijnej dyrektywy, urlop rodzicielski może być wydłużony. Available from https://www.prawo.pl/kadry/byc-moze-trzeba-bedzie-wydluzyc-urlop-rodzicielski-szwed,375585.html (accessed 12 February 2020).

# Bossing or Protecting? The Integration of Social Regulation into the Welfare State

*By*
PHILIPP TREIN

This article is an empirical analysis of how social regulation is integrated into the welfare state. I compare health, migration, and unemployment policy reforms in Australia, Austria, Canada, Belgium, France, Germany, Italy, the Netherlands, New Zealand, Sweden, Switzerland, the UK, and the United States from 1980 to 2014. Results show that the timing of reform events is similar among countries for health and unemployment policy but differs among countries for migration policy. For migration and unemployment policy, the integration of regulation and welfare is more likely to entail conditionality compared to health policy. In other words, in these two policy fields, it is more common that claimants receive financial support upon compliance with social regulations. Liberal or Continental European welfare regimes are especially inclined to integration. I conclude that integrating regulation and welfare entails a double goal: "bossing" citizens by making them take up available jobs while expelling migrants and refugees for minor offenses; and protecting citizens from risks, such as noncommunicable diseases.

*Keywords:*  immigration; immigrant integration; labor market policy; health care; public health; social investment

In the last two decades, the study of regulatory governance has become interesting to political researchers. Scholars have focused on regulatory policy instruments and agencies, which deal with the consequences of economic liberalization (e.g., Majone 1996; Braithwaite 2008; Gilardi 2008; Levi-Faur 2011; Maggetti 2012) in different policy areas (e.g., Ozel 2013; Reynaers and Parrado 2017).

Against this background, researchers have also assessed how regulatory policies have permeated

*Philipp Trein is a senior researcher and lecturer at the University of Geneva. He also holds an Ambizione Research Grant of the Swiss National Science Foundation. His research interests cover comparative public policy, governance, health and social policy, and the politics of data protection.*

Correspondence: josefphilipp.trein@unige.ch

DOI: 10.1177/0002716220953758

social policy and the welfare state. Although scholars have assessed the regulatory dimension of the welfare state for a long time (Kliemt 1993; Swenson 2004), there is a growing interest in the link between regulation and welfare. More recently, scholars have focused on the regulation of private pension schemes (Leisering 2012; Benish, Haber, and Eliahou 2017), welfare-related effects of utility regulation (Haber 2011, 2017), the regulation of job security (Emmenegger 2014; Zohlnhöfer and Voigt 2020), and social assistance (Özel and Parado 2020), as well as the regulatory dimension of social policy at the EU level (Graziano and Hartlapp 2018; Hartlapp 2019). Nevertheless, some broader questions remain (Benish and Levi-Faur 2020). For example, the role of social regulations in the welfare state, which target the behavior of individuals directly, needs more empirical work (Levi-Faur 2014, 607).

In this article, I explore how social regulation and fiscal transfers are linked within welfare state reforms in different policy domains and countries. By using an original empirical dataset, I descriptively analyze (Gerring 2012) the wave of reforms linking regulation and welfare in health, immigration, and unemployment policy across thirteen developed democracies. I explain how integrating regulation and welfare varies between the three policy fields, and I show that there are differences between countries and over time. Harkening back to literature on the complexity of policy fields (Trein and Maggetti 2020), I argue that we see different patterns concerning the integration of regulation and welfare between migration on one hand, and health and unemployment policy on the other. In migration and unemployment policy, integrating regulation and welfare entails a strong conditionality dimension, that is, the receipt of monetary benefits depends on compliance with regulations. In health policy, compliance plays a minor role as target groups have more political clout (Schneider and Ingram 1993). I hold that there are differences between welfare state types regarding such reforms, as Continental European and liberal welfare states are more inclined to use regulations to cover the reduction of benefits and to commodify social services (Iversen and Wren 1998; Häusermann and Schwander 2012; Levi-Faur 2014).

Second, using the idea of the protective state (Ansell 2019), I argue that integrating regulation and welfare has two faces. On one hand, integrating regulation and welfare has the potential to protect citizens from the forces of the market. On the other hand, such reforms and policies have a capability to boss individuals and to put pressure on them; for example, by forcing them to participate in the labor market. I use this distinction to develop an argument that distinguishes two approaches to integrating regulation and transfers through public policy. The first is a "regulation first approach," in which the government uses primarily social regulations to improve welfare, whereas transfer measures have a complementary role. The second is a "transfer first approach," which contains the primary use of transfers and where social regulations play a secondary role. I conclude by linking the idea of bossing and protecting to the uses of welfare and regulation in social policy, and I suggest how future research can address this topic in a theoretical and empirical manner.

## Theoretical Starting Point and Dataset

The theoretical starting point for this research is the concept of the regulatory welfare state (RWS). In two articles, David Levi-Faur developed a regulatory perspective on the welfare state and coined the term *regulatory welfare state* (Levi-Faur 2013, 2014). This term combines the concepts of a welfare state, which aims to "promot[e] equality, solidarity and social justice" through fiscal redistribution with the regulatory state, which works according to "criteria of economic efficiency while keeping politics of equality out" (Benish Haber, and Eliahou 2017, 315–6). Against this background, Levi-Faur suggested two ideal types of the welfare state—the "fiscal-welfare state" and the "regulatory-welfare state." Both types aim to achieve welfare goals but with different means: fiscal welfare policy contains the use of redistributive policy instruments, whereas regulatory welfare policy uses regulatory instruments (Levi-Faur 2014, 608).

In this article, I focus on the integration of regulation and welfare, that is, the merging of policy goals or coordination of public sector agencies, for regulating social behavior with the provision of fiscal transfers or social services. Therefore, the article focuses on three policy fields. First, in unemployment policy, governments have integrated regulation and welfare by making the receipt of welfare benefits conditional upon compliance with regulations that demand benefit claimants participate in job trainings or even accept certain jobs (Clasen and Clegg 2011). Second, another example of regulatory social policies is immigrant integration policy, which obligates immigrants to make use of integration measures (Goodman and Wright 2015, 1886–1887) to receive permanent residency or citizenship, which then entitles them to receive welfare benefits. Third, a further example of integrating regulation and welfare is the integration of health care services with measures that incentivize individuals to take preventative health measures (Trein 2017b, 2018).

I compiled a dataset that measures the integration of regulation and welfare according to the previously mentioned examples. Health, migration, and unemployment represent three very different examples of the integration of regulation and welfare. A description of the data can be found elsewhere (Trein and Maggetti 2020). The dataset covers over 30 years (between 1980 and 2014) and thirteen countries, which represent different welfare state types (Levi-Faur 2014): Liberal (Australia, Canada, New Zealand, UK, and the U.S.), Continental European (Austria, Belgium, France, Germany, the Netherlands, and Switzerland), one Southern European (Italy), and one Social Democratic (Sweden). The data start with the onset of "regulatory capitalism" (Braithwaite 2008, 1), which entails that government bodies (agencies) that are independent from government's immediate control and are in charge of regulatory policymaking and implementation in many policy fields (Jordana and Levi-Faur 2004; Maggetti 2009; Jordana, Levi-Faur, and Fernández i Marín 2011). Originally, the dataset was created to analyze the coordination and integration between policy instruments and public sector organizations (Trein 2017c; Trein, Meyer, and Maggetti 2019; Trein and Maggetti 2020). In addition to policy coordination and integration, the data also measure the integration of regulation and welfare.

TABLE 1
Empirical Identification of Regulation and Welfare in Three Policy Fields

| Policy field | Examples of integration of regulation and welfare |
|---|---|
| Health | Integrating incentives for prevention with health care (for example in health insurance programs); integration of health regulations and (paid) curative services at the level of policy goals (tobacco control and cancer strategies) |
| Migration | Integrating immigration and integration rules with social benefits for immigrants and refugees; receipt of benefits is conditional on compliance with rules |
| Unemployment | Integrating regulations regarding labor market activation with unemployment benefits and social assistance; receipt of benefits is conditional on compliance with rules |

Table 1 operationalizes the integration of regulation and welfare. We collected the data according to the following steps: (1) survey of primary sources, secondary literature, edited books, and policy reports (for instance by international organizations or governments); (2) creation of a time series of formal policy, legislative, and organizational changes; (3) data sheets validated by international experts; and (4) exclusion of reforms that are unclear in their substantial relevance for our analytical focus. A detailed description of the dataset and the data collection is published elsewhere (Trein and Maggetti 2020).

Specifically, I use a binary (0/1) variable, which records whether there is a reform event integrating regulation and welfare in a year, nested in a policy field and country. Coding binary variables to measure change follows the strategy used in diffusion and conflict data (Maggetti and Gilardi 2016) and creates a dynamic measurement for policy change. To analyze cumulated reform activity, we aggregated the binary variables for reform events to create an indicator of reform intensity comparing countries, years, and policies.

# The Integration of Regulation and Welfare in Different Policy Fields

The data on reform events show differences regarding the integration of regulation and welfare among the three policy fields. For migration policy, the number of reforms for immigration and migrant integration policies increased during the 1980s and declined again during the early 1990s when many member states of the Organisation for Economic Co-operation and Development (OECD) experienced economic difficulties. After 1995, the number of these reforms increased again (see Figure 1). For unemployment, policy changes integrating regulation and welfare increased from the early 1980s until the mid-1990s and then again during the early 2000s. These types of reforms declined after 2005. Finally,

FIGURE 1
Reform Trends Integrating Regulation and Welfare in Different Policies (Median Spline)

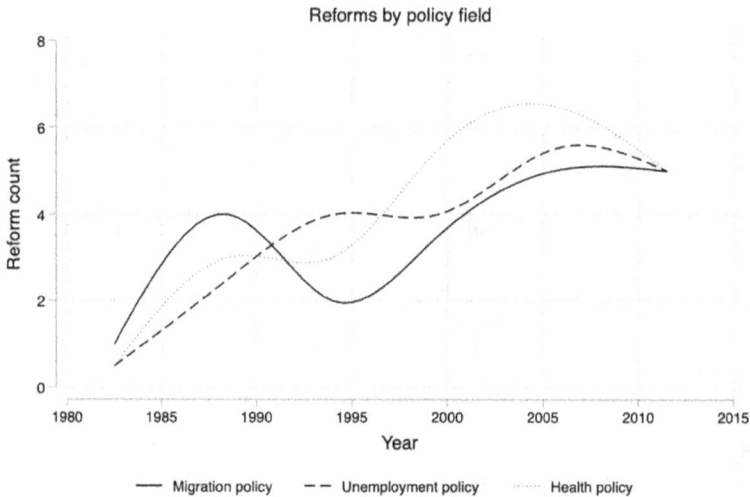

reforms linking behavioral and regulatory with welfare instruments in health policy appeared especially after 1995. The frequency of such reforms peaked before 2005 and declined after that. I show median splines (Figure 1) of the reform events instead of the actual reform events to indicate reform trends.

In *health policy*, the integration of regulation and welfare concerns the integration of health regulations and other behavioral incentives for individuals who pay for health care services. The biggest part of health policy covers the financing and provision of health care services, for example in hospitals (Gerlinger 2010; Klenk and Reiter 2015). Regulatory policies aimed at influencing individual behavior, such as smoking bans, seatbelt laws, and bans on drugs, are distinctive from health care in terms of their legal and organizational foundations (Trein 2018). Nevertheless, conditionality is rare between the welfare part (health care) and the regulatory part (individual public health regulation) in the sense that the receipt of health care services is conditional on complying with public health regulations. Noncompliance with public health regulations will, usually, not result in the loss of health care coverage. Integration entails health care financing organizations and instruments that nudge individuals toward healthier behavior. For example, the German law on preventative health *(Präventionsgesetz)* requires statutory health insurances to provide prevention measures (Gerlinger 2018). Furthermore, in health policy, the integration of regulations and health care services appears often at the level of policy goals, for example in integrated policy strategies such as the Australian Better Health Program (Trein 2018, 132). Nevertheless, in some U.S. states, noncompliance with work requirements can result in the loss of Medicaid coverage (Venkataramani et al. 2020).

For *unemployment policy*, the integration of regulatory and welfare instruments focuses on integrating regulations for individuals with social transfers and can entail conditionality. For example, in Switzerland, regulations requiring individuals to file a certain number of applications or to accept work to receive welfare benefits happened between the federal unemployment insurance's regional office and the municipal social assistance schemes (Champion 2011). The 2004 reform of the German unemployment insurance merged the national unemployment insurance and the municipal social assistance programs (Zimmermann and Rice 2016). Under the new regime, claimants are subject to rather strict regulations if they want to obtain full benefits (Götz, Ludwig-Mayerhofer, and Schreyer 2010; Zimmermann and Rice 2016, 170).

The third case for the integration of social regulation and welfare is *immigration policy*. In this policy field, regulation and welfare are integrated through conditionality. Claimants of social benefits need to comply with rules requiring them to learn the language, acquire knowledge about the country they immigrate to, and accept jobs they are being offered to obtain access to permanent residency and welfare benefits. In this case, regulation and welfare are integrated across different policy fields with different legal foundations and agencies. For example, the Canadian Immigrant Integration Program of 2010 was aimed at "uniting separate programmes for settlement programming. Newcomer services are covered by a single funding agreement, simplifying the administrative process for immigrant-serving organisations, and allowing them to tailor their offerings to suit newcomers' needs" (OECD 2012, 218). The three cases show that there are differences among policy fields regarding the integration of regulation and welfare.

Why do we see these similarities and differences among policy fields? In the following, I provide a tentative explanation using two variables. First, the *complexity* of the policy field matters. The more different the policy sectors (laws and public sector organizations) involved, the more complex the problem that cross-sectoral policies need to address (Peters 2017, 392–4; Christensen, Lægreid, and Lægreid 2019). Integration of regulation and welfare cuts across different policy fields in migration policy, but remains within the wider policy fields for health and unemployment policy, although the latter two policy fields differ regarding their technical complexity (Trein and Maggetti 2020). Therefore, the different reform pattern in migration policy—compared to health and unemployment policy—can be attributed to a larger scope of the integration targets potentially involved in this policy field.

Second, the *political clout of the policy field's target group*, that is, the political influence of those who are affected by the policy (Schneider and Ingram 1993), explains why there is conditionality in the integration of regulation and welfare in unemployment and migration policy but not health policy. In health policy, individuals who do not comply with public health regulations, such as compulsory vaccinations or smoking bans, face charges but they do not lose health care coverage as a consequence of noncompliance. Such a policy is difficult to accept from a moral, legal, and social point of view, as it would interfere with basic human rights. Furthermore, those who do not conform with public health regulations are *contenders*, that is, they have a moral cause and are politically influential

(Schneider and Ingram 1993, 336) of the *Nanny State*, and they can count on some political backing, for example from liberal parties or economic organizations. The term *Nanny State* refers to the accumulation of public health policies, such as tobacco control and anti-obesity measures, indicating that these policies reduce individual freedom (Harsanyi 2007). This implies that policy-makers are likely to take such contending groups politically seriously, although these groups do not necessarily have a positive image (Schneider and Ingram 1993, 343). Recipients of health care services can be considered either an *advantageous* or a *dependent* target group, conditional on the type of services covered by the health care system (Blank, Burau, and Kuhlmann 2017). If these target groups have a positive image, policy-makers will regard their concerns as a political priority (Schneider and Ingram 1993, 336).

In migration and unemployment, the receipt of benefits can be conditional on compliance, with rules and noncompliance resulting in the reduction or loss of eligibility for payments. I argue that target groups are *deviants* in both cases; that is, they are considered to be responsible for their own situation (Schneider and Ingram 1993, 343). In the instance of migration, this applies to those "unwilling to integrate," whereas those fleeing violence and war are *dependents* who deserve special protection. Nevertheless, the distinction between *immigrants as deviants* and *refugees as dependents* is volatile and depends on how many migrants in each group arrive. A high number of immigrants is likely to lead to reforms that increase conditionality not only regarding integration rules but also concerning strictness of background checks (Natter, Czaika, and de Haas 2020). Contrary to contenders, deviants have a lower potential for political mobilization (Schneider and Ingram 1993, 343). Therefore, governments can be tough on target groups for immigration and unemployment policies and design the integration of regulation and welfare in a way that makes the receipt of monetary benefits conditional on compliance with rules. Naturally, there are differences between political parties regarding these policies. Right and market-liberal parties are more likely to use the narrative that the deviants should be punished, whereas Left parties would consider these target groups as dependents deserving of support (Morel, Palier, and Palme 2012).

## Integration of Regulation and Welfare in Different Welfare State Types

In the following, I turn to an analysis of the integration of regulation and welfare in different welfare state regimes and policy fields. Levi-Faur distinguishes among different welfare types in an ideal-typical perspective (Levi-Faur 2014). I differentiate among the real types of Liberal, Continental European, Social Democratic, and Southern European welfare states (Emmenegger et al. 2015; Ferrera 1996). To visualize the data effectively, I created a count index of the reform events. I multiplied the reforms for countries in the group of Liberal welfare states by 0.5 (five countries in the sample) and those in the group of

FIGURE 2
Integration of Regulation and Welfare across Welfare State Types and Time

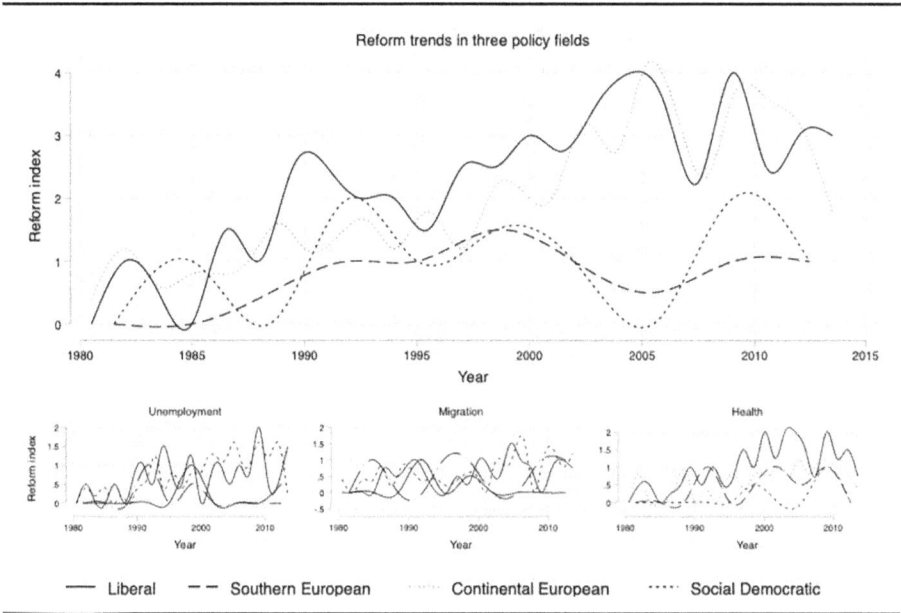

Continental European welfare states by 0.4 (six countries in the sample). This strategy allows me to compare the data with the Social Democratic and Southern European cases in the sample. I created again a median spline curve to describe reform trends over time (Figure 2).

The results indicate differences among welfare state types as well as differences among policy fields. Overall, the curve of reforms integrating regulation and welfare is much steeper in Continental European compared to Liberal welfare states. For unemployment policy, Liberal and Continental European welfare states tend to have more reforms compared to Southern European and Social Democratic welfare states, especially after 2000. For migration policy, the data indicate that there are fewer differences among welfare state types compared to unemployment policy. For health policy, my analysis suggests that especially countries with a Liberal welfare state have pursued measures to integrate regulation and welfare, compared to the governments of countries representing other welfare state types.

To deepen the analysis further, I show the reforms per country over the expenditure for social security transfers on one hand, and labor market activation and family policies on the other, in two time periods. I chose these measures to contrast the reforms integrating regulation and welfare with money spent on cash transfers that claimants received (Emmenegger et al. 2015), as well as to contextualize reforms with social policies that help individuals to find jobs and support their families (Bonoli 2005).[1] The results confirm that the majority of reforms integrating regulation and welfare happened after 1997 and were more common

FIGURE 3
Integration of Regulation and Welfare in Immigration and Unemployment Policy

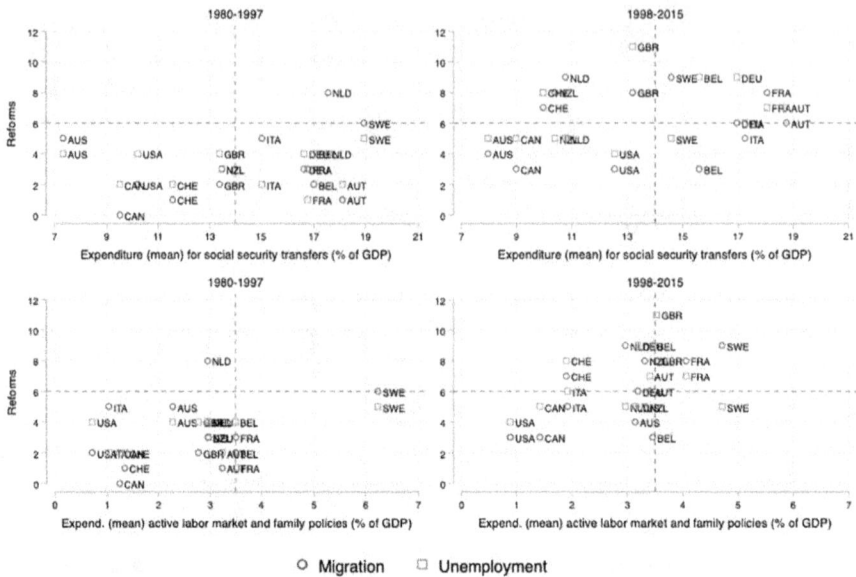

1980-1997

Reforms — Expenditure (mean) for social security transfers (% of GDP)

1998-2015

Reforms — Expenditure (mean) for social security transfers (% of GDP)

1980-1997

Reforms — Expend. (mean) active labor market and family policies (% of GDP)

1998-2015

Reforms — Expend. (mean) active labor market and family policies (% of GDP)

○ Migration    □ Unemployment

in countries that are part of the Continental European and Liberal welfare states (Figure 3). The data reveal further insights. Notably, among the countries with a Liberal welfare state, the UK above all, as well as Australia and New Zealand, created more policy changes, whereas Canada and the United States have fewer reforms. Countries from the group of Continental European welfare states, such as Austria, Belgium, Germany, and France, accompany reforms integrating regulation and welfare with an increase in expenditure for new social risks while mostly maintaining their levels of transfer expenditure. In the Netherlands, reforms integrating regulation and welfare come along with a reduction of social security transfers. Interestingly, Sweden reduces expenditure for transfers and new social risks along with reforms integrating regulation and welfare, whereas other countries increased those expenditures, with France at the top.

I depicted reforms to integrate regulation and welfare in health policy along the development of public and private expenditure for health.[2] The findings indicate that especially countries with a mainly tax-funded health care system— Australia, Great Britain, and New Zealand, but also Italy—tend to pass more reforms integrating regulation and welfare. Contrariwise, countries that have a health care system that largely relies on private health expenditure, such as Switzerland and the United States seem to have fewer reforms integrating regulation and welfare in health policy, at least at the national level (Figure 4).

My findings suggest that integrating regulation and welfare fits with common practices of commodifying and decommodifying welfare services and that there are variations among welfare state types. For example, Social Democratic welfare

FIGURE 4
Integration of Regulation and Welfare in Health Policy

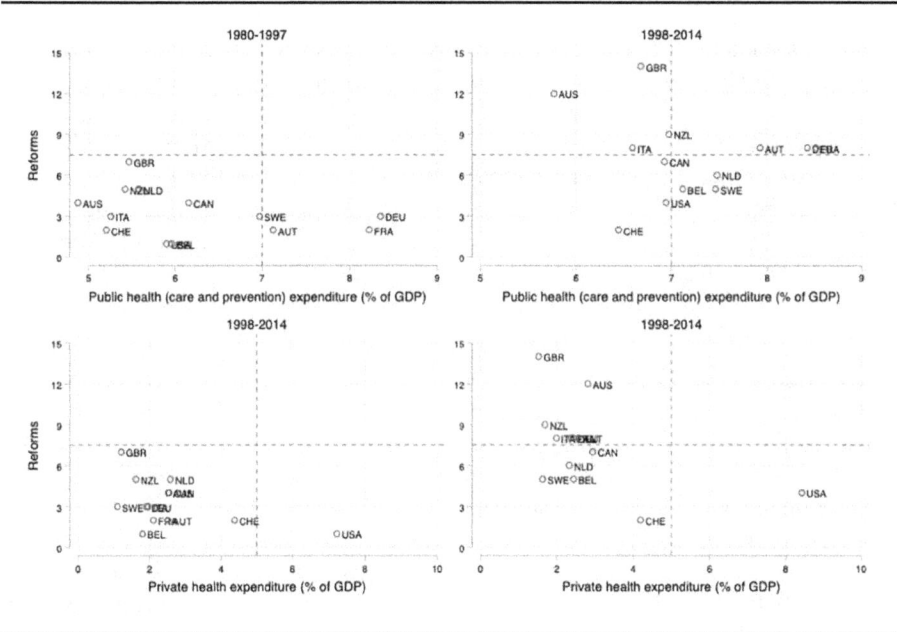

states tend to use social spending and regulation to decommodify, whereas Liberal welfare states use regulation and spending to commodify (Levi-Faur 2014, 609–10), creating what scholars have termed a workfare state where the availability of social services is linked to the acceptance of jobs by benefit claimants (Daguerre 2004).

My data indicate that there is a distinction among welfare state types regarding the integration of regulation and welfare. Particularly, Liberal and Continental European welfare states integrated regulation and welfare regarding immigration and unemployment policy. Liberal welfare states pursued such reforms continuously, whereas in Continental European welfare states integrating reforms appeared later but more frequently. In Sweden, such reforms happened less frequently. My results indicate that there is a convergence of welfare states regarding the integration of specific types of regulation with welfare transfers, which follows with the insight that welfare states pursued a common trajectory toward liberalization reforms (Thelen 2014).

My findings also fit with the argument that economic (including social) policy in the service economy aims at balancing three goals—earnings equality, employment growth, and fiscal discipline—of which only two can be achieved at the same time. According to the literature, Christian Democratic welfare states focus on fiscal discipline and earnings equality, Neoliberal welfare states prefer employment growth and fiscal discipline, and Social Democratic welfare states focus on earnings inequality and employment growth (Iversen and Wren 1998, 514). Against this background, in Continental European (that is, Christian

Democratic) welfare states, the integration of regulation and welfare contributed to creating a second labor market for individuals who have difficulties in integrating into the first labor market (Häusermann and Schwander 2012). The more limited use of such reforms in the Swedish case fits the expectation that policymakers in Social Democratic welfare states pursue earnings equality and full employment (Iversen and Wren 1998, 514). My findings confirm some of the findings from previous case studies about integration of regulation and welfare in health care, which suggest that countries with a tax-financed health care system tend to integrate preventative and curative health policies. In this context, the government uses preventative health policies to protect citizens and to keep the cost for health care under control (Trein 2017a, 2018).

## Two Faces of Regulatory Social Policy in the Welfare State

What are the implications of these data for our understanding the regulatory welfare state and the roles and uses of regulation in social policy in general? According to its original concept, the regulatory welfare state explicitly focuses on redistribution through regulatory instruments, for example through regulations that require private utility providers to offer better conditions for low-income households (Levi-Faur 2014; Benish, Haber, and Eliahou 2017). Nevertheless, governments have also used regulatory instruments to protect citizens from the problem of new social risks that have become more important in postindustrial society broadly defined (Beck 1986; Leisering and Leibfried 2001; Bonoli 2005). Regulatory policy is likewise used as part of what Ansell denotes as the *protective state*, which aims to, ". . . protect against discrete harms, accidents, hazards, threats, and risks . . ." (Ansell 2019, 2). For example, new public health policies aim to protect citizens from smoking, driving without a seatbelt, or diabetes (Trein 2017b, 2018). On the contrary, regulatory measures have also limited individual liberties, for example the liberty to smoke as well as the liberty to choose a job and not having to accept work simply to remain entitled to a minimal level of social benefits (Daguerre 2004).

These policies are examples for what Taylor-Gooby (2006, 275) and Ansell (2019, 15) have named, a ". . . greater regulation of individualized life-styles." Therein, regulatory policy instruments aim to protect citizens from risks, such as unemployment or health hazards, in influencing individual behavior. Such policies are social regulations, which differ from regulations of private providers of social benefits, such as private pension schemes and private health insurances. Social regulations are often integrated or coordinated with fiscal transfers. The goal of such social regulations can either be explicitly formulated or remain hidden, as policy instruments, ". . . may be a useful smokescreen to hide less respectable objectives" (Lascoumes and Le Galès 2007, 17).

In the following, I point out that the use of social regulations can have a double face. On one hand, social regulations I have mentioned aim to protect citizens from all kinds of social risks; on the other, they have a coercive face, which enforces a particular behavior through a Nanny State that limits individual choices (Ansell 2019, 39–40). Furthermore, citizens and observers might perceive such

## FIGURE 5
### Integration of Regulation and Welfare in Different Policy Contexts

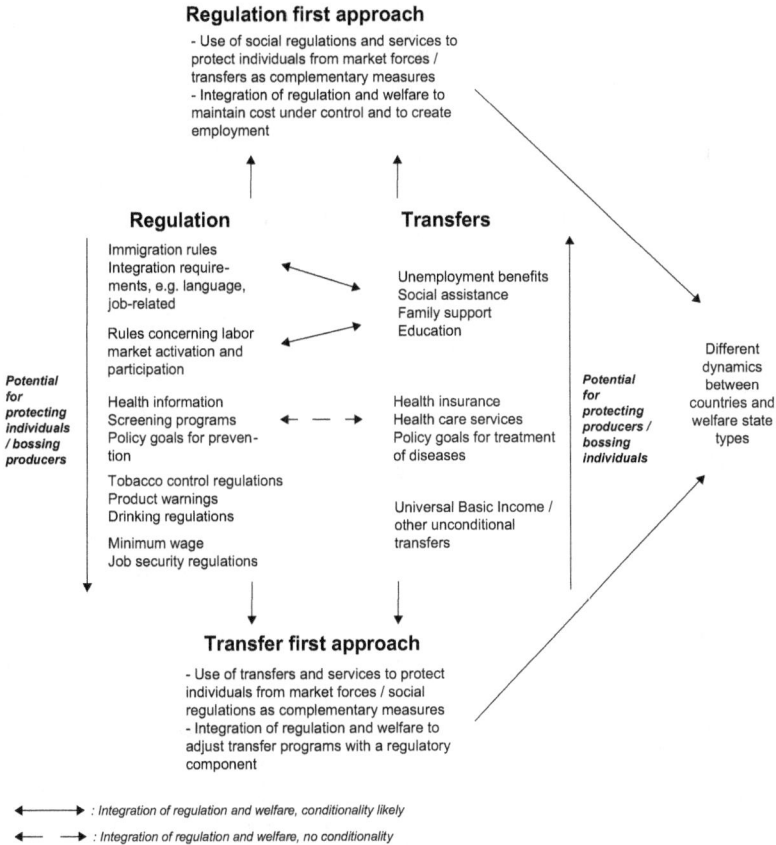

**Regulation first approach**
- Use of social regulations and services to protect individuals from market forces / transfers as complementary measures
- Integration of regulation and welfare to maintain cost under control and to create employment

**Regulation**

Immigration rules
Integration require-
ments, e.g. language,
job-related

Rules concerning labor
market activation and
participation

Health information
Screening programs
Policy goals for preven-
tion

Tobacco control regulations
Product warnings
Drinking regulations

Minimum wage
Job security regulations

**Transfers**

Unemployment benefits
Social assistance
Family support
Education

Health insurance
Health care services
Policy goals for treatment
of diseases

Universal Basic Income /
other unconditional
transfers

*Potential
for
protecting
individuals
/ bossing
producers*

*Potential
for
protecting
producers /
bossing
individuals*

Different
dynamics
between
countries and
welfare state
types

**Transfer first approach**
- Use of transfers and services to protect individuals from market forces / social regulations as complementary measures
- Integration of regulation and welfare to adjust transfer programs with a regulatory component

◄─────► : *Integration of regulation and welfare, conditionality likely*

◄── ──► : *Integration of regulation and welfare, no conditionality*

policies as an augmentation of a coercive state (Fassin 2019). The data presented here show that the integration of regulation and welfare has happened across developed democracies, but that there are also differences among welfare state types and policy fields. In the empirical analysis, I focused on the integration of regulation and welfare through conditionality, concerning immigration and unemployment policy fields. In these two policy fields, integrating regulation and welfare means that the receipt of benefits can be conditional upon compliance with regulations, such as the need to regularly apply for jobs or to obtain benefits. In health policy, there is integration of preventative health programs into health care services and of policy goals for treatment and prevention of diseases, but usually there is no conditionality for individuals attached to them. I did not include policies in my analysis that are "only" social regulations, such as tobacco control policies or minimum wage policies. Neither did I consider transfers that do not depend on regulatory elements, for example, universal basic income or other unconditional cash transfers, which are part of social policy mixes (Figure 5).

In taking a comparative perspective, the regulations and welfare elements discussed here can be distinguished according to their potential for protecting or bossing individuals, that is, citizens in need of social benefits or producers (companies) (cf. Ansell 2019, 25–26; Knoepfel, Larrue, and Varone 2011). The integration of regulation and welfare based on conditionality is an example of potential protection of producers and bossing of individuals because it forces individuals to seek jobs and provides labor supported by the state and potential contracts for firms that deliver job training and placement services, that is, workfare (Daguerre 2004, 2017). From a social investment perspective, the integration of regulation and welfare can be described as "social policy [that] should help to 'make work pay' through positive economic incentives (by improving net income for those who work, first of all at the bottom end of the wage distribution), and that it should assist in promoting the creation of 'quality jobs'" (Morel, Palier, and Palme 2012, 10). The integration of regulation and welfare in health policy has a more limited potential for bossing and offers more protection for individuals compared to integrating regulation and welfare in immigration and unemployment. Beyond the examples discussed in this article, health regulations, such as tobacco control measures, as well as regulations that protect jobs and wages have a higher potential to protect individuals and restrict producers, in comparison to integrated measures. Finally, transfers that are not linked to regulation, such as an universal basic income, are another instrument aimed at protecting individuals from market forces (Figure 5).

The empirical research presented here suggests that, broadly put, governments mix regulation and welfare in two different ways. On one hand, there is a regulation first approach, which uses social regulations above all to protect individuals from market forces; in this case, welfare transfers complement regulatory instruments, and the integration of regulation and welfare aims to create employment and keep public expenditure under control. The empirical cases that come closest to this approach are Liberal welfare states. On the other hand, there is a transfer first approach. This approach aims to use fiscal transfers to protect individuals first and employs individual social regulations as complementary policy measures. The empirical cases representing these approaches are Continental European welfare states (Figure 5).

## Conclusion

In this article, I have analyzed the integration of regulation and welfare, based on a dataset of reform events that link the two. The results of my analysis show that the integration of regulation and welfare differs among immigration and unemployment policy on one hand, and health policy on the other. The main difference is that in the case of immigration and unemployment, integrating regulation and welfare comes along with conditionality; that is, the uses of regulation make the receipt of benefits conditional on compliance with regulation, whereas in health policy the receipt of health care benefits is not conditional on compliance with health regulations or behavioral incentives. My results show that such reforms appeared as of the mid-1980s in all three policy fields. Nevertheless, they take a more cyclical shape in immigration policy compared to unemployment and health, where the integration of regulation and welfare increased during the 1990s. Furthermore, there are differences among welfare states. The integration of regulation and welfare happens most in Liberal and Continental European welfare states concerning unemployment and immigration, and in Liberal states regarding health policy.

Against this background, I have argued that integrating regulatory instruments in social policy links two faces of social policy and can take two different approaches. On one hand, there is a regulation first approach. This approach entails the use of social regulations and services to protect individuals from market forces, and transfers are complementary measures. The integration of regulation and welfare aims to keep costs under control and to create employment. On the other hand, there is a transfer first approach. According to this approach, transfers and services are used to protect individuals from market forces. Social regulations act as complementary measures to transfer programs. The integration of regulation and welfare entails the adjustment of transfer programs with a regulatory component.

With this article, I also open avenues for future research. Scholars could especially focus on the following topics to analyze the integration of regulation and welfare. First, research should concentrate on the complementarity of an integrated approach with instruments that are purely regulatory or transfers-oriented, such as health regulations, universal basic income, and minimum wages. Second, future research needs to explore the drivers of reforms that integrate regulation and welfare, such as the powers of the central government or fiscal imperatives. Third, additional research should take into account the limitations of quantitative datasets, such as the one used in this article, and assess how governments have terminated and discarded policies that integrate regulation and welfare.

# Notes

1. To measure welfare transfers and spending on new social risks, I use the *Comparative Political Dataset* (Armingeon et al. 2016). The measure for welfare transfers uses the variable "sstran," which aggregates spending on transfers as a percentage of GDP. The measure for new social risks aggregates the variables "almp_pmp" and "fallow_pmp". The data use mean values for the two periods.

2. The measure for public and mandatory private health expenditure uses the variables "wdi_exphpu" and "wdi_exphpr" from the *Quality of Government Dataset* (Teorell et al. 2017).

# References

Ansell, Christopher. 2019. *The protective state*. Cambridge: Cambridge University Press.

Armingeon, Klaus, Christian Isler, Laura Knöpfel, David Weisstanner, and Sarah Engler. 2016. *Comparative political data set 1990–2014*. Bern: University of Bern, Institute of Political Science.

Beck, Ulrich. 1986. *Risikogesellschaft. Auf dem Weg in eine andere Moderne*. Frankfurt: Suhrkamp.

Benish, Avishai, Hanan Haber, and Rotem Eliahou. 2017. The regulatory welfare state in pension markets: Mitigating high charges for low-income savers in the United Kingdom and Israel. *Journal of Social Policy* 46 (2): 313–30.

Benish, Avishai, David Levi-Faur. 2020. The expansion of regulation in welfare governance. *The ANNALS of the American Academy of Political and Social Science* (this volume).

Blank, Robert H., Viola Burau, and Ellen Kuhlmann. 2017. *Comparative health policy.* 5 ed. Basingstoke: Palgrave Macmillan.

Bonoli, Giuliano. 2005. The politics of the new social policies: Providing coverage against new social risks in mature welfare states. *Policy & Politics* 33 (3): 431–49.

Braithwaite, John. 2008. *Regulatory capitalism: How it works, ideas for making it work better.* Cheltenham: Edward Elgar Publishing.

Champion, Cyrielle. 2011. Switzerland: A latecomer catching up. In *Regulating the risk of unemployment: National adaptations to post-industrial labour markets in Europe,* eds. J. Clasen and D. Clegg, 121–41. Oxford: Oxford University Press.

Christensen, Tom, Ole Martin Lægreid, and Per Lægreid. 2019. Administrative coordination capacity: Does the wickedness of policy areas matter? *Policy and Society* 1–18.

Clasen, Jochen, and Daniel Clegg, eds. 2011. *Regulating the risk of unemployment: National adaptations to post-industrial labour markets in Europe.* Oxford: Oxford University Press.

Daguerre, Anne. 2004. Importing workfare: Policy transfer of social and labour market policies from the USA to Britain under New Labour. *Social Policy & Administration* 38 (1): 41–56.

Daguerre, Anne. 2017. *Obama's welfare legacy: An assessment of US anti-poverty policies.* Bristol: Policy Press.

Emmenegger, Patrick. 2014. *The power to dismiss: Trade unions and the regulation of job security in Western Europe.* Oxford: Oxford University Press.

Emmenegger, Patrick, Jon Kvist, Paul Marx, and Klaus Petersen. 2015. Three worlds of welfare capitalism: The making of a classic. *Journal of European Social Policy* 25 (1): 3–13.

Fassin, Didier. 2019. *The will to punish.* New York, NY: Oxford University Press.

Ferrera, Maurizio. 1996. The "Southern Model" of welfare in social Europe. *Journal of European Social Policy* 6 (1): 17–37.

Gerlinger, Thomas. 2010. Health care reform in Germany. *German Policy Studies* 6 (1): 107–42.

Gerring, John. 2012. Mere description. *British Journal of Political Science* 42 (4): 721–46.

Gilardi, Fabrizio. 2008. *Delegation in the regulatory state: Independent regulatory agencies in Western Europe.* Northampton, MA: Edward Elgar.

Goodman, Sara Wallace, and Matthew Wright. 2015. Does mandatory integration matter? Effects of civic requirements on immigrant socio-economic and political outcomes. *Journal of Ethnic and Migration Studies* 41 (12): 1885–1908.

Götz, Susanne, Wolfgang Ludwig-Mayerhofer, and Franziska Schreyer. 2010. Sanktionen im SGB II: Unter dem Existenzminimum. *IAB-Kurzbericht* 10.

Graziano, Paolo, and Miriam Hartlapp. 2018. The end of social Europe? Understanding EU social policy change. *Journal of European Public Policy* 1–18.

Haber, Hanan. 2011. Regulating-for-welfare: A comparative study of "regulatory welfare regimes" in the Israeli, British, and Swedish electricity sectors. *Law & Policy* 33 (1): 116–48.

Haber, Hanan. 2017. Rise of the regulatory welfare state? Social regulation in utilities in Israel. *Social Policy & Administration* 51 (3): 442–63.

Harsanyi, David. 2007. *Nanny state: How food fascists, teetotaling do-gooders, priggish moralists, and other boneheaded bureaucrats are turning America into a nation of children.* New York, NY: Broadway Books.

Hartlapp, Miriam. 2019. Revisiting patterns in EU regulatory social policy: (Still) supporting the market or social goals in their own right? *Zeitschrift für Sozialreform* 65 (1): 59–82.

Häusermann, Silja, and Hanna Schwander. 2012. Varieties of dualization? Labor market segmentation and insider-outsider divides across regimes. In *The age of dualization: The changing face of inequality in deindustrializing societies,* 27–51. Oxford: Oxford University Press.

Iversen, Torben, and Anne Wren. 1998. Equality, employment, and budgetary restraint: The trilemma of the service economy. *World Politics* 50 (4): 507–46.

Jordana, Jacint, and David Levi-Faur. 2004. *The politics of regulation: Institutions and regulatory reforms for the age of governance*. Cheltenham: Edward Elgar Publishing.

Jordana, Jacint, David Levi-Faur, and Xavier Fernández i Marín. 2011. The global diffusion of regulatory agencies: Channels of transfer and stages of diffusion. *Comparative Political Studies* 44 (10): 1343–69.

Klenk, Tanja, and Renate Reiter. 2015. The governance of hospital markets—Comparing two Bismarckian countries. *European Policy Analysis* 1 (1): 108–26.

Kliemt, Hartmut. 1993. On justifying a minimum welfare state. *Constitutional Political Economy* 4 (2): 159–72.

Knoepfel, Peter, Corinne Larrue, and Frédéric Varone. 2011. *Public policy analysis*. Bristol: The Policy Press.

Lascoumes, Pierre, and Patrick Le Galès. 2007. Introduction: Understanding public policy through its instruments—from the nature of instruments to the sociology of public policy instrumentation. *Governance* 20 (1): 1–21.

Leisering, Lutz 2012. Pension privatization in a welfare state environment: Socializing private pensions in Germany and the United Kingdom. *Journal of Comparative Social Welfare* 28 (2): 139–51.

Leisering, Lutz, and Stephan Leibfried. 2001. *Time and poverty in western welfare states: United Germany in perspective*. Cambridge: Cambridge University Press.

Levi-Faur, David. 2011. Regulation and regulatory governance. In *Handbook on the politics of Regulation*, ed. D. Levi-Faur, 3–24. Cheltenham, UK: Edward Elgar.

Levi-Faur, David. 2014. The welfare state: A regulatory perspective. *Public Administration* 92 (3): 599–614.

Levi-Faur, David. 2013. The odyssey of the regulatory state: From a "thin" monomorphic concept to a "thick" and polymorphic concept. *Law & Policy* 35 (1–2): 29–50.

Maggetti, Martino. 2009. The role of independent regulatory agencies in policy-making: A comparative analysis. *Journal of European Public Policy* 16 (3): 450–70.

Maggetti, Martino. 2012. *Regulation in practice: The de facto independence of regulatory agencies*. Colchester: ECPR Press.

Maggetti, Martino, and Fabrizio Gilardi. 2016. Problems (and solutions) in the measurement of policy diffusion mechanisms. *Journal of Public Policy* 36 (1): 87–107.

Majone, Giandomenico. 1996. *Regulating Europe*. New York, NY: Routledge.

Morel, Nathalie, Bruno Palier, and Joakim Palme. 2012. Towards a new social paradigm. In *Towards a social investment welfare state?* ed. N. Morel, B. Palier, and J. Palme, 1–32. Bristol: Policy Press.

Natter, Katharina, Mathias Czaika, and Hein de Haas. 2020. Political party ideology and immigration policy reform: An empirical enquiry. *Political Research Exchange* 2 (1).

OECD. 2012. *International migration outlook*. Paris: OECD Publishing.

Ozel, Isik. 2013. Differential Europe within a nation: Europeanization of regulation across policy areas. *Journal of European Public Policy* 20 (5): 741–59.

Özel, Işık, and Salvador Parrado. 2020. Varieties of regulatory welfare regimes in middle-income countries: A comparative analysis of Brazil, Mexico, and Turkey. *The ANNALS of the American Academy of Political and Social Science* (this volume).

Peters, B. Guy. 2017. What is so wicked about wicked problems? A conceptual analysis and a research program. *Policy and Society* 36 (3): 385–96.

Reynaers, Anne-Marie, and Salvador Parrado. 2017. Responsive regulation in public-private partnerships: Between deterrence and persuasion. *Regulation & Governance* 11 (3): 269–81.

Schneider, Anne, and Helen Ingram. 1993. Social construction of target populations: Implications for politics and policy. *American Political Science Review* 87 (2): 334–47.

Swenson, Peter A. 2004. Varieties of capitalist interests: power, institutions, and the regulatory welfare state in the United States and Sweden. *Studies in American Political Development* 18 (1): 1–29.

Taylor-Gooby, Peter. 2006. Social and public policy: Reflexive individualization and regulatory governance. In *Risk in social science*, eds. P. Taylor-Gooby and J. O. Zinn, 271–87. Oxford: Oxford University Press.

Teorell, Jan, Stefan Dahlberg, Sören Holmberg, Bo Rothstein, Anna Khomenko, and Richard Svensson. 2017. *The quality of government standard dataset*. Gothenburg: The Quality of Government Institute.

Thelen, Kathleen. 2014. *Varieties of liberalization and the new politics of social solidarity*. Cambridge: Cambridge University Press.

Trein, Philipp. 2017a. Coevolution of policy sectors: A comparative analysis of healthcare and public health. *Public Administration* 95 (3): 744–58.

Trein, Philipp. 2017b. Europeanisation beyond the European Union: Tobacco advertising bans in Swiss Cantons. *Journal of Public Policy* 37 (2): 113–43.

Trein, Philipp. 2017c. A new way to compare horizontal connections of policy sectors: "Coupling" of actors, institutions and policies. *Journal of Comparative Policy Analysis: Research and Practice* 19 (5): 419–34.

Trein, Philipp. 2018. *Healthy or sick? Coevolution of health care and public health in a comparative perspective*. Cambridge: Cambridge University Press.

Trein, Philipp, Iris Meyer, and Martino Maggetti. 2019. The integration and coordination of public policies: A systematic comparative review. *Journal of Comparative Policy Analysis: Research and Practice* 21 (4): 332–49.

Trein, Philipp, and Martino Maggetti. 2020. Patterns of policy integration and administrative coordination reforms: A comparative empirical analysis. *Public Administration Review* 80 (2): 198–208.

Venkataramani, Atheendar S., Elizabeth F. Bair, Erica Dixon, K. A. Linn, William J. Ferrell, Kevin G. Volpp, and Kristen Underhill. 2020. Association between state policies using Medicaid exclusions to sanction noncompliance with welfare work requirements and Medicaid participation among low-income adults. *JAMA Network Open* 3 (5): e204579–e204579.

Voigt, Linda, and Reimut Zohlnhöfer. 2020. Quiet politics of employment protection legislation? Partisan politics, electoral competition, and the regulatory welfare state. *The ANNALS of the American Academy of Political and Social Science* (this volume).

Zimmermann, Katharina, and Deborah Rice. 2016. Organizational barriers to service integration in one-stop shops: The case of Germany. In *Integrating social and employment policies in Europe: Active inclusion and challenges for local welfare governance*, ed. M. Heidenreich and D. Rice, 162–84. Cheltenham, UK: Edward Elgar Publishing.

# Politics, Markets, and Modes of Contract Governance: Regulating Social Services in Shanghai and Chongqing, China

By
WEI LI
and
BAO YANG

Inspired by the concept of the *regulatory welfare state*, this article identifies four primary modes of governance in regulating contract processes and contract implementation (market-based, hierarchical, professional, and relational), and compares contract governance modes in Shanghai and Chongqing. We find that the governments in these two localities prioritize and integrate the hierarchical and relational modes, relying less on the market-based and professional modes of governance. The emphasis on the hierarchical-relational mode advances the values and mechanisms of trust, adaptation, and alignment with top-down priorities, but may hinder public and legal accountability. We argue that the dynamics of political context and market condition affect the formation and effectiveness of hybrid modes of contract governance, and we advise that regulators in different countries should factor in such dynamics when designing contract governance modes in the regulation of social services.

*Keywords:* regulatory welfare state; hierarchical-relational; contract governance; regulating social services; China; authoritarian; transitional

The concept of the *regulatory welfare state* (RWS) refers to the state pursuing social objectives through regulations. It captures the double expansion of welfare expenditure and regulation to fulfill social objectives in democratic welfare states (e.g., the U K and Israel) (Haber 2011; Levi-Faur 2014a). The purposes, mechanisms, and forms of RWS can vary across sectors and states (e.g. Benish, Haber, and Eliahou 2017). With the global diffusion of

*Wei Li is an assistant professor in the Department of Government and Public Administration at Chinese University of Hong Kong. Her research interests include politics of regulation, public sector reforms, social policy analysis, among others.*

*Bao Yang is an associate professor of public management at Chongqing University of China. His research interests are situated in the fields of government-NPO relations, performance of public service, and civic engagement.*

Correspondence: yangbaoruc@163.com

DOI: 10.1177/0002716220957286

privatization and the delegation of social services to the nonprofit and business sectors, regulating social service contracts is one mechanism through which welfare spending and regulation are expanded to meet social objectives (Levi-Faur 2005; Benish 2010).

Since the 1980s, driven by domestic problems and influenced by New Public Management ideas,[1] Chinese public sector reforms have sought to enhance the efficiency, performance, and accountability of the state in the transition from a planned economy to a market economy. In the 2000s, China witnessed a growing number of social organizations (SOs)[2] to which governments started to contract social services (e.g., poverty alleviation) (Jing and Savas 2009). Chinese governments have also issued an increasing number of documents to regulate social service contracts (SSCs). Due to weak legal institutions, the regulatory style of governance in China differs from that in many Western democratic countries, and the authoritarian context in China presents challenges to integrating the values of new actors into regulation (Lo, Yip, and Cheung 2000; Rooij, Stern, and Fürst 2016).

This article maps the modes of contract governance in regulating social services by Chinese governments and identifies the mix of actors, values, and accountability mechanisms involved. It begins with a review of the literature, identifying four modes of contract governance in democratic welfare states. It then introduces the authoritarian and transitional context of China, which affects the implementation of these modes. Based on official documents, archives, semi-structured interviews, and survey questionnaires, we then analyze and compare the mode of contract governance implemented in two municipalities in China, Shanghai and Chongqing. We then compare this mode with those in democratic welfare states, and we propose policy for regulators.

## Modes of Contract Governance in Regulating Social Services

Regulating contracts in social services is important to ensure accountable and effective service delivery (Braithwaite 1999). A governance perspective on contract regulation goes beyond the legal conception of regulating contractual relations to focus more broadly on how institutions shape, reshape, and reflect the preferences and choices of the actors involved through processes, mechanisms, and strategies (Collins 2002; Levi-Faur 2014b). Considerable attention is paid in

NOTE: Wei Li presented this article at the "Regulation for Welfare?" workshop held at The Hebrew University of Jerusalem, organized by David Levi-Faur and Avishai Benish in May 2019. Wei Li is grateful for the Israel Science Foundation's support for her attendance at the workshop and appreciates the workshop participants' great company and comments. Wei Li is also grateful for those who assisted with the fieldwork in Shanghai and the department students who helped with the project despite unusual circumstances in Hong Kong. Wei Li's contribution to this study was funded by the Direct Grant of Social Science Faculty, Chinese University of Hong Kong (Grant Number 4052202). Bao Yang's contribution to this study was funded by the Fundamental Research Funds for the Central Universities at Chongqing University (Grant number 2019GGXY00).

TABLE 1
Modes of Contract Governance in Regulating Social Services

|  | Regulating contracting processes | Regulating contract implementation |
| --- | --- | --- |
| Market-based mode | Reduces service cost; meets service needs through fair competition; enhances transparency; lowers entry barriers; and enables objective evaluation of proposals (Lane 2001). | Competition motivates contractors to perform well and little monitoring is needed (Romzek and Johnston 2005). |
| Hierarchical mode | Contractors align services with government funders' requirements (Gazley 2008); contract officials follow political or managerial superiors' preferences in decision making (Brown, Potoski and Van Slyke 2006). | Close monitoring by government funders; frequent reporting by contractors (Romzek and Johnston 2005). |
| Professional mode | Evaluates proposals by professional criteria pertaining to social values (i.e., improving people's lives) (Lynch-Cerrulo and Cooney 2011). | Evaluates outcomes based on client and social impacts (Lynch-Cerrulo and Cooney 2011); professional evaluation by contractors or independent inspectorates (Christensen and Ebrahim 2006; Clarke 2008). |
| Relational mode | Negotiation before reaching a contract agreement; trusted service providers are preferred; lacking contractual specificity and great flexibility afforded to contractors (Van Slyke 2009). | Ensuring contractors' good performance by nurturing long-term relations; adaptation of service requirements is allowed in response to contingencies (Bertelli and Smith 2010). |

the literature to four primary modes of contract governance in regulating social services (see Table 1). Each mode represents a form of the regulatory welfare state that advances different values and uses different accountability mechanisms.

The *market-based mode* relies on competition to place pressure on service providers to lower their service costs and respond to the needs of users. This mode, however, is often found to be ineffective in the social service sector because of a lack of competition and difficulties in pre determining the service needs, cost, and quality in the contracts (Van Slyke 2009). The *hierarchical mode* relies on the authority of the state and hierarchical accountability to influence contract decisions and monitor contract implementation. This mode requires considerable resources and capacity on the part of government funders and may stifle service providers' levels of innovation and responsiveness to users (Kim 2005). The *professional mode* defers to professional knowledge, standards, and norms to ensure the accountability of contractors (Lynch-Cerrulo and Cooney 2011). The *relational mode* is built on repeated interactions, resource sharing, and informal accountability mechanisms such as trust, reputation, and opportunities and gains for future collaboration (Van Slyke 2009). To prevent this mode

FIGURE 1

Regulations of Government Contracts in Social Services

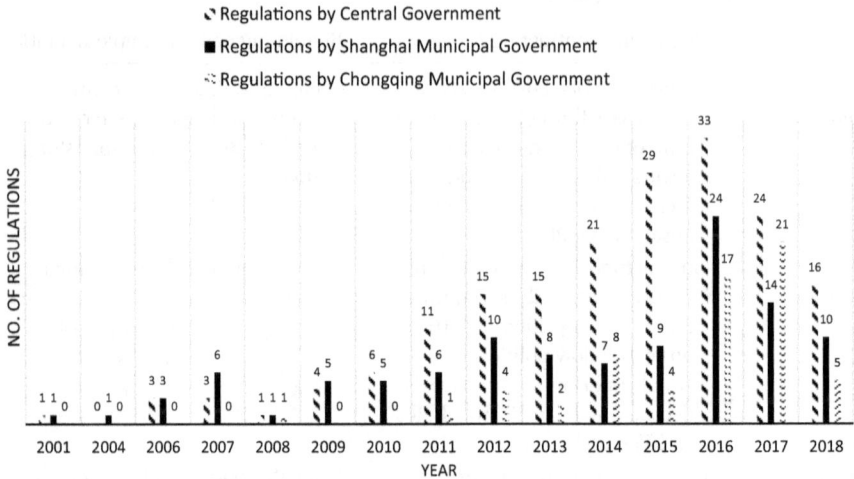

SOURCE: Database PKULAW.CN

from negatively affecting public accountability, penalties should be adopted, such as threats to terminate the contract (Bertelli and Smith 2010).

There are overlaps and trade-offs among the multiple objectives, values, and accountability mechanisms associated with the four modes of contract governance we have listed. For instance, the mechanism of market competition does not fit well with the relational mode, which values trust; the professional mode may contradict the upward accountability required by the hierarchical mode; and the relational mode, which nurtures service providers, could enhance the service providers' professional accountability. We propose that prioritizing and integrating multiple modes of contract governance yields a source of hybridity, relating to other sources articulated by Benish and Mattei (2019), such as the integration of market logic into public organizations, or private actors bringing business culture and civil society values into the codesign and codelivery of public services. One challenge to implementing the hybrid contract governance mode lies in the choice of what primary values to advance (e.g., efficiency and equity) (Windholz and Hodge 2012). Other challenges relate to the integration of different accountability mechanisms that consider the tension and uncertainty involving multiple actors in complex conditions (e.g., top-down control and bottom-up innovation; market competition and control of service quality) (Benish 2014; Jantz et al. 2018).

## Regulating Contracts in Social Services in China

We apply the RWS framework to China's social services in respect to the double expansion of expenditure[3] and regulation (see Figure 1). Like other countries, regulations in China are often ambiguous and are subject to interpretation and re-creation by actors involved in the regulatory processes to cope with prevailing contexts in implementation (Zheng 2009; Lahat and Talit 2015). This section highlights the distinct context that affects the implementation of modes of contract governance in regulating social services in China.

First, while other RWSs integrate social and economic values mainly to adjust their relations with the market economy (Benish and Levi-Faur 2020), Chinese governments do so to sustain economic, social, and political stability (e.g., Braithwaite 2020). To sustain domestic political stability in the post–Mao Zedong era while integrating its economy with the world market, China has been transitioning from a planned economy to a market economy since the late 1970s. The current welfare system in urban China was established to protect employees against economic shocks brought by this transition. Under the planned economy, employees of the public work units[4] (e.g., factories, shops) had low salaries but job security, and their welfare benefits and services were directly provided by their units. With the retreat of the state in many industries and a reform of public work units that aimed to increase their productivity, welfare benefits such as healthcare, pensions, and housing have been jointly financed by employers, employees, and the state through insurance schemes and state subsidies (Guan 2005; Li 2017). Social services—such as care and social assistance for vulnerable groups, job placement for the unemployed, and cultural and sports services for the general population—have been provided by the street-offices[5] in collaboration with private providers and volunteers. To reduce social conflicts and meet the growing social needs brought by economic development, the Chinese government has recently expanded social services by contracting with SOs (Leung and Xu 2015).

Second, the political context in China affects service market conditions. The Chinese government mandates that only SOs that support the Party's leadership, membership activities, and policies are eligible to register and bid for government contracts.[6] These regulations exclude many unregistered grassroots SOs working on sensitive issues and limit the degree of competition among SOs.[7]

Third, the literature on welfare states assumes judicial independence and the capacity of courts to enforce government contracts, with both government funders and private contractors being bound by the rights and obligations specified in the contract or understood by the contracting parties. In China, legal institutions are weak and not independent of the Party-state (Peerenboom 2010). Therefore, the legal accountability mechanism can be implemented differently.

Fourth, in democratic welfare states, regulations are often the products of relatively open and plural processes (Benish 2010). In China, policy processes are often centralized and government actors dominate the processes; hence the values of transparency and service responsiveness may not be safeguarded in regulating SSCs (Chan 2018; Li and Weible 2019). With frequent changes in Party leaders and shifting priorities in mandates (Birney 2013), contract officials have to cope with uncertainty when implementing regulations.

Last, certain values that are exercised through political representation of citizens and delegation of authority, such as the equal protection of individual rights and public accountability, may not be applicable to an authoritarian context (Benish and Levi-Faur 2012). Lacking independent inspectorates and a responsive citizen redress system outside of the executive government in China (Cai and Zhou 2019), a professional accountability mechanism would be weakened by limited input from service users.

Considering the context in China, then, this study investigates: 1) what modes of contract governance in regulating social services are adopted to nurture politically loyal but inexperienced SO contractors while ensuring quality service provision; and 2) how multiple values and accountability mechanisms are integrated and reconciled in implementing the regulations.

## Method and Data

We study two localities that are somewhat similar (Seawright and Gerring 2008): Shanghai and Chongqing. Both are municipalities and have three levels of governments: municipal, district, and street-office. Both are required to follow the central government's priorities, but have the discretion to adjust the implementation of regulations according to local circumstances (Birney 2013).

Shanghai and Chongqing have different levels of economic development, service market conditions, and government capacity, and may implement the regulations of SSCs in different ways. Chongqing's GDP per capita is half that of Shanghai and its social policy spending relies more heavily on central government fiscal transfers. Chongqing has a higher level of household income inequality than Shanghai. Nevertheless, Shanghai began to contract out social services to SOs earlier than Chongqing. Shanghai also has more SOs and a higher level of government expenditure on social services than Chongqing (see Appendix I).

Findings from these two localities have the potential to be widely applicable to the rest of China, because the income levels, fiscal conditions, and social policy expenditure patterns of Shanghai and Chongqing represent two clusters of the provinces inhabited by most of the population of China (Tian et al. 2016; Ratigan 2017).

From December 2018 to July 2019, we conducted twenty-three semistructured interviews in Shanghai and Chongqing involving nine government contract officials and the managers of fourteen SOs. The managers of five additional SOs in Chongqing were invited to complete six survey questionnaires without being interviewed. These SOs were contracted by various government agencies, including civil affair bureaus, street-offices, health commissions, and mass organizations.[8] Their services were of various kinds such as home-based elderly care, cultural services for disabled youth, and counseling services for families who had lost their only child (see Appendix II and IV-A). We also collected public and internal documents during the fieldwork.

We based the design of the semistructured interviews and survey questionnaires on a literature review and pilot interviews conducted in Shanghai and Chongqing (see Appendix III). Informed by the literature, and using qualitative analysis techniques (meaning categorization, analytical memo writing, and open and axial coding) (Corbin and Strauss 2008; Saldana 2009), we developed eleven code categories for the hierarchical mode, six for the market-based mode, sixteen for the professional mode, and thirteen for the relational mode. We analyzed the interview transcripts and survey questionnaire responses according to these categories (see Appendix IV–B1). The purpose of the analysis, following Yin (2009, 130), was to identify evidence that supported our expectations or offered alternatives.

We systematically searched a database sponsored by the Beijing University Law School to identify the regulations that are in effect. We determined which eleven keywords (see Appendix I) to use for the search of the literature, major regulations, and trial searches. Altogether we identified 182 documents issued by the central government, 110 documents by the Shanghai Municipal Government, and 63 documents by the Chongqing Municipal Government from 2001 to 2018 (see Figure 1). We identified the contract governance modes that the central and local governments adopted from the major regulations issued after 2013.

# Analysis and Findings

## Modes of contract governance in national regulations

The national regulations stipulate four modes of contract governance in regulating social services: market-based, hierarchical, professional, and relational.[9] The regulations stipulate that various government agencies and mass organizations shall, in principle, contract out social services through competitive tendering. This initiative also aims to meet growing needs for high quality, fair, and diversified services in areas such as education, healthcare, culture, and sports, both for vulnerable groups (e.g., the disabled) and the general population.

These four modes have potentially conflicting purposes, values, and accountability mechanisms. Some strategies to enhance service quality embody the values of trust and collaboration in the relational mode of contract governance and conflict with the market-based mode of contract governance. For instance, renewing contracts for incumbent providers with good performance records may hinder fair market competition and increase the risk of corruption.

Similarly, some strategies associated with the hierarchical mode could contradict the market-based mode and the professional mode of contract governance. For instance, encouraging pre-tendering communication between bidders and government funders can better align bidders' services with government priorities, but might hinder market competition. To exert political control over SO contractors and to implement performance targets specified in the contracts, the government must closely monitor the whole process of contract implementation. This strategy is costly and reduces the professional autonomy of contractors to innovate and meet diversified service needs.

The potential trade-offs among the four modes of contract governance that the central government adopts leave room for local governments to adjust regulation implementation according to local circumstances.

FIGURE 2
Actors and their Roles in Regulating SSCs in Shanghai

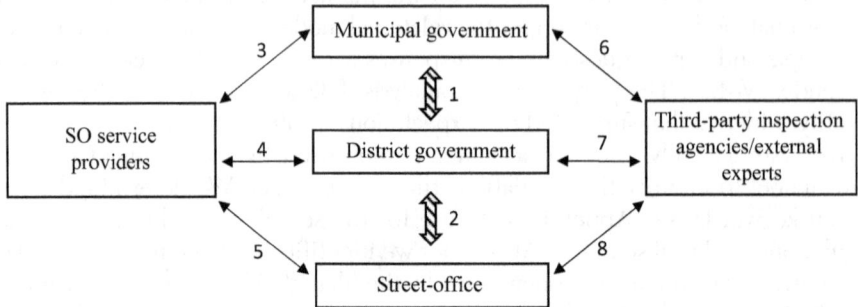

NOTES: 1 and 2 - The government (finance bureau) approves budget applications for services applied by various agencies at the same level or by a lower level government; 3, 4 and 5 - The government administers the tendering processes and monitors contract performance funded from its budget; the government coordinates the implementation of contracts funded by a higher level government; 6, 7 and 8 - The government invites third-party inspection agencies or external experts to evaluate contract bidders' proposals, train contractors and monitor contract performance.

## Regulating social service contracts in Shanghai

The Shanghai municipal and district civil affairs bureaus have launched a philanthropy program to provide funding and capacity training to support new service initiatives designed by grassroots SOs for vulnerable groups (e.g., the elderly, children of migrant workers). Successful programs are then contracted by the government through the fiscal budget.[10] Governments at different levels regulate the SSCs that they fund and coordinate contract implementation for those funded by a higher level of government (see Figure 2). During 2012–2016, government service procurement from SOs increased from 440 million to 699 million CNY, and the number of philanthropic activities undertaken by SOs increased from 294,516 to 840,032.[11]

## Regulating the contracting processes in Shanghai

Following the lead of the central government, four modes of contract governance have been adopted to regulate the contracting processes and realize the multiple objectives of fair competition, efficient and high-quality service contractors, and equalized service provision in accordance with government priorities:[12]

- contractors shall be selected through open and competitive tendering, and government service purchasing shall lower service cost (*market-based mode*);
- external experts or expert agencies shall be involved in, and professional standards adopted for, contract decisions (*professional mode*);

- service contracting shall be led by the government to fulfill the urgent and major livelihood needs of people, and to equalize public service provision (*hierarchical mode*); and
- long term contracts (up to 3 years) can be used to provide continuous and stable services, and the past performance of incumbent contractors shall be considered in re-tendering the same service contract (*relational mode*).

In practice, the government prioritizes the values of collaboration, stability, and trust in the relational mode. Competition for contracts is limited and lowering the price is not a major consideration in contracting decisions. When bidding, SOs usually offer a budget slightly lower than the tendering requirements to appear cost efficient.[13] Prior to the tendering processes, lower level government funders are required to apply for budget approval from higher level governments. Application for budgets is competitive among government agencies.[14] However, government funders usually identify preferred contractors prior to the budget approval.[15] They often prefer incumbent contractors when re-tendering services. For instance, a district women's federation contracted more than half of eighteen service programs to incumbent providers. The major reasons include reducing the uncertainty of new contractors' performance, stabilizing service provision, enhancing service quality through long-term collaboration, and saving on the administrative cost of tendering.[16] Among the six SO service providers that we interviewed, four won more than 80 percent of the contracts for which they had bid.[17] A youth service provider's manager acknowledged that most of the provider's bids for government contracts were successful because it often negotiated and reached an agreement with government funders before entering the tendering process.[18]

In practice, government funders prefer the hierarchical mode. External experts' professional considerations have less impact on contract decisions than hierarchical accountability considerations, such as service providers' support of the Party[19] and whether contractors' services align with the government funders' priorities.[20] For instance, a district women's federation contracted a service program that promoted "family harmony" because this had been mentioned by Xi Jinping as a priority.[21] Government funders prefer SOs that have been recommended by a higher level of government or are in possession of government-certified qualifications. These qualifications evaluate SOs' compliance with regulations and policies, including supporting the Party's leadership and membership activities.[22] Five of six SO service providers confirmed that these qualifications helped them to win government contracts.[23]

Multiple values and accountability mechanisms are integrated and reconciled in the hybrid mode of contract governance implemented in Shanghai. The hierarchical mode that gives advantage to service providers with government-certified qualifications is perceived by service providers to have enhanced their managerial capacity and professional accountability.[24] The relational mode of the contracting process can lower the administrative cost of tendering and offer contractors professional autonomy to innovate services.[25]

## Regulating contract implementation in Shanghai

Multiple modes of contract governance are adopted to regulate contract implementation, as follows:[26]

- The cost of contracted services shall be lower than government provision (*market-based mode*);
- Contract performance shall be evaluated according to professional indicators (e.g., service effectiveness) and by third-party inspection agencies (*professional mode*);
- The whole process of contract implementation shall be monitored by multilevel government funders in accordance with regulations and policies (*hierarchical mode*); and
- The incumbent contractor's performance shall be publicized and considered when re-contracting the same service (*relational mode*).

When implementing these regulations, the professional and market-based modes are downplayed. When SO contractors are subject to frequent self-reporting and government inspections that largely focus on recordkeeping and program management, they are distracted from delivering professional services to the clients.[27] Moreover, the performance indicators that measure the service cost and service effectiveness contribute to only a small part of the contract evaluation scores.[28] Government funders often lack the professional capacity to assess service effectiveness,[29] while third-party inspection agencies (TIAs) often lack the relevant expertise, resources, and independence to professionally evaluate contractors' performance.[30]

To realize the dual purposes of developing SOs and fulfilling top-down performance targets, government funders prioritize and integrate the hierarchical and relational modes to regulate contract implementation. To develop SO contractors and nurture long-term relations, TIAs are requested by government funders to use lenient evaluation criteria in the initial one or two years of contracting and to provide capacity training to contractors.[31] The government funders also mobilize governmental resources to help inexperienced contractors to deliver services. They help high performing contractors to attract positive publicity from state-owned media, obtain contracts from higher level government funders, and win government-sponsored competitions.[32] To save on the expenses of outsourcing inspection, the government funders choose to self-monitor contractors and waive the third-party inspection of contractors with good performance records.[33]

The emphasis on the hybrid hierarchical-relational mode of contract governance hinders legal and public accountability. The fact that TIAs are not independent allows government funders to flexibly request additional services not specified in the contracts according to the superior authority's mandates. However, such adjustment is often not funded and contradicts the notion of legal accountability.[34] Government funders ask TIAs to endorse contractors with average or poor performance,[35] which harms public accountability. For instance, SOs contracted to provide healthcare services to elderly people with physical and/or mental disabilities have been allowed to adjust service targets to younger and healthier groups.[36]

## Regulating social service contracts in Chongqing

The Chongqing government aims to expand community-based social service provision by training social workers, developing new SOs, and contracting services to SOs. From 2013 to 2017, the Chongqing government contracted 688 service programs to SOs in 18 service areas (e.g., services for the youth, the elderly, and the disabled) (Chongqing Daily 2017). The Chongqing government is also mandated to contract social services to 100 "exemplary" SOs to build 400 "exemplary" communities within a short timeframe (Zhang 2015).

## Regulating the contracting processes in Chongqing

The contracting procedures in Chongqing are similar to those in Shanghai. The Chongqing government also stipulates four modes of contract governance to regulate SSCs.[37]

In practice, governments in Chongqing, like those in Shanghai, prioritize and integrate the hierarchical and relational modes of contract governance. The budget for contracting is granted by giving priority to programs that align with government work priorities (e.g., poverty alleviation). Based on the value of fairness, budgets are also evenly allocated according to the distribution of street-office communities.[38] Competition for contracts is limited. Of the eight SOs in Chongqing that we studied, two won all of the contracts they bid for, three won more than 70 percent, and three won less than half. In contracting decisions, lowering service cost is again not a major consideration. In one district, the indicator measuring the service unit cost accounted for 12 out of 103 total marks in evaluating bidders' proposals.[39] The district government often overruled the evaluations by external experts and selected contractors who negotiated and reached agreements with street-office funders prior to the tendering process. One reason for the overrule is that SOs are perceived to have limited service capacity and sometimes lack integrity. Hence, SOs who are trusted and supported by street-office funders are considered more likely to implement contracts successfully. SO contractors could also initiate new ideas and influence program design during the pre-tendering negotiation with street-offices.[40] Contractors' support for the Party is valued: all of the SO contractors that we studied in Chongqing have Party members among their full-time staff (see Appendix II-B).

Due to limited government funding, high demand for social services, and a lack of qualified service providers, the hybrid hierarchical-relational mode is implemented in Chongqing to a greater extent than in Shanghai. In one district, selecting contractors for a community service program progressed through three stages: first, the district government randomly selected three SOs with good performance records from a database; second, if the selected SOs were interested in the contracts, they were expected to negotiate with the street-office governments prior to the tendering process; and third, all of the selected SOs were to bid for the contracts, but only the SO that reached an agreement with the street-office in the previous stage would be contracted. Initially, there were only four SOs in the database, and that number increased to eleven in 2018. The district government had limited choices of service providers for more than forty communities.[41] As a result, not only do the incumbent contractors with good performance records continue to be contracted to deliver the same program, but less competent contractors were also trained by external experts to improve their service design. SOs with a good reputation among higher level governments are highly trusted by lower level government funders; SOs that are recognized as "exemplary" by higher level governments are awarded contracts without competitive tendering.

### Regulating contract implementation in Chongqing

The Chongqing government announced four contract governance modes to monitor contract implementation. In practice, the market-based and professional modes are of relatively little use as in Shanghai; the hierarchical and relational modes are prioritized and integrated by the Chongqing government. Lowering service cost comprises a small percentage of contract evaluation scores.[42] TIAs are not independent of the government funders and have to accommodate the latter's requests for lenient contract evaluation.[43] Street-office officials and community cadres[44] also care less about contractors' performance measured by professional indicators (e.g., service quality) and more about the ability of contracted services to attract positive attention and evaluations by higher level government.[45] Contractors are allowed to adjust their services in the process of implementation due to unexpected users' needs or service requests by governments not specified in the contracts (e.g., preparing presentation materials). Contractors have to negotiate with governments for additional resources or to adjust contract agreements.[46]

The hybrid hierarchical-relational contract governance mode has been emphasized to a greater extent in Chongqing than in Shanghai. Lacking qualified TIAs, six of the eight SO service contractors that we studied had evaluated the contract performance of other SOs. In one case, an external expert was selected to evaluate his own SO's contract performance; this was later investigated by the Party Discipline Committee.[47] To avoid such conflicts of interests, government funders often have to evaluate contractors on their own or, if they have resources, invite inspection agencies from outside Chongqing. The monitoring by street-offices is so lenient that services are often not delivered by professional staff as required.[48] The government funders also have to tolerate underperformance of contractors who are funded and granted "exemplary" status by higher level governments.[49]

## Discussions and Conclusion

The concept of RWS captures the double expansion of expenditure and regulation for SSCs in China. Like its counterparts in other countries (e.g., Benish and Mattei

2019), the Chinese government sought to reconcile the values of equity and efficiency, as well as integrate multiple accountability mechanisms in designing contract governance modes. In practice, both the Shanghai and Chongqing governments prioritize and integrate the hierarchical and relational modes of contract governance, relying less on the market-based and professional modes to regulate SSCs. In democratic welfare states where private service sectors are well developed (e.g., the United States and the UK), the dominance of the hierarchical-relational mode is atypical. Instead, service users and contractors can pressure the government over contracting decisions through coalition building and advocacy. Contractors can defer to professional expertise and norms to resist input-and-task-based scrutiny by the government (Romzek and Johnston 2005; Schwabenland and Hirst 2017). In political systems where both government funders and contractors are subject to criticism and accountability pressure from civil society (e.g., Germany, Denmark, and Israel), the use of the hierarchical-relational mode that may threaten public and legal accountability can be checked (Benish 2014; Jantz et al. 2018).

The similar modes of contract governance implemented in Shanghai and Chongqing can be explained by the authoritarian and transitional context in China, and this explanation can be applied to the rest of the country as well. The governments in both localities need to nurture politically loyal but inexperienced SO contractors to quickly adapt to the shifting priorities of the superior authority; they are also mandated by the central government to fulfill the dual purposes of mobilizing private resources for social service provision and of maintaining political control over civil society. The government officials in the two localities assign extra-contractual tasks to SO contractors in a top-down and unpredictable style, reflecting the features of state-society relations in China's corporatist regime (Unger and Chan 2008). This style constrains the bottom-up and independent input of contractors, service users, external experts, and inspectorates in regulating SSCs, and hinders public and legal accountability.

In Chongqing, the hierarchical-relational mode of contract governance has been emphasized to a greater extent than in Shanghai. Government funders show a higher tolerance for underperformance by contractors and conflicts of interest of external inspectorates. The different practices in Chongqing can be explained by its low government capacity, high demand for social services, and limited number of qualified contractors and external inspectorates. These explanations are transferable to other localities in China with similar levels of economic development, fiscal conditions, and service market conditions.

This study represents a first step in qualifying and explaining the mode of contract governance in regulating SSCs in China. Given the small and unrepresentative sample of respondents, the study does not exhaust various hybrid forms of contract governance modes implemented across China, and hence limits its generalizability to different parts of the country. China's context also differs from the contexts of other countries. Future research can address this limitation by studying and comparing contract governance modes in other places in China and other countries.

The Chinese government has reflected on the limited implementation of the market-based and professional modes of contract governance and has sought to strengthen these modes.[50] We advise that to overcome the difficulties of integrating different values and accountability mechanisms, the government should facilitate nongovernmental actors' participation in and input into regulatory processes.

The study posits that dynamics between political context and market conditions affect the formation and effectiveness of hybrid modes of contract governance. Regulators in different countries should factor in such dynamics when designing modes of contract governance in regulating social services.

# Notes

1. "New public management" includes the adoption of performance and outcome-based management techniques and an emphasis on efficiency and responsiveness to customers in the public sector (see Benish 2014).

2. Social organizations are termed "NGOs" or "nonprofits" in other countries.

3. The government's expenditure on social services increased significantly from 2001 (28.5 billion CNY) to 2016 (544 billion CNY) (Ministry of Civil Affairs 2017; see Appendix IV-C).

4. Public work units refer to government agencies, public institutions, and state-owned and collective-owned urban enterprises that provide employment and welfare for the citizens during the Central Planning era (1950s-1970s) in China (see Li 2017).

5. A street-office is an administrative agency dispatched by the district government.

6. Ministry of Civil Affairs 2016. See Appendix IV-C.

7. Registration for philanthropy/charity organizations, and urban/rural community service organizations has been relaxed; other grassroots groups still find it difficult to register as SOs (Chan 2018).

8. Mass organizations operate as government agencies, such as the Youth League, Women's Federation, and Federation of the Disabled.

9. State Council 2013. These four modes are followed by Shanghai and Chongqing, with details given in the next section. See Appendix IV-C.

10. Shanghai Civil Affairs Bureau 2017. See Appendix IV-C.

11. Shanghai Social Organization Bureau 2017. See Appendix IV-C.

12. Shanghai People's Government 2015. See Appendix IV-C.

13. Interview YGY.

14. For instance, the YP District Civil Affairs Bureau received over 600 applications in 2018, of which it only approved 387. Interview YPM.

15. Interviews YPM and YPC.

16. Interviews HPW and YPC.

17. Interviews AQL, BYL, YZX, ZJS.

18. Interview YGY.

19. All of the SO service providers we studied in Shanghai had Party members among their full- time staff (see Appendix II-B).

20. This particularly applies to government funders with specialized service domains (e.g., the Women's Federation). Interviews YPC, YPM, HPW.

21. Interview HPW.

22. Shanghai Social Organization Bureau 2018. See Appendix IV-C.

23. Interviews YGY, AQL, BYL, YZX, ZJS.

24. Interviews YGY, YZX.

25. Interviews HPW, KJSC, YJSC.

26. Shanghai People's Government 2015. See Appendix IV-C.

27. Interviews LCL and BYL.

28. Service output indicators that can be converted to service unit cost contribute to 10 per cent of the total marks. Service effectiveness indicators only contribute to 9 percent of the total marks (Shanghai Quality Supervision Bureau 2012; see Appendix IV-C). In practice, the weighting can be lower. Interview YPSA.

29. Interviews YZX and LCL.

30. Interviews BYL, JSP, XZJ, ZJS.

31. Interview HPW.

32. Interviews YPM, KJSC, YGY. .

33. Interviews YPC and JSP.

34. Interviews HPW and YPM.

35. Interviews YPSA and JSP.

36. Interviews YPSA, JSP, YZX.

37. Chongqing People's Government 2014. See Appendix IV-C.

38. Interview JLPB.

39. Interview JLPB.

40. Interviews RA, SCB, YYS.

41. Interview RH.

42. In the JL District, service output volumes comprised 13 out of 100 evaluation marks in 2017. Interview JLPB.

43. Interview RH.

44. "Community cadres" refers to the Party organ's secretaries, who direct the residential committees' work for the neighborhoods. They report to the street-office Party work committee. (CCPCC 2019; see Appendix IV-C).

45. Interviews RH, SCB, YYS.

46. Interviews RH, RA, YYS.

47. Interview YYS.

48. Chongqing Civil Affairs Bureau 2018. See Appendix IV-C.

49. Interview YYS.

50. Ministry of Finance 2018. See Appendix IV-C.

# References

Benish, Avishai. 2010. Re-bureaucratizing welfare administration. *Social Service Review* March:77–101.

Benish, Avishai. 2014. The public accountability of privatized activation-The case of Israel. *Social Policy & Administration* 48 (2): 262–77.

Benish, Avishai, and David Levi-Faur. 2012. New forms of administrative law in the age of third-party government. *Public Administration* 90 (4): 886–900.

Benish, Avishai, and David Levi-Faur. 2020. The expansion of regulation in welfare governance. *The ANNALS of the American Academy of Political and Social Science* (this volume).

Benish, Avishai, and Parola Mattei. 29 November 2019. Accountability and hybridity in welfare governance. *Public Administration.*

Benish, Avishai, Hanan Haber, and Rotem Eliahou. 2017. The regulatory welfare state in pension markets: Mitigating high charges for low-income savers in the United Kingdom and Israel. *Journal of Social Policy* 46 (2): 313–30.

Bertelli, Anthony M., and Craig R. Smith. 2010. Relational contracting and network management. *Journal of Public Administration: Research and Theory* January: i21–i40.

Birney, Mayling. 2013. Decentralization and veiled corruption under China's "rule of mandates." *World Development* June:1–43.

Braithwaite, John. 1999. Accountability and governance under the new regulatory state. *Australian Journal of Public Administration* 58 (1): 90–97.

Braithwaite, John. 2020. Meta governance of path dependencies: Regulation, welfare, markets. *The ANNALS of the American Academy of Political and Social Science* (this volume).

Brown, Trevor L., Matthew Potoski, and David M. Van Slyke. 2006. Managing public service contracts: Aligning values, institutions, and markets. *Public Administration Review* 66 (3): 323–31.

Cai, Yongshun, and Titi Zhou. 2019. Online political participation in China: Local government and differentiated response. *The China Quarterly* 238 (June): 331–52.

China Communist Party Central Committee (CCPCC). 2019. *Opinions to strengthen and improve street-level Party building work in cities (in Chinese)*. Available from http://www.gov.cn (accessed 21 March 2020).

Chan, Chak Kwan. 2018. Introduction: Contracting out social services in China. In *China's social welfare revolution: Contracting out social services*, eds. Jie Lei and Chak Kwan Chan, 1–11. New York, NY: Routledge.

Chongqing Daily. 22 May 2017. *Chongqing: Innovating social governance by mobilising social workers and social organizations to strengthen community services (in Chinese)*. Available from http://www.xinhuanet.com (accessed 10 April 2019).

Chongqing People's Government. 2014. *Temporary measures of government purchasing services (in Chinese)*. Document No. 159. Available from http://www.jbczhx.com (accessed 3 September 2020).

Chongqing Civil Affairs Bureau. 2018. *Management guidelines for government purchasing services from social organizations (in Chinese)*. Document No. 1. Available from http://www.cqwomen.org.cn (accessed 8 August 2019).

Christensen, Rachel A., and Alnoor Ebrahim. 2006. How does accountability affect mission? The case of a nonprofit serving immigrants and refugees. *Nonprofit Management & Leadership* 17 (2): 195–209.

Clarke, John. 2008. Performance paradoxes: The politics of evaluation in public services. In: *Public services inspection in the UK. research highlights in social work*, eds. Howard Davis and Martin Steve, 120–34. London: Jessica Kingsley Publishers.

Collins, Hugh. 2002. *Regulating contracts*. New York, NY: Oxford University Press.

Corbin, Juliet, and Anselm Strauss. 2008. *Basics of qualitative research: Techniques and procedures for developing grounded theory*. Newbury Park, CA: SAGE Publications.

Gazley, Beth. 2008. Beyond the contract: The scope and nature of informal government-nonprofit Partnership. *Public Administration Review* January/February:142–54.

Guan, Xinping. 2005. China's social policy: Reform and development in the context of marketization and globalization. In *Transforming the developmental welfare state in East Asia*, ed. Huck-ju Kwon, 231–57. Houndmills, Basingstoke, Hampshire: Palgrave Macmillian.

Haber, Hanan. 2011. Regulating-*for*-welfare: a comparative study of "regulatory welfare regimes" in the Israeli, British, and Swedish electricity sectors. *Law & Policy* 33 (1): 116–47.

Jantz, Bastian, Tanja Klenk, Flemming Larsen, and Jay Wiggan. 2018. Marketization and varieties of accountability relationships in employment services: Comparing Denmark, Germany, and Great Britain. *Administration & Society* 50 (3): 321–45.

Jing, Yijia, and E.S. Savas. 2009. Managing collaborative service delivery: Comparing China and the United States. *Public Administration Review* December:S101–S106.

Kim, S. 2005. Balancing competing accountability requirements: Challenges in performance improvement of the nonprofit human services agency. *Public Performance & Management Review* 29 (2): 145–63.

Lahat, Lihi, and Gal Talit. 2015. Regulation of personal social services—The Israeli experience. *Social Policy & Administration* 49 (3): 335–55.

Lane, J. E. 2001. From long-term to short-term contracting. *Public Administration* 79 (1): 29–47.

Leung, Joe C.B., and Yuebin Xu. 2015. *China's social welfare: The third turning point*. Cambridge, MA: Polity Press.

Levi-Faur, David. 2005. The global diffusion of regulatory capitalism. *The ANNALS of the American Academy of Political and Social Science* 598:33–51.

Levi-Faur, David. 2014a. The welfare state: A regulatory perspective. *Public Administration* 92 (3): 599–614.

Levi-Faur, David, ed. 2014b. From "big government" to "big governance"? In *Oxford handbook of governance*. New York, NY: Oxford University Press.

Lo, Carlos Wing-Hung, To Kwong Plato Yip, and Kai Chee Cheung. 2000. The regulatory style of environmental governance in China: The case of EIA regulation in Shanghai. *Public Administration and Development* 20:305–18.

Li, Bingqin. 2017. Housing welfare policies in urban China. In *Handbook of welfare in China*, eds. Beatriz Carrillo, Johanna Hood and Paul Kadetz, 123–43. Cheltenham, Gloucestershire: Edward Elgar.

Li, Wei, and Christopher M. Weible. 2019. China's policy processes and the advocacy coalition framework. *Policy Studies Journal*. Early View.

Lynch-Cerullo, Kristen, and Kate Cooney. 2011. Moving from outputs to outcomes: A review of the evolution of performance measurement in the human service nonprofit sector. *Administration in Social Work* 35:364–88.

Ministry of Civil Affairs. 2016. *Notice to carry out Party work when registering social organizations (in Chinese)*. Document No. 257. Available from http://www.mca.gov.cn (accessed 18 August 2020).

Ministry of Civil Affairs. 2017. *China civil affairs statistical yearbook-Statistics of China social services (in Chinese)*.Available from https://www.yearbookchina.com/ (accessed 18 August 2020).

Ministry of Finance. 2018. *Government purchasing service administrative measures (Consultation Document) (in Chinese)*.Available from http://www.gongyishibao.com (accessed 9 August 2019).

Peerenboom, Randall. 2010. Introduction. In *Judicial Independence in China: Lessons for global rule of law promotion*, ed. Peerenboom Randall. New York, NY: Cambridge University Press.

Ratigan, Kerry. 2017. Disaggregating the developing welfare state: Provincial social policy regimes in China. *World Development* 98:467–84.

Romzek, Barbara. S., and Jocelyn M. Johnston. 2005. State social services contracting: Exploring the determinants of effective contract accountability. *Public Administration Review* 65 (4): 436–49.

Rooij, Benjamin van, Rachel E. Stern, and Kathinka Fürst. 2014. The authoritarian logic of regulatory pluralism: Understanding China's new environmental actors. *Regulation & Governance* 10 (1): 3–13.

Saldana, Johnny. 2009. *The coding manual for qualitative researchers*. Los Angeles, CA: SAGE Publications.

Schwabenland, Christina, and Alison Hirst. 2017. Hybrid accountabilities and managerial agency in the third sector. *Public Administration*, 1–15.

Seawright, Jason, and John Gerring. 2008. Case selection techniques in case study research. *Political Research Quarterly* 61 (2): 294–308.

Shanghai Civil Affairs Bureau. 2017. *Notice about budgeting for Shanghai tendering and bidding community philanthropy programs in 2018 (in Chinese)*. Document No. 59. Available from http://static.mzj.sh.gov.cn (accessed on 18 August 2020).

Shanghai People's Government. 2015. *Opinions to establish and improve government purchasing service system (in Chinese)*. Document No. 21. Available from http://www.shanghai.gov.cn (accessed 21 March 2020).

Shanghai Quality Supervision Bureau. 2012. *Community philanthropy service program performance evaluation guideline (in Chinese)*. Document No 107. Available from http://www.ssfcn.com (accessed 18 August 2020).

Shanghai Social Organization Bureau. 2017. *Shanghai social organisation development annual report (in Chinese)*. Personal communication with the bureau official.

State Council. 2013. *Guiding opinions about government purchasing services from social forces (in Chinese)*. Document No. 96. Available from http://www.gov.cn. (accessed 17 March 2020).

Tian, Xu, Xiaoheng Zhang, Yingheng Zhou, and Xiaohua Yu. 2016. Regional income inequality in China revisited: A perspective from club convergence. *Economic Modelling* 56:50–58.

Unger, Jonathan, and Anita Chan. 2008. Association in a bind: The emergence of political corporatism. In *Association and the Chinese state: Contested spaces*, ed. Jonathan Unger, 48–68. Armonk,UK: Taylor and Francis.

Van Slyke, David M. 2009. Collaboration and relational contracting. In *The collaborative public manager: New ideas for the Twenty-first century*, eds. Rosemary O'Leary and Lisa Blomgren Bingham, 137–56. Washington DC: Georgetown University Press.

Windholz, Eric, and Graeme A. Hodge. 2012. Conceptualising social and economic regulation: Implications for modern regulators and regulatory activity. *Monash University Law Review* 38 (2): 212.

Yin, Robert. 2009. *Case study research: Design and methods*. Thousand Oaks, CA: SAGE Publications.

Zhang, Chang. 2015. Chongqing will establish 400 exemplary communities (in Chinese). Available from http://trade.swchina.org/trends/2015/1026/24185.shtml.

Zheng, Yin Lily. 2009. It's not what is on paper, but what is in practice: China's new labor contract law and the enforcement problem. *Washington University Global Studies Law Review* 8:595–617.

# Views from Below: Inspectors' Coping with Hybrid Accountabilities

*By*
TANJA KLENK

Regulation of long-term care service provision is a case of hybrid accountabilities. How do inspectors who are responsible for the implementation of regulations handle the uncertainties arising from hybrid accountabilities? While the prevailing scholarly consensus is that hybridity creates tensions that have a negative impact on the quality of regulation, this article shows that different accountabilities can reinforce each other. However, situations in which inspectors can develop a positive stance toward hybridity and integrate competing logics are rare. Hybrid professionalism among inspectors requires training, education, and resources as well as a joint regulatory culture with inspectees—preconditions that are hardly present in recent institutional settings of long-term care regulation.

*Keywords:*  regulatory welfare state; hybridity; accountability; long-term care; quality regulation inspectors

Accountability in the regulatory welfare state is hybrid: providers are held accountable for different, sometimes conflicting, goals. As a result of the intentional mix of the logics of the market, hierarchy, and professionalism, service providers are, for instance, expected to deliver services of high quality, but only for a minimum price to keep public healthcare spending sustainable; service providers should also establish efficient structures and processes without, however, compromising standards regarding the quality of work and the participation of users.

This study analyzes the implementation of a hybrid regulatory framework from the inspectors' perspective. The guiding research

*Tanja Klenk is a professor of public administration and public policy at the Helmut-Schmidt-University Hamburg. Her research interests include institutional and organizational change in public and social policy. Recently, she has been working on the marketization and managerialization of welfare state governance, as well as accountability, quality, and performance management.*

Correspondence: tanja.klenk@hsu-hh.de

DOI: 10.1177/0002716220956587

ANNALS, *AAPSS*, 691, September 2020

question is: How do inspectors, who are responsible for the implementation and enforcement of the regulatory framework, make sense of hybridity? In the literature, we find ample empirical evidence that hybridity creates tensions that are difficult for inspectors to handle. Inspectors—and professionals in general— might even reject the policy they are expected to implement because they cannot make sense of it, a reaction pattern that Tummers (2011) described as policy alienation. However, others are observing the evolution of hybrid professionalism with professionals who have attained new skills and are able to go beyond traditional professionalism by integrating and blending different logics (Noordegraaf 2015). Inspectors who are open to hybrid professionalism are, for instance, willing to learn managerial competences and improve their adaptation skills to navigate contradictions between performance schemes and professional standards.

The article provides an empirical case study of quality inspection in the German long-term care sector, which is a prime example of the regulatory welfare state. The idea of delivering public goods with market means was a guiding principle when the new social insurance for long-term care was introduced as a fifth pillar of the German welfare state in 1995. In subsequent years, the sector developed into a highly competitive field; although, in a parallel movement, we could also observe the rise of a regulatory welfare state (Levi-Faur 2014). A complex regulatory framework has been gradually set up to control clients' access to the services, audit structures, processes, and outcomes of service delivery. So far, the scarce research on the regulation of the German long-term care market has focused mainly on regulatory strategy, or on the tools and instruments and their adjustments to an increasingly hybrid environment (Herr, Nguyen, and Schmitz 2016; Nies and Leichsenring 2018). Views from below, however, are missing: the process of implementing the regulatory framework has remained a black box.

The article proceeds as follows. Section two presents the theoretical background of this study, which draws on three bodies of literature: accountability, hybridity, and street-level bureaucracy. The bodies of literature are closely connected to the research on the regulatory (welfare) state. The rise of the regulatory (welfare) state has fueled an intense debate about accountability. While there were strong concerns about declining accountability in the early years of the regulatory welfare state, particularly with respect to public and democratic accountability, it is today widely accepted in the literature that accountability in regulation is not a question of more or less accountability but of multiple accountabilities and the relationships among them (Benish and Mattei 2019). This is where the literature on hybridity comes in, which acknowledges that accountability in regulation is multifaceted, fluid, and—as a rule—full of tensions. The literature on street-level bureaucracy, in turn, reminds us that inspectors need to implement and enforce accountability mechanisms. Their discretion and their (lack of) ability to cope with hybridity are crucial factors that have substantial impacts on regulatory performance.

In the third section of the article, more information about the institutional background of the German long-term care sector and recent reforms is provided. I then go on to explain the methods for data collection (policy documents, semi-structured expert interviews, and vignettes) and analysis (qualitative content analysis). Next, I present the empirical findings. The empirical analyses show that inspectors fall into different groups. While one group shows active resistance to hybridity, others are able to reconcile the hybrid regulatory framework with their identity as a professional. However, their coping strategy is rather passive: they let situations happen, without bothering about contradictions and dilemmas. The most important finding is that *no* cases of hybrid professionalism were found.

Based on these findings, the discussion section suggests a refined analytical framework: to understand how inspectors deal with hybridity, both the inspectors' attitudes toward hybridity (accepting or rejecting) and their willingness or capacity to use a reflexive approach need to be taken into consideration. The findings also allow us to reflect on the preconditions for hybrid professionalism and to draw conclusions for the design of regulatory architecture. Lessons can be learned from this study, for both quality regulation in the German long-term care market and for accountability systems in the regulatory welfare state in general.

## Theory: Hybridity, Accountability, and Street-Level Bureaucracy

From an institutional perspective, quasi-markets are hybrid arrangements. They deliver public goods—in our case, professional care services—with private means. Hybridity results from the intentional mixture of different logics: market, hierarchy, and professionalism. How to hold providers in the service market accountable for their actions is a central topic in the literature on regulatory welfare state governance (Benish 2014; Jann and Lægreid 2015). The accountability literature assumes that there is an elective affinity between different institutional logics and different accountability mechanisms: hierarchies, markets, and professional networks do not only have their own goals, values, and typical modes of interaction but also ideal typical mechanisms of accountability (Mashaw 2006). In hybrid governance arrangements, where the realms of the state, the market, and civil society collide, accountability relations, too, are hybrid. Providers of public services are held accountable through competition, professional norms, and the hierarchical interventions of regulatory agencies. Often there is not only one but several regulatory agencies to which service providers have to render account (Benish and Mattei 2019; Levi-Faur 2005), and often the accountability obligations of the different regulatory agencies are in conflict. It may even be possible for one regulatory agency to have accountability obligations that are *themselves* hybrid.

Accountability mechanisms need to be put into effect by some agent (Moore 2014). This is particularly true for laws and legal prescriptions that bear only the potential for accountability but do not put it into effect by themselves. The implementation and enforcement of regulatory policies are mainly the responsibilities of inspectors who are what Lipsky (2010) has called "street-level bureaucrats"—that is, actors who fulfill a public task and who are thereby in direct interaction with the target group. Inspectors shadow the people they are inspecting; let them explain how well daily operations are performed; check off boxes on inspection lists; and negotiate with inspected organizations before they decide whether they should hand out inspection tags, issue verbal warnings, or impose fines. Inspectors are thus the human face of regulatory policy (Van de Walle and Raaphorst 2019, 2).

Like every social interaction, the regulatory encounter is shaped by the postures and attitudes of those who interact. Braithwaite (1995) and Braithwaite and Cleland (2017) point to the relational dimension between inspectors and their inspectees, which is often overlooked in the regulatory literature but has a significant impact on both the actual use of enforcement styles and the effectiveness of the regulatory architecture. Among inspectees, we can find a group that is antagonistic toward regulation and expresses this, for example, by treating a regulatory authority as if it is irrelevant or by questioning the legitimacy of a regulator. Others might be willing to "play the regulatory game" and to comply but lack knowledge and/or capacity to do so. Both types of inspectee behavior (and the mixed types in between) can be differentiated for analytical purposes. However, it is even more important to differentiate them in policy practice because they require different treatment. Inspectors thus should be able to adapt their enforcement styles to the situation and look at cues to understand inspectee behavior.

Inspectors thus need the discretion to choose among different enforcement styles, to adapt laws to the circumstances of cases in a manner consistent with policy and hierarchical authority, and to cope with the uncertainties and pressures of their daily work (Van de Walle and Raaphorst 2019). Uncertainties may arise because information is ambiguous or even lacking, because evaluation standards could be interpreted in different ways, or because it is difficult to decide whether an inspected organization or an inspected individual is trustworthy.

However, in light of the ideas of New Public Management (NPM) in the late-twentieth century, discretion in regulation—and in street-level bureaucracy in general—was considered more and more critical. In the scientific but also in the political debate, an increased risk of regulatory capture has been perceived due to the increasing number of private for-profit and semi-autonomous providers as well as the increased choice options of customers (Benish, Halevy, and Spiro 2018; Cohen, Benish, and Shamriz-Ilouz 2016). As a result, political actors have introduced new guidelines and wide-ranging documentation requirements, often on top of already existing practices, to diminish the discretion of street-level bureaucrats. The inspector's role is to ensure the compliance of service providers without, however, giving extensive advice. While hybrid accountability is nothing new in long-term care, the NPM reforms have considerably intensified hybridity through marketization, managerialization, and customer choice.

How do inspectors relate to hybrid accountabilities? When multiple competing logics are in play in the same setting, they can trigger conflict or generate new types of activity. In the literature on inspectors in the care sector, the prevailing interpretation of the NPM accountability reforms is critical: instead of improving the safety and quality of life of patients, NPM practices of routinization and standardization have intensified problems of gaming and ritualistic use of regulatory instruments (Braithwaite, Makkai, and Braithwaite 2007).

Similar empirical findings of professionals who cannot manage competing logics are also reported in other parts of public administration. Tummers (2011) refers to the notion of policy alienation when street-level bureaucrats are not able to make sense of hybridity and thus refuse the policies they are expected to implement. Policy alienation is often caused by feelings of powerlessness or meaninglessness. Street-level bureaucrats can feel powerless when they do not have any influence on the types, quantity, and quality of the policies they implement. Meaninglessness indicates that street-level bureaucrats have the impression that the policies they are expected to implement have no beneficial outcome for society.

However, in the literature on street-level bureaucrats, we also find more positive assumptions about their ability to cope with hybridity. Schott, Kleef, and Noordegraaf (2016, 8) stress the ability of street-level bureaucrats to master hybridity, for instance, by actively integrating and blending competing logics into a new logic. As a result, these street-level bureaucrats become hybridized professionals with new skills that allow them to link professional practices to organizational objectives, as well as to broader social and economic developments. In a similar vein, Benish (this volume) draws attention to situations in which different logics of accountability are perceived as compatible and thus lead to mutual reinforcement.

This article uses the two contrasting modes of coping with hybridity—hybrid professionalism and policy alienation—as a starting point to develop a two-dimensional framework that offers a differentiated understanding of handling hybridity. Thereby, attitudes and postures toward hybridity on one hand, and the degree of activity (or passivity) on the other hand, are considered as relevant to categorizing empirical findings.

## Long-Term Care Regulation in Germany: Hybrid Accountability Arrangements

Long-term care services are provided in Germany in an institutional setting that combines competition among providers and choice for consumers with public funding and public regulation. The Long-Term Care Insurance Act of 1995 not only aimed to provide care for patients for a reasonable price but also to foster innovation in the field through competition. Private for-profit providers were thus explicitly given the same status and the same rights as public and voluntary providers to facilitate their access to the market. Today, the market for ambulatory care is even dominated by private for-profit providers: in 2017, 65.8 percent of the providers had a private for-profit legal form, 32.8 percent were voluntary providers, and only a negligible number of providers (1.4 percent) had a public legal form. Voluntary providers still outweigh the share of private for-profit providers in the market for statutory care, but the share of the latter is on the rise (all numbers are taken from Statistisches Bundesamt [Destatis] 2018).

Parallel to the creation of the new care market, an encompassing and, over the years, even growing regulatory framework has been set up to hold the competing service providers accountable to public values. The regulatory framework was not developed from scratch; rather, it has grown stepwise in a path-dependent way by layering new regulatory mechanisms on top of already existing ones.

The SHI Medical Review Board, which is one of three regulatory agencies, conducts the bulk of the quality inspections. The agency, which is jointly run by the statutory health insurance firms, is thus considered the main regulatory agency. Its regulatory mission is hybrid: the quality care inspections have at least four different objectives that serve different stakeholders (Herr, Nguyen, and Schmitz 2016):

- First, quality inspections aim to improve the transparency of the care market. In particular, they should enable people in need of care to make informed choices among care providers. Collecting and disseminating information is thus one major objective of quality inspections;
- Second, inspections should help to reduce malpractice and fraud among service providers (policing). The preventive and detective functions of quality inspections are of particular importance for funding agencies;
- Third, inspections should help managers and the professional staff of service providers to improve the quality of their services (organizational and individual learning objectives); and
- Finally, quality inspections should contribute to the development of policy recommendations based on the inspection results (policy learning).

The SHI Medical Review Board is thus simultaneously an advisory, control, educative, and policy board. It has vulnerable clients, profit-seeking entrepreneurs, care-providing professionals, bureaucrats, and politicians as stakeholders. From the perspective of the single inspector, this hybrid organizational environment creates dilemmas and paradoxical injunctions. Its missions are not only directed toward different stakeholders but are partly conflicting and require different implementation styles. The preventive and detective functions of quality inspections call for a strict top-down implementation style, whereby compliance is enforced with sanctions. Individual, organizational, and policy learning functions, on the contrary, succeed best in an organizational culture that embraces the lessons that can be learned from failure and that encourages an open discussion about mistakes without immediately blaming the responsible actors. The market transparency expected by citizens, too, might have detrimental effects for individual and organizational learning because it is based on the assumption that compliance is best achieved through public naming and shaming.

The main instruments of the regulatory strategy in force at the time of writing are mandatory quality management for all providers and unannounced inspections. During their inspections, inspectors check the quality according to a standardized list of criteria and pay visits to randomly selected nursing home residents. A particular focus is put on the plausibility of care documentation. The inspector cannot sanction noncompliant providers directly but has to inform the Local Residential Homes Authorities (*Heimaufsicht*), which have the final say about sanctions. To create transparency, the inspection results are published online. From 2009 to 2016, the school grade–based system[1] was used to rate providers according to the results of the inspection. It was, however, withdrawn after a critical public debate. Patient representatives and critical care professionals' associations blamed the system for not being neutral. Indeed, the neutrality of the quality inspections was questioned because the care transparency agreement (CTA) was jointly negotiated by representatives of the funding agencies and service providers, while representatives of patient organizations or nursing associations were not involved at all in the development of quality standards.

In light of the ongoing critical public debate, the regulatory strategy for long-term care quality inspection has been subject to reform initiatives (Wollmann and Bönker 2018). A new regulatory strategy has just become effective during the writing of this article. Instead of putting emphasis on formal compliance (measured by taking the quality of care documentation as a proxy), the new regulatory approach aims to strengthen consultative elements, for instance, thereby providing more room for expert discussions and interviews with care professionals, managers, and residents during the inspection visits (Wingenfeld et al. 2018). We come back to the new regulatory framework and assess the reforms in light of the empirical findings of this study.

# Methods

This is a qualitative study. First, we collected data through an analysis of policy documents, such as reports from expert commissions (e.g., Wingenfeld et al. 2018) and policy statements from different stakeholder groups (e.g., consumer organizations, the umbrella organizations of the health insurance funds, and service providers). Second, we checked the annual reports of the SHI Medical Review Board to assess the administrative capacity of the regulatory agency. The data collected include the number of employees, staff qualifications, training opportunities, and organizational structures.

The main data source, however, was expert interviews with inspectors. We conducted twenty interviews in total, each lasting an average of 60 minutes. As already described, regulating long-term care in Germany is a controversial field, and the regulatory strategy is subject to ongoing reform debates. Because of this, recruiting interviewees was challenging. Potential interview partners could be identified quite easily through the homepage of the SHI Medical Review Board, but there was an atmosphere of fear and distrust that made it difficult to convince inspectors to participate in our research. However, we continued to collect expert interviews until we had saturation, meaning that no new codes occurred in the data but mounting instances of the same codes occurred.

For the interviews, we combined a semi-structured questionnaire with the vignette technique. Whereas the semi-structured questionnaire allowed new ideas to be brought up during the interview while keeping the focus on the topics at hand, the vignette technique helped to explore sensitive topics (e.g., coping strategies for challenging situations such as difficult-to-handle managers of nursing homes). We collected the scenarios for the vignettes through preparatory discussions with scholars, nurses, and service provider managers. After reacting to the vignettes, we asked the inspectors to describe their daily work, how they perceived their role in the long-term care system, and whether the instruments they had on hand were appropriate for their work objectives. We also invited them to report challenging situations during quality inspections and their ways of dealing with such situations. Finally, we asked them to assess the impact the increasing marketization of the long-term care system has had on their work.

We analyzed data along the lines of qualitative content analysis. We developed themes and codes in an iterative process, going back and forth among interview data, secondary empirical material, and the relevant literature. To categorize findings, we used hybrid professionalism and policy alienation—two reactions of street-level bureaucrats toward NPM reform policies previously described in the literature (Noordegraaf 2015; Tummers 2011)—as starting points. In light of the empirical findings, we again refined the framework.

# Findings

## Hybrid accountabilities and role perception

The interviewed inspectors were sensitive to the complex accountability relations in which their work is embedded. When asked to describe their daily work, they reported that they felt obliged to manage diverse expectations generated within and outside the organization:

> When we conduct our work, we are in touch with very different actors: patients, providers, insurances, and also our peers, the professional staff in the nursing homes. And each of these actors wants us to do different things. For insurance firms, ensuring quality means having an eye on financial sustainability; they want us to detect overuse and misuse. Providers want to get the most out of the system, and they push us to approve higher levels of care. The same goes for patients. (Interview 5)

However, inspectors were also aware that they did not have a neutral position in this hybrid setting. When asked about their role, they indicated without hesitation: "We are service providers, and the health insurance firms are our main customers" (Interview 8). Indeed, the institutional framework of quality inspection in Germany encourages inspectors to take sides and adopt a partial perspective. While the regulatory mission of the SHI Medical Review Board, according to law, is fourfold and combines creating transparency, inspection and policing, consultancy for providers, and policy recommendations, inspectors maintain that inspection and policing with a focus on financial issues outweigh other regulatory goals.

## Attitudes toward (limited) discretion

From the inspectors' descriptions of their daily work, it becomes clear how the SHI Medical Review Board as an organization addresses the challenge of hybrid accountability relations: through strict rules and procedures that should help inspectors to cope with administrative ambiguity. Inspectors are expected to implement a predefined work program; they have only limited opportunities to develop their own daily routines. Every evening, they receive a list of where to appear the next day for an unannounced inspection; the quality assessment, too, follows a strictly defined procedure. The inspectors' daily work thus more closely resembles that of bureaucrats than professionals who have leeway to make decisions about the organization of their work. In addition, the regulatory framework has become increasingly dense over the years as a result of regulatory adjustments after scandals. While all interviewees agreed on the result, shrinking room for discretion, their opinions of this development varied. Some of the inspectors explained that they found the detailed form helpful and supportive for navigating difficult situations (Interview 5; Interview 3), such as critical debates with annoyed representatives of the inspected organization: "The detailed regulatory framework helps me to explain my assessment to upset patients or nursing home managers. I can say to them: 'Look, it is not me; it is the law that prescribes doing this or that. I just follow the regulatory guidelines.'" Inspectors, however, referred not only to blame shifting to the regulatory guidelines, but also considered the implementation of these guidelines as their very mission: "When I manage to stick strictly to the official guidelines, then I am truly professional" (Interview 11).

However, some inspectors were more critical about the inspection instruments. They felt restricted in their professional judgment: "I see a lot of deficiencies in nursing homes, which I cannot document just because there are no relevant entry fields in my form!" (Interview 3). Inspectors recognized conflicts between the values and principles of professional care and the regulatory guidelines: "For instance, violence in nursing homes cannot be documented. If I have a reasonable suspicion, I have to depart from the official assessment form and ask in a more hidden way whether patients have experienced inappropriate behavior from nursing staff."

*Enforcement styles*

When asked to describe their enforcement style, it became clear that inspectors viewed their own styles as different from that of the SHI Medical Review Board's hybrid regulatory mission. While some state clearly, "My role is to control. I have worked in the past as a nurse; I definitely know that control is necessary for this field" (Interview 8), others described their enforcement style as advisory, deliberative, and accommodative: "The inspected staff has a huge knowledge and experience of giving care. During my inspections, I try to discuss at eye-level with the inspected organizations and try to find compromises between my expertise and their expertise" (Interview 12).

Inspectors favoring an advisory enforcement style, however, complained that practicing in that way was hampered by their working conditions. Stress from the high workload was indeed a recurring issue in the interviews. Due to the increasing number of people in need of care and the growing number of service providers, as well as the increasing density of the regulatory framework, the daily inspection workload has risen greatly and steadily in recent years. However, it is difficult for the regulatory agency to find well-trained staff, and workforce shortage has become a severe problem. Because of the workload compression, inspectors are concerned that the working conditions do not allow them to conduct the inspections according to their professional standards. The continual time pressure hinders them from handling quality checks with the necessary thoroughness. "The regulatory guidelines have become more and more complex in recent years. New standards were introduced that entailed considerable paperwork—we put more and more effort into the inspection visit without, however, receiving more time per visit!" (Interview 12).

## Relational postures in welfare markets

When asked about challenging situations in their daily work, inspectors often referred to the emotional dimension in the inspector-inspectee relationship, which is quite complex. Several of them stated that they were usually confronted with a hostile atmosphere that prevented them from acting as benevolent and supportive consultants: "Staff and managers don't believe that we are here to support them doing their job in a better way; they only see us as an additional administrative burden and don't see the visit as an opportunity to learn" (Interview 15). It is not only the fact of being assessed and controlled that induces inspected organizations to adopt a critical and sometimes even hostile stance toward the inspectors. The SHI Medical Review Board suffers from a bad organizational reputation: "The Medical Review Board has such a poor standing in the community, but also in the general public debate. It is tough to work against this poor image" (Interview 8); "People pass the buck to the SHI Medical Review Board—we are accused of everything negative in the long-term care system" (Interview 4).

Inspectors also reported that they were accused of having abandoned their former colleagues. "Why are you no longer a nurse? We need you here; we are urgently searching for qualified staff. Why have you escaped to the SHI Medical Review Board?" (Interview 15). The underlying accusation is that the inspectors decided to quit stressful and tiring care work to do a "lazy and unpretentious bureaucratic job." Despite their professional backgrounds, inspectors are no longer considered "one of them": "They ignore the fact that I was once a nurse, that I was their colleague. I'm an outsider now—even worse, they consider me the bad guy" (Interview 6).

Sometimes it is also the nursing home management that labels inspectors as the "bad guys." Inspectors reported experiences in which nurses had confided that their management uses the results of the quality inspections to put additional pressure on their staff to intimidate them and to expect them to do more with fewer resources (Interview 8). Inspectors explained that this type of situation made them feel that they were being instrumentalized—and, at the same time, it made them feel helpless because they did not know how to react.

Another inspector referred explicitly to the management of private for-profit providers that creates challenging conditions:

> I can see a clear difference in the behavior of private for-profit and voluntary providers. Private for-profit providers are new actors in the field and are aware that their legitimacy

is still contested. They thus take the issue of service quality very seriously. Their internal quality management schemes are considerably better developed than those of the long-established voluntary providers. Taking quality seriously, however, also implies that the managers of the private providers watch me closely when I conduct my quality control. They know the guidelines by heart and are better prepared than their colleagues from the voluntary providers. They are often accompanied by lawyers who monitor my work constantly. (Interview 8)

From their daily work experiences, inspectors can see how much the provider landscape has changed in recent years as a result of privatization and marketization. Interestingly, none of the interviewed inspectors referred in a positive way to market-based governance. Instead, they had a rather critical stance toward the recent governance structures of the field, and this critical perspective influenced their inspection styles: "The field is underfunded. If I impose sanctions, I punish the staff—but they are not responsible for the misery" (Interview 14). Inspectors are of the opinion that they cannot hold the staff accountable for quality deficits. Even if they become aware of serious quality deficits in the nursing homes they inspect, they hesitate to impose sanctions: "The nurses do their best—quality problems in nursing homes are produced at the political level, not at the organizational level of the nursing homes or even by individual nurses" (Interview 8). The inspectors' own role in the quality inspection game is considered as rather weak: "We don't have the power to change the structures of the field" (Interview 3); "We cannot impose sanctions, we can only report to other agencies that decide about sanctions" (Interview 12).

# Discussion

The literature suggests that an increasingly hybrid working environment allows street-level bureaucrats to become professionals who have acquired new abilities and skills. In particular, they have internalized managerial thinking that helps them to link professional practices to organizational objectives (Schott, van Kleef, and Noordegraaf 2016, 8). How do our empirical findings relate to this literature?

First, we conclude that inspectors are indeed conscious of the different logics that structure the field of long-term care and are aware of the challenges and conflicts that institutional hybridity causes. They report that they are often confronted with the incompatible demands of their different stakeholders, such as the wish of patients in nursing homes for staff to have time for them and to listen to them versus the expectation of the employer for staff to stick strictly to the schedule. Repeatedly, they see their own professional identity in conflict with external demands, such as when they miss the chance to document the misbehavior of staff or management, or when they lack the opportunity to substantially discuss the results of the visit with those being inspected.

Second, the empirical material reveals that inspectors make sense of hybridity in different ways. Some find it difficult to handle the various logics and thus complain or even reject hybridity, while others are conscious of the competing logics but accept hybridity as a given fact. However, their coping strategy cannot be classified as an active integration or the blending of the different logics into a new one. The inspectors in our sample did not consider themselves the forerunners of renewed professionalism. They did not describe themselves as market regulators controlling a competitive field while at the same time being able to respect professional values. Instead of actively integrating the different logics and combining them, the coping strategy they described is more passive and can be called pragmatic tolerance. Inspectors had value conflicts, but they did not have a clear concept of how to navigate the conflicts. Instead, they let situations happen and relied on formal arrangements to manage them.

While we did not find cases of hybrid professionalism, cases of policy alienation did occur. Inspectors were particularly critical of the increasing marketization of the long-term care field and thus rejected the recent hybrid mode of governance. Inspectors experienced meaninglessness when they wondered whether their interventions made any difference at all. Feelings of powerlessness surfaced when they described the inadequate available instruments they had for sanctioning noncompliant providers. They bowed out because they realized that they could not handle the different expectations of providers. Not all of the inspectors who had a critical stance toward hybrid accountability reacted with inner resignation. Instead, some solved inherent value conflicts by clearly prioritizing one logic. Interestingly, we find both the prioritization of hierarchy ("My main task is to control") as well as the prioritization of professionalism ("I understand inspection as the reflection of professional standards, together with staff and management").

As a single case study, the empirical material is too limited to provide explanations for the inspectors' behavior and to make generalizations. However, the findings allow for the refinement of the analytical framework for how street-level bureaucrats experience hybridity. The findings suggest that two dimensions are relevant for classifying the inspectors' coping strategies. The first is their attitude toward hybridity: do they accept or reject hybridity? The second is the degree of activity and reflexivity in their reaction patterns: are their attempts to deal with hybridity more active and reflexive (either by trying to integrate competing logics or by prioritizing one logic) or more passive (either tolerance or alienation)? Table 1 represents this classification scheme.

When looking at Table 1, it is indeed striking that no cases of reflexive integration of different logics appeared in the analyzed sample. It is interesting to relate this observation to the literature. Noordegraaf (2015, 11) has argued that when the complexity of the work rises, professionalism increasingly becomes organizing work: "Organizing becomes crucial for 'professional' professional action—organizing becomes an intricate part of professional work." Traditional professional and new managerial, hierarchical steering practices are integrated in a reflexive way. However, Noordegraaf (2015, 14) acknowledges that such organization of professional processes cannot suddenly occur within organizational settings. Leveraging the adaptation of inspection processes in a hybrid working environment requires training and education as well as resources (staff, time, financial opportunities, and new technologies). However, in the case of long-term care quality inspection in Germany, the hybridization of accountability relations has occurred alongside a

TABLE 1
Classifying Coping Strategies for Hybrid Accountabilities

| | | Passive or reflexive coping strategies | |
| --- | --- | --- | --- |
| | | Passive practices | Reflexive practices |
| **Attitude towards hybridity** | **Accepting hybridity** | Pragmatism and reliance on formal arrangements <br> • "When I manage to stick strictly to the official guidelines, then I am truly professional." | Integrating or blending different logics <br> • (no cases in this study) |
| | **Rejecting hybridity** | Alienation: powerlessness and meaninglessness <br> • "We don't have the power to change the structures of the field." | Prioritizing one particular logic <br> • "My main task is to control." (prioritizing hierarchy) <br> • "I understand inspection as the reflection of professional standards, together with staff and management." (prioritizing professionalism) |

deterioration in the inspectors' working conditions. Inspectors are expected to handle an increasingly complex regulatory framework and a rising number of cases *without* a complementary improvement in working resources (time, staff, etc.). Thus, inspectors experience hybridization as more demanding—and it is difficult for them to judge whether the hybridization per se or the workload is to blame.

The literature on relational postures in regulatory encounters (Braithwaite 1995; Braithwaite and Cleland 2017) points to the complex inspector-inspectee relationship as another factor that might explain why the inspectors in this case study were not able to integrate different accountability logics in a meaningful way. Effective regulation requires that inspectees be willing to accept the "regulatory game." However, in welfare markets with fierce competition among providers, it is more likely that we find nursing home managers who are not only eager to maximize their profit margins at the expense of regulatory compliance but are also in principle antagonistic toward regulation. Indeed, the inspectors who we interviewed stated frequently that they felt challenged or even blocked and powerless because their counterparts considered the regulatory authority as irrelevant or questioned their legitimacy as a regulator. Interestingly, resistance seems to come more often from voluntary providers who fear losing their market position than from for-profit providers who still seek to stabilize their organizational legitimacy in the social service market, but this assumption needs to be examined more closely in future research.

## Conclusion

Taking the results of this study into consideration, the most recent reforms of the regulatory framework of long-term care in Germany have to be viewed critically.

As we described, a new hybrid regulatory approach that emphasizes the importance of organizational learning in the regulatory encounter became effective in
fall 2019 (Wingenfeld et al. 2018). While the overall objective of the reform—to
encourage learning instead of assessing the quality of documentation—is to be
appreciated, it is doubtful that the reforms will increase the effectiveness of the
system. The new regulatory strategy requires a trust-based and collaborative
relationship between inspectors and inspectees and needs to be accompanied by
appropriate resource allocation. An appropriate adjustment of resources, however, was not part of the reform process, nor was the reform of the regulatory
strategy accompanied by reforms of the overall governance of the field. Without
adjusting the working conditions of the inspectors (e.g., time and workload) and
without decreasing the fierce competition in the field, inspectors will not be able
to integrate the different logics of the new strategy and carry out the learning
approach in a convincing way.

Going beyond the case of Germany, the observations of this study are also
relevant for a general reflection about accountability in the regulatory welfare
state. Gaps in implementation have been identified, the underlying reasons have
been investigated, and possible reasons for regulatory failure can therefore be
better understood. Regulatory failure does not occur because accountabilities in
recent settings of the regulatory welfare state have become hybrid (accountability
in the welfare state has always been hybrid), but because the preconditions for
hybrid professionalism are poorly understood.

The results of the study can inform both research and policy practice, leading
to the design of more effective accountability relations. In light of the empirical
finding that dissatisfaction with working conditions was a recurring issue, we
consider the working conditions of quality care inspectors to be a crucial issue for
future research. Decent work seems to be a necessary, although very likely not
sufficient, condition for enabling inspectors to integrate competing logics in a
meaningful way. The empirical results also indicate that welfare markets with
fierce competition result in relational postures in the inspector-inspectee relationship that hamper the establishment of a joint regulatory culture.

To be clear, these insights have been stated before in the literature on regulation, but they need to be discussed again for two reasons: they are still ignored in
policy practice, and they have become even more pressing in a period in which
austerity policies are combined with marketized and managerialized welfare state
governance.

## Note

1. See pflegenoten.de

## References

Benish, Avishai. 2020. The logic(s) of hybrid accountability: When state, market and professionalism interact. *The ANNALS of the American Academy of Political and Social Science* (this volume).

Benish, Avishai, Dana Halevy, and Shimon Spiro. 2018. Regulating social welfare services: Between compliance and learning. *International Journal of Social Welfare* 27 (3): 226–35.

Benish, Avishai. 2014. The public accountability of privatized activation—the case of Israel. *Social Policy & Administration* 48 (2): 262–77.

Benish, Avishai, and Paola Mattei. 2019. Accountability and hybridity in welfare governance. *Public Administration* (November). https://doi.org/10.1111/padm.12640.

Braithwaite, John, Toni Makkai, and V. A. Braithwaite. 2007. *Regulating aged care: Ritualism and the new pyramid*. Northampton, MA: Edward Elgar.

Braithwaite, Valerie. 1995. Games of engagement: Postures within the regulatory community. *Law and Policy* 17:225–55.

Braithwaite, Valerie, and Deborah Cleland. 2017. *Regulating for workplace health and safety in Queensland: The regulators' perspective*. Available from https://static1.squarespace.com/static/5c05f8595cfd7901fc57139d/t/5c873541ee6eb0145fe5246c/1552364873449/WHSQ+Rgulator+MP+17+Mar+2017.pdf.

Cohen, Nissim, Avishai Benish, and Aya Shamriz-Ilouz. 2016. When clients can choose. Dilemmas of street-level workers in choice-based social services. *Social Service Review* 90 (4): 620–46.

Herr, Annika, Thu-Van Nguyen, and Hendrik Schmitz. 2016. Public reporting and the quality of care of German nursing homes. *Health Policy* 120 (10): 1162–70.

Jann, Werner, and Per Lægreid. 2015. Reforming the welfare state: Accountability, management, and performance. *International Journal of Public Administration* 38 (13–14): 941–46.

Levi-Faur, David. 2005. The global diffusion of regulatory capitalism. *The ANNALS of the American Academy of Political and Social Science* 598 (1): 12–32.

Levi-Faur, David. 2014. The welfare state: A regulatory perspective. *Public Administration* (March). https://doi.org/10.1111/padm.12063.

Lipsky, Michael. 2010. *Street-level bureaucracy: Dilemmas of the individual in public services*. 30th anniversary expanded ed. New York, NY: Russell Sage Foundation.

Mashaw, Jerry Louis. 2006. *Accountability and institutional design: Some thoughts on the grammar of governance*. Research Paper No. 116. Yale Law School.

Moore, Mark H. 2014. Accountability, legitimacy, and the court of public opinion. In *The Oxford handbook of public accountability*, eds. M. A. P. Bovens, Robert E. Goodin, and Thomas Schillemans, 632–46. New York, NY: Oxford University Press.

Nies, Henk, and Kai Leichsenring. 2018. Concepts and strategies of quality assurance in care for older people. In *Cultures of care in aging*, eds. Thomas J. Boll, Dieter Ferring, and Jaan Valsiner, 347–71. Charlotte, NC: IAP.

Noordegraaf, Mirko. 2015. Hybrid professionalism and beyond: (New) forms of public professionalism in changing organizational and societal contexts. *Journal of Professions and Organization* 2 (2): 187–206.

Schott, Carina, Daphne van Kleef, and Mirko Noordegraaf. 2016. Confused professionals?: Capacities to cope with pressures on professional work. *Public Management Review* 18 (4): 583–610.

Statistisches Bundesamt (Destatis). 2018. *Pflegestatistik*. Wiesbaden.

Tummers, Lars. 2011. Explaining the willingness of public professionals to implement new policies: A policy alienation framework. *International Review of Administrative Sciences* 77 (3): 555–81.

Van de Walle, Steven, and Nadine Raaphorst. 2019. Introduction: The social dynamics of daily inspection work. In *Inspectors and enforcement at the front line of government*, eds. Steven Van de Walle, and Nadine Raaphorst, 1–10. Cham, Switzerland: Springer.

Wingenfeld, Klaus, C. Stegbauer, G. Willms, R. Voigt, and R. Woitzik. 2018. Entwicklung der Instrumente und Verfahren für Qualitätsprüfungen nach §§ 114 Ff. SGB XI und die Qualitätsdarstellung nach § 115 Abs. 1a SGB XI in der Stationären Pflege. Abschlussbericht: Darstellung der Konzeptionen für das neue Prüfverfahren und die Qualitätsdarstellung. Bericht im Auftrag des Qualitätsausschusses Pflege. Available from https://www.gs-qsa-pflege.de/wp-content/uploads/2018/10/20180903_Entwicklungsauftrag_stationa%CC%88r_Abschlussbericht.pdf.

Wollmann, Hellmut, and Frank Bönker. 2018. Evaluating personal social services in Germany. In *Evaluating reforms of local public and social services in Europe*, eds. Ivan Koprić, Hellmut Wollmann, and Gérard Marcou, 65–80. Cham, Switzerland: Springer.

Many welfare states have increased their regulatory role, but little attention has been given to historical changes in the regulatory role of government ministries. This study embraces a mezzo perspective and explores the regulatory role of the Welfare Ministry of Israel in the field of personal social services, asking the following questions: 1) What are the changes in regulatory expectations versus practices over the last five decades? and 2) How can we explain these changes and their outcomes? The study is based on the qualitative analysis of comptroller reports and other resources. It reveals a growing gap between society's expectations of the Ministry as a regulator and the Ministry's capacities over five decades. Notably, it points to the variety of regulatory spaces that have appeared in a regulatory welfare state. The Israeli case is relevant for other countries that have experienced processes of outsourcing and privatization in the welfare state and whose ministries had to change their role.

*Keywords:* personal social services; regulation; inspection; welfare; gaps

# Changing Expectations? The Change in the Role of the Welfare Ministry in the Regulation of Personal Social Services

*By*
LIHI LAHAT

In recent decades, the involvement of different sectors, such as the private and voluntary sectors, in the design and supply of social services has created the need for new forms of regulation in the welfare state (Braithwaite 2006; Majone 1994). The expansion of regulation, rather than becoming a substitute for the welfare state, has led to the development of "regulatory welfare states" (RWS) that use regulation to promote their social objectives (Levi-Faur 2014; Haber 2017; Levi-Faur and Benish 2020). This article focuses on the changing role of the Israeli Ministry of Labor, Social Services and Social Affairs (hereafter, the

*Lihi Lahat is a senior lecturer in the Department of Administration & Public Policy at Sapir Academic College and affiliate associate professor, Azrieli Institute of Israel Studies, Concordia University, Montreal. Her research interests are the regulation of personal social services, collaborative governance, and time and policy.*

Correspondence: Lahat_l@mail.sapir.ac.il

DOI: 10.1177/0002716220959310

Welfare Ministry) as the regulator of personal social services. Personal social services (care services) include diverse programs and services providing in-kind services to populations, individuals, and families (Katan 1996); for example, services for addicted individuals or children suffering violence in the home. More specifically, it explores five decades of changes in expectations and practices of regulation in personal social services. It argues that society's expectations of the Welfare Ministry and the abilities of the Ministry itself both affected its regulatory role.

Israel, as elsewhere, has witnessed a continuous growth in the services that non-state sectors supply (Gal and Madhala 2016). Over time, the regulatory role of the Welfare Ministry has faced mounting criticism (Lahat and Talit 2015, Mandelkern 2012). This criticism sparked our interest in the historical development of the regulatory role of the Welfare Ministry. The theoretical term *expectation gap* refers to the gap between society's expectations of the regulator and its actual role (Shikdar et al. 2018). By developing this term and connecting it to government abilities (Bali, Capano, and Ramesh 2019; Howlett, Mukherjee, and Woo 2015), we explore the changes in the regulatory role of the Welfare Ministry.

The following qualitative analysis is based on Israeli State Comptroller Reports, complemented by documents and interviews.[1] The article makes two contributions to the RWS literature. First, it takes a novel mezzo level perspective, offering an "inside look" at the changes in the Welfare Ministry. Second, it identifies different kinds of gaps that may be created in the regulatory spaces of RWSs.

# Regulation of Social Services

Social regulation is not a new topic in the literature, and some studies have dealt with the regulation of personal social services (e.g., Furness 2009; Goodship et al. 2004; Lahat and Talit 2015; Spiro and Frumer 2010). A particularly salient example is the influential work of Braithwaite, Makkai, and Braithwaite (2007). These authors explored the regulation of nursing homes in the United States, the UK and Australia and suggested a model of a regulatory pyramid expressing the escalation of coercion. However, to accomplish their role as regulators, government ministries may need a new set of tools (Elkomy, Cookson, and Jones 2019; Hood et al. 1999).

Hood et al. (1999) mention oversight, competition, mutuality, and contrived randomness as possible regulatory tools. Other possibilities include implementing systems-based regulations or performance-based systems to control the process or

NOTE: I wish to thank Orphee Senouf Pilpoul for her help in gathering the comptroller reports. I also would like to thank the interviewees for their time and patience. My sincere gratitude to the reviewers, the editorial team, and the editors of this special issue of *The ANNALS*, Professor Levi-Faur and Dr. Benish, for their illuminating remarks on previous versions of this article. I would like to thank the Azrieli Institute of Israel Studies, Concordia University, Montreal, the Israel Institute, and the Serling Institute for Jewish Studies and Modern Israel, Michigan State University, U.S., for the time dedicated to this article. First versions were presented at the "Regulating for Welfare?" Workshop at the Hebrew University of Jerusalem, May 14–17, 2019, and at the International Conference of Public Policy, ICPP4, Concordia University, Montreal, June 26–28, 2019.

the outcomes (Baldwin, Cave, and Lodge 2012; May 2007), promoting self-regulation (Black 2002), or using accumulated knowledge and peer-review learning (Benish, Halevy, and Spiro 2018; Lahat and Sabah 2018). These tools can promote a better quality of care, safeguarding service recipients from harm and serving the public interest (Furness 2009). For example, including users' opinions and their families' opinions of the quality of the care would yield more information. The regulatory process could also be well served by asking organizations to create internal quality evaluation systems (May 2007).[2]

Given the new demands, soft and more sophisticated regulatory mechanisms are incorporating various levels of coercion, actors, knowledge, and expertise (Lahat and Sabah 2018).[3] The traditional "command and control" approach has been complemented by "responsive regulation" and "smart regulation" in multi-actor, multi-level, and gradual regulatory systems (Ayres and Braithwaite 1992; Downe and Martin 2007; Gunningham and Sinclair 1998; Munro 2004) to deal with such well-known problems of strict regulation as ritualism and high costs (Braithwaite, Makkai, and Braithwaite 2007) and provide a better solution to the needs of the current social services arena, which is, in effect, a new regulatory space.

Regulatory space comprises interactions between various actors, including regulators and the regulated, organizations and agencies, and formal and informal power (Scott 2001). This space is affected by the capacity, resources, culture, norms, and motivation of the regulatory field, and the regulatory narrative is defined and redefined by the different actors in this space. In the context of care services, the epistemic community of social workers represents the professional actor. Some claim social workers see managerial and regulation trends as corresponding with neo-liberalism and countering the essence of the social process; as such, they might hinder social workers' discretion (Kadushin and Harkness 2014; Marthinsen 2019; McLaughlin 2007; Benish, Halevy, and Spiro 2018; Dubois 2019; Lahat and Sabah 2018; Lahat and Talit 2015).

There are two gaps in the regulation literature. First, studies have tended to ignore the regulatory space in the context of government ministries (for an exception, see Hood et al. 1999), with work looking at European regulatory spaces, regulatory agencies in the United States and UK, and regulation among street-level bureaucracy (Freeman and Rossi 2011; Levi-Faur 2011; Klenk 2020; Van de Walle and Raaphorst 2019). However, regulatory agencies are different from government ministries; they have more autonomy and a clearer regulatory aim, while ministries are more affected by public and political pressures (Gilardi, Jordana, and Levi-Faur 2006; Christensen and Lægreid 2006) and need to adapt to the new demands of the RWS. Second, studies have been less concerned with the effectiveness of the regulatory processes (Jordana and Sancho 2004).

## Gaps in the Regulatory Space: Theoretical Perspective

In the RWS, government ministries need to implement new regulatory tools, but are faced with two problems. One problem is an *implementation gap*. A "perfect implementation" does not exist, and gaps are inherent to implementation (Hogwood and Gunn 1984). Explanations for these gaps include lack of resources and time, administrative traditions, vague policy goals, different interpretations, and resistance to change (Hogwood and Gunn 1984; Hill and Hupe 2002; Ongaro and Valotti 2008). While some researchers say focusing on these gaps is not productive, and some gaps might even be fruitful (see Hill and Hupe 2002), others suggest that exploring gaps can be helpful for our understanding of implementation (Ongaro and Valotti 2008). The second problem is an *expectations gap*. This term comes from the auditing literature and reflects the "gap between society's expectation from the auditors and the performance or role of [the] auditors" (Shikdar et al. 2018, 170).

In other words, there may be an implementation gap, referring to performance or a gap between society's expectations and the reality (Ebimobowei 2010). These expectations might be reasonable or unreasonable. For example, an unreasonable expectation might be the public's perception of the Welfare Ministry as responsible for the well-being of all people; the privacy of families and the lack of information on people's well-being makes this expectation impossible to meet. A reasonable expectation might be that the Welfare Ministry will implement effective regulation vis-à-vis the quality of residents' nutrition and well-being in institutions under its supervision. Determining what aspects create the gaps is important if the regulations are to improve and public trust in the regulator is to increase (Ebimobowei 2010; Shikdar et al. 2018).

Table 1 presents a typology of gaps in the RWS. It includes two axes. The first shows the implementation gaps, based on Bali, Capano, and Ramesh (2019). We specify three requirements for policy effectiveness: the analytical ability (the ability of the agency to choose, adapt, and calibrate policy tools); the operational ability (the ability to implement and coordinate the tools); and the political ability (the ability to gain support and legitimacy for actions from different actors including the professionals in the ministry). The second axis shows society's expectations of a government ministry (Ebimobowei 2010; Shikdar et al. 2018). A society with high regulatory expectations expects regulation will be a ministry's central obligation and one with low expectations expects the regulatory role of the ministry will not be a central aspect of its role.

Based on these axes, we can identify four situations. The first (A) refers to low regulatory expectations with low abilities to execute regulation. In this situation, although the gap is minor, the regulatory space is underdeveloped; there are no demands for regulation and no abilities to implement it. The second (B) refers to relatively high abilities to implement regulatory tools but lower expectations that the ministry has a regulatory role. There is a medium gap between expectation and ability; therefore, the ministry can take incremental steps toward regulation. The third (C) expresses high societal expectations that the ministry has a regulatory role, but the ministry has little ability to implement this role. This situation creates a dramatic gap and stagnation that can be defined as a static regulatory space. In the last situation (D), society has high expectations of the ministry's regulatory role, and the ministry has high capabilities to fulfil this role. There is an extremely minor gap, denoting an optimal regulatory space.

TABLE 1

**Different Expectations-Abilities Gaps and Their Effect on the Regulatory Space**

| Expectations of government ministries as regulators | | Ability to design and implement regulation | |
| --- | --- | --- | --- |
| | | Low | High |
| | Low | A: Minor gap Underdeveloped regulatory space | B: Medium gap Incremental regulatory space |
| | High | C: Dramatic gap Static regulatory space | D: Minor gap Optimal regulatory space |

SOURCE: Adjusted from Bali, Capano, and Ramesh (2019:5) and Howlett, Mukherjee, and Woo (2015:299).

# Method

We used a case study to examine the research questions (Yin 2003). This method is used to explore the way things work (Stake 2010) and, as such, had the potential to shed light on the development of regulation. Using a combined method of textual analysis and grounded theory analysis (Corbin and Strauss 1990), the study examined forty-three Israeli State Comptroller's Reports from 1970 to 2017.[4] We included all the Comptroller Reports that dealt with the Welfare Ministry and personal social services and that mentioned the terms regulation, inspection, standards, bids/tenders, and audit (see Table A1 in the appendix). The reports reflected the expectations of the Welfare Ministry and its roles.

The State Comptroller of Israel is governed by the "Basic Law: The State Comptroller." The Comptroller is an independent body responsible to Parliament (the Israeli Knesset), not to the government. The Comptroller is elected by the Knesset for a fixed term of seven years and s/he submits reports on different subjects to Parliament.[5] Sections 2a and 2b in the Basic Law refer to the areas of audit and function:

> 2(a) the Comptroller will audit the economy, the property, the finances, *the obligations and the administration of the State*, of Government Ministries, of all enterprises, institutions, or corporations of the State, of Local Authorities, and of bodies or other institutions which were defined by law as subject to audit by the State Comptroller. (b) The State Comptroller shall inspect the legality, integrity, managerial norms, efficiency and economy of the audited bodies, as well as any other matter which he deems necessary.[6]

Therefore, the Comptroller Reports reflect external normative expectations of the Welfare Ministry.

Several changes have occurred over the years to the Basic Law. In 1952, a parliamentary amendment to the law added integrity. Amendments referring to the effectiveness and execution of activities were added later. From the 1980s onward, in some cases, the Comptroller examined the results of government action and policy.[7]

Our analysis began with the 1970s to explore the situation before 1985, when Israel adopted a stabilization plan and moved from a social-democratic ideology to a neo-liberal one (Mandelkern and Paz-Fuchs 2018). We complemented the textual analysis with interviews with retired inspectors,[8] as well as with official documents, reports, and studies on the subject.

The analysis comprised two main steps. First, we created a 156-page file; the file included report numbers, general subjects, summaries, regulatory aspects, and first observations. After reading the file several times, we removed four irrelevant reports.[9] Second, we examined the file by decade to determine the main issue being discussed, the main "story," and the main terms (McBeth et al. 2007). Our analysis was guided by the question: what were the unique features of regulation in this decade? We considered four sub-questions for each decade: 1) What were the main regulatory issues being discussed? 2) What were the main tools (strategies) suggested by the Comptroller? 3) What were the main strategies (actions) implemented by the Welfare Ministry? and 4) What were the views of the Comptroller on the responsibility and "guilt" of three actors—the central Ministry (the headquarters), the inspectors, and the NGOs? The analysis also detected certain issues that were discussed repeatedly throughout the decades; examples included deficits in resources, workforce, standards, lack of licensing, and difficulties in finding suitable people to do the job. Examining these diverse aspects can reveal the capabilities and expectations of the Welfare Ministry as a regulator.

*Limitations and ethical issues*

It is important to note two limitations. First, the various personal services differ in their development and features, making it difficult to create a general picture of the regulatory space. Second, the Controller Reports have changed over the years in terms of breadth and style (Sher-Hadar 2019). However, they provide the same point of view, that is, that of an outside formal actor and encompassing society's normative expectations of the Welfare Ministry. Starting in the 1980s, the reports refer to widely ranging topics, but the basic principles of the audit are preserved. Moreover, the reports were complemented by data from other research sources. It is also important to note my familiarity with the issue and the Welfare Ministry because of my previous research and former role in the Ministry.[10] However, my experience may improve my understanding and interpretation of the findings.

The term *regulation* refers to the activities of the Welfare Ministry, such as creating the tools and setting the standards for service delivery, and *inspection* refers to the work of the inspectors (based on Van de Walle and Raaphorst 2019).[11]

# Personal Social Services in Israel

In Israel, personal social services include programs and services provided to populations, individuals, and families. They may include services such as care for the elderly, home care for the intellectually disabled or for people with physical disabilities, and services for families experiencing poverty or domestic violence (Katan 1996; Yanai 2006).

These services are provided based on the Welfare Services Law 5718-1958 that requires local authorities to establish departments of social services to supply these services. The Welfare Ministry has three levels: national, district or regional, and local. Four districts connect the central office to 256 local authorities. Some services are supplied on a regional level and others at a local level. In 2016, 19.5 percent of the families in Israel, totalling 1,300,000 people or 15.4 percent of the population, were registered in the local departments for social services (Ben-Simhon and Gorn 2016). Seventy-five percent of the funding comes from the central government and 25 percent from the local authority. However, it differs based on the local ability to recruit further funding (Auerbach 2007; Katan 1996).

While NGOs were always involved in supplying personal social services, their involvement has grown since the mid-1980s. Today, around 80 percent of the Welfare Ministry's budget is spent on purchasing services from NGOs (Madhala-Brik and Gal 2016). While research has identified the regulatory deficits of the Welfare Ministry (e.g. Gal and Ben-Mordechai 2017; Lahat and Talit 2015; Mandelkern 2012), less attention has been paid to the historical changes in regulation or to the gaps that affected these changes.

# Five Decades of Regulatory Continuity and Change

## The 1970s: Development

In the 1970s, the goal of the Welfare Ministry was to develop its managerial and regulatory functions, based on the suggestions of a committee convened in the 1960s. These included: 1) a division of labor based on the type of service user (family, children, and youth) rather than the unit supplying the service (local or central); and 2) decentralization, whereby the central ministry would design the policy and oversee high-level regulations, and the district level would implement the policy via networks of inspection and guides (Report 22, 481). These changes reflected both the "looseness of the regulation" (Report 22, 484, 498) and the strengthening of regional inspection. The recommendations were inspired by the *Planning, Programming, and Budgeting System* in the United States whose goal was to apply more rational approaches to administration (Report 22). However, the structural changes did not clearly define authority, patterns of work, or coordination. The Comptroller referred to a lack of appropriate managerial and regulatory tools leading to the poor enforcement of the law and emphasized the need for work routines and management to create the proper level of care (Report 22, 506).

These years featured the development of infrastructure, including computer-ized payments and data, but deficits in resources, workforce, instructions, knowl-edge, and information remained a problem. The work of the inspectors needed to be better defined, and their professional development strengthened (Reports 20, 23, 26 and 30). These omissions were blamed on the Welfare Ministry rather than the inspectors (Report 23).

During the 1970s, NGOs were already involved in providing services. For example, fifty-two daycare centers were built by women's organizations; eight were built by the local authorities. However, there were few regulations for man-agers of these facilities (Report 23, 482–83). Similarly, of the 1,000 young people under the Youth Protection Authority, half lived in government housing while the other half lived in private, public, and foster homes (Report 23, 470). The NGOs are referred to equally in the Reports, and the need for systematic regulation refers to all kinds of organizations.

After the mid-1970s there was some development in the regulations. For example, a "route document" on the supervision of local authorities was issued by the Welfare Ministry in 1979 (Labor and Welfare Ministry Committee Report 1997; Hovav 1998). But there was a long way to go. For example, inspections of the homes for the elderly were infrequent and did not meet the standards. Fifty percent were operating without a license, partly because of the time it took to issue one (Report 26, 636–38).

## The 1980s: Pluralistic efficiency

The Comptroller reports emphasized efficiency in the 1980s. For example, the Comptroller suggested that NGOs and the private sector build residential homes for young people because they could do so at one third the cost of comparable government facilities (Report 35, 573). However, the problems of the 1970s per-sisted. The reports highlight a lack of information (e.g. Reports 31, 32, 34, 35, 36, 38). The lack of documentation and data made regulation almost impossible. In 1984, the Comptroller noted that there was inadequate information about the regulation of fourteen government residences (395 residents), home care deliv-ered by eight NGOs (150 residents), and 30 residents in foster families. Regional inspectors were not told to provide a written report, so they often made their reports orally to the state inspector (Report 35, 564–565). In other cases, the reports were not sent to the Welfare Ministry headquarters (Report 34, 381; Report 36). A former inspector said he used the social work regulations that gave the guidelines, but he mentioned a lack of regulatory tools and knowledge.[12] Another former inspector explained: "The role was not structured, and you were thrown into the water... I mainly based on my experience."[13]

During the second half of the 1980s, guides for inspectors were published by the Northern and Haifa districts of the Welfare Ministry and by ELCA[14] (Inspector Guide 1985, 1989) to define the inspector's role. The 1989 guide included eighteen activities, including conveying ministry policies to the services, advising, initiating new programs and services, collecting data, approving budgets, and participating in building the yearly work program. Only three mention supervision and inspection (Inspector Guide 1989, 23–24).

In the 1980s, there were more demands to account for the outcomes of care, to visit facilities more frequently, and to identify the targets of the treatments. The inspectors were required to collect the data and assess the efficiency of the services provided (Reports 32, 34, 38). For example, in the field of rehabilitation, inspectors were asked to track the outcomes of programs to assess their efficiency and the lessons learned from their operation (Report 32, 380). Another change from the 1970s was a move to "blame" the inspectors.

### The 1990s: Widening the gap

The 1990s reflected the challenge and complexity of working in a multi-organizational environment. During this period, government services were contracted out to NGOs; 800 worked with the Welfare Ministry. The focus shifted to contracts, and these became regulatory tools (Labor and Welfare Ministry Committee Report 1997, 11). The Comptroller explained that contracts should clearly define the services and should focus on the efficiency and economy in resource spending, the real and up to date rate of services, and the quality of services. However, many services had no contract at all. For one service, a third of the institutions had no contract (72 out of 210). Similarly, two programs supplying childcare services and services for intellectually disabled people had no valid contracts at the time of the Comptroller's audit (Report 41, 418). Clearly, there was a gap between expectations and reality.

There was some progress in regulation and inspection methods. For example, inspectors visited facilities more often, and there was an attempt to standardize their reports (Report 43, 468). A major advancement was the introduction of the RAF[15] (Regulation, Assessment, Follow-up) method developed in 1987 by the JDC-Brookdale Organization and the Health Ministry for Services to the Elderly and dedicated to the continuous improvement of the quality of care. An outside firm assisted the Welfare Ministry with implementing it (Report 46, 510–11; Labor and Welfare Ministry Committee Report 1997). This method was developed over the years by the Welfare Ministry and JDC-Brookdale and expanded to other services (see Zemach-Marom 2008; Hovav 1998). While it received positive feedback (Hovav 1998, Labor and Welfare Ministry Committee Report 1997, Spiro, Shimon, and Daphna Fromer 2010; Lahat and Talit 2015), its implementation proved demanding (Lahat and Talit 2015), especially because it required a lot of resources to adjust the method to fit all the services (Labor and Welfare Ministry Committee Report 1997). One interviewee said that while it was a useful and simple tool at the beginning, it became more complex; the professionals themselves did not understand some of the demands, making it less effective.[16] Another inspector said, "Friendly tools for gathering information were not developed [and] the RAF is not friendly."[17]

While there was an effort to develop regulations, the demands rose. New populations had new needs, and services became multidimensional. For example, services for those addicted to alcohol were provided by the Welfare Ministry, together with the Ministry of Health, the Social Insurance Institution, and two NGOs. It was hard to coordinate and articulate the division of responsibilities, especially given the continuing lack of data and regulations (Report 44, 544–7). The Comptroller still requested assessments of the needs, outcomes, quality of care, and efficiency and underscored the need to develop comprehensive regulations to ensure services reached their targets (e.g. Report 50, 495–96). However, some argued that the inspection of welfare services should be of the work process and its standards, not of the treatment outcomes (Labor and Welfare Ministry Committee Report 1997, 11).

There was a tendency in the Welfare Ministry to create committees to deal with the new demands, such as "The Public Council for Promoting the Services of the Blind" (Report 50, 486–87), "The Committee for Complaints against the Services for People with Intellectual Developmental Disabilities" (Report 43, 467), and "The Committee on the Role of Inspection" (Labor and Welfare Ministry Committee Report 1997; Hovav 1998). There were also efforts to go to private firms or NGOs for advice and research (e.g. Report 46, 511, 41). Around 20 percent of the inspectors were outsourced (Labor and Welfare Ministry Committee Report 1997). The Comptroller regarded this trend as problematic, particularly when it involved supervision (Report 49, 295). Yet it was challenging to recruit inspectors (e.g. Report 49, 295; Labor and Welfare Ministry Committee Report 1997, 20).

Some of the deficits persisted, including the lack of clarity on the roles of the inspectors, the lack of inspection tools, the lack of guidance or data, and to a lesser degree, the problem of licensing. Furthermore, relationships between managers of the home care facilities and the inspectors were problematic, with tensions emerging between the main office and the regions (Report 41, 541; Reports 46, 48, 50; Report 44, 551–52; Report 42, 468–72; Report 43, 465–69; Reports 46, 48, 49; Labor and Welfare Ministry Committee Report 1997).

At the end of the 1990s, there was an increasing emphasis on the need to supervise NGOs (Report 50, 495) and the need to define the inspector's duties of evaluation and enforcement (Labor and Welfare Ministry Committee Report 1997, 16), but this did not lead to profound change (Hovav 1998).

## 2000–2010: Awareness

In the first decade of the new millennium, the Comptroller reports reflect more awareness of three aspects: 1) a lack of policy, 2) a lack of sophisticated regulation, and 3) a challenge to ameliorate long-standing deficits that needed to be resolved. By this point, it was clear that the privatization trends demanded new developments in inspection (Ahdut et al. 2007).

First, there was a move to a macro perspective and a clear understanding of the need for policy to cover the involvement of other sectors. The Comptroller referred to the government's decision in April 1992 to transfer some services to nongovernmental bodies, based on the findings of the Koversky Committee.

Conditions included the following: the move could not limit the government's authority or its ability to supervise; the services should be handled in a business-like manner; the quality of the services must not decline; and the transfer must demonstrate both efficiency and flexibility. However, the Comptroller refers to the fact that in the Welfare Ministry the outsourcing process was not fully explored before it was pursued (Report 55, 752–3). It is also interesting to note that two decades before, the Comptroller had suggested outsourcing some ser-vices to other sectors (Report 35, 573). The Welfare Ministry established a pri-vatization unit in 1998, but it did not have a meaningful effect and was shut down three years later (Report 55, 753). Furthermore, the Welfare Ministry estab-lished other teams and committees, but the Comptroller maintained that the exploration of the pros and cons of the outsourcing process was insufficient (Report 55, 753–4).

Second, regulations needed to reflect more sophistication in the current multi-organization arena. For example, the Comptroller criticized the depart-ment for people with intellectual developmental disabilities. While there was progress from previous years, there was no structured visitation plan, and inspec-tors did not use a standardized report (Report 55, 730). Another example was the implementation of the RAF method, which, while becoming dominant, was not yet used by all services; nor was it used for benchmarking (Report 55, 730). In 2009, the government made the decision to implement it in all services (Steering Committee 2012). In the area of contracts, the Comptroller called for measura-ble quality outcomes, the implementation of incentive mechanisms, and the reduction of risk by using several suppliers, not just one (Report 55, 748). All these examples represent demands for regulation.

Third, deficits were growing. The Comptroller continued to highlight deficits in basic regulation, knowledge, workforce, and inspection, echoing comments made years before. In a 2007 policy paper on inspection, a group of high-level employees said they found it hard to aggregate data on inspectors in a reliable way (Ahdut et al. 2007, 12). These issues had become increasingly problematic because as demands for regulation grew, resources shrank. Between 1995 and 2004, in some units that were explored by the Comptroller, the number of posi-tions for planning, management, and supervision dropped by 16 percent. For example, the Youth Protection Authority saw a 65 percent increase in the number of service users and a 56 percent rise in the number of organizations supplying those services. However, there was also a 31 percent reduction in the workforce responsible for managerial planning and inspections (Report 55, 756). In 2008, the Comptroller referred to supervision at the district level: although the services and the complexity of the problems had increased, the scale of the inspection was not extended accordingly (Report 59, 932).

## 2011–2017: Tipping point

In many respects, these more recent years reflected the same trends as the previous decade, but different external factors affected the regulatory space. Israel joined the OECD; this offered new knowledge, generated new[18] pressure from the central government to improve regulations (Steering Committee 2012, 4), and some cases were brought to judicial review.[19] However, two emphases are important to note.

The first is the ongoing expansion of the fields of services to include new populations and increase the services offered (Steering Committee 2012). Many of the new services are multidisciplinary and involve different governmental ministries, sectors, and community groups. For example, "The National Program for Children and Youth at Risk" included five ministries as well as other organizations, and was implemented at the local level, making the role of the inspectors even more challenging (Report 62, 899). Another example was centers for children experiencing sexual assault or violence; these involved the education and health ministries as well as the police (Report 62, 1157–1159).

The second emphasis was on the growing gaps in implementation. While there were improvements in the regulatory policy, there were differences among the units. Some had implemented the more sophisticated RAF method (Report 65, 1200), while others lacked the basic processes of regulation, instructions, documentation, and systematic follow-up (Report 62, 1157–59; Report 67, 760). The opening words of a Welfare Ministry steering committee report on the role of inspectors refer to the problems: "However, it seems that this effort did not bring about a fundamental change and alleviation of the root issues" (Steering Committee 2012, 4). Furthermore, the years of a growing divide between the demands on the regulatory system and the ability to meet those demands led, in some cases, to hostile working relationships (e.g., Reports 59, 934; Report 65, 1204; Labor and Welfare Ministry Committee Report 1997). The 2017 Comptroller's Report (Report 67, 756) referred to the Welfare Ministry's intention to create a new department to deal with audits and inspections, and in 2018 the government did establish a new unit, "The Administration for Quality, Inspection and Supervision," aimed at developing a regulatory framework to handle the deficits.[20]

## Discussion and Conclusion

This article explores the changes in the Israeli Welfare Ministry's role as a regulator in the field of personal social services. Throughout the years, various reasons have been suggested for the deficits in regulation in this field, including a lack of urgency; a lack of a general, systematic, and macro perspective; a resistance to change; a lack of maturation, stability or leadership; and a lack of focus on the interests of the actors (Steering Committee 2012, 4; Hovav 1998, Lahat and Talit 2015). However, the preceding exploration of the temporal changes and the use of the theoretical concept of an "expectations-abilities gap" exposes a more nuanced picture. Arguably, both external expectations and inside abilities affect the Welfare Ministry's ability to fulfil its regulatory role.

Three main regulatory spaces can be identified in the Israeli case. The first space emerged in the 1970s. At this time, the Welfare Ministry was occupied with building its organizational structure. Given this stage of the Ministry's development, there were no high expectations of its role as a regulator, and the level of implementation of regulatory tools was low. While the Comptroller expressed the need for further development and stressed the responsibility of the Welfare Ministry, it was apparent that the Ministry was in a building process. The tone on NGO regulation was different, not reflecting a pressing regulatory deficit, and the inspectors were not blamed for the regulatory lack. The gap between expectations and capabilities was relatively small and the regulatory space was underdeveloped (A in Table 1).

The second regulatory space included the 1980s and 1990s. In these decades, Israel experienced trends of privatization and outsourcing influenced by the trends of New-Public Management reforms, together with an economic crisis that led to the creation of a stabilization plan in 1985 (Benish 2008; Mandelkern and Paz-Fuchs 2018). Therefore, while these two decades showed a growing demand for sophisticated regulation, a managerial trend dominated; for example, the emphasis was on efficiency and economy in resource spending in contracts and on outcomes measurements. The Welfare Ministry explored and developed different managerial and regulatory tools, including the RAF method. It improved its regulatory abilities but in a fragmented way that did not incorporate a holistic perspective of the Ministry as a regulator. It is important to note that the privatization of the social services in Israel was not accompanied by a public debate and was mainly guided by the Finance Ministry (Benish 2008). Therefore, the regulatory role of the Welfare Ministry was not high on the public agenda. These decades can be described as an incremental regulatory space (B in Table 1).

The 2000s onward reflect a third regulatory space, with increased expectations of the Welfare Ministry. While the social spending as a percentage of the GDP in Israel has remained relatively low (OECD 2020), since the mid-2000s the Welfare Ministry's budget has grown noticeably, as has its involvement with NGOs (Gal and Madhala 2016). Furthermore, other forces in the central government, the OECD, and the public protest of summer 2011 that led to the creation of the Trajtenberg Committee (Lahat and Sher-Hadar 2015) have begun to emphasize the importance of the regulatory role of the Welfare Ministry, reflected in a much clearer demand to build an encompassing regulatory policy. The demands for regulation have grown, and it is clearer that the ongoing lack of capabilities is acute. Throughout the first two decades of the new millennium, there has been a dramatic gap between expectations and implementation in a relatively static regulatory space (C in Table 1), one that the Welfare Ministry aims to change.

This study makes several important contributions. First, it makes a theoretical contribution by identifying the kinds of gaps that may be created in the RWS, more specifically those between a society's expectations of a government ministry and the ministry's ability to meet those expectations. The study's perspective adds to the implementation literature (Hogwood and Gunn 1984; Hill and Hupe 2002; Ongaro and Valotti 2008) and connects it to the RWS literature. While ideal situations are unlikely to exist, the typology offers a lens through which to examine changes in government ministries' regulatory role while continuing to differentiate them from "regulatory agencies" (Christensen and Lægreid 2006).

Second, the study follows changes in the Israeli regulatory space over five decades. The use of this type of historical perspective and empirical findings at the mezzo level are less common in the literature. In Israel, the privatization processes created regulatory deficits in other social fields, but personal social services represents an extreme case because a larger share of the activity is based on NGOs (Gal and Madhala 2016) than in other fields, such as education.

Third, the findings may be relevant for social services in other countries. The outsourcing and privatization process in Israel has appeared in many other countries as well (Lethbridge 2019). While in some cases the government established a separate regulatory agency, like the CQC in Britain, elsewhere the ministries remained and had to change their role. Therefore, the theoretical perspective of an expectations-capabilities gap, while considering contextual features (Ongaro and Valotti 2008), can help to identify trends in the regulatory space and the change in the role of ministries more generally. Future work in this direction may strengthen the theoretical and empirical claims offered here.

Fourth, the findings have practical implications. There is a need to invest more in the development of different abilities of the regulators, both the analytical and the operational, as well as in professional legitimation. Some scholars have noted the reluctance of social work professionals to adopt regulatory tools because of a fear of losing their discretion and harming the social and treatment process (Benish, Halevy, and Spiro 2018; Dubois 2019; Lahat and Talit 2015). Thus, research needs to develop a unique expertise that connects the social work profession with regulation to enable the implementation of these new duties. While researchers have suggested some directions (Braithwaite, Makkai, and Braithwaite 2007; Benish, Halevy, and Spiro 2018; Lahat and Sabah 2018), more is needed to improve the regulation of care services.

Finally, society's expectations matter. These expectations put external pressure on ministries and lead to the creation of vibrant regulatory spaces. Therefore, bringing regulation into public debates may cause government ministries to assume a clearer regulatory role under the RWS.

# Appendix

TABLE A1
The list of the the comptroller's reports 1970–2017

| The 1970's | The report number/year | Topics covered |
|---|---|---|
| 1 | Report 21 – 1970 | Assistance to Bedouin communities, payments for children in boarding schools |
| 2 | Report 22 - 1971 | The organizational structure of the ministry with an emphasis on supervision |
| 3 | Report 23 – 1972 | Juvenile delinquency prevention and treatment of teenage delinquents, The Rehabilitation Service for youth at risk, The Youth Protection Authority |
| 4 | Report 24 - 1973 | Emergency shelters under the authority of the Ministry of Labor and Welfare, the foundation for vocational rehabilitation center for people with disabilities, the foundation for the management of supportive care institutions |
| 5 | Report 25 - 1974 | The Department of Public Institutions, living facilities licensing |
| 6 | Report 26 - 1975 | The Youth Protection Authority, social services and welfare for senior citizens, supervision over local social services departments |
| 7 | Report 27 - 1976 | Centers for the blind, the main foundation for promoting and developing placement services |
| 8 | Report 28 - 1977 | The youth at risk rehabilitation service, juvenile probation service |
| 9 | Report 29 - 1978 | Volunteering unit |
| 10 | Report 30 - 1979 | Internal audit of the Ministry Supervision over living facilities |
| The 1980's | | |
| 11 | Report 31 – 1980 | Services for youth at risk |
| 12 | Report 32 – 1981 | Social rehabilitation, rehabilitation services |
| 13 | Report 34 – 1983 | Child and youth services |
| 14 | Report 35 – 1984 | The Youth Protection Authority and living facilities under the Ministry of Labor and Welfare |
| 15 | Report 36 – 1985 | Services for senior citizens, implementation of The Youth Law (Treatment and Protection) |
| 16 | Report 37 – 1986 | Addressing the problem of drug use and distribution, community work and neighborhood rehabilitation services |

(continued)

**TABLE A1 (CONTINUED)**

| The 1980's | The report number/year | Topics covered |
|---|---|---|
| 17 | Report 38 – 1987 | Civil Welfare Services |
| 18 | Report 39 – 1988 | Centers for the blind, operation of daycare centers for children |
| 19 | Report 40 – 1989 | Elder care services, supportive care centers under the authority of the Division for the Care of People with Intellectual Developmental Disabilities |
| **The 1990's** | | |
| 20 | Report 41 – 1990 | The Ministry's contacts with non-profit organizations |
| 21 | Report 42 – 1991 | Distribution of relief goods to the needy by nonprofit aid organizations, the treatment for battered women |
| 22 | Report 43 – 1992 | Adoption of children at risk, supervision of supportive care centers for people with intellectual developmental disabilities |
| 23 | Report 44 – 1993 | System of treatment for sufferers of alcohol abuse |
| 24 | Report 45 – 1994 | Employment of people with disabilities, youth rehabilitation – "Miftanim" |
| 25 | Report 46 – 1995 | Issues regarding the supervision and licensing of nursing homes for the elderly |
| 26 | Report 47 – 1996 | Treatment of youth and young adults, outside-the-home living arrangements for handicapped people and people with disabilities: regulations for management and supervision |
| 27 | Report 48 – 1997 | Nursing homes for the elderly, outside-the-home living arrangements in foster families |
| 28 | Report 49 – 1998 | The Department of Public Institutions, emergency centers for treatment of children and their parents: regulations for management and supervision |
| 29 | Report 50 – 1999 | The treatment of senior citizens by the local authorities, services for the blind |
| **The 2000's** | | |
| 30 | Report 51 – 2000 | Budgeting social services for local authorities, international adoption, The Youth Protection Authority's living facilities |
| 31 | Report 52 – 2001 | Integrating people with disabilities into the community, The Division for the Care of People with Intellectual Developmental Disabilities, integrating people with disabilities into the workforce |
| 32 | Report 54 – 2003 | Follow-up findings: addressing violence between spouses |
| 33 | Report 55 – 2004 | Acquiring social services |

*(continued)*

## TABLE A1 (CONTINUED)

| The 2000's | The report number/year | Topics covered |
|---|---|---|
| 34 | Report 57 – 2006 | Aspects of the employment of people with disabilities in "Keren" – the Network of Professional Diagnosis and Rehabilitation Centers, follow-up findings: acquiring social services, follow-up findings: budgeting social services for local authorities - inequality |
| 35 | Report 58 – 2007 | Juvenile probation service, treatment of juvenile delinquents |
| 36 | Report 59 – 2008 | The Youth Protection Authority at the Ministry of Labor and Welfare, follow-up findings: housing arrangements for people with intellectual developmental disabilities - privatization processes and control regulations |
| **2010-2017** | | |
| 37 | Report 61 – 2010 | Aspects of elder care and the needs of senior citizens |
| 38 | Report 62 – 2011 | Situation overview: The National Program for Youth and Children at Risk, treatment of people with autism |
| 39 | Report 63 – 2011 | Course of treatment for single-parent families, work arrangements for planning committees for treatment and evaluation of children at risk, regulation of rehabilitation services the state purchases from outsourced service providers |
| 40 | Report 64 – 2013 | Governmental activities for the integration of people with disabilities in the workforce, bringing children to Israel by non-parents |
| 41 | Report 65 – 2014 | Aspects of treatment of minors who are survivors of sexual assault or violence, physical aspects of outside-the-home living arrangements |
| 42 | Report 67 – 2016 | Youth and children at risk in boarding schools under the authority of the Ministry of Labor and Welfare |
| 43 | Report 68 – 2017 | The support services of the Ministry of Labor and Welfare |

# Notes

1. https://www.mevaker.gov.il/En/About/Pages/yesodot.aspx.
2. https://www.cqc.org.uk/share-your-experience-finder?referer=promoblock.
3. See also www.cqc.org.uk.
4. https://www.mevaker.gov.il/En/About/Pages/yesodot.aspx.
5. https://www.knesset.gov.il/laws/special/eng/basic9_eng.htm.
6. Ibid; emphasis added.
7. https://www.mevaker.gov.il/En/About/Pages/yesodot.aspx.
8. The information from the interview supported the analysis and interpretation, but it focused less on the specific time frame.
9. We started with forty-seven reports.

10. Between June 2013 and December 2014.

11. While regulation inside governance focuses mainly on regulating suppliers from other sectors, in Israel the infrastructure of the regional inspectors includes the services provided by the local authorities. In the article, I focused mainly on the regulation of the NGOs.

12. Interviewee 2, inspector 12/6/2019.

13. Interviewee 4, inspector 1/8/2019.

14. ELCA is the Hebrew name of an association for the development and promotion of workforce in the social services in Israel, also known as JDC Institute for Leadership and Governance founded by Joint Israel and supported by the Israeli government and Joint Israel.

15. The RAF method is based on assessing tracers that can help to evaluate the improvement in care. It includes different stages that are part of a regulation cycle, among them, gathering data on the individual level: the resident, as well as data from family and caregiver and regarding the institutions. Based on needs assessments and discussions, steps for improvement are being implemented in a continuous cycle and based on a defined time frame (see Zemach-Marom 2008).

16. Interviewee 2, inspector 12/6/2019.

17. Interviewee 5, inspector 11/8/2019.

18. Interviewee 1, inspector 29/5/2019.

19. Interviewee 3, inspector 4/7/2019.

20. https://www.gov.il/he/Departments/units/molsa-quality-supervision-examination-administration.

# References

Ahdut, Avner, Shabi Aharon, Shaul Galit, Eltos Devora, Ben-Lavi Dina, Daskal Haya, Neuberger Chana, Azulay Yoram, Yoel Iitzhak, Rozenbawm, Nava et al. 2007. *Policy paper: The regional inspection in the welfare and social services ministry.* Jerusalem: Mandel Institute. (in Hebrew)

Auerbach, Gedalia. 2007. *The relationship of local government and the third sector in Israel* (in Hebrew) (Position Paper). Jerusalem: Knesset Research and Information Center and Hebrew University School of Social Work.

Ayres, Ian, and John Braithwaite. 1992. *Responsive regulation.* Oxford: Oxford University Press.

Baldwin, Robert, Martin Cave, and Martin Lodge. 2012. *Understanding regulation: Theory, strategy, and practice.* Oxford: Oxford University Press.

Bali, Azad S., Giliberto Capano, and M. Ramesh. 2019. Anticipating and designing for policy effectiveness. *Policy and Society* 38 (1): 1–13.

Ben-Simhom, M., and H. Gorn. 2016. Selected data of the target population of the Welfare Ministry and its budget. In *Ministry of Welfare and social services.* Available from https://www.molsa.gov.il/CommunityInfo/SocialServicesReview/Pages/Reviewofsocialservicesin2016.aspx.

Benish, Avishai. 2018. The privatization of social services in Israel. The privatization of Israel, 173–200. New York, NY: Palgrave Macmillan.

Benish, Avishai, Dana Halevy, and Shimon Spiro. 2018. Regulating social welfare services: Between compliance and learning. *International Journal of Social Welfare* 27 (3): 226–35.

Black, Julia. 2002. Regulatory conversations. *Journal of Law and Society* 29 (1): 163–96.

Braithwaite, John. 2006. Responsive regulation and developing economies. *World Development* 34:884–98.

Braithwaite, John, Toni Makkai, and Valerie Braithwaite V. 2007. *Regulation aged care.* Cheltenham, UK: Edward Elgar.

Christensen, Tom, and Per Lægreid, eds. 2006. Agencification and regulatory reforms. In *Autonomy and regulation. Coping with agencies in the modern state,* 8–49. Cheltenham, UK: Edward Elgar Publishing.

Corbin, Juliet, and Anselm Strauss. 1990. Grounded theory research: Procedures, canons and Evaluation. *Qualitative Sociology* 13 (1): 3–21.

Downe, James, and Steve J. Martin. 2007. Regulation inside government: Processes and impacts of inspection of local public services. *Policy & Politics* 35 (2): 215–32.

Dubois, Vincent. 2019. Welfare fraud inspectors between standardization and discretion. In *Inspectors and enforcement at the front line of government*, eds. Steven Van de Walle and Nadine Raaphorst, 167–86. New York, NY: Palgrave Macmillan.

Ebimobowei, Appah. 2010. An evaluation of audit expectation gap: Issues and challenges. *International Journal of Economic Development Research and Investment* 1 (2): 129–41.

Elkomy, Shimaa, Graham Cookson, and Simon Jones. 2019. Cheap and dirty: The effect of contracting out cleaning on efficiency and effectiveness. *Public Administration Review* 79 (2): 193–202.

Freeman, Jody, and Jim Rossi. 2011. Agency coordination in shared regulatory space. *Harvard Law Review* 125:1131–1209.

Furness, Sheila. 2009. A hindrance or a help? The contribution of inspection to the quality of care in homes for older people. *British Journal of Social Work* 39:488–505.

Gal, H., and A. Ben-Mordechai. 2017. *The welfare ministry set the bar (RAF): From a service supplier to a regulator. Methods of regulation in the out of home services* (in Hebrew). Jerusalem: The Federman School, The Hebrew University, Jerusalem.

Gal, John, and Shavit Madhala. 2016. Public spending on social welfare. In *State of the nation report: Society economy and policy in Israel 2016*, ed. Avi Weiss, 233–60 (in Hebrew). Jerusalem: Taub Center.

Gilardi, Fabrizio, Jacint Jordana, and David Levi-Faur. 2006. Regulation in the age of globalization: The diffusion of regulatory agencies across Europe and Latin America. In *Privatisation and market development: Global movements in public policy ideas*, ed. Graeme Hodge, 127–47. Cheltenham, UK: Edward Elgar.

Goodship, Jo, Kavin Jacks, Matt Gummerson, Judith Lathlean, and Stephen Cope. 2004. Modernising regulation or regulating modernisation? The public, private and voluntary interface in adult social care. *Public Policy and Administration* 19 (2): 13–27.

Gunningham, Neil, and Darren Sinclair. 1998. Designing smart regulation. In *Economic aspects of environmental compliance assurance. OECD global forum on sustainable development*. Available from http://www.oecd.org/dataoecd/18/39/33947759.pdf.

Haber, Hanan. 2017. Rise of the regulatory welfare state? Social regulation in utilities in Israel. *Social Policy & Administration* 51 (3): 442–63.

Hill, Michael, and Peter Hupe. 2002. *Implementing public policy: Governance in theory and in practice*. London: SAGE Publications.

Hogwood, W. Brian and Gunn, A. Lewis. 1984. *Policy analysis for the real world*. New York, NY: Oxford University Press.

Hood, Christopher, Colin Scott, Oliver James, George Jones, and Toni Travers. 1999. *Regulation inside government: Waste-watcher, quality police and sleaze-busters*. Oxford: Oxford University Press.

Hovav, M. 1998. *The supervision of social services in Israel. Development, practices and model* (in Hebrew). Tel-Aviv: Chrikover.

Howlett, Michael, Ishani Mukherjee, and Jun Jie Woo. 2015. From tools to toolkits in policy design studies: the new design orientation towards policy formulation research. *Policy & Politics* 43 (2): 291–311.

Inspector Guide. 1985. State of Israel the labour and welfare ministry. Haifa and North district - The Labor and Welfare Ministry the state of Israel (in Hebrew).

Inspector Guide. 1989. ELCA- association for the development and promotion of manpower in the social services in Israel. JDC Institute for Leadership and Governance Founded by the Joint Israel and supported by the Israeli government and Joint Israel. (in Hebrew).

Jordana, Jacint, and David Sancho. 2004. Regulatory designs, institutional constellations and the study of the regulatory state. In *The politics of regulation: Institutions and regulatory reforms for the age of governance*, eds. Jordana Jacint and David Levi-Faur, 296–319. Cheltenham, UK: Edward Elgar Publishing.

Kadushin, Alfred, and Daniel Harkness. 2014. *Supervision in social work*. New York, NY: Columbia University Press.

Katan, Yoseph. 1996. *Personal social services: Trends and contributions* (in Hebrew). Tel Aviv: Ramot.

Klenk Tanja. 2020. Street-level bureaucrats as market regulators – The case of the German long-term care market. *The ANNALS of the American Academy of Political and Social Science* (this volume).

The Labor and Welfare Ministry. Committee Report. 1997. A summary of the committee work and suggestion for discussion prepared to the management on the subject of the roles of the inspection in the Ministry of Labor and Welfare. (in Hebrew)

Lahat, Lihi, and Yakutiel Sabah. 2018. Adapted regulation as a possible model for personal social services: Theoretical and practical aspects (in Hebrew). *Society and Welfare* (38): 149–74.

Lahat, Lihi, and Gal Talit. 2015. Regulation of personal social services: The Israeli experience. *Social Policy & Administration* 49:335–55.

Lahat, Lihi, and Neta Sher-Hadar. 2015. Public value failure and the 2011 social protests in Israel (in Hebrew). *Journal of Welfare and Social Security Studies* 96:29–53.

Lethbridge, Jane. 2019. Project PESSIS+: Promoting employers' social services in social dialogue. Available from: https://www.epsu.org/sites/default/files/article/files/Final-European-Report-PESSIS%2B-Project-26.06.19-EN.pdf.

Levi-Faur, David. 2011. Regulation and regulatory governance. *Handbook on the Politics of Regulation* 1 (1): 1–25.

Levi-Faur, David. 2014. The welfare state: A regulatory perspective. *Public Administration* 92:599–614.

Levi-Faur, David, and Avishai Benish. 2020. The reassertion of the regulatory welfare state: A preface. *The ANNALS of the American Academy of Political and Social Science* (this volume).

Madhala-Brik, Shavit, and John Gal. 2016. The outsourcing of welfare services: Trends and changes. *State of the Nation Report: Society, Economy, and Policy*. Jerusalem: Taub Center for Social Policy Studies in Israel.

Majone, Giandomenico. 1994. The rise of the regulatory state in Europe. *West European Politics* 17 (3): 77–101.

Mandelkern, Ronen. 2012. The politics of partial privatization of social services in Israel: The case of housing for people with intellectual disabilities (in Hebrew). *Social Security Journal* 90:121–53.

Mandelkern, Ronen, and Amir Paz-Fuchs. 2018. Privatizing Israel: An introduction. In *The privatization of Israel: The withdrawal of state responsibility*, eds. Amir Paz-Fuchs, Ronen Mandelkern, and Itzhak Galnoor, 1–18. New York, NY: Palgrave Macmillan.

Marthinsen, Edgar. 2019. Neoliberalisation, the social investment state and social work. *European Journal of Social Work* 22 (2): 350–61.

May, Peter J. 2007. Regulatory regimes and accountability. *Regulation & Governance* 1 (1): 8–26.

McBeth, Mark K., Elizabeth A. Shanahan, Ruth J. Arnell, and Paul L. Hathaway. 2007. The intersection of narrative policy analysis and policy change theory. *Policy Studies Journal* 35 (1): 87–108.

McLaughlin, Kenneth. 2007. Regulation and risk in social work: The general social care council and the social care register in context. *British Journal of Social Work* 37: 1263–1277.

Munro, Eileen. 2004. The impact of audit on social work practice. *British Journal of Social Work* 34:1075–1095.

OECD. 2020. Social spending (indicator). Available from https://www.oecd-ilibrary.org/social-issues-migration-health/social-spending/indicator/english_7497563b-en.

Ongaro, Edoardo, and Giovanni Valotti. 2008. Public management reform in Italy: Explaining the implementation gap. *International Journal of Public Sector Management* 21 (2): 174–204.

Scott, Colin. 2001. Analysing regulatory space: fragmented resources and institutional design. *Public Law* summer:283–305.

Sher-Hadar, Neta. 2019. Pick and roll: Expanded roles for a state auditor. *Financial Accountability & Management* 33 (3): 229–43.

Shikdar, Mohammad Alam, Omar Faruk, and Mohammad Mojahid Hossain Chowdhury. 2018. Reducing the audit expectation gap: A model for Bangladesh perspective. *International Journal of Management, Accounting & Economics* 5 (3): 169–80.

Spiro, Shimon, and Daphna Fromer. 2010. Quality control in the era of privatization: Examination of the RAF method in boarding schools (in Hebrew). *Social Security* 84:105–27.

Stake, Robert E. 2010. *Qualitative research - studying how things work*. New York, NY: The Guilford Press.

Steering Committee. 2012. *The inspector as the initiator of regulation in the welfare and social services ministry: Formulation framework and suggestions for implementation*. Jerusalem: The Ministry of Welfare and Social Services.

Van de Walle, Steven, and Nadine Raaphorst. 2019. Introduction: The social dynamics of daily inspection work. In *Inspectors and enforcement at the front Line of government*, 1–10. Cheltenham, UK: Palgrave Macmillan.

Yin, Robert K. 2003. *Applications of case study research*. 2nd ed. Thousand Oaks, CA: SAGE Publications.

Yanai, U. 2006. *The Welfare Law, 5718-1958: Is it really the basis and guarantee for the population's welfare?* (in Hebrew). Jerusalem: Hebrew University, The Paul Baerwald School of Social Work and Social Welfare.

Zemach-Marom, Tamar. 2008. RAF method in after-school programs in Israel. In *Research for action: Cross-national perspective on connecting knowledge policy and practice for children*, eds. R. Chaskin and J. Rosenfeld. Jerusalem: Myers-JDC-Brookdale Institute–Leader in Applied Social Research.

# Is Service Quality a Driver of the Regulatory Welfare State? Policies for Health Services in Germany and France

By
RENATE REITER

The article analyzes the design and development of health services in Germany and France—two countries with similar welfare states but with striking differences in their national regulatory styles. Using these comparative cases, I show how the interplay of long-term institutional factors and short-term political factors shaped the establishment and development of these regulatory welfare states' (RWS) social services. Specifically, I argue that the discovery of *service quality* in the 1990s had the potential to accelerate RWS development. In Germany, characterized by a corporatist state tradition and a cooperative regulatory style, the political debate on quality (either as a parameter of competition or as a concept for the professional consolidation of service production) had a greater influence on the design of the national quality regulation system (goals, instruments, processes, institutions) than in France, which is characterized by a state-centered Napoleonic tradition and a directive regulatory style.

*Keywords:* regulatory welfare state; regulatory style; health care; quality policy; Germany; France

In the light of growing pressure from globalization and demographic and social change, the "mature" welfare state has been the object of "profound transformation" (Hemerijck 2013, 27ff.) since the late 1980s. A whole body of literature has developed around this theme, arguing that this transformation went hand-in-hand with a move toward the containment of public spending in different sectors; the privatization and/or re-commodification of certain functions, infrastructure, and costs (van Kersbergen and Vis 2014, 9); and the "dismantling" of public

Renate Reiter is a senior fellow in the Department of Political Sciences at the FernUniversität in Hagen, Germany. She specializes in comparative policy analysis, particularly from a Franco-German perspective; public regulation in the welfare state; and public administration. She focuses on the political fields of social and health policy.

Correspondence: renate.reiter@fernuni-hagen.de

DOI: 10.1177/0002716220962407

policies (Jordan, Bauer, and Green-Pedersen 2013). While—driven by the international spread of the New Public Management (NPM) model—cost containment and privatization have indeed become commonly used reform approaches (Hemerijck 2013, 126ff.), the idea of policy dismantling in the sense of deregulation has not proven to be fully convincing. On the contrary, since the beginning of the 1990s, we observe intensified regulatory activity of the welfare state so as to achieve its social ends (Leisering and Mabbett 2011; Levi-Faur 2014; Benish, Haber, and Eliahou 2017). This development is described as the rise of the regulatory welfare state (RWS) (Levi-Faur 2014).

This article explores the development of the RWS in social services. The available literature on the RWS deals primarily with administrative regulation ("output" and "outcome"; Guidi, Guardiancich, and Levi-Faur 2020, 8–9), that is, the implementation and application of [new] welfare state regulations in certain service areas and countries (cf. Benish, Halevy and Spiro 2018). By contrast, the question of which factors ("input") (Guidi, Guardiancich, and Levi-Faur 2020, 8–9) influence the formation and shaping of the RWS in a concrete policy field has not been addressed as much in the literature (Rothstein, Paul, and Demeritt 2020). Accordingly, this article takes health services and the installation of a structure to regulate the quality of such services as an example of regulation of social services. Since the beginning of the 1990s, political and public attention on quality in health care delivery, especially hospital care, has increased in many welfare states and has favored government measures to regulate quality. This pressure to regulate quality was a response to recurring medical scandals, such as those involving contaminated blood reserves or damaged breast implants, and connected to the idea that (better) control of service quality could reduce costs.

This article employs a broad definition of the term *regulation*—regulation as the purposeful, goal-driven use of rules, standards, and other regulatory tools by government in order to influence and—in case—to sanction the behavior of [public, private, charitable] actors (Windholz and Hodge 2012, 217–218; Levi-Faur 2014, 9–10). I start from the thesis that regulation in the welfare state can first and foremost be understood against the backdrop of the existence of normatively embedded and institutionally solidified national styles of regulation (Richardson, Gustafsson, and Jordan 1982; Vogel 1986; Vogel and Kagan 2004; Painter and Peters 2010; Guidi, Guardiancich, and Levi-Faur 2020). These long-term factors that shape the RWS might interact with short-lived factors (e.g., political interests) in moments of change to the welfare state's spectrum of tasks, that is, in moments when state actors are exposed to potentially politically controversial choices about how to conceptualize state regulatory action.

To study the factors influencing the RWS, we investigate the emergence and development of quality regulation in Germany and France, two continental European conservative welfare states characterized by different state and regulatory traditions (Rothstein, Paul, and Demeritt 2020), from the early 1990s to the present. Specifically, we address the following questions: How do the structures of quality regulation in the field of health and notably hospital care in Germany and France look? How has the development of the new field of quality policy in health and hospital care been shaped by the regulatory traditions and institutions in place in the two countries and how did regulatory tradition interact with other factors during the installation of the RWS? What theoretical conclusions can be drawn from the empirical study?

The article is divided into five sections. In the following theoretical section, I discuss the (changing) significance of the concept of regulation in and for the welfare state and use research on national styles of regulation combined with research on the significance of state tradition for public policymaking as a basis to analyze the RWS. I then retrace the development of health services and hospital quality policies in France and Germany since the early 1990s, before I comparatively discuss the significance of regulatory styles and state traditions in the RWS's handling of the quality challenge. Finally, I summarize my findings and draw conclusions about regulatory theory.

## Theoretical Background and Research Design

### Regulation as a (changing) concept of the welfare state

Until the late 1980s, the welfare state was primarily associated with the task of improving the situation of more needy members of society and/or those directly affected by certain risks by means of direct financial redistribution. In (comparative) research on the welfare state, regulation was conceptualized as a mere "secondary instrument" (Levi-Faur 2014, 6), helping to organize financial (re-) distribution and to formally establish individual or group-related social rights to make them enforceable (Van Kersbergen and Vis 2014, 51–52). Since the late 1980s, this perception has changed. By that time, to cut costs and improve the efficiency of their public administrations, many countries used the internationally spreading NPM-model as a blueprint for reform (with decentralization, privatization of tasks, and the establishment of public service markets as typical elements). Regulation, in this context, became interesting for practitioners and representatives of the state as it allowed for the delegation of public tasks and—at the same time—promised a possibility for the state to retain overarching control over the fulfilment of public functions in different sectors, including welfare. For scholars of (comparative) welfare state research, in turn, regulation became ever more interesting as a mechanism of governance. While some researchers in this context saw a replacement of the welfare state by the regulatory state (cf. Majone 1997), others, who reject this dichotomous perspective, have shown that we are witnessing the rise of the RWS. This is characterized by a "polymorphic" (Levi-Faur 2014, 1) form, whereby regulation as the overarching instrument of state action makes it possible to achieve or modify different socially oriented goals (order, behavioral adjustment, redistribution) by various means (regulatory, fiscal, soft) (Levi-Faur 2014; Windholz and Hodge 2012).

In the context of the provision on social services, the welfare state uses regulation with respect to two goals (Levi-Faur 2014; Benish, Haber, and Eliahou 2017, 316f.). On the one side, regulation serves as an overarching mechanism to ensure that *access* for individuals or groups to social services and rights (traditional and new, financial and human) is socially equitable, that is, universal and equal for all members of society (cf. Leisering and Mabbett 2011; Benish, Haber, and Eliahou 2017). On the other side, it serves to control the *production* of social services through the formulation of generally accepted standards to which social services should conform (Evers et al. 1997) through the setup of mechanisms for monitoring compliance (Benish, Halevy, and Spiro 2017) and through the installation of systems to generate expertise regarding the definition and measurement of standards (Freidson 2001).

How can we understand the RWS's functioning related to its tasks in general and to social service provision in particular? In the analysis of the RWS, the literature on national styles of regulation (Richardson, Gustafsson, and Jordan 1982; Vogel 1986, Vogel and Kagan 2004) and on state and/or administrative traditions (Painter and Peters 2010) are acknowledged as important contributions (Rothstein, Paul, and Demeritt 2020, 25). National styles of regulation are defined as well-practiced ways and means of national governance, that is, of the state's handling of (sectoral) policy problems in exchange with nonstate actors (Richardson, Gustafsson, and Jordan 1982, 12–13). The core assumption of this approach is that there are durable "standard operating procedures" (Richardson, Gustafsson, and Jordan 1982, 2), including preferences of those who design regulatory structures and those who regulate certain policy instruments, in addition to a regular, institutionalized way of structuring the relationship between state and other actors (loose, oriented toward economic regulation, coordinative, directive; cf. Windholz and Hodge 2012) in different sectors or policy fields. National styles of regulation find their roots, first, in the nationally prevailing state and administrative tradition, which is reflected institutionally. In particular, this type of regulation concerns the typical structuring of the relationship between the state and societal actors, the relationship of politics and administration and the distribution of roles between them, the political institutional and legal system, and the role of law in controlling state-public action (Painter and Peters 2010, 6–8). Second, most recent studies on the RWS have emphasized that the normative dimension—that is, the basic idea of the state's role in the order of society, bringing forward different ideas about how to cure social illnesses, to compensate market failures, and to regularly ensure the efficiency of welfare state action—must be considered as an element overarching the institutionalist explanation of the regulatory governance in the welfare state (Rothstein, Paul, and Demeritt 2020, 23, 25).

I suggest that the normatively embedded and institutionally prestructured national style of regulation is highly relevant as a factor on the "input" side (Guidi, Guardiancich, and Levi-Faur 2020, 8) to understand the functioning of the RWS in a certain country under conditions of every day policymaking in a settled field of state action (cf. Rothstein, Paul, and Demeritt 2020). However, when the welfare state's spectrum of tasks is being changed, for example, when a new regulatory task is being added, more short-lived factors such as the influence of interest groups, party-political preferences, or political pressures emerge against the background of certain problem constellations as well as in the shaping of the RWS (Loer, Reiter, and Töller 2014).

To be able to investigate the interaction of these bundles of factors, I concentrate on the relatively young welfare state task of regulating the quality of social services and the compliance with according standards (Beckmann 2009). At first glance, quality as a regulatory objective appears to lie beyond the classic welfare state motives of redistribution, distribution, and of "promoting equality, solidarity and social justice" (Benish, Haber, and Eliahou 2017, 315). Yet a closer look reveals the relevance of quality regulation for the welfare state. So, by looking at the concrete interpretation of quality as a parameter of state action, the normative foundations of the regulating welfare state can be made visible: should quality regulation serve as a corrective of market failures to increase the efficiency of service provision in the social service market? Or should it serve to ensure that providers of social services (can) respect the same high professional standards so as to uphold the welfare state's goal of allowing individuals to access social services of equal(ly high) quality (Barr 2020, 47–71)?

In fact, the structure of quality regulation can open up a gateway for the more or less open "retrenchment" of the welfare state (cf. Hacker 2004). Thus, the creation of a new regulatory structure as the new institutional layer of the RWS raises the question of the extent to which it can actually serve to ensure social equality and equal and consistently high quality of service for all; or to what extent, on the contrary, it opens up a new way for the state to withdraw from previous financial involvement in the area of the relevant social (service) provision (cf. Hacker 2004). Confronted with the need to answer this question, state actors might be exposed to claims of political interests and the issue of how to structure quality regulation might thus become a subject of rather short-lived political debate.

I investigate the establishment of a permanent structure for the regulation of quality in the field of health and, especially, hospital services, concentrating on three central dimensions of this structure that I must conceptualize: the *instruments* (Levi-Faur 2014, 604) chosen to guide the behavior of the providers of health and hospital services, the *institutions* established or changed as a foundation for regulators' action, and the *processes* of quality regulation (Richardson, Gustafsson, and Jordan 1982, 12–13).

## Research design

To explore the interaction of the different factors shaping the RWS in the field of health and hospital services, I compare the evolution of health and hospital quality policies in Germany and France, using a combined sector-type-nation design (cf. Levi-Faur 2006).

I have chosen health care and, particularly, the hospital sector, because doing so affords an opportunity to address the question of how to arrange a stable system of service quality control. Even if such a system did not exist as part of the institutional structure of health policymaking in several Western welfare states until the late 1980s, allowing for universal access of the citizens to adequate, needs-based, high-quality services has been a traditional core promise of the modern "health care state," which emerged at the turn of the nineteenth century

(Moran 2000, 139f.). At the same time, health, and notably hospital, services have always been particularly costly. The health sector has always been the second highest expenditure item in the social budget of many OECD states, alongside pensions (OECD 2019, 2). Ever- rising costs against a backdrop of medical, pharmaceutical, and diagnostic progress have increased political pressure to contain costs or make service production efficient and effective. Thus, the tension between social and economic motives of action has always been present in this sector.

Second, I chose Germany and France as two representatives of the continental European "conservative" welfare state. This type of state is known for its preference of status-preservation (Rothstein, Paul, and Demeritt 2020, 23) combined with residual payments as the foundation of social solidarity based on financial redistribution. Moreover, it is also known for its traditional preference for societal self-help ("subsidiarity"), self-regulation based on the state's framework regulation in view of social illnesses. In Germany, this prevailing normative orientation has brought forward a "culture" of negotiation and of cooperation between state and society actors regarding solutions in different social sectors, including health. In France, on the contrary, such a cooperative culture did not emerge. Rather, France is characterized by a traditionally strong central state ("Napoleonic"), and centralism has been enforced in the field of health in the course of the reforms of the French health care state since the 1990s (Hassenteufel and Palier 2008). Consultation, here, has always been the preferred way to integrate society in public policymaking, and, in turn, the state has been acknowledged as the core keeper of the national public interest.

Third, I chose Germany and France because they have major differences in their nationally prevailing styles of regulation. In Germany, cooperative interaction of state and society actors on each level of government and negotiation-based self-regulation by providers of services (physicians, hospitals) and payers (sickness funds) have traditionally been the rules. In France, in contrast, a strong ("dirigiste") central state that hierarchically intervenes in different fields of public interest prevails (Painter and Peters 2010, 21–22; Klenk and Reiter 2012).

In the following section, using the qualitative method of comparative case study analysis based on the in-depth study of a set of primary documents and secondary literature reviews, I inductively retrace the development of policies regarding health and hospital quality in France and Germany from 1990 onward to the present.

# The Emergence of Health and Hospital Quality Policies in France and Germany

In the health sector, the issue of quality was already being discussed internationally from the 1960s onward, against the backdrop of the spread of the first quality models. Germany and France, however, were among those welfare states in which this topic did not play an explicit role in health policy until the late 1980s or early 1990s, respectively. Both countries were characterized by an unquestioned trust in doctors; their medical integrity and high professionalism was "simply assumed" and implicitly accepted as a guarantee for high service quality (De Pouvourville 1997; Rosenbrock and Gerlinger 2014, 382, 384). Therefore, quality had only been an explicit subject of regulation to this point in areas adjacent to medical care (e.g., medical training, further education and training of medical staff).

This situation began to change from the late 1980s onward in France and, with a time lag, from the late 1990s onward in Germany. By then, several developments came together to address the quality issue (cf. Rosenbrock and Gerlinger 2014, 382):

- First, the publication of various international and national expert reports that pointed to quality deficiencies and, especially in France, the crisis in the health care system triggered by the scandal of contaminated blood reserves in 1984 (De Pouvourville 1997; Minvielle 2013; Rosenbrock and Gerlinger 2014, 382).
- Second, increased political pressure, which arose in both countries, in view of the high public expenditure in this social service area (Rosenbrock and Gerlinger 2014, 220; Soual 2017, 3).
- And, third, a trend toward privatization (Germany) or state-sponsored reforms for marketing and managerialization (France), notably in the hospital sector (Klenk and Reiter 2012).

Quality policies emerged from the late 1980s onward in an "incremental process" of increasing interaction between "interrelated problems, actors, institutions and instruments" (Loer, Reiter, and Toeller 2014, 9). In the course of policy evolution, new structures of quality-related regulation of the national (public, private, charitable) providers of health and hospital services developed.

## Quality-related regulation of health and hospital services in France

In France, the first initiatives to establish a quality policy in the health sector, including a special focus on the hospital sector, came from the political Left. The socialist-led government, which had come into office after the election of François Mitterrand in 1981, systematically linked structural reforms, which were primarily intended to reduce the high cost pressure in the health sector, with the goal of securing and improving the quality of services (Weckert 2014, 83f.). Mitterrand's 1988 election campaign program also referenced service quality. The quality-oriented regulation of service providers—the key argument went—serves to release efficiency resources and thus to prevent further cuts in the social security system that would be harmful for solidarity overall (Weckert 2014, 69). On the basis of this argumentation, the first phase of the development of quality-related regulation was characterized by initiatives to create new institutions that would allow the welfare state to effectively control the quality of service providers. So, the Hospital Reform Act entering into force in 1991 (*Loi no 91-748 du 31 July 1991 portant réforme hospitalière*, *"Plan Évin"*) established the ANDEM (*Agence nationale pour le développement de l'évaluation médicale*) as a private law organization of health professionals placed under the supervision of the French Ministry of Health. It functioned to prepare quality-related studies on therapeutic strategies and medical treatment techniques (Weckert 2014, 93f.). Next the comprehensive health reform of the Gaullist conservative government of Prime Minister Alain Juppé, entering into force in 1996 (*"Réforme Juppé"*), replaced the ANDEM with a newly created public law agency, the ANEAS (*Agence nationale d'accrédition et d'evaluation en santé*), which was directly subordinate to the Ministry of Health; it was to implement and administer a system of hospital accreditation (Weckert 2014, 95). Even though the idea that monitoring the quality of health services (especially in hospitals) should primarily be a task of the health professionals themselves and the state should provide only a regulatory framework was discussed in the formulation of the 1991 law (Minvielle 2013, 89), during this first phase of health quality policy the (welfare) state quickly became a central actor of quality regulation in the health sector.

A second phase of the development of health-related quality policy in France began around 2000. Two aspects were important in this context: first, the idea of professional self-regulation as the original approach to quality regulation (Minvielle 2013, 89) was now abandoned. Toward the end of the 1990s, politicians from all political camps recognized the state's supremacy as a core regulator of quality both in the ambulatory sector as well as in the hospital sector. The state's role ultimately also had to be accepted by interest groups, especially doctor's associations (Weckert 2014, 69, 85–86). Second, a differentiation of the welfare state's regulatory instruments, namely regarding quality control in the hospital sector, could be observed. This included the installation of a system of financial incentives ("pay for performance") as well as a system of blaming and shaming of hospital service providers. Based on this carrot-and-stick approach, the French Ministry of Health has, since 2006, regularly published the results of surveys of the quality of care in certain areas of medical treatment in French hospitals (Minvielle 2013, 89ff.). During this consolidation phase, the initial objective of health and hospital quality policy—which had been formulated by Leftist parties but had been adopted quickly by the conservatives, the latter saying that quality policy could serve to achieve cost savings without giving up the welfare state's access-related goals (Weckert 2014, 69)—was now tacitly abandoned as savings did not materialize (Weckert 2014, 79, 118).

In 2012, with the change in office of the French president from the Gaullist Nicolas Sarkozy to the socialist François Hollande, the policy of quality-based regulation of health and hospital services entered its third and latest phase. Assuring quality of health services is now widely accepted as a major task of the welfare state, and the development of related instruments of social regulation of service providers has become a routine exercise for the French health administration, which has developed its own expertise. Interestingly enough, given the continuing low impact of quality regulation in everyday care (Siciliani, Chalkley, and Gravelle 2017, 108), the French RWS in health care now also strives to actively involve the providers of health and hospital services themselves in regulation, thus softening its "hard" interventionist course vis-à-vis the service providers; the goal to design ultimately effective instruments is now a central one (Ferrua et al. 2015).

Overall, France's policy to develop a structure for the social regulation of health and hospital services is an established field. Its evolution follows its own logic of regulatory expansion in response to the differentiation of expertise. Unlike in the initial phase, the coupling of quality and cost savings is no longer drawn; the apprehension that quality policy might become a leeway for (hidden) welfare state retrenchment is ill-founded. In contrast, the aim to continually improve service quality in view of developing professional standards is a fundamental objective of the RWS in France. Whether this goal can be attained remains open; so far, quality-regulation has contributed to stronger bureaucratic burdens on service provision (Nay et al. 2016, 2240).

## Quality-related regulation of health and hospital services in Germany

In Germany, the development of a distinctive field of quality policy in the health sector, notably regarding hospital services, can be observed from the year 2000 onward. The process started after the quality idea had entered health political debate during the 1990s—like in France—on the initiative of the left-wing parties (Weckert 2014, 73f). Notably, the social democrats in the German parliament (*Bundestag*) argued in favor of quality regulation as a means to save costs in the health sector without having to accept cuts in the actual health care of the population. In addition, quality policy was also interpreted as a way of ensuring consistently high standards of care in a field of service provision that was becoming increasingly complex as a result of privatization (Deutscher Bundestag Plenarprotokoll 15/64 2003, 5458; Deutscher Bundestag Drs. 14/1977, 1f; Deutscher Bundestag Drs. 14/6893).

Supported by an expert report of the German Advisory Council on the Assessment of Developments in the Health Care Sector that pointed to quality deficits in the health sector and to potentially negative effects on quality resulting from measures to marketize the financing of hospitals (introduction of "diagnosis related groups") (SVR 2000/2001, 86f), the social democrat-green federal government proposed the SHI-Healthcare Reform Act in 2000 and the SHI Modernization Act in 2004. With these two laws, the basis for the development of a system of provider-oriented regulation of quality in the hospital sector was formed. The 2000 law obliged hospitals to regularly submit quality reports, and the 2004 law contained a requirement for joint self-government actors in the German health care system (Association of SHI physicians, German Hospital Federation, Central Association of Health Insurance Funds) to establish an Institute for Quality and Effectiveness in Health Care (IQWIG). In the legislative process, the federal government had to make compromises. Thus, the conservative-liberal opposition, supported by the powerful interest groups of physicians and the hospital association, urged that the principle of self-administration as a fundamental structural principle of the regulation in the German health care system should be reflected in the emerging system of quality regulation. In addition, the conservative-liberal opposition in the German *Bundestag* successfully advocated that quality regulation was based on soft law, that is, non-obligatory, non-sanction-proven solutions (Weckert 2014, 110–113).

Overall, the two laws represented an entry into the quality-oriented regulation of health and (specifically) hospital services (Rosenbrock and Gerlinger 2014, 381f) which, for the time being, relied on self-regulation and soft measures. Moreover, a consistent definition of quality and its role as a parameter of either economic or social regulation was still lacking.

A second phase of quality policy began by the end of the 2000s, following the change in government to a conservative-liberal (CDU, CSU, FDP) coalition in 2009. It continued up until 2015 and was characterized by refinement of the regulatory instrument and further development of the institutional foundations of health and hospital quality control (SHI Competition Strengthening Act of 2007; SHI Health Supply Structure Act of 2012; Law for the Further Development of the Financial Structure and Quality of the SHI of 2015). In this context, the overarching goal of the welfare state to make sure that the provision of health and hospital services, irrespective of their providers, would meet high-quality standards based on (independently gathered) expertise was lost. Rather, politics put the focus on issues such as the appropriate role of self-government (physician's associations; sickness funds) or the institutionalization of quality control, especially in the hospital sector. At this stage of policy making, the original Leftist idea that the regulation of quality could serve both to realize the welfare state's goal of providing for universal access to high-quality medicine and, at the same time, to contain costs, was fundamentally questioned in view of the continually increasing expenses in the hospital sector (Weckert 2014, 90). In contrast, as physicians complained about excessive bureaucratic demands on their work, inter alia blaming hospital quality regulation (Flintrop and Korzilius 2012), the conservative-liberal governmental coalition began to promote competition as the core "regulatory principle" for achieving the goals of "diversity . . . efficiency . . . and quality of care" in the hospital sector (CDU-CSU, FDP 2009, 85).

Most recently, quality assurance has again been seen as a necessity for the welfare state to be able to effectively use its resources. In 2016, a renewed grand coalition of conservatives and social democrats adopted the Hospital Structure Act, which marks a real change in terms of the state's regulatory orientation vis-à-vis the providers of services. Based on this law, quality standards (which shall be developed by a specialized expert's institution, the IQTIQ, and shall be formally adopted by the Federal Joint Committee) are now directly applicable to hospital planning of the German states (*Bundesländer*). Hospitals that do not meet the required minimum quality standards can now be excluded from the state's hospital planning and thus cut off from access to SHI financing. In addition, further quality-related "hard regulations" (remuneration discounts for bad quality; minimum quantity regulation) have been enacted, strengthening the welfare state's position vis-à-vis the service providers. And, what is more, the installation of a system of negative or positive sanctioning ("pay for performance") is envisaged (Schrappe 2018, 221–223). The recent publication of various expert studies showing persisting process- and outcome-related quality deficits, especially in hospital care, and relating them to deficits in the steering of the sector (SVR 2007; SVR 2014, 132ff.) might help to understand this new step toward the development of the RWS in the health sector. Moreover, it seems that the welfare state's direct intervention to regulate the quality of health services particularly in the hospital is meanwhile being accepted by the providers not only as a means to overcome failure of the hospital welfare market, but also as a means to assure the individual patient's social right of access to high-quality services (Schrappe 2018, 225). Overall, after a long, arduous period of construction, the quality-related social regulation of health and hospital service providers has become part of the welfare state in the health sector in Germany.

## Comparative Discussion

In terms of how they position themselves vis-à-vis the providers of health and hospital services, Germany and France differed in their development of quality-related regulation. In France, the political parties from all sides and the stakeholders in the field of health quickly accepted the central state as the primary regulator of health and hospital service quality; while in Germany, the state's position was subject to political controversy. Both in Germany and France, quality regulation was initially seen as a way to control ever-increasing health costs without compromising the welfare state's goal to ensure universal access to affordable health care for all.

In Germany, only the left-wing parties—especially the Social Democratic Party (SPD)—advocated for this policy, whereas the conservatives and liberals in particular rejected it. As a consequence, the Left argued for a professionally justified definition of quality standards as well as (directive) instruments monitoring compliance ("social regulation"); whereas the conservatives and liberals—supported by the medical profession—advocated the idea that "good quality" could be found via the service provider's competition on the health service market ("economic regulation") (Windholz and Hodge 2012). Only of late has the politicized debate given way to a technical debate on the modalities of institutionalizing and equipping quality regulation, which is now established as a joint project between the public health administration and professionals. In France, on the other hand, party-political differences did not exist from the start. Even though the political Left—as in Germany—first introduced the quality issue in the health policy discourse, the conservative-right parties took up the corresponding arguments (quality control and improvement as a means of cost containment and of providing quality health care to the entire population) very quickly. Moreover, there was no political disagreement over the modalities of a quality regulation. Politicians from all camps saw the state as having the duty, first and foremost. In addition, based on the established system of health policy making, the development of a system of health quality regulation was largely shielded from any stakeholder interest.

If one compares the two countries on the design of instruments to regulate health and hospital quality, it is apparent that the RWS in France was able to use the full range of instruments from the beginning, that is, from the *Juppé* reform in 1996. Hard sanction–proven controls (e.g., hospital accreditation), as well as financial incentives and also soft regulation of behavior, in particular of providers of hospital services, were enacted and made ready for application (e.g., the diffusion of information about individual hospitals). In Germany, the spectrum of instruments envisaged as tools to regulate the quality of health and hospital services has remained limited until recently. Until the adoption of the Hospital Structure Act in 2016, hard measures of social regulation (e.g., allowing for linking the quality of services of individual providers, especially hospitals, to their remuneration) were not envisaged. In turn, the soft instruments were designed to limit their impact from the outset (e.g., quality reports, which are generally noted by professionals).

We can also find differences between the two countries that hint to an interaction of different regulatory traditions and short-lived agency-related factors associated with regulation. In Germany, quality regulation, from the inception, was conceptualized as a task of the actors of the self-regulation (i.e. the providers of services [physicians, hospitals] and the payers [sickness funds]). In this context, the doctors associations, skeptical about hard quality regulation, dominated the debate on the development of a regulatory structure, particularly in its initial phase. On the other hand, the sickness funds, who only gradually built up their own medical expertise and thus became an independent "player" of quality policy (Bode 2002) more open to quality regulation, have gained more weight in the debate only in recent years. In France, from the outset, the state took the typical path of creating its own expert bureaucracy (Hassenteufel and Palier 2008) in terms of health service quality. On this path, however, the original link between the quality idea and the original welfare goals in the field of health quickly lost importance and the question of the most accurate system of quality documentation and examination dominated.

Finally, the comparison of France and Germany reveals the path-dependent continuation of problem-solving practices, processes, institutions, and underlying principles. From the very beginning, quality regulation in Germany was embedded in the system of self-regulation in the health sector. In this context, the state was given the role of a "setter" of a general framework. Only recently, since 2016—at a time when the new structure of quality-oriented regulation of health services was already established—has the state gained more weight in this context. In France, in keeping with the "dirigiste" tradition of regulation that had been enforced in the course of the reforms of the French health care state since the 1990s, the central state became the dominant player in the formulation of rules to define, monitor, and enforce health and hospital service quality right from the start. Interestingly, as of late, the state attempts to more actively involve service providers in the regulation of quality standards and the evolution of methods for their review as quality regulation has not yet delivered the hoped-for results.

# Conclusion

Quality regulation, since the 1990s, has been an important aspect of regulation in the welfare state. This is particularly true in the field of social services, which have been prone to the developments of privatization and marketization since the late 1980s (cf. Evers et al. 1997). Quality, on one side, can be understood as a parameter of social control over the provision of social services. On the other side, it can also be interpreted as a parameter of economic control, that is, as a corrective of failures probably contributing to an increase in efficiency of the social service market. How mechanisms of quality regulation by the state are structured in different social service sectors is important to get an impression of how the welfare state defines the quality parameter and how it strives to utilize it (either as an opportunity for social regulation or for marketization and sometimes, more or less open, retrenchment). This article has shown that to answer the question of how the RWS was shaped in quality regulation in the health care system in Germany and France, we must consider both the rather short-lived political factors and national regulatory traditions, and their corresponding institutional settings.

State and national regulatory traditions—including the openness of regulation to, or compartmentalization from, the influence of societal interests—are indeed important. In Germany and France, health politics took steps to install systems of quality regulation and control from the early 1990s onward. As the comparison has shown, the development of the RWS's supply side–oriented regulation is dependent on the structural and institutional conditions of regulation in the field of health and, generally, is linked to the national regulatory tradition. In fact, the RWS's development in Germany reflects the involvement of powerful non–state actors in defining the concept of quality and making quality-related policy. There, a debate was about whether quality regulation should be understood in the mere sense of a market corrective or in a broader social regulatory sense. Accordingly, the instruments chosen for quality regulation and the institutions and procedures established in this context reflect an (initial) reluctance in terms of the design of the RWS. In contrast, the state's strong position is reflected in the emerging system of social regulation in favor of high quality of health services and monitoring in France.

This study suggests that the RWS is best understood as part of the welfare state and that we, thus, should expect welfare state institutions and traditions to interact with overarching state traditions to shape the RWS. This can be seen in the overall preference for cooperative forms of regulatory governance, notably in the German case; and in that two traditionally strongly physician-centered "conservative" welfare states have discussed for so long the regulation of the quality of health and hospital services by the state.

# References

Barr, Nicolas. 2020. *The economics of the welfare state*. 6th Edition. Oxford: Oxford University Press.
Beckmann, Christof. 2009. *Qualitätsmanagement und soziale Arbeit*. Wiesbaden: VS Verlag für Sozialwissenschaften.

Benish, Avishai, Hanan Haber, and Rotem Eliahou. 2017. The regulatory welfare state in pension markets: Mitigating high charges for low-income savers in the United Kingdom and Israel. *Journal of Social Policy* 46 (2): 313–30.

Benish, Avishai, Dana Halevy, and Shimon Spiro. 2017. Regulating social welfare services: Between compliance and learning. *International Journal of Social Welfare* 27:226–235.

Bode, Ingo. 2002. *Vom Payer zum Player - oder: Krankenkassen im Wandel: der Fall der AOK und ein vergleichender Exkurs nach Frankreich*, Duisburger Beiträge zur soziologischen Forschung.

De Pouvourville, Gérard. 1997. Quality of care initiatives in the French context. *International Journal for Quality in Health Care* 9 (3): 163–70.

Deutscher Bundestag. 2003. Plenarprotokoll 15/64. Stenographischer Bericht 64. Sitzung, Berlin, Freitag, den 26. September 2003. Berlin: Deutscher Bundestag.

Deutscher Bundestag. 2001. Drucksache 14/6893. Gesetzentwurf der Fraktionen SPD und BÜNDNIS 90/ DIE GRÜNEN. Entwurf eines Gesetzes zur Einführung des diagnose-orientierten Fallpauschalensystems für Krankenhäuser (Fallpauschalengesetz-FPG). Berlin: Deutscher Bundestag.

Deutscher Bundestag. 1999. Drucksache 14/1977. Beschlussempfehlung und Bericht des Ausschusses für Gesundheit (14. Ausschuss) 1. zu dem Gesetzentwurf der Fraktionen der SPD und BÜNDNIS 90/ DIE GRÜNEN– Drucksache 14/1245 –Entwurf eines Gesetzes zur Reform der gesetzlichen Krankenversicherung ab dem Jahr 2000 (GKV-Gesundheitsreform 2000), 2. zu dem Gesetzentwurf der Bundesregierung– Drucksache 14/1721 –Entwurf eines Gesetzes zur Reform der gesetzlichen Krankenversicherung ab dem Jahr 2000 (GKV-Gesundheitsreform 2000). Berlin: Deutscher Bundestag.

Evers, Adalbert, Riitta Haverinen, Kai Leichsenring, and Gerald Wistow, eds. 1997. *Developing quality in personal social services. Concepts, cases and comments*. New York, NY: Routledge.

Ferrua, Marie, Benoît Lalloué, A. Girault, S. Jiang, P. Loirat, and Étienne Minvielle. 2015. Incitation Financière à l'Amélioration de la Qualité (IFAQ) pour les établissements de santé français: Résultats de l'expérimentation (2012-2014). *Journal de gestion et d'économie médicales* 33 (4): 277–90.

Flintrop, Jens, and Heike Korzilius. 2012. Bürokratie in Praxen und Krankenhäusern: Vom Versuch, den Alltag in Ziffern zu pressen. *Deutsches Ärzteblatt* 109 (13): A-634.

Freidson, Eliot. 2001. *Professionalism: the third logic*. Chicago, IL: The University of Chicago Press.

Gesetz zur Weiterentwicklung der Finanzstruktur und der Qualität in der gesetzlichen Krankenversicherung (GKV-Finanzstruktur- und Qualitäts-Weiterentwicklungsgesetz–GKV-FQWG) (Law for the Further Development of the Financial Structure and Quality of the SHI) vom 21. Juli 2014. *BGBl.* I (33): 1133.

Gesetz zur Verbesserung der Versorgungsstrukturen in der gesetzlichen Krankenversicherung (GKV-Versorgungsstrukturgesetz–GKV-VStG) (SHI Health Supply Structure Act) vom 22. Dezember 2011. *BGBl.* I (70): 2983.

Gesetz zur Stärkung des Wettbewerbs in der gesetzlichen Krankenversicherung (GKV-Wettbewerbsstärkungsgesetz–GKV-WSG) (SHI Competition Strengthening Act) vom 26. März 2007. *BGBl.* I (11): 378.

Guidi, Mattia, Igor Guardiancich, and David Levi-Faur. 2020. Modes of regulatory governance: a political economy perspective. *Governance* 33:5–19.

Hacker, Jacob S. 2004. Privatizing risk without privatizing the welfare state: The hidden politics of social policy retrenchment in the United States. *American Political Science Review* 98 (2): 243–60.

Hassenteufel, Patrick, and Bruno Palier. 2008. Towards neo-Bismarckian health care states? Comparing health insurance reforms in Bismarckian welfare systems. In *Reforming the Bismarckian welfare systems*, eds. Bruno Palier and Claude Martin, 40–61. Malden, MA: Blackwell.

Hemerijck, Anton. 2013. *Changing welfare states*. New York, NY: Oxford University Press.

Jordan, Andrew, Michael W. Bauer, and Christoffer Green-Pedersen. 2013. Policy dismantling. *Journal of European Public Policy* 20 (5): 795–805.

Klenk, Tanja, and Renate Reiter. 2012. Öffentliche Daseinsvorsorge, privat organisiert? Ein deutsch-französischer Vergleich der Bereitstellung der Krankenhausinfrastruktur. *Zeitschrift für Sozialreform* 58 (4): 401–25.

Leisering, Lutz, and Deborah Mabbett. 2011. Introduction: Towards a new regulatory state in old-age security? Exploring the issues. In *The new regulatory state*, ed. Lutz Leisering, 1–30. New York, NY: Palgrave Macmillan.

Levi-Faur, David. 2014. The welfare state: A regulatory perspective. *Public Administration* 92 (3): 599–614.

Levi-Faur, David. 2006. Varieties of regulatory capitalism: Getting the most out of the comparative method. *Governance* 19 (3): 367–82.

Loer, Kathrin, Renate Reiter, and Annette E. Töller. 2014. Was ist ein Politikfeld und warum entsteht es? *der moderne staat* 8 (1): 7–28.

Majone, Giandomenico. 1997. From the Positive to the Regulatory State. *Journal of Public Policy* 17 (2): 139–67.

Minvielle, Étienne. 2013. Comment évaluer et réguler la performance en matière de qualité de la prise en charge des malades? *Quaderni* 82: 83–98.

Moran, Michael. 2000. Understanding the welfare state: the case of health care. *British Journal of Politics and International Relations* 2 (2): 135–60.

Nay, Olivier, Sophie Béjean, Daniel Benamouzig, Henri Bergeron, Patrick Castel, and Bruno Ventelou. 2016. Achieving universal health coverage in France: policy reforms and the challenge of inequalities. *The Lancet* 387:2236–2249.

OECD. 2019. Public social spending is high in many OECD countries. In *Social expenditure update 2019*. Paris: OECD. Available from www.oecd.org/social/expenditure.htm.

Painter, Martin, and B. Guy Peters. 2010. The analysis of administrative traditions. In *Tradition and public administration*, eds. Martin Painter and B. Guy Peters, 19–30. New York, NY: Palgrave Macmillan.

Painter, Martin, and B. Guy Peters. 2010. Administrative traditions in comparative perspective: Families, groups and hybrids. In *Tradition and public administration*, eds. Martin Painter and B. Guy Peters, 19–30. New York, NY: Palgrave Macmillan.

Richardson, Jeremy, Gunnel Gustafsson, and Grant Jordan. 1982. The concept of policy style. In *Policy styles in Western Europe*, ed. Jeremy Richardson, 1–16. New York, NY: Routledge.

Rosenbrock, Rolf, and Thomas Gerlinger. 2014. *Gesundheitspolitik. Eine systematische Einführung*, 3. Auflage. Bern: Huber.

Rothstein, Henry, Regine Paul, and David Demeritt. 2020. The boundary conditions for regulation: Welfare systems, state traditions, and the varied governance of work safety in Europe. *Governance* 33:21–39.

Sachverständigenrat zur Begutachtung der Entwicklung im Gesundheitswesen (SVR). 2014. Bedarfsgerechte Versorgung Perspektiven für ländliche Regionen und ausgewählte Leistungsbereiche, Kurzfassung, Berlin.

Sachverständigenrat zur Begutachtung der Entwicklung im Gesundheitswesen (SVR). 2007. Kooperation und Verantwortung. Voraussetzungen einer zielorientierten Gesundheitsversorgung, Kurzfassung, Berlin.

Sachverständigenrat zur Begutachtung der Entwicklung im Gesundheitswesen (SVR). 2000/2001. Bedarfsgerechtigkeit und Wirtschaftlichkeit. Band II: Qualitätsentwicklung in Medizin und Pflege, Kurzfassung, Berlin.

Schrappe, Matthias. 2018. Qualität als Wettbewerbsfaktor: Rahmenbedingungen und Umsetzung. In *Krankenhauslandschaft in Deutschland*, eds. Dirk Janssen and Boris Augurzky, 217–230. Stuttgart: Kohlhammer.

Siciliani, Luigi, Martin Chalkley, and Hugh Gravelle. 2017. Policies towards hospital and GP competition in five European countries. *Health Policy* 121:103–10.

Soual, Hélène. 2017. Les dépenses de santé depuis 1950. *Études & Résults (Direction de la Recherche, des Études, de l'Évaluation et de la Statistique, DREES)* 1017 (Juillet 2017). Available from https://drees .solidarites-sante.gouv.fr/IMG/pdf/er1017.pdf (accessed 9 September 2020).

Van Kersbergen, Kees, and Barbara Vis. 2014. *Comparative Welfare State Politics. Developments, Opportunities and Reform*. New York, NY: Cambridge University Press.

Vogel, David. 1986. *National styles of regulation: Environmental policy in Great Britain and the United States*. Ithaca, NY: Cornell University Press.

Vogel, David, and Robert Kagan. 2004. *Dynamics of regulatory change: How globalization affects national regulatory policies*. Berkeley, CA: University of California Press.

Weckert, Elina. 2014. *Qualitätsverbesserung in europäischen Gesundheitssystemen. Ein deutsch-französischer Vergleich*. Baden-Baden: Nomos.

Windholz, Eric, and Graeme A. Hodge. 2012. Conceptualising Social and Economic Regulation: Implications for Modern Regulators and Regulatory Activity. *Monash University Law Review* 38 (2): 212–37.

This study investigates the mechanisms that courts apply to expose private social service suppliers to constitutional duties. In doing so, we suggest two variants of welfare regimes: the *regulatory constitutional welfare state* and the *regulatory constitutional neoliberal welfare state*. We outline how constitutional rights, including social rights, are applied to private entities, and the tests that courts use in doing so. We then analyze the transformation of traditional jurisprudence in Israel since the 1990s, and we discuss developments in British jurisprudence, which embraces a neoliberal approach. We end with an analysis of the differences between British and Israeli jurisprudence to highlight our theoretical framework's contribution to comparative research.

*Keywords:* regulatory state; welfare state; constitutional; neoliberal; publicization; polymorphic regulatory regimes

# The Rise of the Regulatory Constitutional Welfare State, Publicization, and Constitutional Social Rights: The Case of Israel and Britain

By
LILACH LITOR,
GILA MENAHEM,
and
HADARA BAR-MOR

The relationship between the welfare state and the regulatory state has recently been reconsidered by scholars in light of changes in how public services are delivered. The regulatory state is a model in which rule-making regarding markets is used as a means of advancing public policy, whereas the welfare state is a model aimed at advancing social justice and fulfilling social rights. The significance of recent development lies in the understanding that the regulatory state itself—which has always been captured as reflecting a neoliberal ideology—can be a mechanism for enhancing social policy and the model of the welfare state.

One of the recent and promising attempts to grasp the changes taking place in the way

*Lilach Litor is a lecturer at The Open University of Israel. Her research focuses on the intersection of public law, labor relations, and public policy. She is the author of the book* Strike: Law, History and Politics *(2019) and co-author of* Judicial Activism and Passivism *(2008).*

Correspondence: Lilachli@openu.ac.il

DOI: 10.1177/0002716220964385

governments provide social services in recent years involves exploration of the ways in which regulatory regimes interact with welfare regimes. Majone (1994; 1999, 3) viewed the rise of the regulatory state as intertwined with the spread of privatization and contracting services out and as an alternative form of state organization that competes with the welfare state. And yet Levi-Faur (2014, 600) claims that Majone's view of the regulatory state fails to recognize that these state regimes can coexist. Investigating this interaction and the factors shaping it in the welfare services arena is the purpose of the current article.

While focusing on the preservation of welfare norms and social rights within the framework of the regulatory state, we start with the wave of privatization, viewed as the core process shaping the regulatory state's evolution, which began in the 1980s and rapidly diffused throughout the world in the context of neo-liberalism's emergence (Levi-Faur 2005; Kus 2006; Mabbett 2010). Looking into the preservation of welfare norms, we follow Benish and Levi-Faur's (2012) claim that through publicization, which extends public law norms to private entities (Freeman 2003; Metzger 2009; Benish and Maron 2016), public law norms and administrative law requirements can serve as a central accountability mechanism and diagnostic instrument for the state.

Within this conceptual framework, Levi-Faur (2013, 2014) distinguishes between the goals and tools of welfare and regulatory states as regulatory states may pursue various goals and welfare states may use a variety of policy tools. Benish, Haber, and Eliahou (2017) point out that this split between the goals and tools of welfare and regulatory states opens up a space in which both types of state can coexist. We follow this line of reasoning and focus on one tool that both regulatory and welfare states may use: publicization. In most cases, publicization takes the form of declaring nongovernmental organizations (NGOs) as well as those private corporations that supply welfare services to be hybrid bodies having both public and private characteristics. This enables the application of public law norms, originally binding only public authorities, to private entities providing public services (Freeman 2003; Metzger 2009). We suggest publicization to be one type of interaction conducted between goals and tools that may shape a space for coexistence of the regulatory and the welfare state. Braithwaite (2008 in Stewart 2014) suggests that regulatory capitalism represents hybridization between privatization of the public and publicization of the private. While pri-vatization has been widely studied, publicization has been much less documented (Stewart 2014). In this study we attempt to address this gap by investigating the publicization that courts apply to private entities supplying social services. They

*Gila Menahem is a retired professor, Department of Public Policy, Tel Aviv University. She studies policy formulation, policy paradigms, and policy networks. Her recent research deals with collaborative governance in local municipalities. She has coedited two books,* Public Policy in Israel *(Frank Cass 2002) and* Policy Analysis in Israel *(Policy Press 2016).*

*Hadara Bar-Mor is an associate professor in the School of Law at Netanya Academic College, Israel. Her fields of research include labor and employment law, corporate law, and nonprofit law. Her recent articles deal with the nature of strike as a basic right and with lifting the veil in employment tribunals.*

apply this publicization by declaring these bodies to be hybrid, which allows them to be subject to dual systems of law—private and public (Kosar 2011).

Benish, Haber, and Eliahou (2017) refer to systems where regulation is a key policy tool in safeguarding social welfare values and outcomes as "regulatory welfare states." Combining the polymorphic argument and that of the role of publicization in the preservation of public law norms and constitutional rights, we suggest distinguishing between two variants of regulatory regimes: the *regulatory constitutional welfare state* and the *regulatory constitutional neoliberal welfare state*. Within the regulatory constitutional welfare state, the application of constitutional rights on services delivered by private entities is an attempt to preserve the welfare norms in privatized welfare services. Publicization is the major way to protect constitutional social rights in this type of regulatory state. Conversely, the regulatory constitutional neoliberal welfare state preserves the distinction between the public and the private sphere and thus refrains from applying constitutional rights to private entities. These two variants—the regulatory constitutional welfare state and regulatory constitutional neoliberal welfare state—are both subcategories of the regulatory welfare state, given that the regulatory welfare state can take different forms and be of different types (Levi-Faur 2014).

We further suggest that one major factor shaping the differences between the variants is the approach that the jurisprudence embraces regarding the application of constitutional rights through publicization. In attributing this role to courts, we follow previous research that has pointed to the role of judicial decisions in regulatory policymaking. For instance, Miles and Sunstein (2006), when discussing whether judges make regulatory policy, claim that determining new rules regarding the market activity of private bodies is equivalent to formulating regulatory-like decisions. This results from statutory ambiguities often requiring policy-like judgements but also from the courts' duty to monitor the activity of public regulatory agencies and governmental actors regarding their interpretation of vague laws.

## Publicness, Publicization, Hybridity, and Regulatory Welfare Regimes

Benish and Mattei (forthcoming) suggest that hybridity takes on different dynamic arrangements, a reflection of the large range of organizations providing social services. Some are clearly located in either the public or the private domain, namely: they are either public or private entities at their core. Others have both public and private features and are not easily characterized as one or the other. Publicness theory (Bozeman 1984) can be useful for the classification of hybrid bodies. Publicization theory claims that classification of organizations as private or public requires a multidimensional approach that positions organizations along the public-private continuum (Anderson 2012). The concept of publicness is operationalized by a series of interval measures, placed in direct competition with traditional definitions of the public nature of an organization, that is, public as opposed to private ownership (Bozeman and Brestschneider 1994). Following Bozeman and Brestschneider (1994), we suggest such dimensions can include type of resources and public funding, diversity of aim, and whether the organization is an NGO or a for-profit entity incorporated as a corporation enhancing either public interest goals or profit-oriented goals. Other indicators of publicness would be the degree of control exercised by public authorities versus the freedom of operation typical of private bodies. In this respect, at one end of the pole are private entities that are either partially owned or partially managed by public authorities and characterized by significant public authority and consequently a high level of publicness. At the other end are private bodies acting in the market realm, supplying welfare services while regulated by the government. Private or privatized bodies, and those engaged in contracting out with public authorities, lie between the two poles of publicness as the authorities preserve different degrees of control over policy-setting and decision-making.

We argue that courts play an important role in creating a unique mechanism belonging to the hybrid-accountability arrangements characterizing regulatory constitutional welfare governance. Thus, publicization by courts is an additional layer in the accountability arrangements that differentiate between the two variants of the welfare state and carry implications for the ability of those variants to preserve welfare norms. Embracing the welfare variant, courts tend, we suggest, to declare hybridity even upon bodies with low publicness and high privateness; while in the neoliberal variant we suggest that the courts' tendency to exhibit this is diminished.

While our conceptualization builds on the earlier concepts that we have presented, it adds two dimensions: first, it allows for the identification of two diverse variants of the possible relations formed among regulation, social rights, and publicization in the context of a regulatory state. Second, it points to actors and factors infrequently dealt with before: jurisdictions and courts as institutions where the attributes of regulatory regimes are shaped.

To examine the fruitfulness of the suggested distinction between the two regulatory regimes, this article examines two jurisprudences in the welfare services domain, that of Israel and that of the UK. These two countries were selected based on the common law characteristics they share and the large wave of privatization of social services that both underwent (Scott-Samuel et al. 2014). At the same time, the two countries differ, with Britain traditionally liberal and maintaining a minimal welfare state regime, and Israel considered a social democratic state up to the 1970s. Since then, Israel has transformed into a market-oriented system (Benish, Haber, and Eliahou 2017).

Our analysis of both systems shows that differences in the rulings of each jurisprudence have shaped important aspects of two emerging variations of the regulatory state: the regulatory welfare constitutional state and the regulatory constitutional neoliberal state. By doing so, the article contributes to development of a theory on the polymorphic nature of regulatory regimes. On the empirical side, we examine rulings regarding health services, nursing homes, pension payments, and programs for the unemployed, and we offer criteria for distinguishing each variant; we thus contribute to the development of a comparative approach to judicial rulings as part of the study of policy regimes.

The rest of the article is structured as follows: the first part discusses the application of constitutional rights, including social rights, to private entities and the distinction among the two variants of the regulatory state, the regulatory welfare constitutional state and the regulatory neoliberal constitutional state. The first section also presents the tests each judiciary typically uses when deciding whether to apply public law to private entities. The second part analyzes the transformation of the traditional jurisprudence regarding the application of public law norms in Israel since the 1990s. The third part discusses developments in British jurisprudence and its embrace of a neoliberal approach. In the fourth and concluding section, we offer an analysis of the differences between British and Israeli jurisprudence to highlight the theoretical framework's contribution to comparative research.

# Preserving Social Rights in the Regulatory State

The concept of social rights is largely a twentieth-century phenomenon (King and Waldron 1988). In 1967, social rights were entered into the UN's International Covenant of Social and Economic Rights (United Nations 1967).

One result of the privatization of public services that has raised special concern is that the private bodies fulfilling public duties are not, for the most part, subjected to the same constitutional obligations and public law norms to which public authorities are subject, thus giving rise to a lack of constitutional accountability (S. Palmer 2008; Metzger 2009; Frankel 2009). Extension of public law norms to private entities allows for introduction of an accountability mechanism effective in these circumstances.

The distinction between a *regulatory constitutional welfare regime* and a *regulatory constitutional neoliberal regime* lies in the transformation of constitutional rights and publicization into policy tools for the fulfillment of welfare norms, which creates diverse accountability mechanisms. Following Levi-Faur (2014) we suggest that such differences in the application of constitutional rights and publicization shape distinctive modes of the regulatory constitutional state and form morphs of the regulatory states.

## Two applications of constitutional rights within the regulatory state

The two different regulatory constitutional regimes proposed differ in several major respects regarding their adherence to constitutional welfare norms and publicization as a tool to preserve those norms. Regulatory constitutional welfare regimes perceive social rights as human rights with constitutional status, meaning that they should also be applied in the privatized service arena. The neoliberal variant lags behind in recognizing social rights as constitutional rights and applying them to private entities (Kus 2006).

The approaches also differ in their adherence to the public/private distinction as it relates to the imposition of constitutional obligations. These differences rely on two tests; first, whether a close connection to public authorities is a prerequisite for the application of constitutional rights and public law norms, and second, whether a voluntary contractual relationship between the private body and the service recipient denies the possibility of the application of public law norms. Organic tests require a close connection with public authorities and the absence of contractual relationships as preconditions to the application of public duties to private entities, while functional tests look at whether the task the entity performs is a public one (Morris 2000). Close connections to public authorities can be reflected in the involvement of those authorities in the challenged private act or in activities closely meshed with the activities of the public authority.

The regulatory constitutional neoliberal regime typically stresses application of organic tests that limit the implementation of public law primarily to bodies closely connected to the state or acting under state control, meaning bodies characterized with high publicness. Alternatively, the regulatory constitutional welfare approach emphasizes functional tests for the application of public law norms, even to entities characterized by a low degree of publicness, based on the public function of the respective private entities, regardless of any connection to public authorities.

We, therefore, suggest that the more courts are willing to use functional tests on bodies with low-to-medium degrees of publicness, the more they enhance the regulatory welfare accountability regime. In contrast, the more courts use organic tests on bodies with low-to-medium degrees of publicness, the more they enhance the neoliberal regulatory accountability regime.

## Methodology

*Accessing relevant court rulings in Israel and the UK.* To empirically substantiate our claims, we performed a search of all rulings by judicial bodies that dealt with the publicization of services in each site. The court decisions and the areas where these are applied are different in the UK and Israel. In the UK, they refer to housing and to health care in nursing homes, while the Israeli cases refer to medical insurance, treatment of the unemployed, and pension funds. The different areas, between Britain and Israel, reflect differences in the legal systems and differences in the areas that have been privatized in each country. For instance, in Israel as opposed to Britain, public housing has always been supplied by public corporations owned by either the government or the local municipality, such as the governmental corporation "Amidar," with no involvement of the private sector. Since these entities are purely public and have never been privatized, the issue of capturing them as hybrid bodies naturally has never been raised in courts.[1]

The Israeli dataset we analyzed consists of Israeli court rulings from 1990 through 2019, whereas the British dataset consists of decisions handed down from 2000 through 2019. Data reflect the constitutional development and legal context of the two countries. In Israel, two basic laws regarding human rights were passed in the early 1990s: *Basic Law: Freedom of Occupation* and *Basic Law: Dignity and Liberty*, both being considered as having a constitutional status. This means that the application of social rights was looked at in cases dated 1990s onward. In Britain, the Human Rights Act 1998 (here after HRA), when introduced, declared the application of the constitutional rights mentioned in the European Convention of Human Rights within British law. Hence, the search of cases was from the year 2000 onward.

We obtained the Israeli cases by a search for the keyword "hybrid," together with several other terms: "supplementary health services," "from welfare to work program," "the right to a minimum standard of living," and "pension fund." Searching for "supplementary health insurance" in the legal database *Nevo* yielded twenty-seven cases.

Regarding British jurisprudence, the keywords guiding our search in the Westlaw database were "hybrid" and "section 6(3)(b) of the HRA." The search yielded seven court decisions regarding hybrid bodies that relate to health and welfare.

*Operationalizing degrees of publicness.* We used three degrees of publicness. A high degree of publicness reflects an organization whose nature is very close to a core public body. A low degree of publicness indicates an organization whose nature is close to that of a core private body. A medium degree of publicness refers to an organization located in the middle of the private-public continuum.

We operationalized the degrees of publicness by means of several parameters:

(1) *Type of funding*: private funding reflects a low degree of publicness, whereas public funding or partial public funding reflects a high degree of publicness.

(2) *Aims of the private body*: a for-profit corporation or an NGO. NGOs aimed at furthering the public interest reflect a high degree of publicness, whereas for-profit entities exhibit a low degree of publicness; an NGO with no public interest goal is marked by a medium degree of publicness.

(3) *Type of arrangement and form under which public functions are carried out*: with respect to this indicator, a firm partially owned by the state or in which the state has the ability to nominate some of the directors reflects a high degree of publicness; a body engaged in contracting-out arrangements with public authorities reflects a medium degree of publicness since the private authorities can still determine public policy regarding the service. Regulated private bodies reflect only a low degree of publicness since they are subject only to regulation. Privatized bodies reflect a low-to-medium degree of publicness since the services they provide were once governmental and supplied by the state itself.

# The Rise of a Regulatory Constitutional Welfare State in Israel

*The transformation of jurisprudence after the 1980s*

Since its establishment in 1948 and until the mid-1980s, Israel could be characterized as a variant of "social democratic corporatism" stressing welfare interventionism (Mundlak 2007). Since the mid-1980s, Israel has been undergoing a deep shift toward a "neoliberal regime" that, beginning in the 1990s, included liberalization of financial markets, deregulation of labor markets, decreasing welfare allowances, and massive privatization (Ben-Bassat 2001; Maman and Rozenhak 2012).

Within this context, the jurisdiction of Israeli courts up until the end of the 1980s was restricted to the application of public law norms to state authorities as the main actors in the welfare services arena (Barak Erez 2017). In the early 1990s, application of public law norms and constitutional rights to hybrid bodies began. The term "hybrid" was defined in the *Mikrodaf* case as the Israeli Supreme Court held that in addition to state authorities, private entities having major public characteristics, and thus considered hybrid bodies, could also be subject to public law norms (HCJ 731/86.1987). Public characteristics included, for instance, monopolistic status and the supply of essential services or public utilities.

In the early 1990s, following passage of the two basic laws on human rights—*Basic Law: Freedom of Occupation* and *Basic Law: Dignity and Liberty*—Israel's Supreme Court ruled that the two basic laws enjoyed constitutional status (*Bank Hamizrahi v. Migdal* 1993). The human rights now covered by the basic laws were therefore recognized as constitutional.

*Analysis of the application of constitutional rights and public law norms to Israel's privatized welfare services since the 1990s*

The cases retrieved by our search in the Israeli legal database concern three social service sectors: health care services, pension funds, and a government-initiated program intended to channel the unemployed back into the labor market. Provision of these areas of service has been increasingly outsourced to private entities while pension funds have been transferred from public control by the unions to the private market. A short description of each of these areas follows.

In 1995, Israel enacted its National Health Insurance Law, granting all residents medical services financed by a compulsory health tax and delivered by government-regulated health care organizations. Concomitantly, a plethora of private and supplementary medical insurance programs became available to the public. These programs, which go beyond the statutory required minimum health services and do not enjoy public funding, may be voluntarily purchased by the public (Mizrahi and Cohen 2012).

The cases reviewed in Table 1 deal with those same private medical insurers, occupational pensions provided by private corporations, and a third set of cases

TABLE 1

Israeli Court Decisions regarding Publicization of Privatized Services

| Case | Issue | Court decisions | Reasoning | Publicness parameters: public or private funding | Publicness parameters: for profit NGO / aimed at public interest | Publicness parameters: structure / form | Combined degree of publicness | Type of test |
|---|---|---|---|---|---|---|---|---|
| Private medical programs *Shirit 2000; Shiber 2003; Lev 2008; Plony 2008; Rotman 2011* | Appeal to finance a surgical procedure or treatment - not included in the insurance contract. | *Considered subject to public low norms* | Provision of essential services; despite contractual relationship | Private funding- low public- ness | NGO - aimed at public interest high publicness | Privatized service- *low–medium publicness* | Combined publicness *low–medium publicness* | *Functional* |
| Pension funds Leibovich 1996; Fyurst 1998 Eliav1998; Rapaport 2001 Fidelman 2004; Vaingrate 2005; Lahav 2006; Bales 2006; Bashery 2006; Shohat 2007; Abud 2012; Vider 2013; Levi 2014 | A dispute with pension fund over a change in the calculation of payments or terms | *Considered subject to public low norms* | Social security goals; despite contractual relationship | Private funding- low public- ness | NGO aimed at public interest- high publicness | Regulated body- low public- ness | Combined publicness *low public- ness* | *Functional* |
| From welfare to work program Rajbi 2006; Lugasy 2007 Salomon 2007;Galeb 2007, Rahminov 2007 | Denial of an unemployment allowance based on non-attendance at a training program | *Considered subject to public law norms* | Authority to decide on allowances | Public funding- high publicness | For profit body- low publicness | Contracting out corporation medium publicness | Combined *medium publicness* | *Functional* |

197

concerning the "from welfare to work" program initiated in 2004 and operated by private providers based on competitive tendering.

Regarding coverage of medical procedures as shown in Table 1, even though the basis of the relationship is contractual and no public funding is provided, and regardless of either the government's noninvolvement in the entity's management or any close connection to the relevant activity, the Court used functional tests to declare these associations hybrid bodies and therefore subject to public law norms.

For example, in the *Lev* case, the Court ordered a medical insurance corporation (Bituach Mashlim) to finance a surgical procedure in a private hospital based on the positive character of the constitutional social right for health even though the procedure was not included in the contract concluded with Bituach Mashlim (Regional Labor Court case 9914/05 2008). Even though the basis of a relationship is contractual and regardless of the lack of either governmental involvement in the form's management or the provision of public funding, the Court held that Bituach Mashlim was a hybrid body subject to public law norms. Thus, this case, like others, demonstrates that even though the degree of publicness is only low-to-medium, the Court applied functional tests, thus indicating the emergence of a regulatory constitutional welfare regime.

In the area of pension funds, even though the relationship between the private fund and the insured persons was contractual, and despite no public funding nor any tight connection to public authorities, using functional tests led the Court to hold that the funds were subject to public law norms.

With respect to private corporations involved in the "from welfare to work" program, it was held that despite their for-profit orientation, the fact of having the discretion to decide entitlement to unemployment allowances demands that they be considered hybrid bodies.

## British Jurisprudence, 2000–2019

*Analysis of the application of constitutional rights in Britain's privatized welfare services*

Britain's social and economic policies have become subject to a neoliberal regime shift that Prime Minister Thatcher instituted in 1979, one that held even after Labor came to power, as Jessop (2015, 22) notes: "New Labor committed itself to further liberalization and . . . to the privatization or, at least, corporatization of most of what remained of the state-owned sector as well as to the extension of market forces into what remains of the public and social services at the national, regional, and local level."

Within the wave of privatization, a central privatization of welfare relates to public housing. Mostly, housing associations, which are registered social landlords (RSL) under the Housing Act 1996, provide social housing (S. Palmer 2008). Social housing trusts provide affordable housing below market value to those who cannot secure their housing needs in the market. RSLs are regulated in various ways by the Housing Corporation—an executive public body responsible to the Secretary of State. Other privatized welfare services are residential care homes and nursing homes, which are mostly operated by charity associations and financed by public funds. Charity associations provide accommodation to individuals to whom the local authority owed a duty under the National Assistance Act 1948 as amended by the Local Government Act 1972.

Britain's HRA has incorporated the European Convention for the Protection of Human Rights and Fundamental Freedoms CETS No. 5 Rome 1950 into UK law. The human rights included in the convention are considered constitutional rights in Britain, with the HRA declaring that public authorities are subject to compliance with those constitutional rights. With the spread of privatization, the courts were confronted with the dilemma of whether such service providers should be considered hybrid bodies and thus subordinate to the human rights regime in place. Section 6(3)(b) of the HRA demanded application of the human rights listed in the European Convention to any person or entity who provides services of a public nature. The legal definition for "hybrid bodies" was not mentioned explicitly in Britain's HRA, although the term was framed within the British jurisprudence, even as late as 2009. As we show in Table 2 for the British cases reviewed, the *Aston Cantlow* case stated that a hybrid body is any legal body whose functions are considered by the courts to be fulfilled by a public authority according to the HRA (Leslie 2009).

As demonstrated in the rulings presented in Table 2, British jurisprudence, when considering the attribution of public duties to private bodies, has tended to base amenability to compliance with human rights law on either a very close connection to the authorities or the authorities' involvement in the private body's activities.

British courts declared a close connection in cases where the private body either operated in very close harmony with a public authority, its activities were tightly enmeshed with those of that authority, the private body's charitable objectives were specifically determined by the public authority, or the public body's statutory authority was explicitly delegated to the private body.

British jurisprudence thus emphasizes organic tests that base amenability to human rights on a public authority's involvement in the private body's specific actions while stressing the source of the private organization's power. When the source of that power is contractual, it usually prevents the application of constitutional rights and leads to classification of the respective body as a purely private entity.

This approach is reflected in the case of *YL v. Birmingham City Council* (2007, 27), where it was held that a care home contracted out to a local authority was not subject to constitutional rights. The Court distinguished between a local authority having a statutory duty to arrange care and accommodations, and a private company providing services contracted out by the local authority as a means to fulfill its (the local authority's) statutory duty. The Court consequently denied application of the functional test in this case. The court in the case of *YL* based its decision on the *Donoghue* case (included in our analyzed cases, see Table 2) and observed that the court in *Donoghue* did not apply a functional test.

TABLE 2

British Court Decisions regarding Publicization of Privatized Services: Court Decisions, Reasoning, and Type of Test Applied by the Court

| Case | Issue | Court decision regarding public duties | Reasoning behind the decision | Publicness parameters: public or private funding | Publicness parameters: for profit NGO / aimed at public interest | Publicness parameters: structure / form | Combined degree of publicness | Type of test |
|---|---|---|---|---|---|---|---|---|
| **Nursing home Heather 2002- YL v. Birmingham City Council 2007** | Private nursing home's decision to close or evict a tenant. | *Not considered subject to public law norms* | Source of power-contractual; not an inherently governmental function | **Public funding** high publicness | **NGO – aimed at public interest** high publicness | **Contracting out** medium publicness | **Combined-high publicness** | *Organic* |
| **Housing association Donoghue 2004 Weaver 2009** | Housing association evicted tenants | *Considered subject to public law norms* | Activities were closely enmeshed in the activities of the public authority | **Public funding-** high publicness | **NGO aimed at public interest-** high publicness | **Municipality nominated directors** High publicness / **contracting out-** medium publicness | **Combined-high publicness** | *Organic* |
| **Housing association James 2004 Walker 2015** | Disconnecting a tenant from electricity or terminating a social tenancy | *Not considered subject to public law norms* | The association did not act in place of the local government | **Private funding-** low publicness | **NGO – without aim to benefit the public-** medium publicness | **Contracting out** medium publicness | **Low-medium publicness** | *Organic* |
| **Walting 2019** | A firm engaged in contracting out with the police | *Considered subject to public law norms* | Essential services of medicine | **Public funding-** high publicness | **For profit body-** low publicness | **Contracting out-** medium publicness | **Combined-medium publicness** | *Functional* |

Thus, despite public funding of the patient's stay at the nursing home, contracting out services, and operating an NGO aimed at public interest—all reflecting high publicness—the Court denied the application of constitutional rights. Hence, the use of organic tests, regarding bodies characterized by high publicness, reflects the regulatory constitutional neoliberal variant of the welfare state.

# Discussion and Conclusion

The shift toward privatization and contracting out of social services as major policy tools in the second half of the twentieth century has given rise to concerns regarding the preservation of welfare norms. While more traditional views of the regulatory state have considered the regulatory state and the welfare state as tradeoffs, a more recent approach suggests that the two potentially coexist, based on a polymorphic conceptualization of the regulatory state (Levi-Faur 2013, 2014) and the rise of the regulatory welfare state (Benish Haber, and Eliahou 2017). Our analysis builds on these theoretical contributions and on the distinction between publicness and privateness as developed by Bozeman (1987).

The analysis offered in this article lends support to the fruitfulness of the polymorphic conceptualization of regulatory regimes on one hand and contributes to the development of a typology of these regimes' variants on the other. We introduce the concepts of the *regulatory constitutional welfare* state and the *regulatory constitutional neoliberal welfare* state as two such variants. These terms denote differences in adherence to social rights as constitutional rights and application of public law to those private entities performing public functions. In this article we also draw attention to the courts as co-creators of a regulatory constitutional regime, facilitated by their interpretation of the legal framework in a way that enables delegation of public duties to the respective private entities.

To demonstrate how social rights are viewed in a given regulatory regime as well as to provide a basis for further development of the typology we offer, we looked at the specific criteria used when applying public law to private entities and implementing publicization. We suggest that the criteria regarding decisions on publicization be construed as important features that distinguish a welfare constitutional from a neoliberal constitutional regulatory state.

Our analysis of Israeli trends revealed the Court's application of constitutional rights and public law norms, based on functional tests and imposed on a wide range of private bodies regardless of the type of nexus holding between the private body and the public authority, that is, the association of public law to private bodies with even relatively low publicness. This practice also enables application of public law norms in cases where the contractual relationship between the private body and the public authority is apparent. The use of publicization as a policy tool enhances the entrenchment of accountability within the privatized welfare arena.

The constitutional neoliberal regulatory state, as our analysis of the British cases shows, tends to refrain from applying public law norms and constitutional rights to private bodies. The British courts tend to apply organic tests and require a tight nexus between the private body and the public authority as a precondition for applying constitutional rights. As a result, the types of bodies subject to constitutional rights and public law norms are limited; they include only those with high publicness. These tendencies to apply public duties and subject private entities to constitutional rights capture different modes of protecting the citizen's social rights that lie at the heart of the two regulatory regimes.

The two variants developed here, and the tests used, can be applied to other countries as well. We therefore argue that using this conceptualization of organic and functional tests allows interaction and interplay between the regulatory state and the welfare state and shapes important aspects of their coexistence. Further research is required to address several issues.

One question to be addressed is how the differences between the two jurisdictions affect their tendency to apply public norms to nonpublic entities. While they share common law characteristics, the two systems differ in how the courts operate. As we mentioned, British courts operate in a context that has traditionally represented a liberal social policy regime, with a minimal welfare state regime that moved toward the neoliberal pole in the Thatcher era. Israel, however, was considered a social democratic state up to the 1980s (Doron 1985; Litor 2019b), until a deep and far-reaching process of liberalization emerged in the mid-1980s, led by the executive branch (Maman and Rozenhek 2012; Litor 2019a). Israeli courts have thus operated in a context marked by a government-led retreat of the welfare state. Therefore, a related question is whether, in jurisdictions operating in the context of transforming social regimes, courts lean toward the regulatory constitutional welfare pole in an attempt to preserve constitutional social rights.

While the current study pointed to two variants of the regulatory state, further research should investigate and delineate additional variants. Research should also attempt to identify the other factors shaping each variant. In the Israeli case, it appears that the courts played an important role in preserving welfare norms, but further research should look into the role of bureaucracy, elected officials, and epistemic communities.

## Note

1. In Israel, most nursing homes for the elderly have always been private corporations and have not been privatized. Hence, the issue of applying public law norms or capturing them as hybrid bodies has never been raised in courts.

## References

Anderson, Stuart. 2012. Public, Private, Neither, Both; Publicness Theory and the Analysis of Healthcare Organizations. *Social Science and Medicine* 74:313–22.

Barak-Erez, Daphne. 2017. Three questions of privatization. In *Comparative administrative law*. Cheltenham, UK: Edward Elgar Publishing.

Ben-Bassat, Avi. 2001. Conflicts, interest groups, and politics in structural reforms. *The Journal of Law and Economics* 54 (4): 937–52.

Benish, Avishai, and David Levi-Faur. 2012. New forms of administrative law in the age of third-party government. *Public Administration* 90 (4): 886–900.

Benish, Avishai, and Asa Maron. 2016. Infusing public law into privatized welfare: Lawyers, economists, and the competing logics of administrative reform. *Law & Society Review* 50 (4): 953–84.

Benish, Avishai, Hanan Haber, and Rotem Eliahou. 2017. The regulatory welfare state in pension markets: Mitigating high charges for low-income savers in the United Kingdom and Israel. *Journal of Social Policy* 46 (2): 313–30.

Benish, Avishai, and Paola Mattei. Forthcoming. Accountability and hybridity in welfare governance. *Public Administration*.

Bozeman Barry. 1984. Dimensions of publicness, an approach to public organization theory. In *New directions, public administration*, eds. B. Bozman and J. Straussman. Monterey, CA: Brooks Cole

Bozeman, Barry. 1987. *All organizations are public: Bridging public and private organization theory*. San Francisco, CA: Jossy Bass.

Bozeman, Barry, and Stuart Bretschneider. 1994. The "publicness puzzle" in organization theory: A test of alternative explanations of differences between public and private organizations. *Journal of Public Administration Research and Theory* 4 (2): 197–224.

Braithwaite, John. 2008. *Regulatory capitalism: How it works, ideas for making it work better*. Cheltenham, UK: Edward Elgar Publishing.

Doron, Abraham. 1985. The Israeli welfare state at crossroads. *Journal of Social Policy* 14 (4): 513–25.

Frankel, Richard. 2009. Regulating privatized government through § 1983. *The University of Chicago Law Review* 76 (4): 1449–1516.

Freeman, Jody. 2003. Extending public law norms through privatization. *Harvard Law Review* 116 (5): 1285–1352.

Jessop, Bob. 2015. Margaret Thatcher and Thatcherism: Dead but not buried. *British Politics* 10 (1): 16–30.

King, Desmond S., and Jeremy Waldron. 1988. Citizenship, social citizenship and the defense of welfare provision. *British Journal of Political Science* 18 (4): 415–43.

Kosar, Kevin R. 2011. *Quasi government: Hybrid organizations with both government and private sector legal characteristics*. Collingdale, PA: Diane Publishing.

Kus, Basak. 2006. Neoliberalism, institutional change and the welfare state: The case of Britain and France. *International Journal of Comparative Sociology* 47 (6): 488–525.

Leslie, J. 2009. Approaches to Section 6 HRA: Lessons from Weaver v London and Quadrant Housing Trust. *Judicial Review* 14 (4): 327–32.

Levi-Faur, David. 2005. The global diffusion of regulatory capitalism. *The ANNALS of the American Academy of Political and Social Science* 598 (1): 12–32.

Levi-Faur, David. 2013. The odyssey of the regulatory state: From a "thin" monomorphic concept to a "thick" and polymorphic concept. *Law & Policy* 35 (1–2): 29–50.

Levi-Faur, David. 2014. The welfare state: A regulatory perspective. *Public Administration* 92 (3): 599–614.

Litor, Lilach. 2019a. Constitutionalism and anti-privatisation strikes: Introducing an eclectic model. *Israel Law Review* 52 (3): 327–66.

Litor, Lilach. 2019b. The rise of an anti -global doctrine and strikes in public services. In *Transformative law and public policy*, eds. Sony Pellissery, Mathew Babu, Avinash Govindjee, and Arvind Narrain. Abingdon: Taylor & Francis.

Mabbett, Deborah. 2010. The regulatory rescue of the welfare state. The Jerusalem papers in regulation and governance. No. 28. Working Paper.

Majone, Giandomenico. 1994. The rise of the regulatory state in Europe. *West European Politics* 17 (3): 77–101.

Majone, Giandomenico. 1999. The regulatory state and its legitimacy problems. *West European Politics* 22 (1): 1–24.

Maman, Daniel, and Zeev Rosenhek. 2012. The institutional dynamics of a developmental state: Change and continuity in state–economy relations in Israel. *Studies in Comparative International Development* 47 (3): 342–63.

Metzger, Gillian E. 2009. Private delegations, due process, and the duty to supervise. In *Government by contract: Outsourcing and American democracy*, eds. Jody Freeman and Martha Minow, 291–309. Cambridge, MA: Harvard University Press.

Miles, Thomas J., and Cass R. Sunstein. 2006. Do judges make regulatory policy? An empirical investigation of Chevron. *The University of Chicago Law Review* 73:823–81.

Mizrahi, Shlomo, and Nissim Cohen. 2012. Privatization through centralization in the Israeli health care system: The case of the national health insurance law and its amendments. *Administration & Society* 44 (4): 412–37.

Morris, Gillian S. 2000. Employment in public services: the case for special treatment. *Oxford Journal of Legal Studies* 20 (2): 167–83.

Mundlak, Guy. 2007. *Fading corporatism: Israel's labor law and industrial relations in transition*. Ithaca, NY: Cornell University Press.

Palmer, Stephanie. 2008. Public functions and private services: a gap in human rights protection. *International Journal of Constitutional Law* 6 (3–4): 585–604.

Scott-Samuel, Alex, Clare Bambra, Chik Collins, David J. Hunter, Gerry McCartney, and Kat Smith. 2014. The impact of Thatcherism on health and well-being in Britain. *International Journal of Health Services* 44 (1): 53–71.

Stewart, Fenner L. 2014. The corporation, new governance, and the power of the publicization narrative. *Indiana Journal of Global Legal Studies* 21 (2): 513–51.

United Nations. 1967. International Covenant on Social, Cultural and Economic Rights. New York, NY: UN General Assembly.

## British cases:

*Aston Cantlow v. Wallbank UKHL* 37 (2003)

*James v. London Electricity* (2004) EWHE 3226 (QB) (2004)

*R on the application of A v. Partnerships in care ltd. High court (Administrative court)* 2002.EWCH 329. 2002. 1 W.L.R. 2610. 4 WLUK 121. 5 CCL Rep 330.

*R. v. Servite homes exp. Goldsmith* (2001) LGRS

*Donoghue v. Poplar Housing and Regeneration Community Association* (2004) 4 All ER 183

*R on the application of Heather and others v. Leonard Cheshire* (2002) 2 All E.R. 936 (C.A).P. 946

*James v. London Electricity* (2004) EWHE 3226 (QB) (2004)

*Y.l. v. Birmingham city council* (2007) 27

*The application of Weaver v.* London and Qua drant housing trust Court of appeal 2009. 18 June 2009.

*Southward Housing Cooperative Ltd. V. Walker EWHC* 1645 (CH) (2015)

*Walting v. Chief constable of Suffolk.* (2019) EWHC 2342 (QB) 2019

## Israeli cases:

Supreme Court appeal *Bank Hamizrahi v. Migdal* vol 49(4) 221 (1993).

HCJ 366/03 Commitment of peace and social justice association v. Minister of finance (2005)

Supreme Court case 10662/04 *Hasan v. The National Insurance institution* (2012)

Supreme Court case 1105/06 *Kav Laoved v.* The welfare minister (2014)

High court decision 731/86 *Kastenbaum v.* The Kadisha association (1992).

High court decision 731/86 *Mikrodaf v.* Electricity corporation (1987).

HCJ 5587/02 *Manor v. Treasury Minister* (2004)

Regional labor court case 9914/05 *Lev v. Clalit Medical services* (2008)

Labor case (Tel Aviv)7053/00 Yosef v. *Kupat Holim* (2001)

Civil case 850/03 *Duby v. Kupat Holim* (2003); HBR 2018-15-14 *Nahum v. Kupat Holim* (2016)

Regional labor court case (Tel Aviv) 1770/01 *Shiber v. The General Kupat Holim Klalit* (Takdin legal database) 2001

Regional labor court (Haifa) 188712/08 *Rotman v. Kupat Holim Meuchedet* (2008)

Labor appeal 1091/00 *Shitrit v. Kupat Holim* vol. 35 (2000)

Labor Court case 60026/97 *Mivtachim v. Fyurst* (1997) vol. 39, 831 (2003)

High Court case 600026/97 *Mivtachim v. Fyurst* (2010)

Labor Appeal 1341/01 *Rapeport v. Mivtachim* vol. 38, p.630

Labor Court case 629/97 *Eliav v. Mivtachim* pension fund volume 36, (2).

Labor court case 600013/96 *Leibovich v. The Histadrut Pension Fund* (2002).

Labor Court case 17/03 *Vaingrate v. Mivtachim* (2005)

Labor Court case 68/07 *Lugasy v. the Employment Ministry* (2007)

Labor court (Jerusalem) case 1506/06 *Rajbi v. From welfare to work program* (2006)

Labor case (Haifa) 1151/07 *Abu Saada v. The employment municipality* (2007)

Labor case 2495/06 *The employment municipality. Machluf* (2007)

Labor appeal 1465/07 *Salomon v. The from welfare to work*

Labor case 1146/07 *Galeb v. The from welfare to work* (2007)

Labor court case 3293/06 (Beer Sheva) *Rachminov v. The State of Israel* (2007)

# Quiet Politics of Employment Protection Legislation? Partisan Politics, Electoral Competition, and the Regulatory Welfare State

Political parties and party competition have been important factors in the expansion and retrenchment of the fiscal welfare state, but researchers have argued that regulatory welfare is not part of political debate among parties. We explore this claim theoretically, and then empirically examine it in the case of employment protection legislation (EPL) in twenty-one established democracies since 1985. EPL is a mature and potentially salient instrument of the regulatory welfare state that has experienced substantial retrenchment. We test three prominent mechanisms of how electoral competition conditions partisan effects: the composition of Left parties' electorates, the strength of pro-EPL parties, and the emphasis put on social justice by pro-EPL parties. We find that the partisan politics of EPL is conditioned by electoral competition under only very specific circumstances, namely when blame sharing becomes possible in coalitions between EPL supporters.

*Keywords:* employment protection legislation; partisan politics; regulatory welfare state; electoral competition; welfare state retrenchment

The regulatory welfare state (RWS) is considered as a way to cater for "the social needs of vulnerable groups" (Haber 2017, 445) and can be a "redistributive instrument" that is "functionally equivalent to social spending" (Levi-Faur 2014, 604, 606). Nonetheless, there are some relevant differences between regulating for welfare and social spending (as the classic way to deliver social security). As Levi-Faur (2014, 610) observes: "Money is visible and regulations are not." This claim has two implications. First, agents that would need to pay for

*By*
LINDA VOIGT
and
REIMUT ZOHLNHÖFER

*Reimut Zohlnhöfer is a professor of political science at Heidelberg University in Germany. His research interests include German politics, political economy, comparative public policy, and policy process theory. He has published widely, in journals such as the* British Journal of Political Science *and* Comparative Political Studies.

Correspondence: reimut.zohlnhoefer@ipw .uni-heidelberg.de

DOI: 10.1177/0002716220964388

social spending and that have increasingly obtained an exit option due to globalization might be more willing to accept the invisible regulatory welfare state than the visible levying of taxes and social security contributions. Consequently, regulation is often seen as a rather attractive alternative to providing benefits from the public purse in the era of "permanent austerity" (Pierson 1998). Policy-makers hope that regulation will attain similar goals as welfare transfers without eliciting significant public spending. In that sense, the regulatory state is sometimes regarded as a potential "rescue of the welfare state" (Levi-Faur 2014, 610). Therefore, the regulatory welfare state has been on the rise for quite some time now.

Second, the greater visibility of spending compared with regulation may have consequences for the politics of the different "faces" of the welfare state. It is largely undisputed that the development of the spending welfare state was significantly driven by credit-claiming parties that sought to attract voters by either increasing (highly visible) welfare spending or by preventing tax increases for their respective electorates (see, for example, Huber and Stephens 2001). Likewise, retrenchment of the fiscal welfare state often became an exercise in "blame avoidance" (Weaver 1986) due to the high visibility and electoral salience of the respective programs (cf. Pierson 1994, 1996).

In contrast, the "quiet politics" (Culpepper 2010) of the regulatory welfare state were much less salient among the voters and, consequently, parties may have had fewer incentives to compete on this issue. This, in turn, might have led to the irrelevance of partisan politics for the shaping of welfare regulation. Haber (2017, 457), in a recent study on the regulatory welfare state, substantiates this claim empirically: "The politics of regulatory welfare are not the high stakes, ideological and highly conflictual politics of fiscal welfare. . . . regulatory welfare is not politically contested: it is not a matter of party-political debate."

In this article, we study the relation between political parties and the regulatory welfare state in more detail. We do so by analyzing employment protection legislation (EPL) in twenty-one established democracies since 1985. The investigation of EPL promises a number of new insights for the study of the regulatory welfare state. First, EPL is not at all a recent addition to the welfare state and was never meant to substitute social spending. Rather, it was complementing spending programs to begin with.

Second, while the argument about regulation as the "rescue of the welfare state" (Levi-Faur 2014, 610) suggests that the regulatory welfare state tends to be expanded in times of "permanent austerity," the example of EPL shows that more regulation for welfare has not been the only game in town. Rather, while we see that up until the 1980s EPL expanded in all advanced democracies, it was somewhat retrenched in many countries—particularly in temporary employment and after the financial crisis of 2008 (Emmenegger and Marx 2019, 707–11). So, just

*Linda Voigt is a PhD student and an assistant lecturer at the Institute of Political Science at Heidelberg University in Germany. Her research interests include public policy analysis, political psychology, as well as German and European politics. She has published in the journal* German Politics.

like with welfare spending, there is not necessarily a unidirectional development of the regulatory welfare state.

Third, EPL exemplifies a regulatory program that at least at times has been politically salient due to a substantial potential for redistribution. Labor market insiders cherished dismissal protection where it existed, while employers often found EPL an unwanted intervention into their managerial powers associated with potentially considerable costs. Moreover, substantial parts of the academic literature have identified EPL as being responsible for labor market problems in many countries (cf. Siebert 1997; Blanchard 2006).[1] Given what is at stake—a quite visible protection of labor market insiders versus a potential improvement of the employment situation in case of EPL liberalization—political parties may have translated these different views into different partisan positions. Right parties (i.e., Conservatives and Liberals) should side with employers and advocate a liberalization of the labor market to spark employment dynamics, while Left parties (above all Social democrats, but also [Post] Communists) should seek to protect labor market insiders' interests in employment protection (Rueda 2005, 2007).

With some notable exceptions (Jäkel and Hörisch 2009; Potrafke 2010), the literature suggests that the expected partisan differences have indeed materialized in the postwar period (Algan and Cahuc 2006; Rueda 2005, 2007; Siegel 2007), although some differentiation seems to be in order. First, center parties and Christian democrats in particular seem to behave more like Left parties than like Right parties (Botero et al. 2004; Emmenegger 2011; Heinemann 2007; Huo, Nelson, and Stephens 2008; Zohlnhöfer and Voigt 2019). Second, just like with welfare spending, partisan effects seem to diminish over time in the sense that partisan differences were quite strong until the 1980s and have become less relevant since then (Zohlnhöfer and Voigt 2019). Third, partisan effects have been found to depend on other factors, most notably the veto player constellation (Avdagic 2013; Becher 2010), the level of unemployment (Zohlnhöfer and Voigt 2019), and debt or income inequality (Aaskoven 2019).

What follows from these observations is that in a number of key aspects, EPL as an important part of the regulatory welfare state is not too dissimilar from fiscal welfare. It is a mature welfare program with substantial redistributive implications that has also come under retrenchment pressure since the 1980s—although evidently not because it was too expensive, but rather because some claimed that it dampened labor market dynamics. Accordingly, the politics of employment protection could also be similar to those of fiscal welfare.

This would lead us to expect that the liberalization of EPL, which we observe in many advanced democracies between 1985 and 2013, should have been unpopular among substantial parts of the electorate (Avdagic 2013). The literature on the fiscal welfare state and Paul Pierson's (1994, 1996) argument about "the new politics of the welfare state" and the importance of blame avoidance in particular (see Jensen, Wenzelburger, and Zohlnhöfer 2019 for a recent assessment) would lead us to expect that its unpopularity will shape the politics of EPL liberalization. More specifically, partisan differences should generally disappear or should be conditional on the constellation of electoral competition. Surprisingly, though, nobody has analyzed how electoral competition affects EPL yet. In this article, we address this void in the literature.

In the next section, we make a theoretical argument for why parties should make a difference in EPL in principle and why and how electoral competition could affect the politics of EPL reforms. We then take the three most relevant mechanisms from the literature on the fiscal welfare state and adapt them to the case of EPL. Next, we explain our empirical strategy and operationalization before we present our results. We end with a concluding section. We do find very little evidence that electoral competition shapes the partisan politics of the regulatory welfare state except for very specific circumstances. Indeed, Christian democrats have an easier time liberalizing when in a coalition with a Left party that strongly emphasizes social justice, probably because they can share the blame with these strong welfare supporters. Nonetheless, these effects are only statistically significant for employment protection for regular employment.

# Theory: Partisan Politics, Voters, and Issue Emphasis

In the literature, there are two approaches to deduce partisan differences in public policy theoretically. Some authors essentially argue that parties translate their voters' preferences into public policy; and to the extent to which the preferences of voters of different parties differ, the policies these parties adopt will also differ. Others maintain that the preferences and ideologies of party members and party leaders are relevant, and party positions and eventually public policies differ to the extent that the ideologies of various parties differ (for a more detailed discussion, see Wenzelburger and Zohlnhöfer 2020). Although both of these approaches arrive at the theoretical expectation that Left parties tighten employment protection while Right parties liberalize EPL, we keep the two distinct for this article—the reason being the way electoral competition plays out differs between the two.

We start with the voter-based model. Rueda (2005, 2007), for example, argues that labor market insiders, who stand to benefit from dismissal protection, belong to the core supporters of Left, particularly social democratic, parties. Consequently, these parties will translate the preferences of their voters into public policy and will seek strict EPL if they get into government. In contrast, those who vote for Right parties, such as managers, the self-employed, and the better-off in general do not depend on employment protection and feel that this is an impediment to their entrepreneurial freedom and thus prefer EPL liberalization. As Right parties tend to follow the preferences of their core voters, too, they will abstain from regulation and might even deregulate labor markets once in office. Interestingly, just like for the fiscal welfare state (van Kersbergen 1995; Huber and Stephens 2001), some authors also expect Christian democrats not to behave like Right parties with regard to EPL (Emmenegger 2011; Zohlnhöfer and Voigt 2019). Factory workers, who tend to benefit from employment protection, used to be among these parties' core voters, so Christian democrats do not have electoral incentives to resist labor market regulation.

Therefore, according to this approach, the electoral importance of labor market insiders keeps Left parties from liberalizing EPL. What happens, however, if the relative electoral importance of labor market insiders for Left parties declines? Indeed, empirical research suggests that, since the 1980s, the working class voters who are considered as labor market insiders were increasingly replaced by parts of the middle class such as "sociocultural professionals," that is, well-educated individuals working in interpersonal service occupations, as core voters of Left parties (Gingrich and Häusermann 2015; Engler and Zohlnhöfer 2019). Whether these middle-class voters prefer strict labor market regulation to the same extent as classic working-class voters is questionable, because sociocultural professionals typically work in the public sector with a much lower risk of dismissal than workers in the private sector. Moreover, these people are highly educated, which also implies a lower risk of being laid off (and a higher chance of finding a new job quickly in the case of unemployment). Thus, as the composition of the electorate of Left parties changes, the relevance of labor market insiders keen on EPL diminishes, and the relevance of sociocultural professionals who are likely to care less for employment protection increases, we should expect these parties to become less fervent advocates of strict EPL. The opposite should hold true when the share of Left parties' voters from the working class rises. Thus, our first hypothesis is:

(H1) The positive effect of Left parties on the strictness of EPL increases with the share of working-class voters among their electorates.

One can come to virtually identical expectations regarding partisan differences in EPL if one assumes parties seek policy. Left parties, based on an ideology of supporting weak members of society by more state intervention in the economy, will advocate stricter EPL as a means to increase job security and to further the well-being of the less well-to-do. Right parties, in contrast, preferring the market over government intervention, will make the point for EPL liberalization to create dynamic labor markets and employment growth. Finally, Christian democrats are opposed to the unfettered operation of the market ideologically and they consider EPL as a way to protect their favorite model of the family, the male breadwinner model, which depends particularly on safe full-time regular employment for the husband. Thus, also when considering party ideologies, Christian democrats should be in favor of EPL.

Electoral considerations play out differently in the ideology-based model of partisan differences than in the voter-driven approach, however. While in the latter, parties tend to follow the preferences of their core voters, in the former, parties pay attention to the median voter. Dismissal protection is considered very popular among many voters, so it is likely that the median voter would rather support employment protection (Avdagic 2013).

Consequently, EPL expansion should be a vote winner, while liberalization will be electorally risky. Therefore, while rising unemployment—that many economists (Siebert 1997; Blanchard 2006) and some international organizations (OECD 1994) have linked with comparatively strict labor market regulation—may have suggested labor markets should be liberalized, these kinds of reforms are politically challenging. Like most attempts at welfare state retrenchment in the spending area, parties might also fear losing votes if they liberalize EPL, and thus might avoid it.

Just how risky a liberalization of EPL is depends on which party adopts it, however. Left and Christian democratic parties have expanded EPL in the past and voters are likely to be aware of that. Now imagine a Right party liberalizes EPL. Dissatisfied former voters of that party might switch to one of the pro-EPL parties as a result. If pro-EPL parties were in a strong political position in terms of votes and parliamentary seats already prior to the reform, these additional votes could put the Right governing party's reelection into question. Therefore, this Right party might shy away from the reform under these conditions, while it might adopt deregulation if EPL-defending parties are politically weak (for a similar argument cf. Hicks and Swank 1992). Therefore:

(H2) The liberalizing effect of Right (i.e., conservative and liberal) parties' government participation decreases with the electoral and parliamentary strength of Christian democratic and Left parties.

Apart from the sheer electoral and parliamentary strength of the party families that defend EPL, the risk of losing votes due to unpopular EPL reforms depends on whether the defenders of EPL politicize the reform (Armingeon and Giger 2008; Zohlnhöfer 2017). Other things being equal, Left—and to some extent Christian democratic—parties are likely to emphasize issues of social justice in their public statements and their election manifestos. The reason for this expectation is that an increasing salience of these issues among voters is likely to benefit these parties electorally because voters associate these parties with welfare issues (Budge 2015). From that perspective, Left and Christian democratic parties, willing to defend EPL, could point to the potentially negative effects of EPL liberalization and characterize deregulation as a threat to social justice. An increasing emphasis of pro-EPL parties on issues of social justice will in turn lead to a politicization of the (unpopular) EPL liberalizations, which is likely to increase the electoral risk for Right parties to adopt these reforms (Jensen and Seeberg 2015).[2] Therefore, parties that can credibly criticize a government's unpopular policies in principle have a strategic interest in talking about these issues as much as possible. Nonetheless, there are many reasons why they cannot do so all the time (Budge 2015, 770; Jensen and Seeberg 2015, 218). Some of these reasons are beyond their control; in other cases, these parties might tone down their criticism for strategic reasons, for example because they (quietly) agree with the liberalization. Therefore, it is likely that the emphasis EPL-defending parties put on the issue of social justice can vary substantially. Hence, we expect:

(H3) The liberalizing effect of Right (i.e., conservative and liberal) parties' government participation decreases the more Christian democratic and Left parties emphasize issues of social justice in their public statements.

This argument might just as well work if the parties that have expanded EPL previously now aim at liberalizing employment protection themselves. A liberalization of EPL would also be more risky for a Left government if a Christian democratic party emphasizes issues of social justice (and vice versa). Therefore, a Left (Christian democratic) government competing with a Christian democratic (Left) party that emphasizes issues of social justice might be inclined to keep their hands off EPL liberalization. We might need to distinguish between whether the defenders of EPL are in government together in a coalition or whether one of these parties is in opposition, however. While the restraining effect we have discussed should be particularly visible when one party that emphasizes social justice is in opposition, things could look differently when these parties govern jointly. If a coalition partner that emphasizes social justice can be convinced to back an EPL liberalization, this might permit a blame sharing strategy. Thus, Christian democrats in government could dare to liberalize EPL when their Left coalition partners emphasize social justice (and vice versa), because no credible alternative exists for dissatisfied voters if the coalition partner supports the reform. This way, the issue would be insulated from electoral competition. Thus, we hypothesize:

(H4a) The positive effect of Christian democratic (Left) parties' government participation on EPL decreases as Left (Christian democratic) *governing* parties' (i.e., coalition partners') emphasis on social justice increases.

(H4b) The positive effect of Christian democratic (Left) parties' government participation on EPL increases as Left (Christian democratic) *opposition* parties' emphasis on social justice increases.

## Method and Data

Our dependent variable is EPL. Among various existing indicators for EPL, we decided to use the relevant OECD (2019a) indicators. The OECD measures EPL using twenty-one items in three fields: 1) protection of regular workers against individual dismissal, 2) regulation of temporary forms of employment like fixed-term or temporary agency employment, and 3) specific conditions for collective dismissals (OECD 2014). The indicators for each field quantify the strictness of the regulations on a scale from zero to six. Higher values indicate stricter regulations. We chose these indicators for two reasons. First, they are available on a yearly basis for a long period of time and for many OECD countries. Second, we can distinguish between EPL for regular and temporary contracts. Moreover, summing up the two categories (regular and temporary contracts) equally weighted[3] to a composite index picks up all changes in both areas. Since we are interested in the liberalization or tightening of EPL, we employ the changes of the three indices (i.e., an individual index's value in a cabinet's end year minus the value in the start year) as dependent variables.

Our key explanatory variable is the partisan composition of governments. We use the cabinet seat shares of Left parties (social democrats, [Post]Communists), Right parties (conservatives, liberals), and Christian democrats based on Schmidt's (2015) dataset. Cabinets are our unit of analysis (cf. Schmitt 2016). They are defined as governments "with the same party composition (even if there are new elections or the prime minister changes but is of the same party)" (Boix 1997, 483). We slightly diverge from this definition in one respect. If a government of the exact same party composition is re-formed after an election, we still count it as a new cabinet. We think our counting rule is appropriate for our data because our data on parties' issue emphases are available for every election and our way of counting cabinets is able to make use of this data structure. Therefore, our sample consists of 124 cabinets.

The share of working-class voters among Left parties' electorates, which we need to test H1, is from Engler and Zohlnhöfer (2019) who follow Gingrich and Häusermann (2015) in combining data from various waves of the European Social Survey (2002–2012) and the Eurobarometer trend-file (1980–2001).[4] To test whether parties' emphasis on social justice limits the room for maneuver of their competitors, we use the Comparative Manifesto Project (CMP) dataset (Volkens et al. 2018). We measure emphasis on social justice by the sum of the three categories "welfare state expansion positive (per 504)"; "labour groups positive (per 701)"; and "equality positive" (per 503).[5] We code the emphasis for all Left parties falling in the CMP's categories "Socialist Parties or other left parties" and "Social democratic parties,"[6] for all Right parties in the categories "Liberal parties" and "Conservative parties" and for all Christian democratic parties. The emphasis on social justice is weighted by party strength, that is, the sum of the vote and the parliamentary seat share gained in the most recent election. If more than one political party belongs to the same party family, we refer to the parties' combined vote and seat shares.

We test our hypotheses for a sample of twenty-one (sixteen for H1) established OECD countries[7] for the period 1985 to 2013. The period of observation is limited due to the data availability of our dependent variable. We run pooled OLS regression models with standard errors clustered by country.

We include several control variables.[8] High GDP growth (from OECD 2019b) may lead to less need for EPL liberalization. Additionally, we consider the de facto index of economic globalization from the KOF dataset (Gygli et al. 2019). The more economically open a country is, the more we expect a liberalizing pressure on EPL to stay competitive. Furthermore, we include unemployment rates (from Armingeon et al. 2018) in our regression models: EPL is often described as a cause of high unemployment, which in turn should lead governments to liberalize EPL. Trade unions should facilitate stricter EPL and even force governments to strengthen EPL. We capture this effect by including union density (net union membership as share of employees) and strike activity (working days lost per 1,000 workers) from the Comparative Political Dataset (Armingeon et al. 2018). Moreover, to measure a government's institutional room to maneuver we add veto player range according to Jahn et al. (2018). We control for EU membership as a dummy variable. Finally, we include cabinet duration, as

FIGURE 1

Conditional Effect of Left Voters from the Working Class on Left Parties'
Effect on EPL

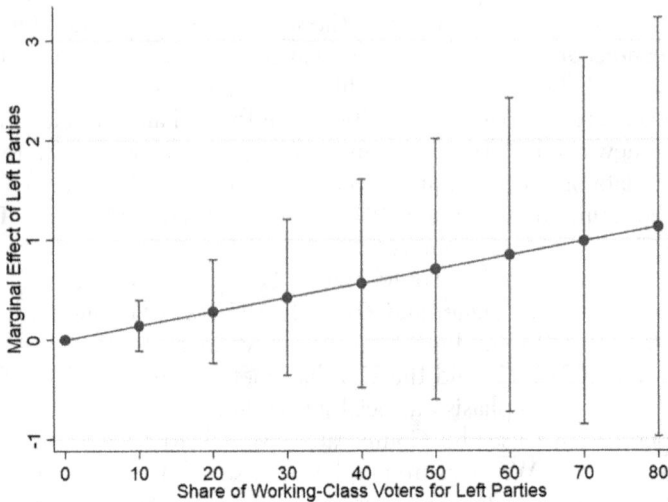

governments could have higher chances of reforming EPL when they stay in government longer, and the level of the dependent variable at the beginning of the respective cabinet to control for β-convergence. The control variables (with the exception of cabinet duration and the level of EPL at the beginning of the cabinet) reflect averages for the first half of the respective cabinet to avoid endogeneity problems.

# Results

As we investigate interaction terms, we provide graphical illustrations in the form of marginal effects plots (MEP) for ease of interpretation. These figures show the marginal effects of the partisan composition of government on EPL changes at different levels of working class shares in the electorate, strengths of EPL defender parties, and emphasis on social justice, respectively. The whiskers show the 10 percent confidence intervals. An effect is significant when the confidence interval does not include the zero line. The complete numerical results including robustness checks can be found in the online appendices. Moreover, we only report results for the composite EPL index unless findings for regular and temporary EPL differ substantially.[9]

First, we turn to Hypothesis 1 (H1). As we can see in Figure 1, the positive effect of Left parties on the strictness of EPL increases with the share of working-class voters among their electorates. Nevertheless, this effect never reaches statistical significance. Thus, H1 cannot be corroborated.[10] Neither does our Hypothesis

FIGURE 2
Conditional Effect of the Combined Strength of Christian Democrats and
Left Parties on Right Parties' Effect on EPL

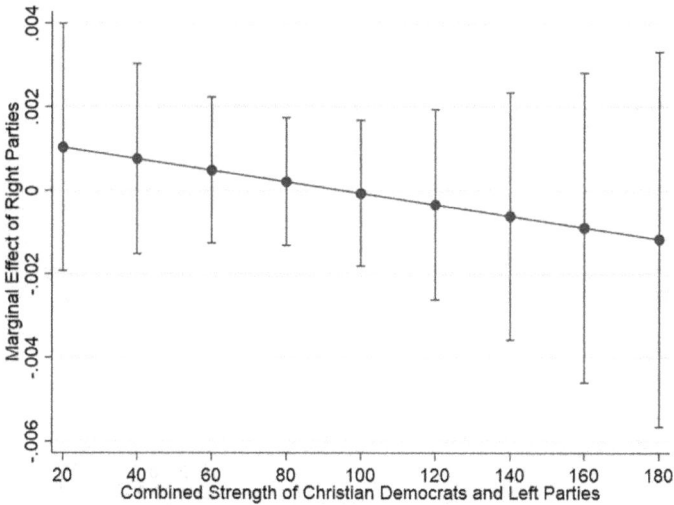

2 hold true (Figure 2): against theoretical expectations, the effect of Right parties on EPL becomes more negative when the strength of Left parties and Christian democrats rises. However, the effect is far from statistical significance.

According to Hypothesis 3, the "power of talk" (Jensen and Seeberg 2015) should play a role. The liberalizing effect of Right parties should decrease as the pro-EPL parties politicize the issue. Figure 3 shows that, against our expectations, the more the defenders of EPL emphasize their issues, the more Right parties liberalize EPL. The effect never reaches statistical significance, however.

Next we turn to Hypothesis 4 (H4), which looks at the interaction of Left parties' emphasis and Christian democratic government participation.[11] Here, distinguishing between regular and temporary contracts makes a significant difference.[12] We start with H4a that deals with Left and Christian democratic parties *governing together in a coalition* (Figure 4). The MEP on the left side shows that Christian democrats in government have a statistically significant positive effect on EPL for *regular contracts* when Left parties in government remain silent about the issue. When Left parties start to politicize the topic, however, the effect of Christian democrats soon disappears. The Christian democrats' effect even turns negative when Left governing parties get stronger and emphasize social justice more. From a weighted emphasis value of 1,250 on,[13] the effect is even significantly negative. This result corroborates H4a. The MEP on the right side shows a different picture: Christian democrats even liberalize EPL for *temporary contracts* more when their Left-wing coalition partners remain silent, and they continue to liberalize up to a weighted Left party emphasis on social justice of around 750.[14] When the Left parties' issue emphasis rises, the effect shows a positive trend but turns insignificant;

FIGURE 3

Conditional Effect of Christian Democrats' and Left Parties' Weighted Emphases on Social Justice on Right Parties' Effect on EPL

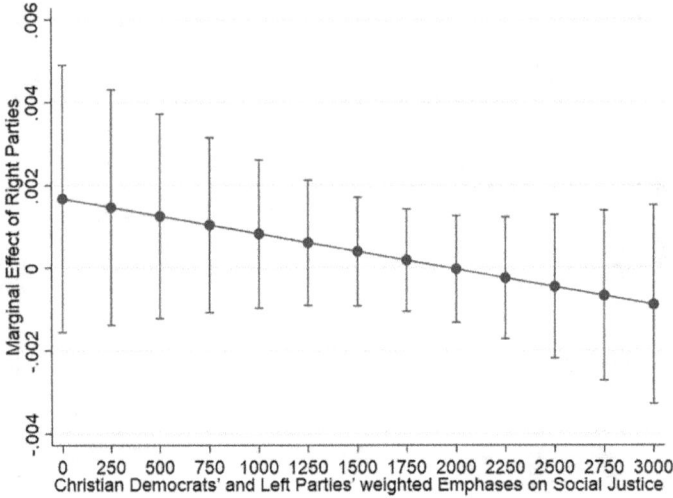

FIGURE 4

Conditional Effect of Left Governing Parties' Weighted Emphases on Social Justice on Christian Democrats' Effect on EPL (regular contracts left, temporary contracts right)

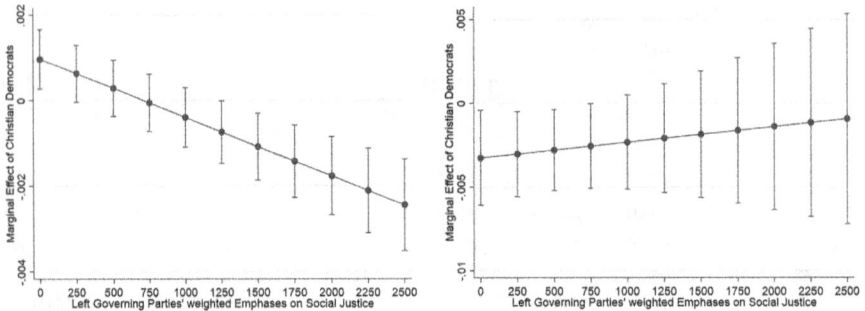

that is, Christian democrats facing a strong politicizing Left coalition partner stop liberalizing EPL for temporary contracts.

These effects turn around when Christian democrats face strong Left *opposition* parties. The left side of Figure 5 shows that Christian democrats liberalize EPL for *regular contracts* when Left opposition parties remain (nearly) silent. However, they tighten EPL further as the Left opposition increasingly emphasizes social justice. The effect reaches statistical significance on a 10-percent level at weighted emphasis scores from 1,400 upward.[15] On the right side, the effect gets more negative and is significant at moderate levels of Left issue

FIGURE 5

Conditional Effect of Left Opposition Parties' Weighted Emphases on Social Justice on
Christian Democrats' Effect on EPL (regular contracts left, temporary contracts right

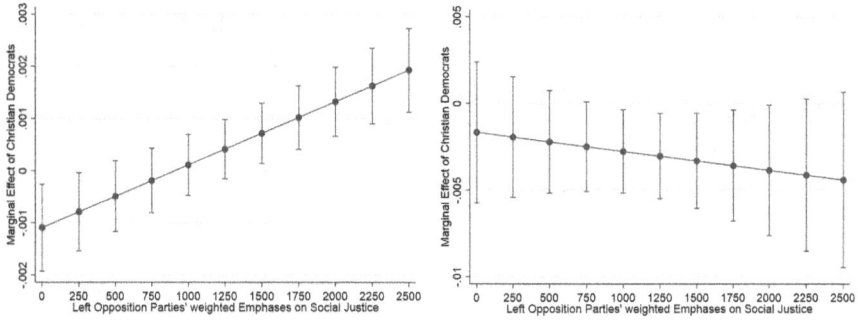

emphasis for *temporary contracts*. Thus, only the results for regular contracts are mostly in line with H4b.

While our results conform to H4a and H4b when analyzing regular employment, this is not the case for temporary employment. One possible explanation for these different patterns could be that Christian democrats have started to liberalize employment protection for atypical work as a response to rising unemployment to protect the male breadwinner model, which depends upon EPL for regular jobs (Zohlnhöfer and Voigt 2019). If Christian democrats themselves aimed at deregulating the labor market for temporary contracts, it would make sense that they would only do so when Left opposition parties do not strongly emphasize these issues (Figure 5), and that it would take very committed and strong Left coalition partners to achieve a significant positive effect (Figure 4).

The control variables corroborate our expectations or fail to reach statistical significance. We ran several robustness checks including long-term unemployment (OECD 2019c) instead of unemployment rates and a dummy for the financial crisis (1 = all cabinets in power in or after 2008, 0 = otherwise). Results do not change substantially (see online appendices).

## Conclusion

We have investigated whether theoretical approaches from the study of the fiscal welfare state based on partisan politics have explanatory power for the regulatory welfare state (RWS). The results are somewhat sobering. We do not find much evidence that electoral competition shapes the partisan politics of the regulatory welfare state. Testing the main arguments regarding the conditioning effect of electoral competition on partisan differences from the literature on the fiscal welfare state does not yield particularly conclusive results.

The composition of Left parties' electorates does not condition their effects significantly nor are Right parties deterred from liberalizing EPL by the strength or issue emphasis of those parties that can credibly claim to support employment protection. Surprisingly, politicizing strategies of pro-EPL parties do have an impact when focusing only on the competition between themselves. At least when confining the analysis to EPL for regular contracts, we find a pattern of blame sharing when Christian democrats and Left parties form coalitions, while even parties that have expanded EPL previously are kept from liberalizing employment protection when a credible competitor in opposition emphasizes issues of social justice. That is to say: when the Left opposition is strong and emphasizes the issue, Christian democrats fear to lose voters to a credible alternative claiming that they would act differently when in government and abstain from liberalizing.

What accounts for the lack of evidence for our hypotheses that have been adapted from the literature on the fiscal welfare state and that we argued could plausibly be transferred to the regulatory welfare state? An explanation for the lack of evidence for H1 on the support-base of Left parties could be that the new middle-class voters of Left parties do not care so much for employment protection, as they do not benefit directly from liberalization. This would allow even those Left parties that are experiencing a strong inflow of middle-class voters to cater to their traditional constituency regardless of the working-class voters' relative importance. Alternatively, parties might simply not care that much for the specific interests of individual voter groups but might behave more policy oriented (cf. Wenzelburger and Zohlnhöfer 2020).

Turning to our other hypotheses, one could argue that employment protection, like many other elements of the regulatory welfare state, is characterized by a quiet politics, which is not salient and thus not affected by electoral competition. Looking at qualitative evidence from Germany as an example, however, this seems unlikely. There, the infamous Hartz reforms, which contained some EPL liberalization, remained highly salient for years and have substantially affected the party system (Schwander and Manow 2017; Fervers 2019). Moreover, our results concerning blame sharing among pro-EPL parties show that electoral concerns may play some role in specific circumstances (for example, when two large pro-welfare parties compete).

Finally, one might suggest that we find neither conditional nor unconditional partisan effects because parties' programs have converged with regard to EPL. A recent study, however, that looked at the programmatic positions of all major parties on nonstandard employment in four European countries between 2007 and 2013 still finds important programmatic differences. Nonetheless, the most vocal opposition to liberalization comes from smaller Left parties such as (Post) Communists and Greens, while this kind of opposition "is expressed more mutedly" by the major parties of the Left (Picot and Menéndez 2019, 914). Although that study is based on data from only four countries and only looks at what we have analyzed as temporary EPL, it might provide an interpretation for our results, namely that the major parties that are also most relevant for forming governments and influencing public policies could indeed have converged somewhat (at least temporarily). This convergence might only have been a partial one, however. Parties in countries with a history of stubborn structural unemployment or comparatively low employment rates in the 1990s and 2000s (like the ones that Picot and Menéndez [2019] analyzed) might have concluded that liberalization is a reasonable response to the labor market problems, irrespective of the programmatic positions. That would mean that partisan differences in EPL are conditioned by the labor market situation in a country (cf. Zohlnhöfer and Voigt 2019).

What do our findings mean for the politics of the regulatory welfare state? Regarding its substance, our article makes clear that the regulatory welfare state is not only about regulation to the benefit of vulnerable groups as a side aspect of economic reforms (cf. Haber 2017), but also that programs genuinely aimed at social protection should be considered (Levi-Faur 2014). These programs are often older, more mature, more salient, and less a compensation for retrenchment of the fiscal welfare state. Rather, they have often become an object of retrenchment themselves. Therefore, it is likely that the politics also differ substantially between different areas of the regulatory welfare state. While its more recent parts may be characterized by quiet politics, as implied by Haber's (2017) important contribution, this is not necessarily the case for EPL. Although the effects we find are nuanced and subtle at best, the reasons for the lack of partisan differences in EPL since the mid-1980s are likely to be different. Rather than quiet politics, it is probably the partial programmatic convergence of mainstream parties in the face of high structural unemployment that drove EPL reforms in the last decades. This ultimately implies that it may well be worth applying theoretical approaches from the study of the fiscal welfare state at least to the salient parts of the regulatory welfare state, as we have done in this article.

# Notes

1. The empirical evidence for a negative effect of EPL liberalization on unemployment is mixed (Avdagic 2015). Nonetheless, our argument does not rest on the assumption that EPL liberalization is an effective way of fighting unemployment empirically; rather, we assume that parties may have expected that liberalization might help to fight unemployment.

2. Right parties can try to convince voters of the necessity of EPL liberalization, of course, and they can refer to their perceived economic policy competence in this context. Nonetheless, they are likely to be more successful in their attempt to convince voters when the opposition does not emphasize the issue, while the electoral risk of an EPL liberalization increases, at any given level of government justification, as the opposition politicizes the issue.

3. By choosing equal weights for EPL for regular and temporary EPL, we follow the literature. Moreover, we do not see an obvious alternative. We exclude collective dismissals from the analysis because the data are not available prior to 1998.

4. No data are available for this variable for Australia, Canada, Japan, New Zealand, and the United States. Thus, the number of cabinets drops to seventy-six in the relevant regression.

5. Given our theoretical argument, we would have also liked to use data on parties' emphasis on employment regulation. The CMP data do not include such an item, however.

6. The CMP data erroneously code the Partido Social Democrata in Portugal as a Left party, while it actually is a Right party (and is coded as such in our cabinet data). We changed the respective coding for the emphasis data.

7. Australia, Austria, Belgium, Canada, Denmark, Finland, France, Germany, Greece, Ireland, Italy, Japan, the Netherlands, New Zealand, Norway, Portugal, Spain, Sweden, Switzerland, the UK, and the United States.

8. See online Appendix 1 for detailed descriptive statistics of the variables.

9. Results not reported are available from the authors on request.

10. Note that the number of cabinets is lower than in the other regressions due to missing data.

11. We refrain from reporting results on how Christian democratic parties' emphasis on social justice conditions the effect of Left parties on EPL. The reason is the rather low number of countries in which Christian democrats are relevant. If we distinguish between Christian democrats in government and in opposition, the number of zeros becomes exceedingly high, which makes interpretation of the results highly problematic. Results available from the authors on request.

12. As the signs of the conditional effects differ between regular and temporary EPL, we do not report results for the composite index, which (unsurprisingly) are not statistically significant. Results available from the authors on request.

13. That would be a Left party that gained 35 percent of both the votes and seats and spent slightly less than 18 percent of its manifesto on issues of social justice would receive such a score, for example.

14. That would be a Left party that gained 25 percent of both the votes and seats and spent 15 percent of its manifesto on issues of social justice, for example.

15. That would be a Left party with 40 percent of votes and seats that spends 17.5 percent of its manifesto on social justice.

# References

Aaskoven, Lasse. 2019. Redistributing under fiscal constraint: partisanship, debt, inequality and labour market regulation. *Journal of Public Policy* 39 (3): 423–41.

Algan, Yann, and Pierre Cahuc. 2006. Job protection: The macho hypothesis. *Oxford Review of Economic Policy* 22 (3): 390–410.

Armingeon, Klaus, and Nathalie Giger. 2008. Conditional punishment: A comparative analysis of the electoral consequences of welfare state retrenchment in OECD nations, 1980–2003. *West European Politics* 31 (3): 558–80.

Armingeon, Klaus, Virginia Wenger, Fiona Wiedemeier, Christian Isler, Laura Knöpfel, David Weisstanner, and Sarah Engler. 2018. *Comparative political data set 1960–2016.* Berne: University of Berne, Institute of Political Science.

Avdagic, Sabina. 2013. Partisanship, political constraints, and employment protection reforms in an era of austerity. *European Political Science Review* 5 (3): 431–55.

Avdagic, Sabina. 2015. Does deregulation work? Reassessing the unemployment effects of employment protection. *British Journal of Industrial Relations* 53 (1): 6–26.

Becher, Michael. 2010. Constraining ministerial power: The impact of veto players on labor market reforms in industrial democracies, 1973–2000. *Comparative Political Studies* 43 (1): 33–60.

Blanchard, Olivier. 2006. European unemployment: The evolution of facts and ideas. *Economic Policy* 21 (45): 5–59.

Boix, Carles. 1997. Privatizing the public business sector in the eighties: Economic performance, partisan responses and divided governments. *British Journal of Political Science* 27 (4): 473–96.

Botero, Juan C., Simeon Djankov, Rafael La Porta, Florencio Lopez-de-Silanes, and Andrei Shleifer. 2004. The regulation of labor. *The Quarterly Journal of Economics* 119 (4): 1339–1382.

Budge, Ian. 2015. Issue emphases, saliency theory and issue ownership: A historical and conceptual analysis. *West European Politics* 38 (4): 761–77.

Culpepper, Pepper D. 2010. *Quiet politics and business power: Corporate control in Europe and Japan.* Cambridge: Cambridge University Press.

Emmenegger, Patrick, and Paul Marx. 2019. Regulierung der Arbeitswelt: Der Kündigungsschutz. In *Handbuch Sozialpolitik*, eds. Herbert Obinger and Manfred G. Schmidt, 697–718. Wiesbaden: Springer VS.

Emmenegger, Patrick. 2011. Job security regulations in western democracies: A fuzzy set analysis. *European Journal of Political Research* 50 (3): 336–64.

Engler, Fabian, and Reimut Zohlnhöfer. 2019. Left parties, voter preferences, and economic policy-making in Europe. *Journal of European Public Policy* 26 (11): 1620–1638.

Fervers, Lukas. 2019. Economic miracle, political disaster? Political consequences of Hartz IV. *Journal of European Social Policy* 29 (3): 411–27.

Gingrich, Jane, and Silja Häusermann. 2015. The decline of the working-class vote, the reconfiguration of the welfare support coalition and consequences for the welfare state. *Journal of European Social Policy* 25 (1): 50–75.

Gygli, Savina, Florian Haelg, Niklas Potrafke, and Jan-Egbert Sturm. 2019. The KOF Globalisation Index – revisited. *Review of International Organizations* 14:543–74.

Haber, Hanan. 2017. Rise of the regulatory welfare state? Social regulation in utilities in Israel. *Social Policy & Administration* 51 (3): 442–63.

Heinemann, Friedrich. 2007. The drivers of deregulation in the era of globalization. In *Political competition and economic regulation*, eds. Peter Bernholz and Robert Vaubel, 245–66. New York, NY: Routledge.

Hicks, Alexander M., and Duane H. Swank. 1992. Politics, institutions, and welfare spending in industrialized democracies, 1960-82. *American Political Science Review* 86 (3): 658–74.

Huber, Evelyne, and John D. Stephens. 2001. *Development and crisis of the welfare state. Parties and policies in global markets*. Chicago, IL: The University of Chicago Press.

Huo, Jingjing, Moira Nelson, and John D. Stephens. 2008. Decommodification and activation in social democratic policy: Resolving the paradox. *Journal of European Social Policy* 18 (1): 5–20.

Jahn, Detlef, Nils Düpont, Sven Kosanke, Christoph Oberst, Thomas Behm, and Martin Rachuj. 2018. PIP – Parties, Institutions & Preferences: PIP Collection, Version 2018- 02. Greifswald: University of Greifswald, Chair of Comparative Politics.

Jäkel, Tim, and Felix Hörisch. 2009. Die Deregulierung von Arbeitsmärkten im OECD-Vergleich zwischen 1990 und 2005. In *Deutschland zwischen Reformstau und Veränderung. Ein Vergleich der Politik- und Handlungsfelder*, ed. Uwe Wagschal, 83–104. Baden-Baden: Nomos.

Jensen, Carsten, and Henrik B. Seeberg. 2015. The power of talk and the welfare state: Evidence from 23 countries on an asymmetric opposition-government response mechanism. *Socio-Economic Review* 13 (2): 215–33.

Jensen, Carsten, Georg Wenzelburger, and Reimut Zohlnhöfer. 2019. *Dismantling the welfare state?* After twenty-five years: What have we learned and what should we learn? *Journal of European Social Policy* 29 (5): 681–91.

Levi-Faur, David. 2014. The welfare state: A regulatory perspective. *Public Administration* 92 (3): 599–614.

OECD. 1994. *The OECD jobs study*. Paris: OECD.

OECD. 2014. Calculating summary indicators of EPL strictness: Methodology. Paris: OECD. Available from www.oecd.org/els/emp/EPL-Methodology.pdf (accessed 10 July 2019).

OECD. 2019a. OECD indicators of employment protection. Paris: OECD. Available from www.oecd.org/employment/emp/oecdindicatorsofemploymentprotection.htm (accessed 01 May 2019).

OECD. 2019b. Data on the real gross domestic product. Paris: OECD. Available from https://data.oecd.org/gdp/real-gdp-forecast.htm (accessed 01 May 2019).

OECD. 2019c. Data on long-term unemployment. Paris: OECD. Available from: https://data.oecd.org/unemp/long-term-unemployment-rate.htm#indicator-chart (accessed 01 May 2019).

Picot, Georg, and Irene Menéndez. 2019. Political parties and non-standard employment: An analysis of France, Germany, Italy and Spain. *Socio-Economic Review* 17 (4): 899–919.

Pierson, Paul. 1994. *Dismantling the welfare state? Reagan, Thatcher, and the politics of retrenchment*. Cambridge: Cambridge University Press.

Pierson, Paul. 1996. The new politics of the welfare state. *World Politics* 48 (2): 143–79.

Pierson, Paul. 1998. Irresistible forces, immovable objects: Post-industrial welfare states confront permanent austerity. *Journal of European Public Policy* 5 (4): 539–60.

Potrafke, Niklas. 2010. Labor market deregulation and globalization: Empirical evidence from OECD countries. *Review of World Economics* 146 (3): 545–71.

Rueda, David. 2005. Insider–outsider politics in industrialized democracies: The challenge to social democratic parties. *American Political Science Review* 99 (1): 61–74.

Rueda, David. 2007. *Social democracy inside out: Partisanship and labor market policy in advanced industrialized democracies*. Oxford: Oxford University Press.

Schmidt, Manfred G. 2015. Partisan composition of government in OECD democracies, 1945–2014, unpublished data. Heidelberg: University of Heidelberg.

Schmitt, Carina. 2016. Panel data analysis and partisan variables: How periodization does influence partisan effects. *Journal of European Public Policy* 23 (10): 1442–1459.

Schwander, Hanna, and Philip Manow. 2017. "Modernize and Die?" German social democracy and the electoral consequences of the Agenda 2010. *Socio-Economic Review* 15 (1): 117–34.

Siebert, Horst. 1997. Labor market rigidities: At the root of unemployment in Europe. *Journal of Economic Perspectives* 11 (3): 37–54.

Siegel, Nico A. 2007. Moving beyond expenditure accounts: The changing contours of the regulatory state, 1980–2003. In *The disappearing state? Retrenchment realities in an age of globalisation*, ed. Francis G. Castles, 245–72. Cheltenham, UK: Edward Elgar Publishing.

Van Kersbergen, Kees. 1995. *Social capitalism. A study of Christian democracy and the welfare state*. London: Routledge.

Volkens, Andrea, Werner Krause, Pola Lehmann, Theres Matthieß, Nicolas Merz, Sven Regel, and Bernhard Weßels. 2018. The manifesto data collection. Manifesto Project (MRG/CMP/MARPOR). Version 2018b. Berlin: Wissenschaftszentrum Berlin für Sozialforschung (WZB). Available from https://manifesto-project.wzb.eu/datasets (accessed 01 May 2019).

Weaver, Kent R. 1986. The politics of blame avoidance. *Journal of Public Policy* 6 (4): 371–91.

Wenzelburger, Georg, and Reimut Zohlnhöfer. 2020. Bringing agency back into the study of partisan politics. A note on recent developments in the literature on party politics. *Party Politics* online first. DOI: 10.1177/1354068820919316.

Zohlnhöfer, Reimut, and Linda Voigt. 2019. Prioritizing employment over protection? The conditional effect of unemployment on partisan politics in employment protection. Paper prepared for the panel: New perspectives on the study of partisan politics and public policies at the ECPR General Conference, 2019. Wroclaw.

Zohlnhöfer, Reimut. 2017. Zum Einfluss des Parteienwettbewerbs auf politische Entscheidungen. In *Parteien unter Wettbewerbsdruck*, eds. Sebastian Bukow and Uwe Jun, 15–37. Wiesbaden: Springer VS.

# Varieties of Regulatory Welfare Regimes in Middle-Income Countries: A Comparative Analysis of Brazil, Mexico, and Turkey

By
IŞIK D. ÖZEL
and
SALVADOR PARRADO

The expansion of social welfare regimes in middle-income countries (MICs) has become a global trend that has involved the adaption of robust social assistance programs aiming to alleviate poverty and diminish inequalities. We analyze conditional cash transfers in Brazil, Mexico, and Turkey, identifying the types of regulatory regimes that exist in each, namely "loose decentralism" in Brazil, "strict centralism" in Mexico, and "subcontracted *dirigisme*" in Turkey. We argue that regulatory design is key to understanding how the newly flourishing welfare regimes can control political manipulation, and that where manipulation occurs, social assistance programs can deviate from their initial objectives and endanger the welfare of the poor and hazard trust in the government and political institutions. However, when social welfare regimes work in line with their objectives and eschew political discretion, regulatory welfare states can enhance trust in and legitimacy of political institutions. Our analysis indicates that a centrally regulated social assistance governance nurtured by local knowledge is key to avoiding political manipulation and to alleviating poverty, major issues in MICs.

*Keywords:* social assistance; conditional cash transfers; regulatory welfare state; Brazil; Mexico; Turkey

Since the late 1990s, the expansion of social welfare in the Global South has become a prevalent phenomenon in the face of globalization,

*Işık D. Özel is a visiting professor at Universidad Carlos III de Madrid and a member of the Carlos III-Juan March Institute. Broadly situated in comparative political economy, her research examines the politics of institutional change and its diverse outcomes in middle-income countries, with a focus on social policy, education, and market regulation.*

*Salvador Parrado teaches public administration at the Spanish Distance Learning University (Madrid). He has carried out comparative research on executive politics, public management, public values, public-private partnerships, civil service, and reform policies. He is the director of Governance International and associate editor of* Public Administration.

Correspondence: iozel@clio.uc3m.es

DOI: 10.1177/0002716220965884

which, in contrast, exhorted welfare retrenchment in advanced countries (Haggard and Kauffman 2008; Holland and Schneider 2017; Mares and Carnes 2009). Aiming to fight against poverty and alleviate inequalities, while garnering support from the poor, social assistance programs have become major constituents of these flourishing welfare regimes. These programs have been adopted by divergent regimes and governments in all corners of the ideological spectrum, defying views of democratic-authoritarian and Left-Right divides in welfare expansion (Garay 2016). An increasingly popular component of the social assistance programs is the noncontributory and nondiscretionary means-tested conditional cash-transfers (CCTs) to the poor—adopted widely, from Brazil to Burkina Faso and Mexico to Indonesia—as a cost-effective redistribution tool for which governments can claim credit.

Tied to strict eligibility criteria and conditionalities like the recipients keeping their children at school and attending medical check ups, CCTs—delivered mostly to women as representatives of the household—aimed to break the cycle of intergenerational poverty by advancing human capital (World Bank 2009). Based on their means-tested provision linked to strict conditions and rather parsimonious benefits, the CCTs resemble the poverty relief instruments of the "liberal welfare states" à la Esping-Andersen (1990). Tied to concrete eligibility criteria and co-responsibility of the beneficiaries, they are often considered panacea against political discretion and, hence, a major break with the past (IDB 2015; Sugiyama and Hunter 2013).

We argue, however, that the ways in which governments regulate these programs might hinder or facilitate political discretion, which is a common practice in many developing countries. Based on their implementation at multiple levels and substantial reach—more than 20 percent of the population in Mexico and Brazil (Cecchini and Atuesta 2017)—CCTs may provide ample ground for political discretion. The regulatory design is key to understanding how the newly flourishing welfare regimes in these countries can eschew clientelism,[1] which deteriorates the welfare of the poor (Díaz-Cayeros and Magaloni 2009), muddles their political preferences, and, hence, hampers political competition, an essential constituent of democracies (de la O 2015).

Focusing on the selection and recertification of CCT beneficiaries—the processes where regulatory instruments come into play—we examine the varieties of regulatory regimes in the CCT programs in Brazil, Mexico, and Turkey. Adopting Mill's method of difference, we select these cases with similar levels of per capita income [2] and parallel legacies of highly stratified Bismarckian conservative welfare states and treat them as the "most similar cases" (Eckstein 1975). All three countries are trapped in the upper-middle-income group[3] and are members of the G20. They simultaneously went through similar drastic transformations, shifting from state-led import-substituting industrialization strategy (1930s–1980s) to a market-oriented model with varying nuances (Özel 2011, 2014; Schneider 2013).

Unlike most advanced countries, they adopted neoliberal policies in the 1980s in the absence of well-established welfare states and the presence of large informal markets (Holland and Schneider 2017). Their welfare regimes expanded starting in the 1990s at the critical juncture of accelerating integration of their national markets to the global and regional ones. They evolved from "truncated" welfare states—that offered restricted social insurance tied to employment; provided flat or regressive transfers; and kept barriers to access, resembling Bismarckian conservative typology (Esping-Andersen 1990), yet in a highly limited fashion due to the sole coverage of urban formal labor—to more universalistic ones (Díaz-Cayeros Estévez, and Magaloni 2016; Holland 2018).

Echoing the "hybridization" that Leisering (2011, 2012) conceptualized, we show the ways in which hybrid forms have been incorporated into the regulation of fiscal transfers, bringing complex sets of actors together in these three countries. The adoption of regulatory instruments makes social assistance a policy field where fiscal transfers intersect with the regulatory state, exemplifying the regulatory welfare state (RWS). Adding up to Levi-Faur's (2014, 599) emphasis that "the regulatory state may strengthen the welfare state," we suggest that an appropriately regulated welfare state situated at the intersection of social policy and regulation might also strengthen democratic institutions through limiting politically driven redistribution.

Given that redistribution is germane to political manipulation, regulatory instruments would (ideally) function to eliminate such manipulation by means of setting, enforcing, and monitoring varying rules in fiscal transfers at distinct stages of selection (targeting, identification, and registering) and recertification of beneficiaries. Analyzing the roles of multifarious actors (public and private alike) in implementation, as well as regulatory instruments and processes set in the selection and recertification processes, this article poses the following questions: How do the regulatory processes adopted in distinct polities mold discretionary spaces? What accounts for varieties of regulatory welfare states in different countries? The article explores the room for political discretion embedded in respective regulatory regimes—either created intentionally or emerging as unintended outcomes.

To understand the ways in which regulatory instruments are adopted in these three upper-middle income countries, we carried out extensive archival research on official documents and policy papers of public authorities related to conditional cash transfers; reports and assessments of international organizations and evaluating agencies; along with press releases and media sources on the subject matter. Additionally, we conducted eighteen semi-structured in-depth interviews with the officials in charge of selection and recertification processes of the CCT programs as well as experts of social policy in the respective countries (five in Brazil, six in Mexico, and seven in Turkey, face-to-face, and via email and phone). Bringing together and cross-checking the findings of the interviews with archival data, we analyze the variation across these three cases regarding the formation of distinct types of regulatory welfare states.

Drawing on these three cases with well-established CCT programs run by central governments, we find noteworthy differences in the regulatory design of selection and recertification and the roles of agents in those, leading to the varieties of CCT regulatory regimes, namely loose decentralism in Brazil, strict centralism in Mexico, and subcontracted *dirigisme* in Turkey. Our analysis suggests that contingent upon the regulatory instruments established in the selection and recertification processes, the space for political discretion can be minimized or expanded. We argue that regulatory instruments might diminish the likelihood of gearing redistribution at opportunistic gains, as they may help to maintain neutrality in granting benefits or becoming the tools of political patrons (Knott and Miller 2008).

## Regulating Social Assistance against Political Discretion

Scholarship on expanding social welfare regimes in the Global South has tackled the emergence, expansion, sustainability, content, and effectiveness of these regimes, along with their ideology-related determinants and consequences (Mares and Carnes 2009; Hanlon, Barrientos, and Hulme 2010; Huber 2005; Huber and Stephens 2012). While a number of studies emphasize the electoral pay-offs of social assistance programs (Cornelius 2004; De la O 2013; Díaz-Cayeros, Estévez, and Magaloni 2016; Hunter and Power 2007; Zucco 2013), others highlight their mobilizing effect rather than their ability to boost pro-incumbent votes (de la O 2015; Layton and Smith 2015). Several studies demarcate the regime-level implications of social assistance (Holland and Schneider 2017; Layton, Donaghy, and Rennó 2017; Özel and Yildirim 2019).

Social policy provides an apt ground for reinforcing political manipulation. De la O (2015) argues that the strict design of the CCTs with clear operational guidelines limiting discretion may, indeed, erode clientelism, as indicated by the example of the Mexican *Prospera* program, endowed with elaborate rules and robust operation. Likewise, Garay (2016) denotes the Zedillo government's zealous effort to disassociate *Progresa* from clientelistic linkages. Sugiyama and Hunter (2013) assert that Brazil's *Bolsa Família* by-and-large evaded clientelistic pitfalls. De la O (2015) suggests that the checks and balances in CCTs, installed through elaborate rules and robust operations, are more likely to be set when the president faces checks on his own power, contingent upon a strong legislature.

Regulation of social assistance regimes is indispensable for minimizing the potential for political manipulation, as rules and administrative procedures may operate as shields against politicization by tying the hands of the principals (Moynihan, Herd, and Harvey 2014). Regulatory regimes—as bundles of regulators, rules, administrative procedures, and enforcement agents—are germane to shaping the complex dynamics between principals and agents at different levels of government. These regimes, then, interact in multifarious ways with the welfare states in the field of social policy.

Deconstructing the dichotomous positioning set by Majone (1997) regarding the properties, instruments, and outcomes of the welfare state (WS) and the regulatory state (RS), recent studies point to the intersection between the WS and RS, rather than looking at them as binary opposites. Underscoring the redistributive character of regulation and its embeddedness within the welfare state, Levi-Faur (2014, 600) suggests that regulatory instruments may indeed be used for redistributive ends, indicating the intertwined and mutually constitutive nature of regulatory and welfare states. In line with Tanzi (2002), who addresses the use of regulatory instruments in the pursuit of social objectives, Haber (2017) shows that utility regulation engenders substantial redistributive outcomes, operating like a functional equivalent of welfare instruments filtered by the existing welfare regimes. Leisering (2011, 2012) also points to a similar dynamic where regulation of pensions works like social welfare instruments. Similarly, Benish, Haber, and Eliahou (2017) examine the ways in which the regulation of pension markets in Israel and the UK generates varieties of "regulatory citizenship," shaped by an egalitarian approach in the former, and minimal regulatory social protection in the latter, in line with the WS traditions in the respective countries.

As regulation generates significant welfare-state-like outcomes (intentionally or unintentionally), it also permeates into the WS through setting and monitoring the rules of the game regarding how the social policy is designed and who is targeted on which criteria (Levi-Faur 2014). Based on such complex interactions, distinct varieties of regulatory welfare states are formed, resembling liberal, neoliberal, or workfare welfare states contingent upon their traits regarding the level of decommodification, conditions linked to labor markets, while introducing new regulatory traits (Esping-Andersen 1990; Jessop 1993).

Two strands of the extant literature envisage administrative rules and procedures as regulatory instruments of the executive. The first one considers administrative rules as "burdens on citizens," inevitably engendering political control (Herd and Moynihan 2019). It suggests that these procedures induce compliance with the rules but offer a limited range of feasible policy actions, in line with the actual policy objectives of politicians (McCubbins, Noll, and Weingast 1987). In social policy, politicians may use administrative *burdens* to achieve policy objectives by undertaking "hidden or subterranean" political control mechanisms (Hacker 2004) as beneficiaries may give up enrollment due to such burdens, regardless of their eligibility (Brodkin and Majmundar 2010). For instance, the application procedures might be complex, or the potential recipients of social assistance may be asked to attend meetings scheduled at inconvenient time slots or held at far-away places, which might be hard to get to for the poor. Alternatively, conditionality may be so rigid that dismissal of beneficiaries would be a likely outcome, swiftly reducing fiscal spending. For example, conditionality might require the proof of an official rental contract or bills, which the applicant might not possess because such documents are not used in the country. Therefore, administrative burdens might be attractive for politicians who do not disclose their actual objectives (Moynihan Herd, and Harvey 2014) of cutting welfare, engendering welfare retrenchment without direct political intervention.

In the second strand, however, standard operating procedures constitute safeguards against the utilitarian calculations and interference of politicians (Knott and Miller 2008). Administrative procedures, considered neutral because they follow general rules, would restrain politicians' discretionary capacity, facilitating fairness and legitimacy (Stewart 1975). Neutrality would inevitably be undermined when the procedures are used as political instruments aligning with electoral concerns (McNollgast 1990). Given that the administration of public resources may result in moral hazard—public officials might engage in risky behavior whose cost would be borne by others such as, for instance, the political actors or the society as a whole—only an appropriate regulatory system could offset the manipulation by the principal. To minimize the moral hazard risk, Knott and Miller (2008) point to well-entrenched trustee systems, acting on behalf of the electorate, and thwarting the principal's control. Rules and standard operating procedures are trustees' key to constraining principals' interference. Notwithstanding its costs, these regulatory instruments offer the potential to limit the risk of moral hazard based on blind rules. Independent auditors might enhance administrative neutrality and help to keep political manipulation at bay.

Given that the social assistance programs this article focuses on are designed and funded by central governments yet implemented locally, we tackle the regulatory instruments at both levels: central and local. First, we consider how the ways in which different levels of government are involved in the implementation might empower political principals at distinct levels. In the case of the CCTs, potential discretionary space at the local level might help to eschew the eligibility criteria and loosen up the rules of recertification, as keeping beneficiaries longer in the system would generate important payoffs for local principals (Medellín et al. 2015). Regulatory regimes may either become shields against political discretion favoring particular constituencies or, rather, turn into political instruments to shift priorities at different governmental levels. We would expect that centralist systems might design regulatory regimes with some leeway for political discretion of the central government. However, in the federal systems, the center is likely to tighten regulations and embedded operating procedures to avoid political influence of subnational governments.

Second, regulatory instruments endowed with well-established information systems as *modus operandi* of selection and recertification processes are likely to alleviate the potential political manipulation of CCTs at the local and national levels. Besides information systems, monitoring instruments from higher organizational/territorial levels helps to reduce the level of political discretion. Studies on street-level bureaucracy indicate the role of individual-level discretion in enforcing administrative procedures (Evans 2016). Given that CCTs may be politically manipulated, we discuss the ways in which regulation is designed to leave room for or prevent political discretion. We would expect that a strict regulatory design regarding the selection and recertification of beneficiaries (i.e., use of national information and monitoring systems to cross-check household information among other instruments) would diminish the discretionary space, while "loose" design might enable the discretionary space.

## From the Bismarckian to the Liberal Welfare States: Mexico, Brazil, and Turkey

Conditional cash transfers were launched in the aftermath of severe financial crises in all three countries that we focus on (Mexico 1994, Brazil 1999, Turkey 2001) under the aegis of international financial institutions such as the International

Monetary Fund (IMF), which provided loans based on conditionality. In the context of those loans, the respective governments needed to comply with the conditions set by the IMF, such as budgets consistent with the fiscal framework approved by the organization to facilitate macroeconomic adjustment programs. In a way, the respective governments transposed the conditionality approach of those institutions, carrying it from the national to the household level, as the policy-makers linked cash transfers to households complying with the set conditions. Therefore, in all three cases, CCTs portray the characteristics of "liberal" WS with limited decommodification. Rather than being tied to citizenship rights, they are tied to strict criteria and compliance with (behavioral) conditionalities. Recent articulation of labor market incorporation conditionality in the Turkish case made it akin to Jessop's (1993) "workfare state," endowing it with a rather "neoliberal" character (Benish and Levi-Faur, this volume).

While Turkey has a highly centralized administrative Napoleonic tradition, Mexico and Brazil are federal systems with different subnational constellations. Nevertheless, this difference mollifies when we consider the historical reflexes of centralization of social policy stemming from authoritarian pasts in Mexico and Brazil (Díaz-Cayeros, Estévez, and Magaloni 2016; Draibe 2002). Endowed with similar features, all three counties have established CCTs since the late 1990s. Despite that Mexico was the global pioneer, its "iconic *Prospera*" program (World Bank 2009), designed to eliminate clientelism, was dismantled in 2019 following 22 years of operation and having reached 6.6 million households.[4] Based on the claims of its alleged political manipulation and "neoliberal quality" tied to conditions, the MORENA Government led by Andrés Manuel López Obrador replaced *Prospera* with Benito Juárez Scholarships for students, divorced from health and nutrition components and conditionalities. In contrast, two right-wing populist leaders with authoritarian overtones, namely Bolsonaro and Erdoğan, continue the respective CCTs in Brazil and Turkey. Yet the Bolsonaro Government reduced the beneficiaries by 1 million in January 2020, planning to replace Bolsa Familia with the program "*Renda* Brazil" (Brazil Income) (*Economist* 2020).

Until dismantling in 2019, the Mexican CCT program evolved from "*Progresa*" (1997–2002), initially geared toward the rural poor, to the nationally expanded *Oportunidades* (2002–2014) and to *Prospera* (2014–2019), widely referred to as POP (CONEVAL 2019; UNDP 2011). In 2014, *Prospera* reached over six million families (21 percent of the population) in almost 2500 municipalities. Its 2015 budget constituted 1.6 percent of the federal budget and 0.4 percent of the GDP (*Prospera* 2015). In addition to the conditionalities regarding school enrollment and regular health check ups, mimicked in all countries adopting CCTs following the Mexican example, *Prospera* also allowed recipients to attend basic courses on preventive healthcare and hygiene and to take part in community services.

Despite Mexico's pioneering role in establishing a nationally administered CCT program, Brazil's *Bolsa Familia* might be the most popularly known CCT, reaching about 13.6 million households or 21 percent of the population, with its budget constituting 0.6 percent of GDP by 2019 (IDB 2019). Initiated as a subnational program, *Bolsa Familia* was launched at the federal level in 2003, merging four existing programs—*Bolsa Escola, Bolsa Alimentação, Cartão Alimentação,* and *Auxilio Gas*—and later adding the Child Labor Eradication Program in 2006 (World Bank 2009).

In Turkey, the CCT was launched in 2001 and adopted nationally in 2004 through the "Social Risk Mitigation Project" (SRMP) funded by the World Bank (2008, 2). It offered conditional emergency cash transfers to the poor linked to education and health. Successive Justice and Development Party (AKP) governments embraced and funded the CCT following the SRMP's termination in 2007, combining it with a range of regular and irregular—cash and in-kind—social assistance programs (Öktem 2018). Due to the opacity of funding and lack of transparency about the recipients, along with the existence of numerous social assistance schemes, the exact figures on CCT per se are not accessible. By 2017, the budget of the Ministry of Family, Labor and Social Services (MoFLSS) constituted 4 percent of the central budget, and social assistance made up 84 percent of the MoFLSS's budget and 1.6 percent of GDP (World Bank 2017).

## Modalities of Governance: Roles of Different Agents and Levels of Government

The constellation of actors varies among the three scrutinized cases; in particular, the role of the national versus the subnational level and public versus private actors varies in the design and the implementation of these regulatory instruments. As modalities of governance, this section shows the varying role of the agents in the federal-only system in Mexico, a federal-municipal duo in Brazil, and the interplay of a centralized system implemented by a public-private partnership at the district level in Turkey.

In Mexico, centralization was considered a "shield against political manipulation" since the launching of the CCT program in 1997, based on the belief that "the absence of intermediaries between the federal government and the beneficiaries helps to limit the opportunities of political manipulation and possibility of corruption" (Levy 2006, 98). *Prospera* National Coordination Office (PNCO) affiliated with the Ministry of Social Development (SEDESOL), in coordination with the Ministry of Health, Institute of Social Security and the Ministry of Education, steered the system. The PNCO had thirty-two *Prospera* delegations at the state level, each containing eight to twelve zones of operation with designated "micro-zones" and "customer service units" in charge of enrollment and recertification. "Customer care managers" had direct contact with the beneficiaries at the micro-zone level where the government organized bimonthly seminars and workshops. An important feature of the Mexican system was the presence of an autonomous national agency in charge of monitoring and evaluating *Prospera*. Operational since 2006, the National Council for the Evaluation of Social Development Policy (CONEVAL) generated multidimensional poverty measures, periodically updated at the subnational and municipal levels (Ibarrarán et al. 2017).

In the case of Brazil, municipalities are the key players in the implementation of *Bolsa Família*, a national program administered by the National Secretariat for

Citizen Incomes (SENARC) at the federal level. Although *Bolsa Familia* is centralized regarding the incorporation of all beneficiaries into the Single Registry (*Cadastro Unico*), the municipalities register households into *Cadastro* and monitor and report their compliance with designated conditionality. Municipalities are provided with monthly transfers by the federal government in return for their administration of *Bolsa Familia*, and those transfers depend on the municipality's "decentralized management index" value along with the number of beneficiaries they serve. They have a certain level of discretion about the use of transfers, as a robust cross-check from the federal government is missing. Formed by the government and civil society organizations, Social Accountability Units monitor *Bolsa Familia*'s implementation, yet the challenges persist regarding the difficulty of finding independent organizations, especially in small municipalities (Tapajós et al. 2010).

Centralizing the control and monitoring of data and decentralizing implementation, the Turkish regime has a hybrid modality of governance, entailing private and public actors alike. The General Directorate of Social Assistance (GDSA), associated with MoFLSS, administers the social assistance schemes. These schemes are funded by the *sui generis* extra-budgetary "Fund for the Encouragement of the Social Cooperation and Solidarity" (FESCS), comprising mainly public funds and private contributions.[5] Supervised by the GDSA, the Fund Committee consists of the undersecretaries of MoFLSS; Ministries of the Interior, Health, Finance; the chairs of the GDSA; and the Directorate General of Foundations (KHK 633-§34). FESCS disseminates funds to semi-autonomous social assistance and solidarity foundations (SASFs) established at the district level (1,002 in total by 2019).[6]

Designated as parastatal organizations authorized to distribute FESCS funding—besides generating individual funds through private donations and corporate revenues[7]—SASFs are the agents that implement social assistance at the district level, operating as subcontractors to steer CCT throughout Turkey.[8] They are governed by the Boards of Trustees, which consist of both nationally appointed high-level bureaucratic officials at the provincial level—including the governor, who chairs the board—and elected officials such as the mayor, along with local philanthropists and representatives of (selected) civil society. Boards have decision-making authority and some discretion to override eligibility criteria in selection and recertification.[9] Although this setup seemingly opens discretionary space for local agents, discretion has been relatively restrained since 2010[10] through controls undertaken by an e-government database, the Integrated Social Assistance System (ISAS), based on data across twenty-two public institutions (World Bank 2017).

Like in the Turkish case, some discretionary room also prevails in Brazil, where the federal government sets quotas of beneficiaries for municipalities, whose discretionary use may be likely (Hellman 2015; Eiró and Koster 2019). A striking feature of CCT regimes in all three countries is the formation of periodically updated rigorous information systems by the central governments. The Mexican CCT regime also installed an autonomous evaluator, which the others lack (other than the offices of audit/evaluation set in the state apparatus, such as the General Controller's Office, the Federal Audits Court, and the Office of the Public Prosecutor in Brazil).

## Regulatory Instruments in Selecting and Recertifying Beneficiaries

The selection process for CCTs starts with identifying eligible households for which three methods are used. The first, a geographical method, entails the selection of all households in certain areas, contingent upon meeting the respective criteria; the second, a categorical method, grants automatic beneficiary rights to specific groups, independent of the eligibility criteria; and the third, means-testing through the eligibility criteria (Medellín et al. 2015).

Mexico and Brazil have combined different targeting methods, while the Turkish CCT uses means-testing. The targeting in *Prospera* was conducted annually as a two-step process undertaken at the national level based on proxy means-testing (combining census data on assets and demographics with information collected through surveys). The first step entailed geographical targeting, done by the PNCO, while the selection of municipalities corresponded to their position in national databases and indices: registry in an information system (*Sistema de Focalización del Desarrollo* [*SIFODE*]), social lagging, and marginalization index. In the second step, *Prospera's* thirty-two state delegations, containing eight to twelve operation zones each, used an algorithm to select households, or the PNCO conducted house visits at distinct municipalities based on their scores in the indices. Social workers applied surveys containing a proxy means-test employing thirty-one variables to assess eligibility (Dávila 2016, 15). Communities played some role in verifying the beneficiary lists, often to expand them to correct exclusion errors (IDB 2015).

Compared to *Prospera*, both eligibility and conditionality criteria of Brazil's *Bolsa Família* are relatively looser, and poor households without children are also included. The selection process, based on geographic and categorical targeting, coordinated by the National Secretariat of Citizen Income (SENARC), does not have the same level of robustness as in Mexico. In the first step, the Institute for Geography and Statistics establishes an estimated number of households living in poverty in each municipality and at the national level. SENARC sets a quota for each municipality. In the second step, potential beneficiaries file applications at the municipalities based on a self-declared per capita family income. In 2014 only 6.1 percent of certifications were done with house visits, while 77 percent were done without such visits (Hellman 2015, 9). In addition, SENARC engages in categorical targeting above the quotas set for municipalities. Disadvantaged groups (like indigenous families) that meet the eligibility criteria automatically receive the benefits even if the estimated quota of beneficiaries for a municipality has been reached.

The selection process in the Turkish CCT takes place through the engagement of national- and district-level actors, bureaucrats and politicians, and public and private stakeholders alike. As in Brazil, the first step takes place at the local level in Turkey, but at the district rather than municipal level. Potential beneficiaries file their applications at the district SASF, which standardizes the applicants' data and generates a socioeconomic profile based on an ID number and self-declaration, and then integrates and verifies that data with the national ISAS database. In the second step, SASF officers undertake house visits where they apply a standard questionnaire, double check the applicant's socioeconomic profile, make further assessments, and provide the applicant with a poverty score. They then upload these questionnaires to ISAS, which uses a proxy means-test aggregating socioeconomic data, household characteristics, and geographical variables. The final step is the evaluation of the applicant's profile based on the updated ISAS data by the Board of Trustees of the district SASF, the principal decision-making authority regarding selection (World Bank 2017).

The variation between the three cases regarding the selection of beneficiaries is rather puzzling. In the Turkish case, which is the most central of all, the implementation at the local/district level is contracted to semiautonomous foundations, which are run in a concerted fashion by appointed and elected public actors as well as private stakeholders (representatives of selected organizations and philanthropists). The decentralized nature of the Brazilian system is similar to its Turkish counterpart, as local agents are granted discretionary space in selection, yet private actors are not involved. The selection processes in both Brazil and in Mexico bypass the subnational actors. In Mexico, it was run by the state-level representatives of the federal agency PNCO and, hence, sidestepped municipalities; whereas in Brazil, municipalities are involved. All three countries rely on centralized information systems to eschew discretion and manipulation.

The *recertification* process determines whether beneficiaries can remain in the program by means of assessing the continuation of their eligibility and their compliance with conditionalities. Removing beneficiaries may incur important electoral costs for politicians; therefore, recertification has crucial importance for politicians, who may use strategies to keep beneficiaries in the program longer, such as postponing recertification or not dismissing those who are not eligible or did not comply with conditionalities.

The three cases in our sample adopted different recertification procedures. Recertification happens annually in Turkey, every other year in Brazil, and every eight years in Mexico. The Mexican system used house visits; the Brazilian system mostly relies on beneficiaries' self-declaration of the beneficiaries (subject to checks by municipal authorities); and the Turkish system combines database checks with house visits. In Mexico, the social workers of PNCO delegations undertook recertification based on house visits to update data, which was analyzed through a centralized information system (CONEVAL 2019). The beneficiaries were sanctioned in cases where they failed to go through recertification and when they did not comply with conditionalities that were both extensive (seminar attendance besides obtaining certificates for health check-ups and school attendance) and strictly monitored.

The recertification process in Turkey is undertaken through automatic controls performed by the ministry using the ISAS database and the house visits conducted by the SASF social workers. Since the establishment of ISAS in 2010, recertification is handled in a more rigorous fashion, cross-checking for both continuing eligibility and conditionality compliance. Accordingly, sanctioning mechanisms (benefit cuts for a certain period or complete dismissal) are applied more strictly than before in Turkey. Although conditionality was not as extensive as in Mexico previously, the labor market insertion program, incorporated in 2017 (22/6/2017, Official Gazette, #30104), extended the conditionalities. Nevertheless, this new regulation came into force in 2018 on paper, yet was only implemented partially by 2020.[11]

In Brazil, the municipality officials carry out recertification through the updates of beneficiaries' data based on self-declaration. Beneficiaries, reminded of recertification scheduling via messages sent with their payment receipts, are expected to update their information at the respective municipal offices. The recertification process was much more robust in Mexico than in Brazil and Turkey.

## Varieties of Regulatory Regimes

The three CCT regimes that we analyzed installed a range of similar principles, yet they were adopted through various procedures and by distinct constellations of actors at the central-local nexus. Central governments in all three aimed to deter clientelistic practices at the subnational/local level and tie the hands of politicians by means of different institutional arrangements. Well-established information systems integrated into national databases, which facilitate targeting and selection based on objective data, enabled administrative neutrality in all regimes. Although all three cases present high technical capacity (see the Table 1), Mexico and Turkey display higher state capacity to combine the results of means-testing and house visits, which has been a limited practice in Brazil.

Federal governments in Mexico and Brazil employed varying strategies to bypass the potential interference of subnational governments. The former controlled the whole process in a highly centralized fashion, while the latter relied on municipalities to manage the CCTs. In the centralist system of Turkey, however, selection and recertification were institutionalized in a hybrid fashion *a la* Leisering (2011), as they brought together public and private sectors and appointed and elected officials at the national and local levels. Both Turkey and Brazil incorporate local knowledge in their certification and recertification of beneficiaries, yet their national governments cross-check local agents' performance with a different degree of detail due to their varied capacity to reach, control, and coordinate the local agents. Such disparities gave rise to different varieties of regulatory regimes installed in the CCTs in the three countries. The first variety is loosely monitored decentralism in Brazil, designed and funded by the center and implemented by the local agents with relatively loose controls of the former, along with relatively loose monitoring of conditionalities. Strict centralism, epitomized by Mexico, has the traits of highly bureaucratized vertical governance tightly controlled by the central government to minimize potential manipulation at the local level, along with strict conditionalities set for behavioral change. Finally, subcontracted *dirigisme*, exemplified by the Turkish case, relies on the design and control of the central government and the administrative implementation by the semi-autonomous parastatal entities that bring together

TABLE 1
Traits of Conditional Cash-Transfers (CCTs) in Brazil, Mexico, and Turkey

| | Selection ( eligibility ) | | Recertification ( conditionality) | |
| --- | --- | --- | --- | --- |
| | Explicit criteria and information system | National / local | Extent /content of conditionality | Nature of conditionality, monitoring and sanctioning |
| **Brazil** | | - Centralized management of information, conditions and payment<br>- Municipal implementation of monitoring<br>- Absence of states | - Explicit, but shallow<br>- School attendance and health check<br>- Training programs | - Loose<br>- Imperfect monitoring<br>- Minimal enforcement |
| **Mexico** | - Explicit eligibility criteria<br>- Extensive national information system | - Central information system and centrally implemented administered<br>- Consulting role of communities<br>- Absence of municipalities and states | Explicit and extensive<br>- School attendance and health check<br>- Courses, workshops<br>- Community work<br>- Self-registry (health visits) | - Strict<br>- Effective monitoring<br>- Effective enforcement (sanctioning) |
| **Turkey** | | - Central information system<br>- Local knowledge in implementation applied by SASFs-discretion | - Explicit and increasingly extensive (previously shallow)<br>- School attendance and health check<br>- Labor market insertion, yet partially adopted | - Increasingly strict<br>- Effective monitoring (since 2012)<br>- Mid-level enforcement |

public (appointed and elected) and private actors at the district level, and take charge in selection and recertification processes. Unlike decentralization, in this variety the central power is administratively *deconcentrated* since the Turkish governors, like their equivalent French prefects, play a coupling role in bringing together national and local elites. Table 2 describes the central traits of the regulatory regimes set in the three countries on which we focus.

The Mexican CCT was designed based on extensive conditionalities and proxy-based targeting, a system strictly steered from the center to eliminate political discretion particularly at the subnational level. Yet the weakness of local links (hence use of local knowledge and monitoring) brought about by the extremely centralized Mexican system created certain targeting failures, causing some "exclusion and inclusion errors" (CONEVAL 2019). These errors, then, were used as "evidence of corruption" by the MORENA Government that

TABLE 2
Varieties of Regulatory Regimes in Social Assistance

|  |  | Degree of regulation (selection and recertification of beneficiaries) | |
|---|---|---|---|
|  |  | Loose | Strict |
| **Mode of governance** (role of different agents and levels of government) | **Centralised** |  | Strict centralism (Mexico) |
|  | **Deconcentrated** |  | Subcontracted *dirigisme* (Turkey) |
|  | **Decentralised** | Loosely monitored decentralism (Brazil) |  |

replaced *Prospera* with scholarships solely in 2019. Although administrative neutrality seemed to reign at the systemic level, the government dismantled the CCT based on claims of corruption and manipulation; its "ineffectiveness" in eliminating poverty; conditionalities constituting a major burden especially on women, along with rejecting conditionality as a distant perspective from social assistance as a citizenship right.[12] Paradoxically, the critiques pointed to the very procedures that were designed to avoid clientelism as culprits of clientelism, though they do not pinpoint clear mechanisms invalidating *Prospera's* administrative neutrality. In a way, the tight grasp of the central government, aiming to avoid subnational and municipal interference, might have contributed to the dismantling of *Prospera*.

The design of Brazilian and Turkish systems allows for a certain level of local discretion at the municipal and district levels, respectively. In Brazil, municipalities play an important role in selection, albeit under the constraints of quotas provided by the federal government. Although several studies assess that the selection process is untainted by clientelism (Fenwick 2009; Sugiyama and Hunter 2013), Brollo, Kaufmann, and La Ferrara (2019) find political manipulation at the municipal level based on the lenient behavior of local politicians in the enforcement of conditionalities to deter beneficiaries' penalizing mayoral candidates at polls.

In a puzzling fashion, Turkey, as an extremely centralist country, established a relatively decentralized governance of CCT whose implementation is contracted to semi-autonomous local agents with decision-making authority over selection and recertification, generating a hybrid decentralized regime with centralized monitoring. Since 2010 this regime has been bound by a national information system, which sets certain limits on the discretion that those foundations may enjoy.[13]

The discretionary space granted to the local SASF boards is justified as "setting the priorities at the local level based on a hands-on approach with accurate information about those who really need social assistance."[14] Although this is considered a strength of the Turkish program because it enables local reach, improving the accuracy of targeting (World Bank 2017), some scholars have criticized it for having facilitated discretionary enrollment and fostering patronage-based exchanges (Aytaç 2014; Eder 2010; Öktem 2018). Only in the Turkish case can nonstate actors be involved in the CCT administration, exemplifying a path-dependent legacy regarding the Turkish (and Ottoman) state's reliance on privatized, charity-based welfare (Özbek 2006). The opaque nature of private contributions (at both national and district levels) and the list of beneficiaries subject the system to probable clientelistic exchanges/patronage networks between firms or individuals (philanthropists included in the SASF boards) and municipalities or the central government (Özdemir 2020).

As the extant literature states, WS legacies shape the ways in which the RWS operates (Leisering 2011, 2012; Marschallek 2011; Taylor-Gooby 2011). Pointing to the hybridization, Leisering (2011, 270) argues that WS legacies leave their marks in the degree and form of delegation to nonstate actors. As the range of institutional hybridization has widened, bringing together public and private actors and norms, the RWS delegates some welfare functions to private actors, gearing privately operated dynamics to "social" goals while "redefining" the social (Leisering 2012, 148; 2011, 257, 268). This is evident in the Turkish case—where the public actors delegated authority and responsibility to private actors, which coincides with a centuries-long charity tradition and the incorporation of traditional communitarian forms of welfare into the modern WS apparatus.

The historical legacy that marks the CCT regulation in the Mexican case is the centralist, vertical governance structure. Despite the federal system, centralization of power and concentration of fiscal resources are the legacy of the long-lasting dominant-party regime with authoritarian overtones in which the last incumbency of the Institutional Revolutionary Party (PRI) gave rise to the emergence of the CCT (Diaz-Cayeros, Estévez, and Magaloni 2016). Such a legacy seems to be "sticky" with respect to RWS, despite the changing regime and governments over the years. Although Brazil is subject to similar historical legacies—where the federal system operated as a de facto central state regarding the concentration of power as an imprint of the authoritarian past and social policy was institutionalized at the federal level (Draibe 2002)—the 1988 Constitution highlighted the need for decentralized and participatory governance of social policy, which was articulated in the design of *Bolsa Familia* (Guimarães and Schettini 2014).

# Conclusion

More than two decades into their emergence, CCTs have had a noteworthy impact on alleviating poverty and diminishing inequalities in the countries in which they were adopted; however, extant literature is divided as to their long-term effects on human capital, health, and breaking intergenerational poverty cycles (Molina et al. 2019; Saad Filho 2016). By examining the modalities of governance established in the selection and recertification of CCT beneficiaries in Brazil, Mexico, and Turkey, this article identified a variety of RW regimes. All three regimes display regulatory instruments that are set to avoid political discretion. However, the deployment of these instruments and the role of different agents show variation, much of which seems embedded in path-dependent legacies of social welfare and lie at the centralism-decentralism nexus in the respective countries.

Although centrally steered and strictly controlled social assistance regimes (strict centralism epitomized by the Mexican case) are considered strong in terms of their "formula-based" identification of poverty and, hence, beneficiaries, they might cause targeting failures since they are detached from local knowledge due to their vertical structures. Such knowledge could be facilitated by the local agents with ties to the communities, yet by design, their role in selecting and recertifying the beneficiaries is discarded to eschew potential political manipulation, based on the previous experiences of social assistance.

The three cases that we examined and the varieties they exemplify indicate the importance of state capacity in the design and implementation of RWS. Vertical formula-based systems necessitate a very high capacity of the states to access, gather, process, and monitor information about citizens in general and poverty in particular. In the absence of such capacity, duplication and dismissal errors might be likely, which would then jeopardize the legitimacy of the system and provide justification for political actors to attack the system as such, as observed in the Mexican case in 2019. Decentralized systems based on horizontal collaboration between the center and the local agents require not only solid capacity to coordinate the central governments, but also the capacity of the local agents to fulfill monitoring of eligibility and conditionality compliance. Where the latter lacks or varies across different localities, as in the case of Brazil, duplication and dismissal errors as well as inconstancies become likely, leading to concerns about fraud (Hall 2006). From the other side of the coin, local agents with solid capacity fostered by the incorporation of a wide range of actors, public and private alike, might diminish such errors yet expand the patronage networks. Yet in the Turkish case, the opaque nature of data, particularly about the functioning of the SASF boards, hinders definite claims on this issue linked to the AKP governments.

There are some caveats and limitations regarding our findings. First, CCTs are just one of the social assistance programs implemented in these countries. Fairly expansive unconditional transfers and in-kind social assistance schemes juxtapose the CCTs, especially in the Turkish case. Second, regulatory instruments are not mere mechanisms to tie/untie the politicians' hands to manipulate the redistribution based on their interests. Watchdogs, the ways in which field-workers are recruited and trained, and transparency mechanisms, among other features, can also play important roles in keeping administrative neutrality. In countries where democratic institutions are challenged through different means, boundaries between bureaucracy and political executives might become blurry, so that regulatory processes could be automatically tainted by politicization. In such cases, central or bureaucratic control might bluntly mean political control. In Turkey, which has gone through substantial democratic backsliding in the 2010s, key bureaucratic positions at both the national and provincial levels are filled through presidential appointments (SIGMA 2019); therefore, the distinction between elected and appointed becomes murky, a dynamic that should be taken into account regarding the decision-making bodies of the local foundations/SASFs.

Despite their popularity throughout the developing world, sustainability of these programs cannot be taken for granted as they might be subject to drastic changes and dismantling in line with partisan preferences, as shown by the drastic transformation of Mexico's emblematic *Prospera* in 2019. Future research should explore the dynamics that might help to sustain CCTs as well as other social assistance programs, along with the ways in which they bring about better results in alleviating poverty and diminishing inequalities untainted by political manipulation.

# Notes

1. We define clientelism as an exchange relationship between a patron, who is an individual politician or a political party running for office, and a client, a voter who receives discretionary benefits in return for their political support (Yıldırım and Kitschelt 2020).

2. GDP per capita (current prices, 2019) of Brazil is US$8,717.2, while it is US$9,863 in Mexico and US$9,042.5 in Turkey. See https://data.worldbank.org/indicator/NY.GDP.PCAP.CD.

3. According to the World Bank's classification, upper-middle-income economies are those with a GNI per capita between US$3,956 and US$12,235. See https://www.worldbank.org/en/country/mic/overview.

4. See https://www.gob.mx/cms/uploads/attachment/file/442955/Reglas_de_Operacion_PROSPERA_2019.pdf.

5. See https://ailevecalisma.gov.tr/sygm/hakkimizda/sosyal-yardimlasma-ve-dayan%C4%B1smayi-tesvik-fonu/ (accessed 5 February 2019).

6. https://ailevecalisma.gov.tr/sygm/hakkimizda/sosyal-yard%C4%B1mlasma-ve-dayan%C4%B1smavak%C4%B1flar%C4%B1/ (accessed 5 February 2019).

7. https://ailevecalisma.gov.tr/sygm/hakkimizda/sosyal-yard%C4%B1mlasma-ve-dayan%C4%B1smavak%C4%B1flar%C4%B1/ (accessed 5 February 2019).

8. Defined as "distinct workplaces" by Law #5737 and #4857, SASFs have legal personality of private law.

9. Interviews with SASF officials. Istanbul, Turkey. 08/01/2019.

10. Interviews with SASF officials. Ankara, Turkey. 09/01/2019.

11. See https://www.resmigazete.gov.tr/eskiler/2017/06/20170622-1.htm

12. https://www.jornada.com.mx/ultimas/sociedad/2019/01/30/acaba-el-clientelar-prospera-surge-el-programa-becas-benito-juarez-4641.html

13. Interviews with SASF officials, Balikesir,Turkey. 04/01/2019.

14. Interviews with SASF officials, Istanbul, Turkey. 08/01/2019

# References

Aytaç, Selim Erdem. 2014. Distributive politics in a multiparty system: The conditional cash transfer program in Turkey. *Comparative Political Studies* 47 (9):1211–1237.

Benish, Avishai, and David Levi-Faur. 2020. The expansion of regulation in welfare governance. *The ANNALS of the American Academy of Political and Social Science* (this volume).

Benish, Avishai, Hanan Haber, and Rotem Eliahou. 2017. The regulatory welfare state in Pension markets. *Journal of Social Policy* 46 (2): 313–30.

Brodkin, Evelyn Z., and Malay K. Majmundar. 2010. Administrative exclusion: Organizations and the hidden costs of welfare claiming. *Journal of Public Administration Research and Theory* 20 (4): 827–48.

Brollo, Fernando, Katia M. Kaufmann, and Eliana La Ferrara. 2019. The political economy of program enforcement: Evidence from Brazil. *Journal of the European Economic Association* https://doi.org/10.1093/jeea/jvz024.

Cecchini, Simone, and Bernardo Atuesta. 2017. Programas de transferencias condicionadas en América Latina y el Caribe: Tendencias de cobertura e inversión. CEPAL.

Consejo Nacional de Evaluación de la Política de Desarrollo Social (CONEVAL). 2019. El Progresa-Oportunidades-Prospera: A 20 años de su creación. Mexico City: CONEVAL.

Cornelius, Wayne A. 2004. Mobilized voting in the 2000 elections: The changing efficacy of vote buying and coercion in Mexican electoral politics. In *Mexico's pivotal democratic election*, eds. Jorge I. Dominguez and Chappell Lawson, 47–65. Palo Alto, CA: Stanford University Press.

Dávila, Laura G. 2016. How does Prospera work? Best practices in the implementation of conditional cash transfer programs in Latin America and the Caribbean. Technical Note. IDB-TN-971, IDB Social Protection and Health Division.

De La, O, and Ana Lorena. 2013. Do conditional cash transfers affect electoral behavior? Evidence from a randomized experiment in Mexico. *American Journal of Political Science* 57 (1): 1–4.

De La, O, and Ana Lorena. 2015. *Crafting policies to end poverty in Latin America*. New York, NY: Cambridge University Press.

Díaz-Cayeros, Alberto, and Beatriz Magaloni. 2009. Aiding Latin America's poor. *Journal of Democracy* 20 (4): 36–49.

Díaz-Cayeros, Alberto, Federico Estévez, and Beatriz Magaloni. 2016. *The political logic of poverty relief: Electoral strategies and social policy in Mexico*. New York, NY: Cambridge University Press.

Draibe, Sonia M. 2002. The Brazilian Welfare State in perspective: old issues, new possibilities. In *The state of social welfare: The twentieth century in cross-national review*, eds. J. P. Dixon and R. Scheurell. London: Praeger Publishers.

Eckstein, Harry. 1975. Case study and theory in political science. In *Handbook of political science*, vol. 7, eds. Fred I. Greenstein and Nelson W. Polsby. Reading, MA: Addison-Wesley.

*Economist*. 30 January. 2020. Bolsa Família, Brazil's admired anti-poverty programme, is flailing.

Eder, Mine. 2010. Retreating state? Political economy of welfare regime change in Turkey. *Middle East Law and Governance* 2:152–84.

Eiró, Flávio, and Martijn Koster. 2019. Facing bureaucratic uncertainty in the Bolsa Família Program: Clientelism beyond reciprocity and economic rationality. *Focaal* 85:84–96.

Esping-Andersen, Gøsta. 1990. *The three worlds of welfare capitalism*. Princeton, NJ: Princeton University Press.

Evans, Tony. 2016. *Professional discretion in welfare services: Beyond street-level bureaucracy*. London: Routledge.

Fenwick, Tracy Beck. 2009. Avoiding governors: the success of *Bolsa Família*. *Latin American Research Review* 44 (1): 102–31.

Garay, Candelaria. 2016. *Social policy expansion in Latin America*. New York, NY: Cambridge University Press.

Guimarães Duarte Sátyro, Natália, and Eleonora Schettini Martins Cunha. 2014. The path of Brazilian social assistance policy post-1988: The significance of institutions and ideas. *Brazilian Political Science Review* 8 (1). https://doi.org/10.1590/1981-38212014000100004.

Haber, Hanan. 2017. Rise of the regulatory welfare state? Social regulation in utilities in Israel. *Social Policy and Administration* 51 (3): 442–63.

Hacker, Jacob S. 2004. Dismantling the health care state? Political institutions, public policies and the comparative politics of health reform. *British Journal of Political Science* 34 (4): 693–724.

Haggard, Stephan, and Robert R. Kaufman 2008. *Development, democracy and welfare states*. Princeton, NJ: Princeton University Press.

Hall, Anthony. 2006. From Fome Zero to Bolsa Família: Social policies and poverty alleviation under Lula. *Journal of Latin American Studies* 38 (4): 689–709.

Hanlon, Joseph, Armando Barrientos, and David Hulme. 2010. *Just give money to the poor: The development revolution from the Global South*. Sterling: Kumarian Press.

Hellman, Aline G. 2015. How does Bolsa Familia work? Best practices in the implementation of conditional cash transfer programs in Latin America and the Caribbean. Inter-American Development Bank.

Herd, Pamela, and Donald P. Moynihan. 2019. *Administrative burden: Policymaking by other means*. New York, NY: Russell Sage Foundation.

Holland, Alisha C. 2018. Diminished expectations, redistributive preferences in truncated welfare states. *World Politics* 70 (4): 555–94.

Holland, Alisha C., and Ben Ross Schneider 2017. Easy and hard redistribution: The political economy of welfare states in Latin America. *Perspectives on Politics* 15 (4): 988–1006.

Huber, Evelyn. 2005. Globalisation and social policy developments in Latin America. In *Globalisation and the future of the welfare state*, eds. M. Glatzer and D. Rueschemeyer. Pittsburgh, PA: University of Pittsburgh Press.

Huber, Evelyn, and John D. Stephens 2012. *Democracy and the Left: Social policy and inequality in Latin America*. Chicago, IL: The University of Chicago Press.

Hunter, Wendy, and Timothy J. Power. 2007. Rewarding Lula: Executive power, social policy, and the Brazilian elections of 2006. *Latin American Politics and Society* 49 (1): 1–30.

Ibarrarán, Pablo, and Nadin Medellín, Ferdinando Regalia, Marco Stampini, eds. 2017. *Así funcionan las transferencias condicionadas*. Inter-American Development Bank.

Inter-American Development Bank (IDB). 2015. How does Bolsa Familia work? Best practices in the implementation of conditional cash transfer programs in Latin America and the Caribbean. IDB-TN-856, IDB Social Protection and Health Division.

Jessop, Bob. 1993. Towards a Schumpeterian workfare state? Preliminary remarks on post-fordist political economy. *Studies in Political Economy* 40:7–39.

Knott, Jack H., and Gary J. Miller. 2008. When ambition checks ambition: Bureaucratic trustees and the separation of powers. *The American Review of Public Administration* 38 (4): 387–411.

Layton, Matthew L., and Amy Erica Smith. 2015. Incorporating marginal citizens and voters: The conditional electoral effects of targeted social assistance in Latin America. *Comparative Political Studies* 48 (7): 854–81.

Layton, Matthew L., Maureen M. Donaghy, and Lúcio R. Rennó. 2017. Does welfare provision promote democratic state legitimacy? Evidence from Brazil's Bolsa Família program. *Latin American Politics and Society* 59 (4): 99–120.

Leisering, Lutz. 2011. Transformation of the state: Comparing the new regulatory state to the post-war provider state. In *The new regulatory state*, ed. Lutz Leisering. New York, NY: Palgrave Macmillan.

Leisering, Lutz. 2012. Pension privatization in a welfare state environment: Socializing private pensions in Germany and the United Kingdom. *Journal of Comparative Social Welfare* 28 (2): 139–51.

Levi-Faur, David. 2014. The welfare state: A regulatory perspective. *Public Administration* 92 (3): 599–614.

Levy, Santiago. 2006. *Progress against poverty: Sustaining Mexico's Progresa-Oportunidades Program*. Washington, DC: Brookings Institution Press.

Majone, Giandomenico. 1997. From the positive to the regulatory state. *Journal of Public Policy* 17 (2): 139–67.

Mares, Isabel, and Matthew E. Carnes 2009. Social policy in developing countries. *Annual Review of Political Science* 12:93–113.

Marschallek, Christian. 2011. Back to the state? The public policies of private and public pensions in Britain. In *The new regulatory state*, ed. Lutz Leisering, 103–26. New York, NY: Palgrave Macmillan.

McCubbins, MatthewD., Roger G. Noll, and Barry R. Weingast. 1987. Administrative procedures as instruments of political control. *Journal of Law, Economics, & Organization* 3 (2): 243–77.

McCubbins, Matthew D., Roger G. Noll, and Barry R. Weingast. 1990. Positive and normative models of procedural rights: An integrative approach to administrative procedures. *Journal of Law, Economics, & Organization* 6:307–32.

Medellín, Nadin, Pablo Ibarrarán, Marco Stampini, and Juan Miguel Villa. 2015. *Moving ahead: Recertification and exit strategies in conditional cash transfer programs*. Washington DC: IDB.

Molina, Teresa, Tania Barham, Karen Macours, John. A. Maluccio, and Marco Stampini. 2019. Long-term impacts of conditional cash transfers: Review of the evidence. *The World Bank Research Observer* 34:119–59.

Moynihan, Donald P., Pamela Herd, and Hope Harvey. 2014. Administrative burden: Learning, psychological, and compliance costs in citizen-state interactions. *Journal of Public Administration Research and Theory* 25 (1): 43–69.

Öktem, Kerem Gabriel. 2018. Turkey's social assistance regime in comparative perspective: History, administrative structure, programmes and institutional characteristics. Blickwechsel-Contemporary Turkey Studies, Working Paper #1.

Özbek, Nadir. 2006. *Cumhuriyet Türkiyesi'nde Sosyal Güvenlik ve Sosyal Politikalar* [*Social Security and Social Policy in Republican Turkey*]. İstanbul:Tarih Vakfı.

Özdemir, Yonca. 2020. AKP's neoliberal populism and contradictions of new social policies in Turkey. *Contemporary Politics*. DOI: 10.1080/13569775.2020.1720891.

Özel, Işık D. 2014. *State-business alliances and economic development: Turkey, Mexico and North Africa*. London: Routledge.

Özel, Işık D. 2011. Emerging and hybrid: The cases of Turkish and Brazilian market economies. *Desenvolvimento em Debate* 1 (3): 65–95.

Özel, Işık D., and Kerem Yıldırım. 2019. Political consequences of welfare regimes: Social assistance and support for presidentialism in Turkey. *South European Society and Politics* 24 (4): 485–511.

Saad Filho, Alfredo. 2016. Social policy beyond neoliberalism: From conditional cash transfers to Pro-poor growth. *Journal of Poverty Alleviation and International Development* 7 (1): 67–94.

Schneider, Ben Ross. 2013. *Hierarchical capitalism in Latin America: Business, Labor and challenges of equitable development*. New York, NY: Cambridge University Press.

SIGMA 2019. *Monitoring report of Turkey*. Paris: SIGMA-OECD.

Stewart, Richard B. 1974. The reformation of American administrative law. *Harvard Law Review* 88:1667–1813.

Sugiyama, Natasha Borges, and Wendy Hunter. 2013. Whither clientelism? Good governance and Brazil's Bolsa Família Program. *Comparative Politics* October 2013:43–62.

Tanzi, Vito. 2002. Globalization and the future of social protection. *Scottish Journal of Political Economy* 49 (1): 116–27.

Tapajós, Luziele, Júnia Quiroga, Fernando Pereira, and Alexandro Pinto. 2010. O processo de avaliação da política de segurança alimentar e nutricional entre 2004 e 2010: a experiência do MDS. In *Fome Zero: Uma historia Brasileira*, eds. Adriana Veiga Aranha, 44–57. Brasília: Ministério do Desenvolvimento Social.

Taylor-Gooby, Peter. 2011. Limits to the regulated market: The UK experiment. In *The new regulatory state*, ed. Lutz Leisering, 80–100. New York, NY: Palgrave Macmillan.

United Nations Development Program (UNDP). 2011. Mexico: Scaling up Progresa /Oportunidades. New York, NY: UNDP.

World Bank. 2017. *Turkey's integrated social assistance system*. Washington, DC: World Bank, IBRD and IDA in collaboration with the Ministry of Family and Social Policy of the Turkish Republic.

World Bank. 2009. Conditional cash transfers: Reducing present and future poverty. Policy Research Report. No. 47603. Washington, DC: World Bank.

World Bank. 2008. Implementation, Completion and Results Report on a Loan in the amount of US$500 Million to the Republic of Turkey for a Social Risk Mitigation Project. 26/6/2008. Washington, DC: World Bank.

Yıldırım, Kerem, and Herbert Kitschelt. 2020. Analytical perspectives on varieties of clientelism. *Democratization* 27 (1): 20–43.

Zucco, Cesar. 2013. When pay-outs pay-off: Conditional cash transfers and voting behaviour in Brazil 2002-10. *American Journal of Political Science* 57 (4): 810–22.

# Indirect and Invisible Regulations Set in Stone: A Driving Force behind the Rise of Private Health Insurance in Sweden

*By*
JOHN LAPIDUS

The Swedish welfare model is gradually losing its former characteristics. Notable is the extensive privatization of provision and the emerging privatization of funding, primarily through new and half-private services in health care, education, and elderly care. The clearest example of this trend is the rise of private health insurance, which is now signed by every tenth person of working age. This article points out different types of regulations that have provoked the rise of private health insurance, and discusses types of regulations that could potentially slow privatization. Further, this article analyzes three official welfare investigation reports. These reports avoid the decisive regulations they are supposed to discuss, and sometimes go against directives to do so. I argue that regulations for private health insurance have occurred without much debate, while every potential regulation against private health insurance is very much disputed by industry interests and many of the political parties.

*Keywords:* private health insurance; privatization; regulation; Swedish welfare model; hidden welfare state

From the early 1990s onward, Sweden has privatized large parts of its welfare provision. But the government has also privatized welfare funding to a certain extent, mainly through new services in health care, education, and elderly care. The clearest example of this is the rapid rise of private health insurance, which today is taken up by 680,000 Swedish citizens.

There are different types of private health insurance in different countries, mainly substitutive, complementary, and supplementary (Thompson and Mossialos 2009). The Swedish version is the supplementary one; that is, the

*John Lapidus is a research fellow in the Department of Economy and Society at University of Gothenburg. His research interests include comparative welfare states. He is the author of* The Quest for a Divided Welfare State: Sweden in the Era of Privatization *(Palgrave Macmillan 2019).*

Correspondence: john.lapidus@econhist.gu.se

DOI: 10.1177/0002716220964426

insurance covers services that are already part of the public commitment but the policyholder is guaranteed quick access to these services. The policyholders, with quick access, often go to the same clinic as the publicly funded patients. This is so because most private clinics have agreements both with the private insurance companies and with the public county councils (Lapidus 2019a).

The difference between the two queues—one publicly funded and the other privately funded—to the same private provider is significant. The publicly funded patients come under the public health guarantee, which stipulates a maximum wait of 3 days before seeing a general practitioner, then a maximum wait of 90 days before seeing a specialist and a maximum of 90 days before starting treatment (Vårdanalys 2017). Private policyholders, on the other hand, are guaranteed a maximum of between 10 to 15 days for the whole process. If the insurance companies fail to live up to the time guarantees, the policyholder is reimbursed for every day that passes.

The rapid rise of private health insurance represents a parallel health care (Ethical Committee of the Swedish Society of Medicine 2020) in conflict with the Swedish Healthcare Act, which states that health care shall be given due to needs and on equal terms for all citizens. If a growing proportion of the population steps out of the universal and common-to-all-citizens public health system, then, by definition, it is no longer a universal and common-to-all-citizens public health system (Lapidus 2019). Further, the support for a universal health system is reduced when more and more people start to seek private solutions (e.g., Busemeyer and Iversen 2020), something that has consequences for the willingness to pay taxes and for the general trust in the system (e.g. Rothstein 1998).

This article demonstrates how privatization of provision was a prerequisite for the rapid rise of private health insurance. I examine the regulatory steps that enabled the rapid rise of private health insurance, as well as the steps that would be needed to slow it down. The article also reviews some official investigations on this topic, finding that they avoided discussion of decisive regulations at all costs and rather focused on less controversial and less important aspects of welfare reform.

## A Regulatory Perspective on the Rise of Private Health Insurance in Sweden

One of the most distinctive features of the Swedish welfare model was the public monopolies providing publicly funded welfare services (Cox 2004; Premfors 1991; Pontusson 1987). The public sector had a special status in the sense that public delivery was not allowed to be challenged by private interests (Blomqvist 2004). This so-called Social Democratic welfare model (Esping-Andersen 1990) was built on compromises with the employers who, in times of rapid economic growth, affirmed many aspects of the general welfare policy (Andersson 2000).

Eventually, however, the employers' willingness to compromise came to an end (Boréus 1994; Blyth 2001) and instead they turned against many elements of the Swedish welfare model, not least the publicly provided welfare services. The offensive coincided with the international wave of neo liberalism (Harvey 2005) affecting also the European Social Democracy, which saw a significant shift in political and economic thinking (Kitschelt 1994; Ryner 2002), often referred to as the Third Way (Giddens 1998).

One of the results was that Sweden, from the early 1990s, started to privatize large parts of the provision of welfare services in sectors that were still supposed to be publicly funded. This kind of decoupling of public funding and state delivery is found to be one of two main strategies of the so-called regulatory welfare state (RWS; Benish, Haber, and Eliahou 2017), which is a polymorphic approach focusing on "the dialectic relations between the regulatory state and the welfare state as manifestations of the ever-expanding and diversifying dimensions of the administrative state" (Levi-Faur 2014, 600).

What are the consequences of regulatory arrangements such as privatization of provision in a welfare model like the Swedish one? Regulation as such does not say anything about distribution and redistribution (Levi-Faur 2014), but this specific regulatory arrangement was a prerequisite for the rapid rise of private health insurance. It is an axiom: policyholders cannot use their insurance at publicly run caregivers, and the rapid rise of private health insurance is therefore dependent on the creation of a nationwide net of private providers at all levels of health care (Lapidus 2019a; Norén 2008; Dahlgren 1994).

The rapid rise of private health insurance forms part of the hidden welfare state (Howard 1999), which is one of three examples used to "demonstrate the regulatory perspective on the welfare state" in a seminal article on the regulatory welfare state (Levi-Faur 2014, 610). The hidden welfare state mainly refers to welfare services that are not directly tax-funded, but which have indirect elements of public funding through various types of tax breaks. In some countries, it implies large sums in lost tax revenue. One example is the United States, where public health care spending is approaching northern European levels (Adema, Fron, and Ladaique 2014) when adding the hidden welfare to the "visible welfare" (Medicare and Medicaid), producing a sum that has been called the divided welfare state (Hacker 2002; Lapidus 2019a).

The hidden welfare state brings new types of inequality and new types of welfare relations. First, it is a sort of reverse means-testing, where the less well-off are informally and sometimes formally excluded from the multitude of tax breaks. Second, welfare relations shift from citizen-state to employee-employer. The employers normally appreciate the goodwill obtained from being the ones who, instead of the state but at the expense of the state, can offer welfare services (Hacker 2002; Mettler 2011; Lapidus 2019a).

The emergence of a hidden welfare state requires a number of new regulations and creates its own form of RWS. All states are regulatory to some degree (Levi-Faur 2014), but one thing that characterizes the hidden welfare state is that many of its regulations tend to be indirect or hidden and subterranean (Hacker 2004). Since large segments of the population continue to prefer the traditional Swedish welfare model (Svallfors 2011), the "advocates of change" (Pierson 1996) are dependent on invisible and indirect regulatory changes. Further, because of a general skepticism toward privatization among the population, politicians feel obligated to refer to the traditional Swedish welfare model even when their policy recommendations are the exact opposite of that model (Cox 2004).

The gradual regulatory changes, however, reduce support for the universal welfare model. Here, some scholars have concluded (e.g. Busemeyer and Iversen 2020, 685) that once private alternatives are introduced and high-income citizens opt out of public schemes, they "become more supportive of a selective rather than a universalist model of the welfare state." It may be that the universal welfare model still has some supporters in the middle class, but "they can no longer rely on allies in the upper-middle classes." Gradual changes strengthening the hidden welfare state can be referred to as layering, drift, and conversion (Streeck and Thelen 2005; Mahoney and Thelen 2010), and they are often not even perceived as regulations.

The opposite goes for every regulatory step that would be required for preserving the traditional Swedish welfare model, such as taxation of benefit and a ban on profits in welfare. This type of action promotes a less complex and less regulated welfare model based on welfare services on equal terms for all citizens, but such actions are now regarded as regulations of the most ambitious and far-reaching kind.

## Private Health Insurance in Sweden: Scope and Consequences

Private health insurance is currently taken up by about 10 percent of the working age population, about 680,000 people. Until 2000, it was a relatively unknown phenomenon in Sweden. The insurance was taken up by relatively few—mainly CEOs and the like (Skoglund 2012)—and the use was concentrated in big cities, primarily in Stockholm. Since 2000, however, the number of policyholders has been growing each year. The rapid rise has been made possible by the creation of a nationwide network of private caregivers receiving policyholders, and also by the new infrastructure (booking systems, care coordinators, loss adjusters, and so on) built around the private health insurance industry (Lapidus 2019a).

About 70 percent of the insurance policies are taken up by employers and paid through gross salary deductions by the employees. Up until 2018, it was advantageous for the employee to make these gross salary deductions, because the insurance was not taxed as a benefit. Since 2018, however, there is a law on benefit taxation; although this legislation is, in some ways, relatively diluted.

Second, an increasing number of insurances are taken up through the unions. While the blue-collar federation LO criticizes private health insurance (LO and The Swedish Medical Association 2019), more and more unions within the two large white-collar federations TCO and Saco are now offering insurance to its members. This has been internally debated. For example, members of the Saco union ST have raised the issue at the congress, and the chairman of the TCO-union, the Swedish Association of Health Professionals, has warned of the effects of a rapid rise of private health insurance (Ribeiro 2020).

In a wider perspective, today's decisions made by the unions may have a great impact on the future evolution of semi-private health care solutions in Sweden. For example, many scholars have pointed to the crucial role the unions played in the U.S., where their acceptance of private health insurance was one of the most decisive factors in creating the U.S. health system (Dobbin 1992; Hacker 2002; Starr 2008).

Third, private health insurance can be taken up by individual policyholders, but only after filling in a detailed health declaration. Without declarations, there is a risk for adverse selection (Barrett and Conlon 2003; Jacobs and Sommers 2015), that is, an increased influx of sick, cost-intensive individuals, which leads to increased premiums for all policyholders, which in turn means that healthy policyholders are incentivized to go to another insurance company.

What will be the consequence of the emerging parallel health insurance system? Representatives of the Swedish private industry often argue that the parallel system has a relieving effect on the public system (Morin 2016; Erlandsson 2019). This is so because policyholders continue to pay taxes to the public health system—in Sweden it is not like in Germany, where policyholders step out of the public tax system (Thomson and Mossialos 2006; Greß 2007)—and thus contribute to the public system without using it to the same degree as they did previously. The effect, then, is that there are more resources to share for those who remain in the public health system.

However, there are many counteracting factors that imply that the parallel system actually erodes, rather than relieves, the public system. The most obvious one is that the support for a universal health system is reduced when more and more people start to seek private solutions (e.g., Busemeyer and Iversen 2020), something that has consequences for the willingness to pay taxes and for the general trust in the system (e.g. Rothstein 1998). Further, a parallel and semi-private system is not only free-riding on the public system through different types of tax breaks and publicly supported infrastructure and education (Lapidus 2019a), but also driving general and societal health care costs in different ways, for example by a fragmented payment system (Reinhardt, Hussey, and Anderson 2004), an unregulated distribution and utilization of expensive new technologies (Bodenheimer 2005), high administrative costs (Woolhandler, Campbell, and Himmelstein 2003), high advertising costs (Applequist and Ball 2018), high salaries and remuneration levels to doctors (Schroeder and Frist 2013), and defensive medicine (Panella et al. 2015), that is, doctors who order unnecessary samples and treatments because of fear of being sued for malpractice.

Further, if a growing proportion of the population steps out of the universal and common-to-all-citizens public health system, then, by definition, it is no longer a universal and common-to-all-citizens public health system. All in all, private health insurance is a deviation from a decommodified health care sector, and a more relevant question is probably the moral-philosophical one: shall health care be regarded as a universal right distributed on equal terms for all citizens, or shall health care be treated as a commodity (Daniels 1985; Rumbold 2017)?

## Regulating Private Health Insurance

How did private health insurance emerge in Sweden? One indirect but absolutely crucial regulatory change was the large-scale privatization of provision that began in the early 1990s. Before discussing how and why, however, we must first say that privatization of provision was made possible by a number of new laws and regulations. When it comes to, for example, the school sector, we find a very explicit legislation, the Free School Reform in 1992, according to which private schools would be entitled to public funding via a school voucher that accompanied each student to the school chosen (Wiborg 2015).

In the case of health care, there was initially no such explicit legislation, but several other laws nevertheless made it possible for privatization of provision to take off. One of these laws was the Competition Act in 1993. This law prohibited anticompetitive agreements (cartels) and prohibited the abuse of a dominant position. In this context, it is important to note that the state and municipal bodies conducting economic activities (for example, running hospitals) were included in the concept of enterprise. Thus, the law included the public sector, and it was even a "conscious choice to let the principles of the Competition Act, as far as possible, apply also to publicly run operations" (Bernitz 2011, 220). The law, inspired by EU competition legislation, was a paradigm shift in Swedish competition legislation (Edwardsson 2003).

From that point on, it was possible for public authorities to buy privately run health care in accordance with the Public Procurement Act. Later, a new law—LOU, the Law on Freedom of Choice—was introduced, according to which private care providers were reimbursed by the public for each patient who chose to visit that particular facility.

But what does privatized provision have to do with privatized funding and in particular with private health insurance? Very much indeed. In fact, private health insurance in today's scope would have been impossible without the prior privatization of provision on a large scale. This is so because it is still impossible to use private health insurance at a public provider. To use private insurance, one must seek out a privately run provider; and for the insurance system to grow and operate smoothly across the country, there must be a network of private care providers at all levels of care, all across the country.

If there had not been such a national network of private providers created across the country, that is, if Sweden had not privatized provision on a large scale but instead kept the public monopoly for health care provision, then the insurance companies would have nowhere to send their 680,000 customers.

It is an axiom that private health insurance is dependent on privately provided health care as long as the publicly provided health care does not receive insurance patients, and scholars have pointed this out: "The insurance companies' opportunity to expand is therefore dependent on the expansion of private health care in Sweden. This expansion is currently rapid, which should benefit private insurance" (Norén 2008, 42).

The expansion continued rapidly, even after 2008, thus enabling the rapid rise of private health insurance. Even in 1994 scholars pointed out (Dahlgren 1994, 242) that the supply of private health care providers was still insufficient to achieve a rapid expansion of private health insurance:

> One limiting factor, however, is that the private healthcare supply is still too limited to offer a comprehensive range of care services to people with private health insurance. With the increased supply of publicly funded but privately delivered healthcare that characterizes the development—and the healthcare policy of right-wing political parties—the market for private health insurance is of course also increasing.

Thus, private health insurance in mass scope requires previous privatization of provision on a large scale. Private provision drives private insurance. This is the exact opposite of how it was portrayed by those who advocated privatized provision in the early 1990s. Prime Minister Olof Palme had previously warned about the consequences of privatization (Antman and Schori 1996), but then said that privatized provision in no way threatened the universal welfare model's joint financing through the tax system (Rothstein 1988).

In theory, there are four possible combinations of provision and funding (Donahue 1989; Starr 1988). First, something can be publicly run and publicly funded. Second, something can be privately run and privately funded. Third, privately run and publicly funded. And, fourth, publicly run and privately funded (in the latter case, for example, one can imagine publicly run national parks where private entry covers a large portion of the costs).

In theory, it is possible to imagine a system that is 100 percent privately run and 100 percent publicly funded, but in practice it is very difficult to maintain such a system. As soon as provision is privatized, the private caregivers begin to seek income from different sources, not just from public authorities. It is about profit maximization and risk diversification. It can be risky for a private care provider to rely solely on the agreement with the region and, besides, the insurance companies normally pay more for each customer in Sweden (Lapidus 2019a) as well as in other countries (Decker 2012; Anderson, Hussey, and Petrosyan 2019).

The private caregivers want income from different sources and that is why they set up price lists for people who want to pay out of pocket and, above all, that is why they sign agreements not only with the county councils but also with the insurance companies. In a study of 108 private care providers, I found that 62 of them had double agreements (both with the county council and with the insurance companies), thus welcoming different patient groups on very different terms and conditions (Lapidus 2019a).

Welcoming different patient groups on different terms to one and the same clinic has been heavily criticized by medical associations and blue-collar trade unions (Ethical Committee of the Swedish Society of Medicine 2020; LO and The Swedish Medical Association 2019) as going against the intentions of the Swedish Healthcare Act.

However, there is no direct regulation that has made this violation of the Healthcare Act possible, but instead it is mainly the privatization of provision that has enabled the parallel and growing health care system. Thus, the rapid rise of private health insurance is mainly due to an indirect regulation just in line with what has been called layering, that is, the introduction of new rules on top of or alongside existing ones, something that gradually can change the original rules and/or institutions (Streeck and Thelen 2005; Mahoney and Thelen 2010). Privatization of provision is a regulation that foments the rise of private health insurance, even though the regulation as such has nothing to do with private health insurance.

Privatization of provision drives the rapid rise of private health insurance, but it is also triggered by other layering-like regulations that were also in place before private health insurance started to grow. Two of them are the exemption of benefit taxation for private health insurance and the right for private companies to conduct agreements with whom they want, but none of them could have a boosting effect on private health insurance before the decisive regulation—privatization of provision—came into effect.

## Regulating against Private Health Insurance

The large-scale privatization of provision enabled the rapid rise of private health insurance. In theory it is possible to regulate within the privately provided system and create a system that is 100 percent privately run and 100 percent publicly funded, but it is almost impossible in practice, especially since the ever-stronger private welfare industry opposes every regulation and more and more actors (for example 680,000 policyholders and many white-collar unions) are drawn into the new system and benefit from it (Lapidus 2019a).

Thus, the most effective way to regulate against private health insurance is probably to regulate against the private provision that enabled the new system. But before discussing the attempts that have been made in this regard, let us first look at two less comprehensive regulations—benefit taxation and the Stop Law—which, without attacking private provision as such, have aimed to slow the growth of private health insurance.

Freedom from benefit taxation and the right to receive different patient groups under different conditions were already in place when the insurance market began to grow. In the former case, it was a piece of legislation that was passed without public attention nor debate as early as the 1980s, a typical example of subterranean (Hacker 2004) tax decisions within the framework of the hidden welfare state (Howard 1999). In the latter case, it was more about regular free enterprise procedure, that is, private caregivers taking for granted that they could, and still can, have agreements with whom they wanted to, including insurance companies.

But on July 1, 2018, the government introduced a law on benefit taxation of private health insurance, and to this date it is one of few attempts to slow down the growth of private health insurance. Before the legislation, the policyholder was exempt from benefit taxation. This meant that the employer could buy the insurance and withdraw the cost from the employee's gross salary without the employee having to pay tax for that benefit, that is, the typical loss of state tax revenue within the framework of the hidden welfare state (Adema, Fron, and Ladaique 2014).

The Left Party and the Social Democrats introduced the law, and it was voted through in parliament despite the opposition of the center right-wing parties. Something that was not much discussed, however, was that while the insurance was now taxed for the employees, the insurance now became tax deductible for the employers (before the law, the insurance was not tax deductible for employers). But not only that: the new law was subjected to massive criticism from the actors of the private welfare industry, ranging from insurance companies and private care providers to editorial pages in the largest Swedish newspapers (Gudmundson 2017; Mårder and Bjur 2018).

The trade association, Swedish Insurance, even filed a protest against the Swedish Tax Agency's original interpretation (Swedish Tax Agency 2018) of the law, and six months later the Swedish Tax Agency had changed its position in favor of the demands made by the private welfare industry. The new interpretation (Swedish Tax Agency 2019a) was an exact copy of these demands, and it meant that as much as 40 percent of the insurance policies were now exempt from benefit taxation for the employees.

On what grounds did the Swedish Tax Agency change its position? Before contacting its leading experts, I studied the fragmentary appendix innovatively designed by Swedish Insurance and now published on the Swedish Tax Agency's website (Swedish Tax Agency 2019b). According to the appendix, health care can be divided into three categories with regard to tax liability: 1) taxable, 2) tax-free, and 3) partially tax-free.

The third category includes specialist care as well as lab and x-ray. How can these health care segments be partially tax-free in a law aimed at taxing? I contacted one of the Swedish Tax Agency's legal experts, and I asked for the underlying calculations mentioned in the Swedish Tax Agency's statement (Lapidus 2019b). The expert replied that the Swedish Tax Agency had no access to them. I asked if there was more material than Appendix 1, and I was told that there was also an Appendix 2.

Swedish Insurance shared that, "The data itself is of course corporate secrets." However, they sent me the mentioned Appendix 2, which turned out to be a random categorization of specialist care to be taxed and not taxed as a benefit. According to Swedish Insurance, their point of departure is the so-called ICD-10, but there has not been a single word about how this classification system has been used and why (Lapidus 2019b).

Thus, it is possible that Swedish Insurance had made a random or profit-maximizing categorization of specialist care, which need not at all be categorized since all specialist care is taxed according to the law. With the new interpretation, however, the insurance companies have managed to change the legislation on such grounds that, at a later stage, it may be possible to argue that all segments of health care should be exempt from taxation.

This is a telling example of how the private welfare industry interferes with the rare regulations that go against its interests. In sum, the Benefit Taxation Act was an attempt to regulate and slow down the rapid rise of private health insurance, but the result (tax-free for companies and 40 percent of the benefit tax for employees negotiated away) is probably that the insurance is now more subsidized than ever before.

Heavier artillery against private health insurance is the attempt to distinguish between public and private by prohibiting private providers from receiving different patient groups on different terms. These attempts are also fraught with both technical difficulties and a massive resistance from the welfare industry.

The main attempt to keep public and private separate was the so-called Stop Law, instituted by a Social Democratic government in 2006 and unraveled one year later by a center right-wing government (Lapidus 2017). According to the Stop Law, private care providers were forced to choose one side: either they had an agreement with the county council and were not allowed to receive insurance customers, or they had agreements with the insurance companies and could not conclude an agreement with the county council.

The purpose of the Stop Law was to avoid a mix of different patient groups on different terms and to avoid violating the Healthcare Act's section on health care on equal terms. The law, however, was so full of exceptions and loopholes that it had no appreciable effect. First, all primary care was exempt from the law. Second, some hospitals were also excluded, while others quickly redefined themselves into community care units so not to be targeted by the law. Third, there were no possibilities of sanctions against the county councils that violated the law and signed agreements with providers that welcomed insurance customers (Lapidus 2017).

Here is not the place to discuss the Social Democratic ambivalence and discrepancy between rhetoric (toward members and grassroots movements) and practice (toward the private welfare industry), so let us just briefly conclude that the law was toothless. Still, despite all its shortcomings, it was met with resistance and was unraveled by the center right-wing government that took office later that year.

Recently, the Social Democratic and Green Party governments have made new attempts to distinguish between public and private care in this way, but these attempts have been even less extensive than the limited Stop Law. In 2016, a proposal was made to add one nonbinding sentence to the existing Healthcare Act (Socialdepartementet 2016), and in 2020 the issue has once again been discussed in parliament, resulting in a new official investigation that will publish its results in September 2021.

It is difficult to regulate against the rapid rise of private health insurance as long as there are private providers enabling the insurance system and opposing any counter-regulation whatsoever. Ultimately, therefore, opposition to privatized provision of welfare services is probably the most meaningful form of opposition to private health insurance and the emergence of a hidden welfare state. In the next section, we take a closer look at the investigations that have dealt with, or were supposed to deal with, issues concerning private health insurance and private provision of welfare services.

## Investigating or Not Investigating?

The basis for the rapid emergence of private health insurance is the extensive privatization of provision that began in the early 1990s. In Sweden, the debate over private provision has been called *profits in welfare*, and in 2015 an inquiry— The Welfare Investigation—was appointed and tasked with proposing a welfare service sector without profit-making actors (Välfärdsutredningen 2016). However, the inquiry, led by Social Democratic politicians, deviated from its directives. Instead of proposing a ban on profits, it proposed a seven percent (plus the government borrowing rate) ceiling for the welfare companies' return on operating capital. In addition to this being a violation of the directives, it also led to a technically complicated, economical debate about what this type of profit regulation would actually mean. The technical debate was incomprehensible for most people and it was a contributing factor to the slowdown in the public debate over profits in welfare (Lapidus 2019a).

The Welfare Investigation departed from its directives, but even before that, one of the welfare services—health care—was excluded from its area of responsibility. Initially, the investigation would apply to three major welfare service sectors, but now it would apply only to the school sector and the elderly care sector. Health care was lifted out of the controversial investigation and received its own investigation, possibly because the welfare industry is particularly strong in the health care sector. Here, we look at two investigations that specifically pertained to health care, the Trust Delegation (Tillitsdelegationen 2018) and Governance for Equal Healthcare (SOU 2018, 55; SOU 2019, 42).

According to its directives, Governance for Equal Healthcare aims to "remove the hunt for profits from the health care sector." The name and purpose of the investigation make two issues—private health insurance and profits in welfare— impossible to ignore, but it is precisely these questions that the investigation ignores.

The question of private health insurance can be derived from the name of the investigation—equal health care—and can focus on the inequality that arises when hundreds of private providers welcome different classes of society and patient groups on different terms. Policyholders are prioritized, and the same applies to those who pay out of pocket. A third group, the vast majority, comes via the agreements that the county council politicians negotiate with the private caregivers.

The question of profits in welfare can be derived from the purpose of the investigation, which is to remove the hunt for profits from the health care sector. The profit hunt is a result of private provision on a large scale, that is, hundreds of providers that are run in accordance with the Swedish Companies Act's (Aktiebolagslag 2005, 551) credo on profit maximization. Governance for Equal Healthcare has published two reports with a total of 859 pages (SOU 2018, 55;

SOU 2019, 42). How many pages are devoted to private health insurance and profits in welfare? Zero.

The same goes for the Trust Delegation (Tillitsdelegationen 2018). Private providers are consequently referred to as "external providers," and they are not at all included in the delegation's studies of different (publicly run) providers. Why are there no profit-making providers included in the reports? The Trust Delegation's justification for the absence of private providers is in line with the New Public Management philosophy (Hood 1991)—that there is no relevant difference between profit-making and non-profit-making activities. Framing it this way leaves them with no need to analyze the natural lack of trust that results from having profit-maximizing actors in the welfare sector.

In a debate article (Lapidus 2018), I asked why the Trust Delegation paints a peaceful still life of a fragmented and increasingly privatized welfare sector, but I have not received an answer. Nor has the chairman of Governance for Equal Healthcare answered my questions (Lapidus 2019c) of why his investigation chooses to exclude what I consider the most relevant issues. In his presentation of the final report, he says that he is a "warm supporter of the existence of private actors in healthcare," a notable starting point for a chairman of an inquiry aimed at stopping the hunt for profits in that sector.

## Conclusion

The rapid rise of private health insurance is one of many steps away from the traditional Swedish welfare model. Private health insurance implies a more unequal access to health care than before, and it forms part of a general trend toward greater inequality in the Swedish society as a whole (Almqvist 2016; Therborn 2018; Lundberg and Waldenström 2018). Moreover, private health insurance challenges the first paragraph of the Swedish Healthcare Act, stating that health care shall be given due to needs and on equal terms for all citizens.

It is true that "the application of regulatory instruments and fiscal transfer do suggest neither fairness nor egalitarianism" (Levi-Faur 2014, 600), and it all depends on which instruments and which transfers and, especially, for whom. Private health insurance creates a new type of inequality in the Swedish health care system, where some groups and classes now get better access to care than others. The rise of private health was enabled by indirect and invisible regulations, especially the extensive privatization of provision from the early 1990s onward, but also by the generous legislation on benefit taxation and the right for private providers to welcome different patient groups on different terms.

The extensive privatization of provision of health care was a prerequisite for the rapid rise of private health insurance. This is so because policyholders cannot use the insurance in the publicly run health care system. As long as welfare services were provided by public monopolies, policyholders had no one to turn to. The rise of private health insurance therefore required a nationwide net of private providers on all levels of health care.

Invisible regulation includes the generous legislation on benefit taxation that promoted the rapid rise of private health insurance, and the right for private providers—in violation of the principles of the Healthcare Act—to welcome different patient groups on different terms. As for the latter regulation, it is so invisible that it does not even exist. As for the former regulation, benefit taxation, it was silently established long before the insurance market started to grow, and recent changes in the legislation have been successfully renegotiated by the industrial organization, Swedish Insurance.

Going in the other direction—regulating against private health insurance—is everything but indirect and invisible. Regulating against private health insurance may be an obvious policy implication for everyone who wants to comply with the Swedish Healthcare Act, but all of the three possible regulations mentioned in the article—benefit taxation, Stop Law, and profit prohibition in the welfare sector—face a compact opposition from the ever-stronger private welfare industry and its increasing number of affiliated actors.

# References

Adema, Willem, Pauline Fron, and Maxime Ladaique. 2014. How much do OECD countries spend on social protection and how redistributive are their tax/benefit systems? *International Social Security Review* 67 (1): 1–25.

Aktiebolagslag. 2005. Available from www.riksdagen.se.

Anderson, Gerard F., Peter Hussey, and Varduhi Petrosyan. 2019. It's still the prices, Stupid: Why the U.S. spends so much on health care, and a tribute to Uwe Reinhardt. *Health Affairs* 38 (1): 87–95.

Almqvist, Anna. 2016. *Den ekonomiska ojämlikheten i Sverige*. Stockholm: Bantorget Grafiska AB.

Andersson, Bengt-Olof. 2000. *Den svenska modellens tredje kompromiss: Efterkrigstidens välfärdspolitik med utgångspunkt från industrins kompetenssäkring och skolans reformering*. Göteborg: Ekonomisk-historiska institutionen.

Antman, Peter, and Pierre Schori. 1996. *Olof Palme: den gränslöse reformisten*. Stockholm: Tiden.

Applequist, Janelle, and Jennifer Gerard Ball. 2018. An updated analysis of direct-to-consumer television advertisements for prescription drugs. *The Annals of Family Medicine* 16 (3): 211–16.

Barrett, Garry F., and Robert Conlon. 2003. Adverse selection and the decline in private health insurance coverage in Australia: 1989–95. *Economic Record* 79 (246): 279–96.

Benish, Avishai, Hanan Haber, and Rotem Eliahou. 2017. The regulatory welfare state in pension markets: mitigating high charges for low-income savers in the United Kingdom and Israel. *Journal of Social Policy* 46 (2): 313–30.

Bernitz, Ulf. 2011. *Svensk och europeisk marknadsrätt 1*. Stockholm: Norstedts juridik.

Blomqvist, Paula. 2004. The choice revolution: Privatization of Swedish welfare services in the 1990s. *Social Policy & Administration* 38 (2): 139–55.

Blyth, Mark. 2001. The transformation of the Swedish model: Economic ideas, distributional conflict, and institutional change. *World Politics* 54 (1): 1–26.

Bodenheimer, Thomas. 2005. High and rising health care costs. Part 2: Technologic innovation. *Annals of Internal Medicine* 142 (11): 932–37.

Boréus, Kerstin. 1994. *Högervåg: nyliberalismen och kampen om språket i svensk debatt 1969– 1989*. Stockholm: Tiden.

Busemeyer, Marius, and Torben Iversen. 2020. The welfare state with private alternatives: The transformation of popular support for social insurance. *The Journal of Politics* 82 (2).

Cox, Robert. 2004. The path-dependency of an idea: why Scandinavian welfare states remain distinct. *Social Policy & Administration* 38 (2): 204–19.

Dahlgren, Göran. 1994. *Framtidens sjukvårdsmarknader*. Stockholm: Natur och kultur i samarbete med Institutet för framtidsstudier.

Daniels, Norman. 1985. *Just health care*. New York, NY: Cambridge University Press.

Decker, Sandra L. 2012. In 2011 nearly one-third of physicians said they would not accept new Medicaid patients, but rising fees may help. *Health Affairs* 31 (8): 1673–1679.

Dobbin, Frank R. 1992. The origins of private social insurance: Public policy and fringe benefits in America, 1920–1950. *American Journal of Sociology* 97 (5): 1416–1450.

Donahue, John. 1989. *The privatization decision: Public ends, private means*. New York, NY: Basic Books.

Edwardsson, Eva. 2003. Konkurrenslagen och konkurrensbegränsande offentliga regleringar. PhD diss.

Erlandsson, Eva. 9 December 2019. Sjukvårdsförsäkringar avlastar den skattefinansierade vården. *Dagens Nyheter*.

Esping-Andersen, Gøsta. 1990. *The three worlds of welfare capitalism*. Cambridge: Polity Press.

Et hical Committee of the Swedish Society of Medicine. 2020. *Privata sjukvårdsförsäkringar leder till vård på olika villkor*. Available from www.sls.se.

Giddens, Anthony. 1998. *The third way: The renewal of social democracy*. Cambridge: Polity Press.

Greß, Stefan. 2007. Private health insurance in Germany: Consequences of a dual system. *Healthcare Policy* 3 (2): 29.

Gudmundson, Per. 5 April 2017. Hur många gånger måste man betala för att få träffa doktorn. *Svenska Dagbladet*.

Hacker, Jacob S. 2002. *The divided welfare state: The battle over public and private social benefits in the United States*. Cambridge: Cambridge University Press.

Hacker, Jacob S. 2004. Privatizing risk without privatizing the welfare state: The hidden politics of social policy retrenchment in the United States. *American Political Science Review* 98 (2): 243–60.

Harvey, David. 2005. *A brief history of neoliberalism*. Oxford: Oxford University Press.

Hood, Christopher. 1991. A public management for all seasons? *Public Administration* 69 (1): 3– 19.

Howard, Christopher. 1999. *The hidden welfare state: Tax expenditures and social policy in the United States*. Princeton, NJ: Princeton University Press.

Jacobs, Douglas Bernard, and Benjamin Daniel Sommers. 2015. Using drugs to discriminate— Adverse selection in the insurance marketplace. *New England Journal of Medicine* 372 (5): 399–402.

Kitschelt, Herbert. 1994. *The transformation of european social democracy*. New York, NY: Cambridge University Press.

LO and The Swedish Medical Association. 9 December 2019. Privata sjukvårdsförsäkringar underminerar offentlig vård. *Dagens Nyheter*.

Lapidus, John. 2017. Private health insurance in Sweden: Fast-track lanes and the alleged attempts to stop them. *Health Policy* 121 (4): 442–49.

Lapidus, John. 14 November 2018. Tillitsdelegationen undviker de viktiga frågorna. *Dagens Medicin*.

Lapidus, John. 2019a. *The quest for a divided welfare state: Sweden in the era of privatization*. London: Palgrave Macmillan.

Lapidus, John. 2019b. 5 July 2019. Skatteverket dansar efter försäkringsbolagens pipa. *Dagens Samhälle*.

Lapidus, John. 2019c. 16 December 2019. När ska S kliva ut ur skuggorna och kämpa för välfärden. *ETC*.

Levi-Faur, David. 2014. The welfare state: A regulatory perspective. *Public Administration* 92 (3): 599–614.

Mahoney, James, and Kathleen Thelen, eds. 2010. *Explaining institutional change: ambiguity, agency, and power*. Cambridge: Cambridge University Press.

Mettler, Suzanne. 2011. *The submerged state: How invisible government policies undermine American democracy*. Chicago, IL: University of Chicago Press.

Morin, Anders. 20 October 2016. Privata försäkringar förstärker sjukvården. *Svenska Dagbladet*.

Mårder, Günther, and Thomas af Bjur. 2 May 2018. Nya straffskatten gör Sverige sjukare. *Expressen*.

Norén, Lars. 2008. Att göra patienter till kunder – om sjukvårdsförsäkringar och entreprenörskap. In *Perspektiv på förnyelse och entreprenörskap i offentlig verksamhet*, eds. A. Lundström and E. Sundin. Örebro: Forum för småföretagarforskning

Panella, Massimiliano, et al. 2015. Defensive medicine: Defensive medicine: Overview of the literature. *Igiene e sanita pubblica* 71 (3): 335–51.

Pierson, Paul. 1996. The new politics of the welfare state. *World Politics* 48 (2): 143–79.

Pontusson, Jonas. 1987. Radicalization and retreat in Swedish social democracy. *New Left Review* 165:5–33.

Premfors, Rune. 1991. The "Swedish model" and public sector reform. *West European Politics* 14 (3): 83–95.

Reinhardt, Uwe E., Peter S. Hussey, and Gerard F. Anderson. 2004. US health care spending in an international context. *Health Affairs* 23 (3): 10–25.

Ribeiro, Sineva. 4 February 2020. Vårdförbundet kritiskt mot privata sjukvårdsförsäkringar. *Arbetsvärlden*.

Rothstein, Bo. 1988. Socialdemokratin och välfärdens institutioner. *Tiden* 88 (8): 467–74.

Rothstein, Bo. 1998. *Just institutions matter: The moral and political logic of the universal welfare state*. New York, NY: Cambridge University Press.

Rumbold, Benedict E. 2017. The moral right to health: A survey of available conceptions. *Critical Review of International Social and Political Philosophy* 20 (4): 508–28.

Ryner, Magnus 2002. *Capitalist restructuring, globalization and the third way: Lessons from the Swedish model*. London: Routledge.

Schroeder, Steven A., and William Frist. 2013. Phasing out fee-for-service payment. *The New England Journal of Medicine* 368 (21): 2029–2032.

Skoglund, Caj. 2012. Privata sjukvårdsförsäkringar i Sverige–omfattning och utveckling. Rapport till SKL, 2–49.

SOU. 2018. Styrning och vårdkonsumtion ur ett jämlikhetsperspektiv. Available from www.regeringen.se.

SOU. 2019. Digifysiskt vårdval. Available from www.regeringen.se.

Starr, Peter. 1988. The meaning of privatization. *Yale Law & Policy Review* 6 (1): 6–41.

Starr, Peter. 2008. *The social transformation of American medicine: The rise of a sovereign profession and the making of a vast industry*. New York, NY: Basic Books.

Streeck, Wolfgang, and Kathleen Ann Thelen, eds. 2005. *Beyond continuity: Institutional change in advanced political economies*. New York, NY: Oxford University Press.

Socialdepartementet. 2016. Privata sjukvårdsförsäkringar inom offentligt finansierad hälso- och sjukvård. Available from www.regeringen.se.

Svallfors, Stefan. 2011. A bedrock of support? Trends in welfare state attitudes in Sweden, 1981–2010. *Social Policy & Administration* 45 (7): 806–25.

Swedish Tax Agency. 2018. Förmån av hälso- och sjukvård. Available from www.skatteverket.se.

Swedish Tax Agency. 2019. Beräkning av sjukvårdsförsäkringsförmån. Available from www.skatteverket.se.

Swedish Tax Agency. 2019b. Appendix. Svensk Försäkrings klassificering av insatser inom sjukvårdsförsäkringarna. Available from www.skatteverket.se.

Therborn, Göran. 2018. *Kapitalet, överheten och alla vi andra: klassamhället i Sverige - det rådande och det kommande*. Stockholm: Arkiv förlag.

Thomson, Sarah, and Elias Mossialos. 2006. Choice of public or private health insurance: Learning from the experience of Germany and the Netherlands. *Journal of European Social Policy* 16 (4): 315–27.

Thomson, Sarah, and Elias Mossialos. 2009. *Private health insurance in the European Union*. European Commission, 320–23.

Tillitsdelegationen. 2018. Med tillit växer handlingsutrymmet. Available from www.tillitsdelegationen.se.

Vårdanalys. 2017. *Löftesfri garanti? En uppföljning av den nationella vårdgarantin*. Stockholm.

Välfärdsutredningen. 2016. Ordning och reda I välfärden. Available from www.regeringen.se.

Lundberg, Jacob, and Daniel Waldenström. 2018. Wealth inequality in Sweden: What can we learn from capitalized income tax data? *Review of Income and Wealth* 64 (3): 517–41.

Wiborg, Susanne. 2015. Privatizing education: Free school policy in Sweden and England. *Comparative Education Review* 59 (3): 473–97.

Woolhandler, Steffie, Terry Campbell, and David U. Himmelstein. 2003. Costs of health care administration in the United States and Canada. *New England Journal of Medicine* 349 (8): 768–75.

# Missing in Action: Bridging Capital and Cross-Boundary Discourse

*By*
SORA LEE
and
VALERIE BRAITHWAITE

The regulatory welfare state illuminates path dependencies and tendencies to mutual growth in markets, welfare, and regulation. This article uses two specific welfare-to-work programs, one in Korea and one in Australia, to illustrate the institutional interconnections that are in play within the regulatory welfare state. Governance of these programs is hampered by lack of discursive capacity to identify where problems exist and how they can be fixed. When faced with new programs, implementers look to higher authorities to make sense of and to solve the problems on the ground, but authorities are blinded by old institutional categories that pit market mentalities against welfare mentalities with regulation as an ideological tool, rather than an integral part of solutions. Transparency and cross-boundary listening are necessary to create the bridging capital to make these programs work and reconnect democratically elected governments with their citizens.

*Keywords:* welfare; regulation; regulatory capitalism; transparency; values

As governments outsource welfare services to private providers, providers compete and markets grow to deliver services. As markets expand, regulation expands, often to ensure that quality services are provided at a competitive price that satisfies users. Regulation shapes the market (sometimes sharpening the focus of services), more welfare needs become visible, more markets emerge, and more regulation is introduced. At an abstract level, Levi-Faur (2014) theorizes that institutions that traditionally have been siloed intellectually as regulation, welfare, and markets actually flourish in response to growth in the others. It is as if institutions are in

*Sora Lee is a doctoral student in the Menzies Centre for Health Governance, School of Regulation and Global Governance, Australian National University. Her doctoral thesis is on values governance for health equity in the elderly in Korea. She was an affiliated scholar with the Korean Women's Institute at Ewha Womans University.*

Correspondence: Valerie.Braithwaite@anu.edu.au

DOI: 10.1177/0002716220965439

competition and cooperation with each other, each constantly adapting and taking advantage of opportunities presented by the other to expand and to exert influence. As markets or welfare or regulatory institutions expand their reach, J. Braithwaite (2020) argues that "new path dependencies that sustain their own future growth paths" are created. There are more opportunities to expand and capture "old path dependencies" than to break down such pathways. In the context of this argument, path dependence means "the dependence of outcomes on the paths of previous routines, processes, and outcomes." Importantly, new paths will capitalize on the routines, patterns, and outcomes already established and redefine them (Jackall 1983), be they in a government's market, welfare, or regulation silo.

This means, as this special issue illustrates, complex webs of interconnections develop across market, welfare, and regulatory institutions. The connections are situation specific and opportunistic. Because institutional connectedness or interdependency is occurring does not mean that politicians, policy-makers, bureaucrats, service providers, users, and citizens understand what is happening, have control, foresee problems, and can manage these problems. Neither the state nor citizens can see clearly because familiar words acquire new meanings as new interconnections form. Competitive markets in welfare delivery can quickly morph into one dominated by oligopolies. As Benish and Levi-Faur point out in their introduction, expansion does not mean necessarily desirable outcomes, particularly for the least powerful in our society.

One research agenda, the primary concern of this special issue, is to understand the intermingling of regulation, welfare, and market institutions and the implications for governance. A parallel agenda, and one that is important for sustaining democracy, is to understand how people are engaging or failing to engage with these institutional changes. "How institutions think" in Mary Douglas's (1986) terms may constrain an individual's understanding, but as institutional changes occur it is not necessarily the case that people have the language or knowledge to make sense of those changes, or that they even experience them in the same way. In short, policy-makers, implementers, and service users may not be on the same page in terms of what is happening and why: are there benefits? Is it fair? Disruption in how things are done creates diversity in experiences and interpretations of the events. Those wedded to the efficiency of markets in principle may disagree on whether a program should pass costs on to users who are infirm and vulnerable. Those wedded to generous welfare provisions may disagree on whether there should be targeting and streamlining of services to make better use of the budget allocated. Different narratives are constructed depending on values, expectations, social groups, political identities, and trust in authority (V. Braithwaite 2009a). If these different narratives are not given voice and problems resolved, defiance and social fragmentation are likely to result (V. Braithwaite 2009b).

---

*Valerie Braithwaite is an emeritus professor in the School of Regulation and Global Governance, Australian National University. She is the author of* Defiance in Taxation and Governance *(Edward Elgar 2009), editor of* The ANNALS *special issue 592, "Hope Power and Governance," and co-editor (with Gale Burford and John Braithwaite) of* Restorative and Responsive Human Services *(Taylor & Francis 2019).*

As contributors to this issue explore the regulatory welfare state (RWS) as a radically different conceptualization of governance, this article asks whether citizens (defined broadly as those affected by a state's policy and actions) are on board to change their way of thinking. If there is truth to the arguments that the rise of populist leaders is associated with the rejection of experts (Kriesi 2014), we might presume that many of the ideas in this issue will unsettle people's consciousness and, in some cases, be resisted as threatening the status quo. This is the issue of concern in this article. More specifically: (a) how are citizens personally affected by changes in how regulation, welfare, and markets are interconnecting? (b) Are these changes affecting the democratic fabric in the sense that citizens feel they no longer see soundness or sense in the actions of their governments? (c) Do citizens feel that what is asked of them is fair and reasonable? Are citizens being treated with respect? And finally, (d) What are the implications for trust in institutions and in government?

We use two case studies from societies with different welfare histories to show that in both cases citizen resistance to government policy and implementation is present and damaging. Government officials and the public alike experience tension as users, managers, and implementers of government programs within the regulatory welfare state. Their expectations and understandings of government are discordant. Many citizens are befuddled by governance arrangements that belie an expectation that a democratic government will care for its people.

## We the People: View from Below

This article is concerned with the interface between the RWS and its beneficiaries. Our starting point is the people who are in the mind's eye of politicians, particularly in democracies as elections loom. Marshall's (1950) social contract is in play as electors look to their politicians for policies that protect them from social risks to their individual and collective well-being. These risks relate to security concerns around law and order, economic prosperity, reward for effort, self-sufficiency, and achievement. Equally important to the public are harmony concerns around social cohesion, compassion, equity, and social justice (V. Braithwaite 2009a). In a practical sense this means that governments have responsibility for ensuring safety nets while encouraging economic growth. Most recently, this has been visible during the COVID-19 pandemic, with many governments (including those under study here) devising policies that simultaneously steer their economies and safeguard the health of their citizens.

Governments do not have to deliver protection of the security or harmony kinds: how much they do themselves depends on the type of welfare state that has developed historically and that frames public expectations (Esping-Anderson 1990). But the responsibility of all governments traditionally has been to oversee the systems of delivery, which generally rely on families, informal networks, and private organizations, as well as government agencies to varying degrees. Recent decades have seen increased complexity in the targets of welfare from multinationals to the unemployed; in the networks of delivery across different levels of government with public and private providers; and in the laws, rules, contracts, standards, and computer systems that regulate delivery. The regulation-welfare-markets conceptualization suggests that leaders are everywhere, and that power is exerted everywhere in moments of opportunity, on occasion crippling and at other times enhancing the performance of other institutions. Confronted with so many moving parts, legitimate questions from citizens include, "Who is in charge?"; "Who should be in charge?"; "What does it mean to be in charge?"; and, finally, "What is all this in aid of?" For the public, what is missing in this new governance era is sense-making, accountability, and transparency. Understandably the public look to their political leaders. Trust ratings across democratically elected governments suggest that answers are not consistently satisfying (OECD 2019).

Regulatory scholars might argue that their contribution to the regulation-welfare-markets juggernaut is accountability and transparency. Unfortunately, such mechanisms are not connected with sense-making for the public. What they see is something technocratic and bureaucratic. Marver Bernstein (1955) wrote of the problem of the U.S. railways commission becoming so intricate in its rule-making that it became disconnected from other arms of government and from those being regulated. This is a telling case study because rail travel had a shockingly high mortality rate in the nineteenth century, before the rise of the Progressive Era version of the regulatory state, and a very low accident rate by Marver Bernstein's time. Today's regulators run a similar risk from regulatory life cycles of being disconnected from the people whom, on many fronts, they want to protect from harm. In the face of regulation-welfare-market interconnectedness, people crave leadership to explain and justify new systems of welfare delivery and governance arrangements.

The point this article makes is that the public needs to be part of a conversation about the regulatory welfare state. The two case studies discussed in this article show public discontent and absence of leadership or bridging capital for carrying sense-making messages down, up, and across networks. In these case studies, the blinkers of old institutional forms prevent cross-boundary thinking to solve new problems. This is to be expected with new institutional forms. We have yet to acquire the language and understanding to communicate the essence of the changes. In the meantime, however, democratic governments struggle with skeptical citizens because authorities cannot convincingly explain who is at the table when decisions are made, who wins, and who pays. We illustrate the problems through two specific programs that fall under the welfare-to-work umbrella in the Republic of Korea and Australia.

## Two Programs Illustrating Regulation-Welfare-Market Alignments

The cases discussed here are taken from two independent studies of government-sponsored welfare-to-work programs: the Korea Senior Employment Program

(KSEP), which supports participation in the workforce for Koreans over 65 years of age (Lee, forthcoming), and the Australian Robodebt Program designed to efficiently capture welfare overpayments for those with low incomes or those out of work (J. Braithwaite, this volume; V. Braithwaite 2020).

While the programs differ in purpose and context, they are both examples of institutional innovations that interconnect regulation, welfare, and markets. Both created tremors that rippled through their respective populations. Experienced policy-makers sometimes contend that all new policies create resistance and in time settle down. There is evidence to the contrary (Ahmed and Braithwaite 2004). This article extends understanding of what has previously been an observation—the public are confused by the priorities and actions of governments as they actively engage in coupling institutions that politicians have historically and rhetorically pitted against each other. For example, the public are used to hearing accounts of how markets commodify and diminish the quality of welfare, welfare undermines incentives for markets, and regulation chokes markets and stifles welfare. Sense-making around successful coupling is sadly lacking. A notable exception is welfare-to-work programs, which have won wide acceptance captured by the dictum, "The best form of welfare is work." Even so, at the point of imple-mentation, successful coupling was not the experience of welfare recipients in our two programs: we show how criticism and discord on what the programs offered to Australians and South Koreans were rife inside and outside government.

## The Korea Senior Employment Program (KSEP): Regulating job creation through welfare and markets

Government sponsored welfare programs are relatively recent phenomena in the Republic of Korea. A subpopulation of particular concern in recent times has been older Koreans (OECD 2018, 2019). Koreans look forward to a healthy old age—their life expectancy is among the highest in the world (Kontis et al. 2017). Yet they also face the highest rates of old age poverty in the OECD. As Korea has become an advanced economy, traditional intergenerational patterns of family support have broken down (Klassen and Yang 2014), and so the state has been called upon to help the almost 50 percent of senior Koreans living in poverty, often alone, and sometimes homeless. Geriatric mental health is a major public health issue (Shin and Hwang 2018) and work has been seen as part of the solution.

While employment is being used to address mental health and poverty issues for Korea's elderly population, there is also a national economic imperative for increasing their work participation rates (OECD 2018). Korea has a population that is ageing rapidly, with projections that by 2050 more than one third of the population will be over 65 (United Nations Department of Economic and Social Affairs 2015). Extending work and alleviating poverty present particular chal-lenges for Korea because many firms prefer a younger workforce and have man-datory retirement policies for older Koreans (Klassen and Yang 2014). The OECD has urged the South Korean government to expand its job-creation and welfare activities and to develop policies that address discrimination against older workers, the structural reasons for discrimination, and offer incentives to mid-career and older workers to remain engaged in work and retraining (OECD 2012).

Korea has quite quickly developed a mixture of programs in an effort to provide a minimum standard of living for elderly citizens. They include private pension funds and public support programs that are targeted to groups of variable income security and work histories (Thakur 2018). KSEP is one program designed specifically to bring older Koreans into the workforce. It began in 2008, under the umbrella of the Ministry of Health and Welfare, and has continued its expansion despite pushes within the government to rationalize welfare expenditure in favor of job creation in the private sector (Ji 2015). KSEP provides work opportunities under two broad categories: social contribution jobs (public service, caregiving, and education) and market entry jobs (labor-dispatch and self-employment).

Eligible participants (over 65 years of age) are required to submit an application to KSEP, which is reviewed for eligibility and suitability for the available jobs. Most jobs offered by KSEP fall in the public service category. They constitute 67.7 percent of KSEP work opportunities (KORDI 2016). These jobs are low skill and require low educational attainment. The remuneration is less than half the national average hourly income. Participants in social contribution jobs receive fixed monthly salaries of 200,000 won (approximately US$165) during a 9- to 12-month participation period.

KSEP jobs that are created in partnership with the private sector are called market entry jobs. They are much preferred because the work contracts are longer and often the pay is better, and they may potentially be a pathway to regular employment. To increase market-entry jobs, the Ministry of Health and Welfare in 2018 began to offer incentives for companies that provided longer contracts for older workers. Companies where the majority of employees are elderly are accredited as "merited enterprises for elderly employment" and have been offered incentives such as social insurance and subsidies for company promotion and improved working environments.

KSEP participants must not work more than 3 to 4 hours a day and 3 to 5 days a week. The rationale is to protect older workers from the physical and mental burden caused by overwork. It is of note that work injury is not an inconsequential problem in Korea and exploitation of an elderly workforce is something to be guarded against (Congressional Audit 2019a). Until recently, those who found work through KSEP were not systematically insured against work-related injury. Contested within government has been the practice of classifying social contribution jobs as welfare for the elderly and not as "real jobs" where insurance is appropriate. The dispute was worsened when responsibility for insurance was shifted to local bodies administering the program. Some implementing organizations were able to cope with the insurance premium, but many others struggled to cope with the financial and administrative burden of making sure KSEP participants had the same protections as other workers. The payment burden in the end fell on the shoulders of participants, but many refused to pay because the financial burden was too great. Others were excluded from insurance because of work conditions; for example, they had too short a contract or insufficient hours of work. The implementing organizations and participants were persistent in communicating these problems to the Congress and the ministry to achieve change. In 2018, a newly modified KSEP acknowledged KSEP participants as employees and provided insurance against injury.

Hence, KSEP is an example of a welfare-to-work program, specifically for older Koreans, that uses markets and welfare to address care for the elderly population and economic growth. The regulatory framework for delivery is expanding rapidly and has changed as KSEP has developed. Intervening between the Ministry of Health and Welfare and local grantee organizations is KORDI, which has taken on an expanded governance role, overseeing the overall KSEP budget, program administration, grantee organizations, and evaluation. KORDI, while officially in the Department of Health and Welfare, is well-networked with the central government. Since the inception of KSEP, KORDI has had the task of creating jobs and partnering with private businesses that wish to participate in providing work positions for older people. While the welfare arm (specifically social contribution jobs) remains dominant, there is little doubt that the momentum is with building work opportunities in the private sector under KORDI's leadership.

Six provincial KORDI offices have recently been opened to create more locally specialized jobs. KORDI allocates jobs through five types of local implementing bodies that oversee work contracts for successful KSEP applicants: provincial government offices, Senior Clubs, the Korean Association of Older People, local community centers, and local senior centers. Local governments that have had prime responsibility for coordinating pre-existing social delivery systems have a limited role in KSEP management and evaluation. Most growth has occurred in the Senior Clubs, newly established semi-public organizations that aim to grow local KSEP jobs (KORDI 2016).

KSEP has multiple levels of administration that extend across government departments, across public and private service providers, and across public and private employers. We should acknowledge that some of the changes that we have described have been welcomed by South Koreans. It is fair to say that older Koreans prefer work in the private sector, and so increases in the availability of such jobs has been met with approval. But these movements privilege some more than others in ways that do not make sense to Koreans. The gold standard for older Koreans is a particular program from the Ministry of Labour. This program is open to those over 60 years of age with three years' work experience and appropriate licenses. Entry into this scheme is much sought after because it offers higher income and longer working hours, but it is limited to 2,500 jobs. This is a quarter of the number of jobs supported by a comparable employment program for those over 50 years of age (Congressional Audit 2019b).

In this case study, we see the interconnectedness of welfare and markets, each driving the other forward, with the regulatory mechanisms available to KORDI and to the Department of Human Services steering and adjudicating the flow of events to ensure all parties have reason to cooperate. Yet while regulation, welfare, and markets are reinforcing each other at a policy level, there are innu-merable tensions playing out at the coalface that explain why individuals might be forgiven for thinking in win-lose terms about the relationships among regula-tion, welfare, and markets. Conditions differ across programs and different min-istries compete and firewall their programs and practices to the detriment of service delivery. For example, the different levels of coverage for injury that per-sisted for so long was a boundary issue within the government but made no sense and was seen as unfair by KSEP beneficiaries. Some private sector jobs offered coverage and some national jobs did as well, but individuals assigned to local social contribution jobs missed out. Furthermore, the hierarchical nature of the KSEP program meant that there was no transparency in the way jobs were allo-cated to individuals, and support to tailor jobs to individual needs was lacking. The experience of individuals and organizations working in KSEP is less positive than the picture portrayed at the macro level of policy and design.

## The Australian Robodebt Program: Regulating overpayment of welfare benefits

The welfare system in Australia is elaborate and the calculation of payments can be complex. Payments from a diverse range of welfare programs can be affected by a range of factors, including income, assets, age, caring responsibili-ties, relationships, living situation, being a student, and capacity to perform activities of daily life. Just over half of households and around a third of adult Australians receive income support (Whiteford 2015).

Within this system, overpayment of benefits and welfare fraud have always been of concern, particularly so because the costs of detection and recovery are so high (Prenzler 2011). Robodebt, the Australian public's vote for "Word of the Year" in 2019, refers to the controversial methodology introduced mid-2016 for recovering presumed overpayments to social welfare recipients (Senate Community Affairs References Committee 2017). The Robodebt program is a data matching algorithm that compares data from the Australian Taxation Office with the data that welfare recipients are legally required to provide to the govern-ment welfare service provider, Centrelink. Recipients are responsible for inform-ing Centrelink of changes to their circumstances within 14 days of those changes to ensure accurate payments are made. An overpayment is assumed when the declarations made by recipients to Centrelink are lower than the estimates extracted from tax office data. An automatically generated letter is then posted to the welfare recipient demanding payment or proof that the debt was invalid.

The administrative workload associated with debt calculation was shifted entirely to technology in the form of the data matching algorithm. A costly addi-tional step of human oversight, which previously involved checking records after a data matching process, contacting employers, understanding the reason for discrepancies, and then deciding who had received an overpayment, was aban-doned. This was a program to make street-level bureaucracy (Lipsky1980) and responsiveness obsolete. The onus of proof for checking and collecting documentation to change the computer-generated decision was passed to the welfare recipient. Debt calculation was retrospective up to seven years.

If the welfare recipient could not prove that the debt was invalid because they had not retained up to seven years of employee pay records, because they could not contact former employers for records, or because they had not been given adequate documentation in the first place, options were limited. The Department of Human Services was intent on recouping revenue to improve the government's budgetary position. There were myriad features of the scheme that made it very difficult to avoid paying the alleged debt. Call centers were understaffed, debts routinely were not explained, and it was difficult to assemble and lodge the documentation that was a prerequisite for having a case reviewed. Taking the matter to court resulted in success in a significant number of cases in so far as debts were reduced or wiped out. But taking the matter to court was daunting for many and time lines for payment of the debt without penalty were tight. Stories of successes at court, however, led to a groundswell of protest against Robodebt involving opposition politicians, administrative lawyers, legal aid lawyers, welfare advocacy groups, professional bodies, and the public. #NotMyDebt was a web site that was set up by those affected. It attracted supporters, shared stories and advice, and organized resistance.[1]

A substantial proportion of the debts turned out to be incorrect. The estimate taken from tax office data was based on annual income and the assumption was made that this money was earned at the same rate across welfare payment periods. This became known as the averaging fallacy, that is, Robodebt's assumption that people on welfare consistently earn the same amount of money each fortnight throughout the year. Those designing Robodebt failed to take account of the fact that seasonal work, being in and out of work, irregular payment, and ill-health disrupted the income earning capacity of those on welfare. The averaging assumption led to the most egregious form of false debts. Many paid the false debts, even though they did not believe they owed the money—they were afraid of harassment by debt collectors or being cut off from future payments by Centrelink. The payments were referred to by critics outside government as "extortion" (Carney 2018a). The Robodebt Scandal triggered two Commonwealth Ombudsman Reports, two Senate Committee inquiries in the Australian parliament (the second to report in December 2020[2]), a Federal Court case that found the government program to be illegal because it was issuing false debts, and a pending class action against the government seeking compensation (Commonwealth Ombudsman 2017, 2019; Carney 2018a, 2018b, 2019; Senate Community Affairs References Committee 2017).

The Robodebt Program was a regulatory solution that the government chose as an innovative way to detect fraud and overpayment without need for human oversight. The government's goal was arguably reasonable. It was looking for efficiency through simultaneously recovering overpayment and reducing expenditure on skilled welfare staff. The opening quote from the Senate Community Affairs References Committee Inquiry (2017) into the Program underlined the shared view of Australians: "I do not support or condone the abuse of the welfare system in any way, and strongly feel that anyone who wilfully rorts the system by providing false information should be caught and punished" (p. 1). It was not the objective that was contentious, but rather the regulatory process that was put in place to achieve the objective. In short, most Australians believed that Robodebt should be shut down (Essential Report 2019). To complete the quote above: "The system of debt recovery needs to be respectful and it needs to be fair and ethical."

The regulatory missteps occurred at four stages of the debt recovery process: calculation, communication, conciliation, and collection. First, the Robodebt calculation had a fundamental flaw. Welfare agencies sprung into action to protect the vulnerable who neither understood nor were able to initiate corrective action. The second misstep was restricting the government's human interface and closing down communication. This gave people limited opportunity to understand the source of the debt and resolve their situation with the government. Instead welfare groups, legal aid, and consumer groups provided much-needed support and advocacy. The third regulatory misstep of government was game-playing the legal system and avoiding accountability. Magistrates of the Administrative Appeals Tribunal (AAT), which hears cases from citizens (and organizations) aggrieved by the administrative decisions of the Australian Government, recognized the "averaging fallacy" early in the history of Robodebt. Magistrates sent cases back to the department for review. The department did not appeal these decisions by the magistrates: on review, debts were commonly reduced. If the department had pursued an appeal in the court, the case would have progressed to being one on the public record. Settling out of court prevented disclosure of what was happening. Meanwhile, the workload for correcting the errors of Robodebt were quietly shifted from the government to an overburdened court system. It was not surprising, therefore, that administrative lawyers became some of the most vocal opponents of Robodebt.

The fourth and final regulatory misstep occurred with debt collection. Debts were collected before complaints were reconciled, using actions that, according to administrative lawyers, departed from model litigant policy. Model litigant policy requires the government to uphold the principle of fair play and avoid conducting litigation in ways oppressive of citizens (Carney 2018b, 9). This is the idea that the state should be a moral exemplar of justice in regulatory welfare capitalism. Those giving evidence to the Senate Inquiry reported that without warning or explanation they were subjected to garnisheeing of debts from income tax returns, deductions from government benefits, and harassment and coercion from private debt collectors.

In reflecting on the government's foray into big data with Robodebt, Galloway (2017) concluded that there had been "a breakdown in standards of governance" (p. 94) and government had "lost its way" (p. 95). With so much new surveillance technology at its disposal, Galloway raised the question of whether "government can be effectively constrained in its exercise of power" (p. 95). Those adopting a regulation-welfare-markets conception would answer yes, that it can be constrained, given time. Evidence to date supports this prediction. It took three and a half years, but constraint was exercised. This was, however, cold comfort for those whose lives fell apart as a result of Robodebt (see Senate Community Affairs References Committee 2017).

The story of Robodebt is one of powerful government actors trapped in thinking that they were part of an old-style welfare system, separated from mainstream society and unaccountable for welfare abuses. As Murphy (2019) stated upon reviewing the scandal: "Robodebt was hatched for a simple, clinical purpose: to return money to the budget at a time when the budget was firmly in the red. . . .Better to go after people you like to characterize as spongers on the public purse than people who might get angry enough with you to vote for someone else." In contrast to times past when injustice to welfare recipients was swept under the carpet, Robodebt became a very public scandal for the government, largely because welfare is so interconnected with job markets and social regulation that it can no longer be successfully siloed. Private and public interests were enrolled in the regulatory processes to action Robodebt, and not all were on board ethically with the way it was used. Those affected had networks that they could marshal to constrain the program. This they did: networks of politicians, welfare advocates, and private interest groups, including lawyers, financial advisors, professional bodies, debt collectors, and private law firms were mobilized. Law may have been the final nail in the coffin of Robodebt, but the issue of illegality became far more lethal for government thanks to a broad coalition of support from a diverse community, as well as the rise of Australia's industry of class actions led by private law firms. At the time of writing this article, the government has agreed to refund overpayments (Henriques-Gomes 2020).

## KSEP and Robodebt as Lived Experience

V. Braithwaite's (2017) wheel of social alignments provides the methodological framework for illustrating how experience and understanding of the KSEP and Robodebt programs generate public unease over the consequences of regulation-welfare-markets interconnections. When individuals or organizations recognize that there are benefits to cooperating with the regulatory requirements of a program, when the program is administered in a fair and reasonable manner, and when there is moral obligation to do what authority requires, cooperation is most likely to emerge and will generate its own community inertia such that cooperation continues— even as the program hits inevitable bumps in the road. However, when belief in benefits fades, or unfairness becomes intolerable, or moral obligation wanes on a large enough scale in the community, the wheel will stop. On such occasions, alternative authorities can make their presence felt to the point of undermining the legitimacy of the presiding authority. In our case studies, the wheel did not stop: strong welfare, strong markets, and strong regulation came into play at different points to temper (Krygier 2019) the poor decisions of the other. Individuals were not spared, however, as institutional forces slowly realigned. The data presented here show feelings of betrayal at the hands of market ideology, welfare dogma, and clunky automation of regulation, singly or in combination.

The data used to illustrate doubts about benefits, fairness, and obligation are taken from two different studies. The study of KSEP undertaken by Sora Lee (forthcoming) involved forty-four interviews with KSEP participants and stakeholders. The data are part of a larger project investigating welfare policy governance in Korea. The study of Robodebt was undertaken by Valerie Braithwaite and relied on 126 written submissions[3] provided to two public inquiries initiated by nongovernment members of the Senate in the Australian parliament. Both studies provided access to the views of civil servants, private providers and implementers, welfare recipients, and advocacy and support groups whose lives were affected by these programs.

## Perceptions of benefits

Clients, civil society actors helping clients, and government employees implementing the programs all perceived program failures with KSEP and Robodebt. An ex-KSEP participant reflected on his experience:

> Can you imagine how deserted you might feel as an older man, worked throughout all his life, and left with just pocket money (Basic Pension)? You don't want to burden your children, because their lives are just as hard. But the government is just ashamed to have this much poverty, and this much unemployment. For the government, we are a useless old bunch. Something's not right.

A similar feeling of being trampled by an uncaring system occurred with Robodebt clients. This client had been successful in having the debt overturned:

> A demanding debt notice of such a magnitude, with no explanation, from over six years ago, with a very limited amount of time to respond, just plunges a financially stressed person into shock, panic, despair and depression. . . . . Increasing a person's level of poverty for no good reason is unethical and inhumane. (Senate Inquiry 2017, Submission 005)

Both KSEP and Robodebt placed social distance between policy designers and those working with clients. Front line organizations were in the vacant space trying to repair the damage that the programs inflicted.

A private sector KSEP implementer questioned program benefits:

> I think the government has to decide what really is the purpose of the program. Is it an employment program or welfare program? The current evaluating components are all revenue related . . . revenue, incentive payment, months of employment . . . If they really want to foster a market type program . . . other benefits for "ethical companies" need to be in place. Right now, the values are misplaced.

Victoria Legal Aid, with many Robodebt cases on their books, was scathing in its criticism of the government's inability to balance its value commitments responsibly:

VLA supports efficiency and expediency as hallmarks of good government decision-making and administration. We also support the intelligent, lawful, and valuable application by government of technology, including to manage government funds. [But]. . . in our experience, the [Robodebt] Initiative undermines key tenets of proper and lawful government action. . . .The cumulative impact will damage the overall integrity of the Centrelink system. (Senate Inquiry 2017, Submission 111)

Last, but not least, failures of both programs to actually benefit the public in ways promised by their respective governments were obvious to officials working within the system. For KSEP, a stand off developed higher up between ministries over injury and illness among participants. This comment from one of central government's welfare data management staff illustrated a highly visible problem that was for a long time ignored to the detriment of KSEP participants:

Who is actually concerned in this cross-boundary issue? Who is taking responsibility? Actually . . . no one in the ministry. Roles are highly compartmentalized and clearly divided, and last time I checked, no one is looking into the problem of "insurability" of KSEP participants in the ministry. You are welcome to dig out who is, and let me know if you do.

For those working within the department administering Robodebt, frustration was expressed not just on behalf of others but also on behalf of fellow staff:

DHS is well and truly broken. In the 24 years that I have been employed here, the place has never been so dysfunctional, so many bad decisions being made at a senior management level, so resource strained, have so much arrears, having rolled out stupid tools and systems that make our jobs more inefficient than they were before the new system or policy was implemented. (Senate Inquiry 2017, Submission 065)

Together, these comments show the governments' failure to deliver on their democratic social contract with their citizens and how they allowed harms generated by these programs to persist. In the words of one Robodebt official, "DHS continues to ignore everything staff and customers are saying, and are in their own fairy world that 'everything is great!'" In the case of KSEP, frustration was equally palpable for this local implementer: "I wonder if they recognize what it would be like to absorb their separate policies at the local level. People are all just one person with complex needs that are intertwined. If they don't understand that, there's only so much we can do."

*Fairness*

Both unfairness and unreasonableness were rife in KSEP and Robodebt. Those implementing KSEP saw hierarchical structures, bureaucratic silos, and rules that denied them the flexibility to place senior citizens in work that was suitable for them. Local implementers and program participants felt cornered and without a voice: "It feels like we are filling a leaking jar hopelessly. No matter how hard we try our voice just doesn't get heard." One agency confirmed the problem of prejudice: "We are bound to avoid older and disabled applicants because participating companies do not prefer them. . . . The private sector makes complaints about us for sending those participants." A disappointed applicant made sense of failure to get a job in a different way: "I suspect the jobs are distributed among those who know someone in the government. . . . It just feels like it would never reach normal people like me."

Robodebt touched the lives of so many people in such an unjust way. The final report of the 2017 Senate Inquiry captured the experiences of the many Australians caught up in the program:

> The system was so flawed that it was set up to fail. . . . This lack of procedural fairness disempowered people, causing emotional trauma, stress and shame. This was intensified when the Government subsequently publicly released personal information about people who spoke out against the process. (p. 107)

## Moral obligation

Within democratic societies, the social contract with the government requires that citizens and residents of the country obey the laws. One might extend this to rules and regulations, with the understanding that noncompliance more broadly can be costly—materially, socially, and psychologically. We know that flouting law occurs when injustice is rife. Nadler (2005) applies the concept of flouting the law to situations where people experience injustice in one context and then transfer that sense of injustice and flout the law in other contexts. Robodebt, in theory, could have the unexpected consequence of welfare recipients finding work in the cash economy to even out the fluctuating income that has made them vulnerable to the averaging fallacy and Robodebt (V. Braithwaite 2020).

If we assume that rules were breached or bent in both Korea and Australia in a bid to find justice, we should ask, why did authorities not respond to complaints and create legitimate pathways for those aggrieved by unfair rules? Regulation-welfare-markets interconnections require the government to see the bigger picture. Neither the Korean nor Australian governments were equipped for such oversight.

The Korean government embarked in 2010 on an initiative called "Raising Efficiency in Centrally-Funded Employment Policies" (Korea Ministry of Labour 2010). The Ministry of Labour led the initiative and sought a merger of all the employment-related programs across sectors, including old-age work programs (KORDI 2014; Ji 2015). Resistance came from the Ministry of Health and Welfare and from many KSEP managers, both public and private, as well as the community, because the Ministry of Labour's "redundancy" agenda did not recognize that different work programs had different purposes and were meeting different community needs. More specifically, social contribution jobs were at risk because they were not seen by the National Budget Office as sufficiently beneficial to the economy. Those opposing the change wanted a government review that took into account interdependence of different work programs and the "organic connectivity of policies from different ministries."[4]

A meaningful dialogue on how different programs could be better coordinated in the interests of older Koreans did not ensue. The ministries did not come together to learn from each other and work through their conflicting value priorities. Instead the Board of Audit and Inspection quickly dampened the looming controversy with a bureaucratic and technocratic solution (Lee, forthcoming). Anyone under 65 would be managed by the Ministry for Labour. Anyone over 65 would seek work through the Ministry for Health and Welfare. The ministries "firewalled" their programs rather than integrating them into a whole-of-government approach. Issues that were giving rise to mistrust among those involved in KSEP on the ground were left unresolved.

In the case of Robodebt, similar tribalism shaped the actions of the Department of Human Services. Trusted sources close to or within the government warned of the illegality of averaging tax data; a confidential, early judgment from the Administrative Appeals Tribunal, advice from the Department of Human Services lawyers, and advice from the Australian Taxation Office lawyers all raised red flags around Robodebt.[5] As in Korea, there was unwillingness to listen to and be responsive to different voices with relevant experience and knowledge. As with KSEP, concerns from below were ignored. The Commonwealth Public Service Union documented the frustration over failures to learn and listen within the department: "Many members stated that concerns were raised during the design process but were simply ignored" (Senate Inquiry 2017, Submission 065).

Once problems started to emerge, communication was blocked: "Many DHS [Department of Human Services] staff have been concerned about disclosing the Robodebt debacle, particularly as staff have been sent numerous emails warning them about doing so" (Senate Inquiry 2017, Submission 065). The Senate Inquiry revealed the schism within the department between the higher and lower echelons of public service: "We've completely lost faith in our leaders. . . . Our systems are failing, it seems like 'head office' is making decisions regarding how we do our work with the primary motivator being 'how to hide mistakes and how to make the stats look good'" (Senate Inquiry 2017, Submission 065).

## Conclusion

This article supports the argument that regulation, welfare, and markets are becoming interconnected and stronger institutions, and that the premise holds even in the traditionally siloed case of care for the vulnerable. As such, there is potential for each to guard against the excesses of the others in the evolution of good governance. At the same time, we have demonstrated that on the ground, beliefs about the integrity and trustworthiness of these interconnected institutions, at least in relation to KSEP and Robodebt, are less affirming.

Scale and time can reconcile these different perspectives. Given enough time, regulation, welfare, and markets are strong and rich enough as institutions to correct the errors of the other. But who decides what is an error and what is not? The warning that emerges from this article for practicing democracies is the importance of strengthening pathways for feedback about programs from the grassroots and investing in the social infrastructure for collaborative responsiveness.

In both Korea and Australia, these pathways were blocked by regulation that was too oriented to the interests and ideological preferences of more powerful players. How best to balance and steer the path dependency of regulation, welfare, and markets is yet to be discovered. What is clear, however, is that greater efforts must be made to allow the experiences of those affected by programs such as KSEP and Robodebt to be heard before an accumulation of missteps, covered up and dismissed as unimportant, wreak havoc and weaken the social fabric of our democracies. Perhaps what is required in a world of more intertwined regulation-welfare-markets is more intertwined administrative law, parliamentary oversight, and trade union mediation, and more civil society activists and street-level bureaucrats who listen and are listened to.

# Notes

1. https://www.notmydebt.com.au/.

2. https://www.aph.gov.au/Parliamentary_Business/Committees/Senate/Community_Affairs/Centre linkcompliance.

3. A further 40 submissions were provided to the second Inquiry after this analysis was undertaken. Of the 156 submissions to the first Inquiry, 99 were publicly available and 57 were submitted to the Inquiry on a confidential basis.

4. Researcher, government research institution.

5. Evidence given in hearings to the second Senate Inquiry, see Henriques-Gomes (2020).

# References

Ahmed, Eliza, and Valerie Braithwaite. 2004. When tax collectors become collectors for child support and student loans: Jeopardizing the revenue base? *Kyklos* 57:303–26.

Bernstein, Marver. 1955. *Regulating business by independent commissions*. Princeton, NJ: Princeton University Press.

Braithwaite, John. 2020. Meta governance of path dependencies: Regulation, welfare, and markets. *The ANNALS of the American Academy of Political and Social Science* (this volume).

Braithwaite, Valerie. 2009a. The value balance model and democratic governance. *Psychological Inquiry* 20 (2–3): 87–97.

Braithwaite, Valerie. 2009b. *Defiance in taxation and governance: Resisting and dismissing authority in a democracy*. Cheltenham, UK: Edward Elgar.

Braithwaite, Valerie. 2017. Closing the gap between regulation and the community. In *Regulatory theory: Foundations and applications*, ed. Peter Drahos, 25–41. Acton: ANU Press.

Braithwaite, Valerie. 2020. Beyond the bubble that is Robodebt: how governments that lose integrity threaten democracy. *Australian Journal of Social Issues* (online).

Carney, Terry. 2018a. Robo-Debt Illegality: A Failure of Rule of Law Protections? *AUSPUBLAW*. Available from https://auspublaw.org/2018/04/robo-debt-illegality/.

Carney, Terry. 2018b. The new digital future for welfare: Debts without legal proofs or moral authority. *University of New South Wales Law Journal Forum* 1:1–16.

Carney, Terry. 18 September 2019. Robodebt class action could deliver justice for tens of thousands of Australians instead of mere hundreds. *The Conversation*.

Commonwealth Ombudsman. 2017. Centrelink's automated debt raising and recovery system: A report about the department of human services' online compliance intervention system for debt raising and recovery. Report No 02/2017. Available from https://www.ombudsman.gov.au/__data/assets/pdf_file/0022/43528/Report- Centrelinks-automated-debt-raising-and-recovery-system-April-2017.pdf.

Commonwealth Ombudsman. 2019. Centrelink's automated debt raising and recovery system: Implementation report. *Report No 01/2019*. https://www.ombudsman.gov.au/__data/assets/pdf_file/0025/98314/April-2019-Centrelinks-Automated-Debt-Raising-and-Recovery-System.pdf.

Congressional Audit submission by the Korea Labor Force Development Institute for the aged. 2019a. A Report on Congressman Kim Kwangsu's inquiry on Workplace Injury among Korean Senior Employment Program Participants.

Congressional Audit submission by the Korea Labor Force Development Institute for the aged. 2019b. A Report on Congresswoman Kim Seunghee's inquiry on Overlapping Senior Employment Programs from Multiple Ministries.

Douglas, Mary. 1986. *How institutions think*. Syracuse NY: Syracuse University Press.

Esping-Anderson, Gøsta. 1990. *The three worlds of welfare capitalism*. Cambridge: Polity Press.

Essential Report. 6 August 2019. Support or oppose calls to shut down 'Robodebt' program, Available from https://www.essentialvision.com.au/wp-content/uploads/2019/08/Essential-Report-050819-V2-1.pdf.

Galloway, Kate. 2017. Big data: A case study of disruption and government power. *Alternative Law Journal* 89:93–4.

Henriques-Gomes, Luke. 12 February 2020. Coalition warned Robodebt scheme was unenforceable three years before it acted. *The Guardian Australia*. Available from https://www.theguardian.com/australia-news/2020/feb/12/coalition-warned-robodebt-scheme-was-unenforceable-three-years-before-it-acted.

Jackall, Robert. 1983. Moral mazes: Bureaucracy and managerial work. *Harvard Business Review*. September–October:118–130.

Ji, Eun-Jeong. 2015. A study on the overlap and duplication of senior job programs. (In Korean).*The Korea Local Administration Review* 29 (4): 229–64.

Kontis, V., J. E. Bennett, C. D. Mathers, G. Li, K. Foreman, and M. Ezzati. 2017. Future life expectancy in 35 industrialised countries: projections with a Bayesian model ensemble. *The Lancet* 389 (10076): 1323–1335.

Krygier, Martin. 2019. What's the point of the rule of law. *Buffalo Law Review* 67:743–91.

Korea Labor Force Development Institute for the Aged. 2016. Performance Report for 2015 Korean Senior Employment Program. Seoul: Korean Labor Force Development Institute for the Aged.

Korean Ministry of Labour. 2010. Guideline for 2011 Budget efficient employment programs. Press release. Sejong City: Korean Ministry of Labour.

Klassen, Thomas R., and Yunjeong Yang. 2014. *Korea's Retirement Predicament: The Ageing Tiger*. London: Routledge.

Kriesi, Hanspeter. 2014. The populist challenge. *West European Politics* 37 (2): 361–78.

Lee, Sora. Forthcoming. Governing values of multiple stakeholders: Evidence from Korean senior employment program and housing pension scheme. PhD thesis, Australian National University.

Levi-Faur, David. 2014. The welfare state: A regulatory perspective. *Public Administration* 92 (3): 599–614.

Lipsky, Michael. 1980. *Street-level bureaucracy: Dilemmas of the individual in public services*. New York, NY: Russell Sage Foundation.

Marshall, Thomas H. 1950. *Citizenship and social class: And other essays*. Cambridge: Cambridge University Press.

Murphy, Katharine. 30 November 2019. The Robodebt horror was all about boosting the budget. That's the brutal truth. *The Guardian Australia*. Available from https://www.theguardian.com.

Nadler, Janice. 2005. Flouting the law. *Texas Law Review* 83 (5): 1399–1441.

OECD. 2012. *Thematic follow-up review of policies to improve labour market prospects for older workers in South Korea (situation mid-2012)*. Paris: OECD. Available from https://www.oecd.org/els/emp/Older%20Workers%20Korea-MOD.pdf.

OECD. 2018. *Working better with age: Korea, ageing and employment policies*. Paris: OECD. Available from https://doi.org/10.1787/9789264208261-en.

OECD. 2019. *Society at a Glance 2019: OECD Social Indicators*. Paris: OECD. Available from https://doi.org/10.1787/soc_glance-2019-en.

Prenzler, Tim. 2011. Welfare fraud in Australia: Dimensions and issues. *Trends and Issues in Crime and Criminal Justice* 421. Doi: https://www.aic.gov.au/publications/tandi/tandi421.

Senate Community Affairs References Committee. 2017. *Design, scope, cost-benefit analysis, contracts awarded and implementation associated with the Better Management of the Social Welfare System initiative*. Canberra: Commonwealth of Australia.

Shin, Sujin, and Eunhee Hwang. 2018. Factors influencing depressive symptoms among Korean older adults with chronic illnesses: Using the 2014 National Survey on Older Adults. *Korean Journal of Adult Nursing* 30 (6): 577–85.

Thakur, Gajender. 2018. Ageing in East Asia challenges and policies: A comparative study of welfare services for the elderly in Korea and Japan. *Lensa Budaya: Journal Ilmiah Ilmu-Ilmu Budaya* 13 (2). DOI:http://dx.doi.org/10.34050/jlb.v13i2.5295.

United Nations Department of Economics and Social Affairs. 2015. World population prospects: The 2015 revision, key findings and advance tables. Technical Report: Working Paper No. ESA/P/WP. 241. New York, NY: United Nations Department of Economic and Social Affairs, Population Division.

Whiteford, Peter. May 11 2015. Fact Check: Is half to two-thirds of the Australian population receiving a government benefit? *The Conversation*. Available from https://theconversation.com.

Governments around the world have turned to higher education to sustain economic development and social welfare. This article uses the concept of the *regulatory welfare state* (RWS) to examine how state authorities in the United States and Germany have sought to spur structural changes in the education sector. I argue that policy-makers in both countries have pursued the goal of organizing competition among universities by combining fiscal and regulatory policies that strengthen universities' self-reliance, rivalry, and decentralized decision-making. The analysis shows that understanding cross-national patterns of institutional transformation requires putting countries' evolving regimes of state-university relations into historical perspective, and that states' shifting governance strategies are important drivers of higher education's contemporary reimagination. It also clarifies how regulatory approaches to welfare provision have fostered the re-composition of public infrastructures, raising pressing questions about the quality and scope of the welfare that regulatory approaches promote.

*Keywords:* higher education; university; welfare state; regulation; competition; United States; Germany

# Organizing Competition: Regulatory Welfare States in Higher Education

*By*
TOBIAS SCHULZE-CLEVEN

Around the world, governments have placed higher education at the center of their attempts to sustain economic development and social welfare, hoping that colleges and universities will help to generate the human capital that policy-makers see as necessary for the twenty-first century's "global knowledge economy." The discursive embrace of higher education has driven substantial growth in the sector, particularly in its more advanced offerings. Between 1995 and 2011 alone, the average expected cohort share of graduates from theory-based academic

*Tobias Schulze-Cleven is associate professor and co-director of the Center for Global Work and Employment at the School of Management and Labor Relations, Rutgers University-New Brunswick. His research examines the comparative political economy of labor markets and higher education across rich democracies.*

Correspondence: tobias.schulzecleven@rutgers.edu

DOI: 10.1177/0002716220965891

programs across the OECD rose by 20 percentage points and graduation rates for doctorates doubled, while rates for shorter and more practical vocationally oriented tertiary qualifications remained stable (OECD 2013, 55). Transformative structural changes abound, both within universities and in their relationships with broader society.

Core institutional features of higher education have rapidly evolved, including universities' forms of legal incorporation, their funding streams, approaches to budgeting, human resource management practices, and modes of instruction delivery. While local contexts continue to exhibit a wide degree of variation, there have been clear cross-national tendencies: for the higher education sector's growth to increase the relative importance of private and for-profit universities; for student tuition to develop into an important complement to (and even substitute for) state subsidies; for universities' internal financial allocations and steering to become more flexible and "responsibility-centered"; for the labor conditions of many academic workers to become more precarious; and for virtual teaching and so-called MOOCs (massive open online courses) to gain prominence. Across particular national contexts, many commentators see higher education as being in "crisis," which is a testament to the real tensions between the rising expectations of the sector's contributions to individual and collective aspirations on one hand, and the significant financial, organizational, and individual costs associated with its structural reform on the other.

This article explores contemporary institutional changes in higher education through the lens of the *regulatory welfare state* (RWS), a concept that David Levi-Faur (2014) proposed to capture the growing role of regulation in states' attempts to sustain the well-being of citizens. The purpose of the analysis is twofold. First, it seeks to leverage the RWS concept to uncover underappreciated commonalities in higher education's transformation across different national contexts. Such findings are valuable for a better understanding of the global dynamics of higher education reform, as well as for theorizing their broader implications for national systems of democratic capitalism. Second, the analysis strives to use newfound clarity on sector-level dynamics to refine theorizing on the RWS itself, including Levi-Faur's notion that regulation has come to the rescue of fiscal expenditures (Levi-Faur 2014, 610), which had supposedly "grown to limits" by the end of twentieth century (Flora 1986).

The analysis focuses on state strategies to spur structural changes in higher education across the United States and Germany, homes to world-leading university systems.[1] Each country closely represents a different institutional ideal type identified in comparative political economy scholarship, with the "liberal" United States relying far more heavily on market-based social coordination than "conservative" and corporatist Germany (Esping-Andersen 1990; Hall and Soskice 2001). In other words, from systems of social and labor protections to corporate governance and finance, American institutions prioritize the choices of consumers, workers, managers, and investors, leaving individuals exposed to the vicissitudes of markets. Germany, in contrast, provides stronger institutional mechanisms to pool resources for collective long-term benefit, whether through state-sponsored social insurance or by empowering cooperation between unions and employer associations. These broader patterns are mirrored in the two countries' higher education systems, where the United States has long featured a larger scope for private funding and a weaker role for faculty voice than Germany (Clark 1983). By concentrating on important countries that exhibit clear and conceptually relevant differences, the case selection provides leverage to develop a theoretical perspective that can unite contrasting local contexts and has probable applicability beyond them.

The article argues that policy-makers in both countries have pursued the goal of organizing competition among universities. They have done so by combining fiscal and regulatory policies to strengthen universities' self-reliance, rivalry, and decentralized decision-making. Understanding cross-national patterns of institutional transformation, the analysis contends, requires putting countries' evolving regimes of state-university relations into historical perspective. Such an approach reveals that states' shifting governance strategies are important drivers of higher education's contemporary reimagination. I also clarify how regulatory approaches to welfare provision have fostered the re-composition of the public infrastructures through which welfare states seek to promote the well-being of citizens. The scope of these changes in higher education, from the increasing role of for-profit providers to the shifting priorities of both public and nonprofit private universities, raises pressing questions about the quality and scope of the welfare that regulatory approaches promote.

I develop these claims in four steps. The first section of this article clarifies the main parameters of welfare states' changing relationships to the sector and spells out the promise of the RWS concept for a comparative political economy perspective on contemporary higher education. The second section invokes the notion of the RWS to define central parallels in how American and German state authorities have sought to shape competition among universities as a way of spurring broader institutional changes during the past three decades. Beyond demonstrating the strengthening of market principles in both countries' higher education systems, this section also discusses how historical legacies have pushed national reforms in particular directions. The third section provides short case narratives to contrast outcomes of shared agendas. The final section reviews the findings of the analysis to elaborate on their implications for the contributions of welfare states and universities to the future of democratic capitalism.

## Welfare States and Higher Education

Higher education has long been neglected in comparative research on the welfare state. Not only is access to universities restricted to citizens deemed to have sufficient merit, higher education also has complex effects on social stratification. As such, the sector did not appear to be an important means for policy-makers to manage the tensions between democratic commitments to citizens' political equality and labor markets' continual generation of economic inequality among workers. Other public social programs—particularly transfer schemes such as unemployment insurance and pensions, but even public services such as health care and non-tertiary education—provided clearer and more direct ways for welfare states' selective decommodification of the working citizenry, and have thus rightfully featured more prominently in scholarship.

Yet higher education's growing prominence in socioeconomic adjustment leaves this void increasingly indefensible. The "massification" of higher education— that is, the increased access to higher learning from what were once a selected few "elite" students to significant shares and often broad majorities of age cohorts— has turned the sector into a central battleground for, and means of mediating, distributional conflict in contemporary societies. It is, thus, time to develop a political science of higher education, particularly as it relates to the shifting conceptions of "welfare" that contemporary states seek to provide (Schulze-Cleven 2017).

Even though countries dedicate only a small share of GDP to higher education, policy-makers see the sector—and reforms in it—as central to the future of their societies. Across the OECD, countries have recently spent 1.6 percent of GDP on average on higher education, with the United States significantly above at 2.6 percent and Germany below at 1.2 percent. In terms of *public* expenditures on higher education, the United States and Germany are quite close at about 1 percent of GDP, which signals that *private* spending is the big difference between the two countries. Both commit significantly less in terms of public funds than Scandinavian "social democratic" countries such as Denmark, where state spending on higher education stands at 1.6 percent of GDP (OECD 2016, 207), providing both tuition-free public higher education (which Germany also has but the United States does not) and living allowances for students.

In the United States, a longtime leader in the massification of higher education, almost three-fourths of cohorts now access tertiary education and more than half of all young adults are currently expected to obtain tertiary degrees in their lifetime, from associate- to doctoral-level qualifications (OECD 2016, 68). Yet other countries have gone even further in boosting degree attainment, relegating the United States to twelfth place for 25- to 34-year-olds worldwide (OECD 2016, 42). Moreover, some of the most impressive growth has taken place in nations that had once restricted university attendance to elite students and channeled most students into vocational education. Germany, for instance, more than doubled cohorts' tertiary degree attainment shares in fewer than two decades after the mid-1990s.[2] With German students finishing their degrees at rates far above American students, Germany quickly reached 80 percent of the United States' lifetime cohort share for graduates from theory-based programs (OECD 2013, 63).

The remainder of this section lays out a three-part foundation for the analysis of contemporary reforms. It first places the current transformation of higher education within the historical experience of state-building, elaborating how universities have long been *part of* the state while also remaining *apart from* it, as both the United States and Germany recognized professional privileges in the governance of the sector. It then discusses recent paradigmatic changes in the perceived role of higher education, which act to put pressure on inherited institutional arrangements. Finally, it turns to the potential contributions of the RWS concept for theorizing how policy-makers have sought to pursue institutional realignment.

## Higher education and state-building

Higher education has played a central role in state-society relations across countries, with universities providing crucial vehicles for the state and its citizens to relate to one another, and individual institutions serving as "parastates" that convey state interests by proxy (Loss 2014). Clearly, state authorities have been the most important driving force behind the growth of national higher education systems. Even the most basic historical sketch of initiatives demonstrates this irrevocably, whether one looks at the early establishment of dedicated research institutions in Germany—with the University of Göttingen (est. 1734) seeking to realize enlightenment ideals and the University of Berlin (est. 1810) striving to realize Humboldt's vision of unified research and teaching—or the expansion of public higher education in the United States through federal land grants in 1862 and 1890.[3]

It is also true that higher education has, since its early days, been a central element of public initiatives to support the population's welfare, including through policies supporting national economic development and defense. The history of Germany's technical universities or the enmeshing of U.S. universities—particularly the Massachusetts Institute of Technology and Stanford University—in the military-industrial complex represents only the proverbial tip of the iceberg. Furthermore, in terms of social citizenship, one can point to the G.I. Bill of Rights of 1944, which laid the foundation for the massification of the U.S. higher education system, and to the Higher Education Act of 1965, which boosted access for women. In Germany, the post-1970s flanking of the existing research university system with institutions (*Fachhochschulen*) that have focused instruction on the applied sciences and operated with less restrictive admissions criteria has similarly expanded citizens' educational opportunities.

Throughout this history, universities have fulfilled core social functions, acting as "sieves for sorting and stratifying populations, incubators for the development of competent social actors, temples for the legitimation of official knowledge, and hubs connecting multiple institutional domains" (Stevens, Armstrong, and Arum 2008, 127). At the same time, they have remained "peculiar organizations" that have enjoyed "a substantial margin of jurisdiction over their own boundaries and internal affairs" (Eaton and Stevens 2020, 1). This on-the-ground reality has been a function of state authorities' reliance on the cooperation of societal actors, such as professional associations and private benefactors, to extend their own reach within and through higher education.

So far, the cooperative character of the state's university-based extension into society has been mainly theorized for the American case (Stevens and Gebre-Medhin 2016), where it resembles a broader pattern of "associational" state-building (Balogh 2015), which created a form of welfare capitalism that was more "enabling" than "interventionist" (Gilbert and Gilbert 1989). Yet, national differences notwithstanding, the associational path to state-building has been a broader transatlantic story, as scholarship on the role of corporatism in Europe demonstrates, whether with respect to the continent's twentieth-century models of welfare capitalism or the governance of contemporary economic institutions.

In higher education, this kind of associational governance has proceeded based on states recognizing the claims of academics to professional privileges, often framed in terms of "academic freedom." The particulars of countries' initial institutionalizations of professional prerogatives have varied, and the institutions protecting academic freedom have been reproduced to differing degrees over time. What unites these institutions is their contemporary effect on severely restricting the direct leverage that both legislatures and executives have to lead structural change in the sector.

In Germany, academic freedom is enshrined in the constitution, which guarantees the freedom of science (*Wissenschaft*), research (*Forschung*), and teaching (*Lehre*). The implementation of these rights provides professors with command over resource-endowed teaching chairs and also grants them the status of civil servants (*Beamte*), which comes with remuneration according to nationally coordinated pay scales and generous pensions. Universities have traditionally been run as constituent parts of subnational states' secondary bureaucracies (*nachgeordnete Behörde*). While subject to administrative law, decisions in academic matters have typically been reserved to the professoriate, although different "status groups"—from junior scientists to students—also have a formal voice. Importantly, the country's constitutional court has interpreted academic freedom to extend to university students, who—as participants in the scientific enterprise—enjoy the freedom to study (*Studier-* or *Lernfreiheit*) and are thus legally entitled to attend university after graduating from secondary education with the appropriate credentials.

In the United States there are fewer statutory protections guaranteeing academic freedom, but the constraints on government agency are formidable nonetheless. By the 1960s, an "academic revolution" had taken place that left the academic profession with significantly more power (Jencks and Riesman 1968). Helped by the scarcity of qualified academic labor during higher education's expansion, the American Association of University Professors (AAUP) succeeded in cementing the faculty tenure system as a cornerstone of universities' "shared governance," thus significantly curbing the managerial leeway that benefactors and presidents had once enjoyed. While professional rights mainly derive from norms promulgated by the AAUP and are only enshrined in enforceable collective bargaining contracts at a subset of institutions, they have been endorsed by the collective organizations of universities and colleges.

Moreover, academic freedom in the United States shows up prominently in the high degree of independence enjoyed even by "public" colleges and universities, which roughly three-quarters of American students attend, thus leaving relationships between government and universities arm's-length at best. Reflecting this, universities have long run their own peer-review accreditation systems, which the federal government endorsed as the appropriate authority to determine providers' eligibility for its student support in 1952. Moreover, universities have effectively guarded this autonomy through extensive lobbying. "One Dupont Circle," the Washington, D.C., address of the college presidents' association (the American Council on Education, ACE), as well as numerous other organizations representing public, private, land-grant, and community colleges (and even registrars and accreditors), has become synonymous with the political influence wielded by providers in the sector.

Across countries, the peculiarities of universities have frequently hampered citizens' experiences of higher education as a state-provided "welfare" benefit. With the state having a "submerged" role in the provision of services (Mettler 2011), higher education has arguably contributed less than other social programs to generating pro-public preferences among the populace, and has also left the sector with less salience in electoral politics. This has been particularly true in the United States where the growth of tuition financing and the tendency of public funding to increasingly take the form of tax breaks and credits (so-called tax expenditures) have effectively hidden public transfers. But even in Germany, where students have not faced high tuition burdens, universities have long appeared less like publicly provided training grounds for a democratic citizenry and more like fiefdoms for professors who resist students challenging their authority (Leibfried 1967).

## The new paradigm: Higher education for the knowledge economy

While the positive effects of higher education on a variety of desirable social outcomes have long been recognized, economists' analysis of contemporary socioeconomic dynamics have put the sector at the forefront of government policy on economic development and social security. Grounded in the concept of "human capital," the explanatory models of disciplinary economics rationalize rising income inequality as driven by skill-biased technological change (SBTC) and emphasize increasing returns in theories of economic growth. Together, they provide a new (neo)liberal policy paradigm that has shifted the universe of political discourse on the purpose of higher education. "Social investment" in education has become the dominant vehicle to fight rising inequality, underwrite social mobility, and ensure that countries can engage effectively in the changing structures of global economic competition (e.g., Hemerijck 2017). Moreover, debates within higher education policy circles reveal the dual desire to boost access and build "world-class" research universities (Meyer 2017), goals that are made compatible with an increasing commitment to organizational differentiation in university systems, with individual institutions focusing on their comparative advantages (Altbach, Reizberg, and de Wit 2017).

The potential positive impact of expanded higher education notwithstanding, there are real problems with the analyses underlying policy prescriptions. Displaying clear disciplinary biases, such as the commodity view of education and deep normative commitments to efficient market allocation, they generally neglect social and political factors. SBTC theorists, for instance, tend to simply assume that workers' wages are a function of their human capital. This fails to consider the impact of workers' varying collective power on patterns of wage setting (whether through unions' collective bargaining with employers or the lobbying of policy-makers) and blends out the consequences of credential inflation for displacements among groups with different education endowments. The assumption also flies in the face of a lot of work on gender and racial inequalities in contemporary societies. Methodologically, it seems questionable to operate with a narrow conception of higher education focused on employability while blending out the actual dynamics of employment. Finally, by viewing worker-citizens primarily through their worker role, these economistic prescriptions embrace the market as the main vehicle for social integration, challenging the primacy of the political realm over economic affairs in traditional conceptions of the welfare state (Berman 2006). But none of these considerations seems to have stopped proponents from advocating for this agenda with technocratic fervor, including in many publications by international organizations such as the OECD or the World Bank.

Rather than centering on a critique of the new paradigm, policy debates have focused on managing rising costs as the obvious side effect of higher education's ongoing expansion. Crucially, the fiscal drain on welfare states' budgets goes beyond proportionally matching the sector's growth with increased expenditures. Given that productivity improvements in higher education lag capital-intensive manufacturing, there is potential for economy-wide wage increases to drive up higher education's relative cost—a fate the sector shares with other labor-intensive, state-financed services including care for the ill, elderly, children, and even the incarcerated, and that is frequently described in terms of "Baumol's cost disease." Moreover, in the United States, "Bowen cost effects" have also received attention, that is, the tendency of universities to collect and spend as much money as possible in an attempt to rise within the university pecking order through investments in research prowess, real estate, or college sports.

American observers have been particularly vocal about the need to increase higher education's efficiency. Judging current institutional arrangements as too expensive, socially exclusive, and simply under-performing with respect to combining excellence and access, they have called for the disruption and fundamental redesign of organizational models for higher education delivery (Christensen and Eyring 2011; Crow and Dabars 2015). To them, American universities' history of "structural accretion" (Smelser 2013)—that is, continually adding new functions without shedding old ones—has left the sector ripe for significant unbundling (Craig 2015). MOOCs in particular are viewed as a promising innovation, not because they would be as effective as traditional methods, but because their minimal marginal costs could provide large-scale savings through scaling. In Germany, elites have been more concerned about the international competitiveness of public research universities, demanding that universities be released from direct regulations and granted more flexibility to reach their goals (Müller-Böling 2000).

## Toward a comparative political economy of higher education

The concept of the regulatory welfare state holds great promise for formulating a comparative political economy perspective on contemporary higher education. Broadening the measurement of welfare state activity beyond fiscal outlays, which had long been the yardstick for analyses of comparative social policy, it also draws on regulatory policy, which became a focus in the analysis of market-led European integration at the end of the twentieth century (Majone 1997).

Offering a polymorphic rather than a one-dimensional conceptualization of contemporary states' welfare efforts, the RWS concept effectively addresses "the dependent variable problem" that plagues many studies (Green-Pedersen 2004).

So far, scholars invoking the RWS concept have focused on publicly regulating private markets for social purposes (e.g., Benish, Haber, and Eliahou 2017). Yet the concept could also be applied to analyzing the regulation of public transfers and social services, which would imply examining the relations (and interactions) between regulatory and fiscal policies (Benish and Levi-Faur, this volume). Here, the RWS concept offers a powerful means of exploring new conditionalities that states have attached to citizens' receipt of benefits, including tying eligibility to particular individual behaviors. By facilitating improved measures of qualitative policy changes, the RWS concept can be an important resource for appropriately conceptualizing contemporary political conflicts over social welfare provision. After all, while scholars have rightly found the "new politics of the welfare state" not to simply be about retrenchment (Pierson 2001), they still need a much better toolbox to examine the reorientation of institutionalized solidarity from economies' demand sides to their supply-side foundations via social investment in human capital.

The RWS concept opens up three interconnected areas of potential analytical progress regarding the shifting politics of higher education. First, going beyond examining state action as a dependent variable, there is great promise in using the RWS concept for analyzing states as relatively autonomous actors with their own specific interests, including maintaining political stability and shoring up their own long-term efficacy. The capacity for state agency has long been an important theme in the political economy literature, but it has gained new urgency as the collective action capacities of both workers and companies have declined. Across rich democracies, shrinking membership in unions and employer associations has underwritten processes of institutional liberalization that have opened up once dominant collective decision-making processes among organized social interests (Streeck and Thelen 2005, 30). Market-based forms of resource allocation and individualized modes of political contention have frequently taken their place. The reduced reach of national systems for collective wage bargaining might well be the best example of this broader trend, which has allowed the centrifugal forces of capitalism to take their toll on political stability (Schulze-Cleven 2018). Scholars are now debating whether states can address the increasing imbalance of national political-economic constellations (Rothstein and Schulze-Cleven 2020). Balancing capitalism's tendency toward expansion and crises through substantive efforts is important for states themselves, since resurging capitalism threatens their own sustainability (Jacobs and King 2009).

Second, by broadening the lens on welfare states' repertoires, the notion of the RWS provides much needed conceptual space to assess states' efforts to shape the evolution of competition-increasing processes of liberalization. Given public authorities' fundamental role in setting the ground rules for the functioning of private markets, there is significant room for governments to craft sophisticated regulation that aligns the dynamics of market competition with broader social goals, including whether competition focuses on cost or quality (Vogel 2018). At this point, liberalization has typically shifted power from workers to employers (Baccaro and Howell 2011). But this is not inevitable, as governments' minimum wage regulations or anti-discrimination provisions demonstrate.

Third, states can shape the locus and form of competition in their own service provision as well. This market making *in*—not just *by*—the welfare state arguably offers an extended set of options, including nurturing competition through quasi-markets that do not use the price mechanism to balance supply and demand (Gingrich 2011). Here, governments can decide if they want to restrict competition to public entities or extend it to include nonprofits or even for-profit providers. Moreover, these markets could allow—or even require—private co-financing, which, in turn, will determine if these services are "state-provided," "state-financed," or merely "state-supported." In any case, these decisions will have significant consequences for the composition of public infrastructures and the boundaries of the welfare state, which are important elements of the changing character of statehood that the RWS concept speaks to.

The next section seeks to realize some of this promise of the RWS concept by analyzing the attempts of state authorities in the United States and Germany to spur structural changes in higher education through shaping competition among universities. It demonstrates how the relatively open conceptual framing of the RWS makes the analysis compatible with many lines of scholarly inquiry, including higher education specialists' use of a public management lens to study the growth of market elements in the steering of higher education systems (e.g., Gornitzka and Maasen 2000). By supporting the aggregation of knowledge across different research programs, the RWS concept provides a solid basis for the high level of abstraction that is necessary to analyze commonalities in state strategies across national regimes with quite distinct institutional arrangements.

# Regulatory Welfare States in Higher Education

This section illuminates how policy-makers have combined fiscal and regulatory policies to strengthen universities' self-reliance, rivalry, and decentralized decision-making. Clarifying the state-sanctioned nature of institutional liberalization in higher education, the analysis demonstrates that states' shifting governance strategies are important drivers of the sector's contemporary reimagination. Organizing competition among providers has been a way for state authorities across regimes to stimulate institutional change and provider differentiation in line with the new policy paradigm for higher education.

## Strengthening market principles across regimes

With academic freedom severely restricting direct state interference in the behavior of individuals in Germany and of organizations in the United States, public authorities in both countries have adopted a piecemeal and indirect approach to nurturing change. Encouraging universities to become entrepreneurial organizational actors (Krücken and Meier 2005), reforms have provided incentives for higher education providers to focus on specific missions, take steps to address structural accretion, and work toward a more efficient division of labor (see Table 1).

Universities' increased self-reliance has come from reductions in unconditional public appropriations per student. U.S. state and local per-student appropriations for public institutions declined by roughly 25 percent in real terms between 1999 and 2011, while base financing per student at German universities fell by about 10 percent over the same period.

Rivalry between universities has been strengthened through competition-increasing regulation. In the United States, the federal government has financially backed both nonprofit and for-profit universities, and numerous (subnational) states have experimented with performance-based funding of public universities and colleges. In Germany, public authorities have increased the share of public financing that is allocated through competition-based mechanisms, including launching new teaching-focused programs and expanding research funding available through the German Research Foundation (DFG).

The enlarged scope for decentralized decision-making has turned on expansions of universities' autonomy. In the United States, many states have relinquished attempts to plan the development and local provision of tertiary education and have shifted to indirect means of controlling institutions' performance. In Germany, the federal states (so-called *Länder*) have revised the laws governing higher education, boosting universities' freedom and introducing governing boards with memberships drawn from society to compensate for reduced direct state guidance.

To be sure, state strategies across regimes have differed substantially—with U.S. policy-makers sanctioning markets that rely on variable (tuition) prices, and German policy-makers focusing on building quasi-markets. Yet the general modality of state intervention has been the same, shaking up inherited national mixes of governance instruments. Across regimes, there has been a common movement toward strengthened indirect state guidance and the expanded recourse to market forces, at the expense of traditional professional prerogatives— though the latter has at times been mobilized as "peer review" for judging offerings in quasi-market competition. In terms of broader outcomes, this new form of state steering has had two important shared consequences:

*Re-composition of public infrastructures.* Competition-based steering has underwritten significant shifts in the boundaries and makeup of welfare states in higher education, making it ever harder to specify where the welfare state begins and where it ends. Public universities have gained more independence, either expanding what they already had (as in the United States) or becoming independent for the first time (as in Germany). Given that tuition finance now accounts for about half the sector's revenue in the United States, many formally "public" institutions have become "public-private hybrids" in practice, with the imperative to meet consumer demands sitting in increasing tension with commitments to serve the common good. Moreover, even the growth of the for-profit sector in the United States during the early 2000s—enrolling as many as

10 percent of American undergraduates at the high point—was overwhelmingly financed by public coffers. A 2010 U.S. Senate investigation found that 86 percent of the revenues received by fifteen publicly traded for-profit institutions during the year before came from federal sources. From the Department of Education's student aid program funds alone (i.e., excluding military and veterans' benefits), $32 billion—a fourth of total outlays—flowed to the for-profit sector from 2009 to 2010 (HELP Committee 2010).

*Differentiation as stratification.* Increased differentiation has come with a tendency to sharpen stratification among universities and to deepen their impact on social stratification. As the scope for market forces has grown, so have the opportunities for actors rich in marketable capital—whether universities, professors, or even students—to take advantage of their market might. Indeed, sustained liberalization has effectively turned national worlds of higher education into varieties of academic capitalism (Schulze-Cleven and Olson 2017). While Germany does not curb stratification as well as its Scandinavian neighbors, the country's overwhelming focus on public provision and financing has moderated stratification compared to the United States, where differences in actors' capital are most striking. For instance, the richest private American universities enjoy average returns on their endowments of one to three billion dollars annually. Given that the exalted collective status of these institutions depends on admitting the most promising students and educating them to the highest educational standards, they lavishly spend on the selected few, creating strong winner-take-all tendencies. At the same time, underserved minority students often end up in lower-ranked institutions, including at for-profit universities. With education at the latter tending to be structured in the interests of owners and investors, their graduation rates have, in some years, failed to hit double digits, and their loan default rates in some cases have outstripped those of graduation rates by a factor of ten (Shireman 2015).[4]

## Institutional roots of national differences

While this article cannot provide a thorough discussion of the factors driving national variation, a few words are in order about the effects of historically rooted institutions in each country's higher education system. In addition to the particular national institutionalization of professional prerogatives and universities' independence, one crucial factor that has strongly conditioned the politics of higher education reform in both countries is public authorities' federal organization, which leaves the primary responsibility for funding higher education with the constituent states.

Federal fragmentation has made it harder to create coherent higher education policy in both countries. The United States and Germany have had to similarly grapple with subnational units' frequent failure to increase fiscal commitments in line with higher education expansion, which has prompted federal authorities across both regimes to assume a growing role—whether through increases in Pell

Grants (to cover tuition for low-income students) and expanded opportunities for student loans in the United States infrastructure investments and financial support for needy students in Germany, or expanded research funding in both countries.

Countries' particular limits on state interference in academic affairs in combination with their division of responsibility among state actors has weighed heavily on federal policy-makers' choice sets, presenting quite distinct opportunities and constraints across the two cases. Specifically, state authorities in the two countries had differential capacities for effective intra-government coordination and state-society concertation—different forms of collective action that are equally necessary to align market forces with broader social goals.[5] Rule-making and rule enforcement are complex tasks that require public authorities to coordinate across different levels of government and to engage in concerted action with a range of actors outside of government, whether they are independent "public" entities (such as universities) or stakeholder groups. Without sufficient internal coordinating capacity, state authorities could be quickly outmaneuvered by predatory private actors, including for-profit universities.

## Contrasting National Reform Pathways

Brief sketches of contrasting reform pathways in the United States and Germany vividly illustrate how common reform strategies could play out very differently across institutional settings. In the United States, recent reforms have effectively allowed self-interested private-sector actors to play American public authorities, and by extension the public, for their own narrow benefit. The limited leverage that the Higher Education Act has provided and the competitive nature of the country's federalism, without fora for joint decision-making by the states and with the federal government, have left public authorities with little room to develop coordinated policy positions through which they could engage and contain societies' special interests.

In Germany, by contrast, public authorities have been locked into cooperation. Although the Länder enjoy constitutional autonomy in cultural matters, horizontal coordination through a standing conference of education ministers has been common. Moreover, vertical coordination between the Länder and the federal government has been buttressed by federal framework legislation (which has been repeatedly changed), a Science Council, and a Federal-State Commission for Educational Planning and Research (which was recently replaced by a Joint Science Commission). Higher capacities for intra-government coordination have, in turn, curtailed the ability of special interests to get their way, and moderated some of the most negative aspects of academic capitalism.

### The United States: Private actors playing the market

American policy-makers have certainly tried to develop a coordinated reform effort, as evidenced by President Bush's Secretary of Education Margaret

Spellings tasking a "Commission on the Future of Higher Education" with developing a "comprehensive national strategy on postsecondary education" in 2005 through 2006. During the commission's deliberations, transparency (particularly about financials) and accountability (including through better performance indicators) emerged as important themes, which members of the commission believed had the potential to inform a far-reaching national overhaul of higher education. Highly critical of perceived deficiencies in the country's accreditation system, the commission envisioned more central control and the potential to save public money by reducing the costs of the federal financial aid system.

Yet little came of this envisioned reform. Without leverage to get the states to ramp up higher education offerings through greater fiscal subsidies to public institutions, federal policy-makers in both Congress and the executive branch faced real challenges around how to increase accessibility. Enamored with the promise of private-sector innovation—which some commentators claimed would diffuse to public providers through competition—and with a former private-sector lobbyist serving as the Assistant Secretary for Post-Secondary Education, federal policymaking during the Bush administration loosened rules levied in 1992 on institutions that wanted to qualify for student loans and grants (including through veterans' benefits). These regulatory changes included requirements for the share of in-person (rather than online) teaching, funding mixes, and strategies for recruitment. Together, they significantly increased profit opportunities and fueled the growth of the for-profit sector.

The Obama White House eventually sought to step in with tougher and more extensive regulation of the whole sector. But these efforts were successfully rebuffed—both by lobbyists from for-profit companies and those at One Dupont Circle, who similarly wanted to avoid additional government oversight. While the growth of for-profit providers had expanded higher education capacity and increased competition, little progress was made in growing the federal regulatory footprint in higher education. Neither the college rating system proposed by the Obama administration, nor the "gainful employment rule" seeking to link the eligibility of for-profits for federal assistance to the employment status of their alumni, came into effect. This left performance funding initiatives at the state level as a realm for experimentation with increased regulation. However, the Obama administration did have success reforming the origination of student loans, which the government took over, cutting out private banks in the process.

The concurrence of interests among very different higher education providers in blocking federal interference highlights how much the submerged policy stance of the American government also serves providers at the very top. As the for-profit sector has itself pointed out, the tax-free/low-tax status of endowment returns channels tax expenditures to the richest nonprofit private institutions, which, on a per-student basis, far exceed public financial support to both for-profit private and public institutions.[6] Finally, when elite institutions did take steps to moderate their positional arms race with an "arms control agreement" (which had universities pledge to focus financial aid on the most needy students), their efforts ran afoul of the Justice Department's interpretation of rules against market collusion (Frank 2001, 11). In turn, the American welfare state has not only been unable to sponsor state-society concertation to reduce cost and ensure access, it appears to have actively undermined at least one of society's own concerted efforts.

## Germany: Public authorities locked into cooperation

Just as in the U.S., core elements of Germany's reform pathway were pursued by the subnational states themselves, including changes to the legal status of universities (in one instance evocatively presented under the label of a "University Freedom Law") as well as the introduction of target agreements between Länder governments and these newly "freed" institutions. Yet most reforms in the country proceeded as a series of pacts between the federal government and the Länder. These included various rounds of the Excellence Initiative, which provided additional competition-based research funding after 2005; a pact that increased joint funding for non-university research organizations; and the so-called Higher Education Pact. The latter pact committed federal authorities to spend almost €10 billion between 2011 and 2018 to help the Länder expand student capacity. In return, the Länder agreed to match these increases in federal funding and to invest more funds in the expansion of public institutions with a focus on applied research and teaching (a crucial cost-saving measure given that most expansion up to that point had taken place at expensive public research universities). Finally, two rounds of the Quality Pact on Instruction have provided additional funding for teaching through a competitive allocation process through 2020.

This cooperative style of policymaking has been far from conflict-free. For instance, Länder governed by conservatives successfully sued the center-Left federal government over its outlawing of tuition fees in the 2002 overhaul of the federal framework legislation. After the constitutional court's decision in 2005 that the legislation violated constitutionally guaranteed Länder prerogatives, some Länder introduced uniform tuition fees of €500 per semester at public institutions. This affected two-thirds of German students, but the practice has been discontinued across the country since 2014. Nor have the Länder always followed through on the commitments they made. In the decade before 2010, twelve out of sixteen Länder reduced their unadjusted expenditures per student (Dohmen and Krempkow 2014, 27).

In turn, just as in the United States, the German federal government has ended up covering a growing share of public higher education funding. Yet it has been far more able to use pacts to contain that increase. While Germany's federal share of public funding for higher education only grew from 13 to 22 percent in the first decade of the new century (Dohmen and Krempkow 2014, 27), national-level expenditures in the United States—including research funding and student grants, but excluding loans and tax expenditures—started *exceeding* those of the states in 2010, up from less than 60 percent of spending by states merely a decade earlier (Pew 2015, 5).

TABLE 1
Strengthening Market Principles Cross-Nationally

| Market Principle | Action | Countries | |
| --- | --- | --- | --- |
| | | United States | Germany |
| **Self-reliance** | **Reducing unconditional funding** | Reduction in state and local per-student appropriations for public institutions by roughly 25% in real terms between 1999 and 2011 | Reduction in base financing per student by roughly 10% in real terms per student between 1999 and 2011 |
| **Rivalry** | **Promoting competition for public funds** | Promotion of competition between public, private non-profit and for-profit universities; experiments with outcome-linked financing | Shift in public financing toward competition-based allocation, e.g., the Excellence Initiative and expansion of research funding provided by the German Research Foundation (DFG) |
| **Decentralized decision-making** | **Increasing autonomy** | Relinquishing of states' attempts to plan for the provision of tertiary education; shift to indirect means of controlling institutions' performance | Revision of state laws governing universities, increasing universities' freedom but retaining states' ability to shape their room for maneuver |

SOURCE: Adapted from Schulze-Cleven and Olson (2017, 818).

# Conclusion

This article has examined the role played by states' shifting governance strategies in the contemporary reimagination of higher education. Using the concept of the RWS as a prism, the analysis demonstrates how state authorities in the United States and Germany have flanked—or tried to flank—fiscal outlays on higher education with new regulatory approaches to steer higher education growth during the past three decades. The comparison highlights the strengthening of market principles as a means for public authorities to disrupt the sector and recast it in line with reconceived goals. At the same time, the analysis also clarifies how historical legacies have conditioned state strategies.

Operating at a high level of abstraction, the analysis naturally remains suggestive. Two implications of the analysis deserve further elaboration. The first one pertains to the purported growth, rather than simply qualitative change, of regulation in the original conceptualization of the RWS—including how this growth has "rescued" the fiscal state. Obviously, the sectoral focus of this article's analysis means it cannot speak to the validity of the broader claim. Nevertheless, higher education's role in state-building suggests both that regulation has long been part of the welfare state, even essential in empowering universities as "parastates," and that recent changes in regulation have often been about quality rather than quantity. This finding is consistent with the analysis provided by other articles in this volume (e.g., Zohlnhöfer and Voigt, this volume) and could be extended to many labor market regulations, from the eight-hour work day to provisions against child labor, both of which preceded the growth of fiscal expenditures financed via income taxes. This suggests that scholars would do well to treat regulation as one of the long-standing levers of welfare states.

The second implication relates to the re-composition of public infrastructures. This phenomenon will likely become an important theme within the broader debates about changing statehood in the twenty-first century. Arguably, this re-composition is already implied in the RWS concept, and it is also underscored by other contributions to this special issue, such as the study of public procurement (Hartlapp, this volume). The main objective of the RWS concept is to highlight welfare provision outside of core fiscal transfers. Yet this also raises questions about the quality (and scope) of the welfare that publicly regulated—though not necessarily publicly financed or publicly provided—schemes promote.

In contemporary higher education, the predatory practices of for-profit higher education institutions, as well as the racial, gender, and socioeconomic biases that pervade routines at notionally public institutions, remind us that there are clear limits to, and inequities in, welfare states' promotion of individual welfare. This is old news for some, given that the "control" of certain populations has long been part of welfare state activity, with the expansion of social citizenship for one group often involving the exclusion of another (e.g., Piven and Cloward 1971). Yet there is a new quality to the changes outlined in this article, particularly in the United States, which threatens to produce universities that are much less able to support the welfare state's core function of sustaining the strength of democracy in the face of capitalism. While it seems too early for social scientists to speak of "the post-welfare state university," as humanists have in the field of critical university studies (Williams 2006), this threat is real.

# Notes

1. These countries' leadership in higher education is evidenced both by the regionally dominant sizes of their respective student populations and their preeminence in research, with scientific citations placing them in the top three countries globally and publication output in the top five (Royal Society 2011, 7–25).

2. The introduction of the BA/MA degree structure through the Europe-wide Bologna Process after 1999 played an important supporting role, as did the context of the European Union's Lisbon Strategy between 2000 and 2010 (Schulze-Cleven 2017). Germany was one of four signatories of the 1998 Sorbonne Declaration that preceded the Bologna Process and called for harmonizing the architecture of the European Higher Education system. The Lisbon Strategy was an action and development plan that sought to turn the EU into "the most competitive and dynamic knowledge-based economy in the world, capable of sustainable economic growth with more and better jobs and greater social cohesion." It is also

worth noting that there are real hurdles to constructing comparative measures of qualification levels. For instance, some forms of education provided by American *tertiary-level* community colleges, such as the GED curriculum and the certification of particular practical skills, are arguably equivalent to those delivered in Germany's *secondary-level* vocational schools.

3. A note about my use of the term "federal," which follows diverging national conventions: while I apply it to both the subnational states (*Bundesländer*) and the national government (*Bundesregierung*) in Germany, I reserve the term for referring to the national government in the United States.

4. Plagued by scandals, the for-profit model has undergone significant reorganization during the past few years.

5. The use of coordination and concertation as two concepts capturing collective action is adapted for this analysis from Ornston and Schulze-Cleven (2015).

6. The 2017 tax reforms recently imposed a 1.4% excise tax on investment income at private schools that have at least five hundred tuition-paying students and endowments of at least half a million dollars per student. According to estimates from the Internal Revenue Services, these changes affect twenty-five to forty institutions.

# References

Altbach, Philip G., Liz Reizberg, and Hans de Wit, eds. 2017. *Responding to massification*. Hamburg: Körber Foundation.

Baccaro, Lucio, and Chris Howell. 2011. A common neoliberal trajectory: The transformation of industrial relations in advanced capitalism. *Politics & Society* 39 (4): 521–63.

Balogh, Brian. 2015. *The associational state*. Philadelphia, PA: University of Pennsylvania Press.

Benish, Avishai, Hanan Haber, and Rotem Eliahou. 2017. The regulatory welfare state in pension markets: Mitigating high charges for low-income savers in the United Kingdom and Israel. *Journal of Social Policy* 46 (2): 313–30.

Benish, Avishai, and David Levi-Faur. 2020. The rise of regulation in welfare governance. *The ANNALS of the American Academy of Political and Social Science* (this volume).

Berman, Sheri. 2006. *The primacy of politics*. New York, NY: Cambridge University Press.

Christensen, Clayton M., and Henry J. Eyring. 2011. *The innovative university*. San Francisco, CA: Jossey-Bass.

Clark, Burton R. 1983. *The higher education system*. Berkeley, CA: University of California Press.

Craig, Ryan. 2015. *College disrupted*. New York, NY: Palgrave Macmillan.

Crow, Michael M., and William B. Dabars. 2015. *Designing the new American university*. Baltimore, MD: Johns Hopkins University Press.

Dohmen, Dieter, and René Krempkow. 2014. *Die Entwicklung der Hochschulfinanzierung*. Berlin: Konrad-Adenauer-Stiftung.

Eaton, Charlie, and Mitchell L. Stevens. 2020. Universities as peculiar organizations. *Sociology Compass* 14 (3): e12768.

Esping-Andersen, Gøsta. 1990. *The three worlds of welfare capitalism*. Princeton, NJ: Princeton University Press.

Flora, Peter, ed. 1986. *Growth to limits*. Berlin: de Gruyter.

Frank, Robert H. 2001. Higher education: The ultimate winner-take-all market? In *Forum futures*, eds. Maureen Devlin and Joel Meyerson, 3–12, San Francisco, CA: Jossey-Bass.

Gilbert, Neil, and Barbara Gilbert. 1989. *The enabling state*. New York, NY: Oxford University Press.

Gingrich, Jane R. 2011. *Making markets in the welfare state*. New York, NY: Cambridge University Press.

Gornitzka, Åse, and Peter Maasen. 2000. Hybrid steering approaches with respect to European higher education. *Higher Education Policy* 13 (1): 267–85.

Green-Pedersen, Christoffer. 2004. The dependent variable problem within the study of welfare state retrenchment. *Journal of Comparative Policy Analysis* 6 (1): 3–14.

Hall, Peter A., and David Soskice, eds. 2001. *Varieties of capitalism*. Oxford: Oxford University Press.

Hartlapp, Miriam. 2020. Measuring and comparing the regulatory welfare state: Social objectives in public procurement. *The ANNALS of the American Academy of Political and Social Science* (this volume).

Health, Education, Labor, and Pensions (HELP) Committee. 2010. For profit higher education. Washington, DC: U.S. Senate.

Hemerijck, Anton, ed. 2017. *The uses of social investment*. Oxford: Oxford University Press.

Jacobs, Lawrence, and Desmond King, eds. 2009. *The unsustainable American state*. New York, NY: Oxford University Press.

Jencks, Christopher, and David Riesman. 1968. *The academic revolution*. New York, NY: Doubleday.

Krücken, Georg, and Frank Meier. 2005. Turning the university into an organizational actor. In *Globalization and organization*, eds. Gili S. Drori, John W. Meyer, and Hokyu Hwang, 241–57, Oxford: Oxford University Press.

Leibfried, Stephan. 1967. *Wider die Untertanenfabrik*. Cologne: Pahl-Rugenstein.

Levi-Faur, David. 2014. The welfare state: A regulatory perspective. *Public Administration* 92 (3): 599–614.

Loss, Christopher P. 2014. *Between citizens and the state*. Princeton, NJ: Princeton University Press.

Majone, Giandomenico. 1997. From the positive to the regulatory state: Causes and consequences of changes in the mode of governance. *Journal of Public Policy* 17 (2): 139–67.

Mettler, Suzanne. 2011. *The submerged state*. Chicago, IL: University of Chicago Press.

Meyer, Heinz-Dieter. 2017. *The design of the university*. New York, NY: Routledge.

Müller-Böling, Detlef. 2000. *Die entfesselte Hochschule*. Gütersloh: Bertelsman Stiftung.

OECD. 2013. *Education at a glance 2013*. Paris: OECD.

OECD. 2016. *Education at a glance 2016*. Paris: OECD.

Ornston, Darius, and Tobias Schulze-Cleven. 2015. Conceptualizing cooperation: Coordination and concertation as two logics of collective action. *Comparative Political Studies* 48 (5): 555–85.

Pew (Charitable Trust). 2015. Federal and state funding of higher education. Washington, DC: Pew.

Pierson, Paul, ed. 2001. *The new politics of the welfare state*. New York, NY: Oxford University Press.

Piven, Frances Fox, and Richard Cloward. 1971. *Regulating the poor*. New York, NY: Pantheon.

Rothstein, Sidney A., and Tobias Schulze-Cleven. 2020. Germany after the social democratic century: The political economy of imbalance. *German Politics* 29 (3): 297–318.

Royal Society. 2011. Knowledge, networks and nations. London: Royal Society.

Schulze-Cleven, Tobias. 2017. Higher education in the knowledge economy: Politics and policies of transformation. *PS: Political Science and Politics* 50 (2): 397–402.

Schulze-Cleven, Tobias. 2018. A continent in crisis: European labor and the fate of social democracy. *Labor Studies Journal* 43 (1): 46–73.

Schulze-Cleven, Tobias, and Jennifer R. Olson. 2017. Worlds of higher education transformed: Toward varieties of academic capitalism. *Higher Education* 73 (6): 813–31.

Shireman, Robert. 9 September 2015. For-profit colleges have no right to point fingers at endowed universities. New York, NY: Century Foundation. Available from https://tcf.org.

Smelser, Neil. 2013. *Dynamics of the contemporary university*. Berkeley, CA: University of California Press.

Stevens, Mitchell L., Elizabeth A. Armstrong, and Richard Arum. 2008. Sieve, incubator, temple, hub: Empirical and theoretical advances in the sociology of higher education. *Annual Review of Sociology* 34:127–51.

Stevens, Mitchell L., and Ben Gebre-Medhin. 2016. Association, service, market: Higher education in American political development. *Annual Review of Sociology* 42:121–42.

Streeck, Wolfgang, and Kathleen Thelen. 2005. Institutional change in advanced political economies. In *Beyond continuity*, eds. Wolfgang Streeck and Kathleen Thelen, 1–39, Oxford: Oxford University Press.

Vogel, Steven K. 2018. *Marketcraft*. Oxford: Oxford University Press.

Williams, Jeffrey J. 2006. The post-welfare state university. *American Literary History* 18 (1): 190–216.

Zohlnhöfer, Reimut, and Linda Voigt. 2020. Quiet politics of employment regulation? Partisan politics, electoral competition and the regulatory welfare state. *The ANNALS of the American Academy of Political and Social Science* (this volume).

# The Logics of Hybrid Accountability: When the State, the Market, and Professionalism Interact

By
AVISHAI BENISH

The delivery of public services increasingly operates under hybrid accountability regimes, but we have much to learn about how these regimes interrelate. I develop a framework for systematic analysis of hybrid public, market, and professional accountability arrangements, looking at the compatibility of their content, steering mechanisms, and relationships. The analysis is informed and illustrated by empirical studies on accountability in welfare state services, which offer evidence on hybrid accountability arrangements. The article concludes by discussing the interplay between accountability regimes and the conditions in which they undermine or reinforce each other. I argue that compatibility between regimes depends on the content of accountability rather than on the accountability mechanisms, and I highlight the importance of the trust between the parties entering into accountability relations and the proximity of their institutional logics.

*Keywords:* regulatory welfare state; accountability; new public management; social policy; social administration; social services

With the rise of the regulatory welfare state (RWS), welfare services increasingly operate under *hybrid*—public market and social—forms of accountability. Hybrid accountability results from the blurring and shifting of boundaries between these accountability regimes, mixing actors, logics, norms, and mechanisms (Benish and Mattei 2019). Such hybridity is evident, for instance, when nonstate agencies and workers are subject to public-law requirements of legality and fairness or when public sector agencies and workers are subject to performance-based management. Hybrid accountability is, of

*Avishai Benish is an assistant professor (tenured) at the Paul Baerwald School of Social Work and Social Welfare at the Hebrew University of Jerusalem. His fields of expertise are social law and administration, and his main research is on regulation and governance reforms in welfare states.*

Correspondence: avishai.benish@mail.huji.ac.il

DOI: 10.1177/0002716220965905

course, not new in welfare state services (Clarke and Newman 1997), but hybridization has radically accelerated with the trends of "new public management" (NPM), collaborative governance, and various other regulatory reforms in social welfare (Gilbert 2013; Levi-Faur and Gilad 2004; Christensen and Lægreid 2017). For quite some time now, scholars have acknowledged the increasingly hybrid nature of accountability (see, e.g., Scott 2001; Halliday 2004), but we are still far from understanding how multiple accountability regimes relate to one another.

Against this backdrop, this article seeks to develop a conceptual framework for hybrid accountability arrangements and the interaction between them in the context of the RWS. It does so by identifying the prevailing logics of the various accountability regimes and assessing the factors influencing their interaction. While existing literature tends to focus on instances of tension and conflict, the article focuses on the compatibility between regimes, including cases of mutual reinforcement. The conceptual frame developed in the article is informed and illustrated by the empirical literature on social administration, which offers a wealth of empirical evidence on the ways hybrid accountability plays out in the field.

The article is structured as follows. The first section develops an analytical framework for understanding the logics of accountability regimes. The second section defines the hybridity of accountability and creates a framework for analyzing the level of compatibility between regimes in terms of their content, mechanisms, and relational aspects. The article then systematically explores how public, market, and professional accountability and their respective underlying logics relate to one another in dyadic hybrids. The article concludes with an overview of the compatibility between accountability regimes and discussing whether and under what conditions they undermine or reinforce each other.

## The Logics of Accountability

The term accountability has leapt to public prominence in the last three decades (Mulgan 2003). The core of accountability is agency theory. Simply stated, agents are required to give an ex-post account of their actions to others for whom they perform tasks or who are affected by the tasks they perform (Bovens, Goodin, and Schillemans 2014). In an effort to unpack the building blocks of these agency relations, Mashaw (2006) lists six questions, the answers to which compose the process of accountability: (1) who is accountable (2) to whom, (3) about what, (4) through what processes, (5) by what standards of appraisal, and (6) leading to what consequences. In addition, Mashaw suggests grouping accountability regimes, usually analyzed separately, into three distinctive types: public regimes, market regimes, and social regimes. According to Mashaw, each type of regime answers the questions of accountability differently in terms of the normative framework and the organizational practices underlying the accountability relations.

In the language of institutional logics (Thornton, Lounsbury, and Ocasio 2012), each of Mashaw's accountability regimes has unique institutional logics, that is, organizing principles, practices, and beliefs that give identity and meaning to the actors on both sides of the accountability relations. The theory of institutional logics makes sense of how the different components add up to create a coherent regime of accountability and connect it to the well-established literature on the logics of the state, the market, and the community. Integrating Mashaw's accountability regimes and the theory of institutional logics provides a framework for understanding the three accountability regimes and their underlying logics.

The first, the *public accountability regime*, is based on the bureau-legal logic of the state. The organizing principle is holding public actors to citizens' democratic will by institutionalizing legality and rule of law as the prevailing mechanisms in controlling state power. Under this regime, public officials are simultaneously subject to two mechanisms of accountability—administrative and legal. Through mechanisms of administrative accountability, they are accountable to their superiors for implementing public policy and are expected to apply administrative rules and procedures accurately and consistently (Halliday 2004). This process of accountability is internal, hierarchal, and formal. At the same time, through legal accountability arrangements, public officials are accountable for respecting and securing the rights of affected individuals as these are set in public law. Such rights may be part of a specific law (such as a right to income support in social welfare law) or based on general administrative law principles of legality and fairness (such as due process, equal treatment, and transparency). Public officials' noncompliance with these laws and regulations may be claimed by affected individuals through mechanisms of review by judicial or administrative tribunals who can validate or nullify an official act or decision.

The second, the *market accountability regime*, is based on the managerial logic of corporate governance and the consumerist logic of competitive markets. Both logics are driven by the same organizing principle—the ultimate goal of maximizing a firm's profits in competitive markets. Managerial and consumerist models of market accountability are closely related, but they are analytically distinct. Managerial accountability is about holding organizations to performance criteria, while consumerist accountability is about competing for customers by satisfying their wants. The consumerist logic reflects the notion of "consumer sovereignty"; that is, the power of consumers to hold producers to account for the quality and price of their service (or product) and for their ability to meet consumers' preferences and desires (Stirton and Lodge 2001). The process of accountability is economic and is based on the willingness of consumers to pay for the service at the offered price, given the competition. The managerial logic is reflected within the firm itself. These accountability relations are hierarchal; managers are given the prerogative to manage the corporation as long as they satisfy the bottom line interests of the owners. This is done by increasing income (mainly through recruiting and retaining paying customers) and by cutting operational costs. Managers exercise control over workers, who are often required to achieve results efficiently; the promise of performance-based bonus payments and the threat of job dismissal for poor performance are the reward and sanction mechanisms underlying these work relations.

*Social accountability regimes* replicate the logic of communities and cultures. Many collaborative governance reforms rely on social forms of accountability (see Lahat and Sher-Hadar 2019); so, too, do families and voluntary organizations, which play a central role in welfare states. Here, we focus on *professional accountability*, the most prominent variant of social accountability in the administration of social services at the street level. Professional accountability reflects the logic of professionalism. It rests on the trust placed by society in professional associations (Friedson 2001). A member of a professional community is accountable to her peers for satisfying professional norms. As a professional, she is expected to provide client-tailored care according to the client's needs and based on the best available knowledge and skills. This form of accountability is horizontal and informal, and it is based on the ability of the professional group to create a sense of duty within a network of colleagues (Romzek 2014). The mechanism driving these collegial relations is peer pressure, which, in turn, is essentially based on esteem, status, and social exclusion (though under some circumstances, formal professional institutions can penalize members and revoke their licenses if they breach the profession's code of ethics; Adler 2003).

This integrated framework of the logics of accountability, as summarized in Table 1, provides a useful analytical prism through which to study hybridity. It breaks the concept of accountability down into its component parts, showing how different accountability components mix and match. At the same time, it provides a theory for the taken-for-granted normative and cognitive underpinnings of the various regimes; this is important if we are to understand the interplay generated by hybrid accountability arrangements.

## Hybrids of Accountability Regimes

Hybrid accountability results from the blurring and shifting of boundaries between traditional accountability regimes. It mixes actors, logics, norms, and mechanisms from public, market, and social accountability regimes by applying two or more of these differing regimes to the same situation at once (Skelcher and Smith 2015). Social services often operate under hybrid accountability arrangements. This was already the case in the "old" public administration, where administrative and professional models of accountability were often intertwined (Clarke and Newman 1997). But recent reforms in public governance generally and welfare governance in particular have profoundly accelerated the diffusion of accountability logics between and across sectors (Benish and Mattei 2019). Moreover, often these reforms bring in new accountability logics without replacing the old ones, simply layering them over existing structures (Jantz, Klenk, Larsen, and Wiggan 2018; Klenk and Cohen 2019).

The layering and mixing of accountability arrangements occur, for instance, when NPM strategies "import" the market logics of managerialism and consumerism into

TABLE 1
The Logics of Accountability

| Accountability regime | Public | | Market | | Social |
|---|---|---|---|---|---|
| Prevailing logic | Bureaucratic | Legal | Managerial | Consumerist | Professional[*] |
| Goal | Implementing public policy | Securing legal rights of affected citizens | Maximizing firm's profits | Satisfying consumer wants | Treating client needs |
| Values and principles | Accuracy, consistency, efficiency (administrative) | Legality, fairness (due process, equal treatment, transparency) | Efficiency (economic) | Customer satisfaction | Expertise, client care |
| Steering logic Steering mechanisms | Authoritative Rules | Authoritative Rights | Managerial Performance standards, economic incentives | Competitive Consumer choice | Collegial Professional standards, peer pressure |

NOTE: [*]Professional accountability is one of several variants of social accountability; it is usually the most dominant form of social accountability in the context of social services.

the realm of public services by adopting performance-based management of public services and setting up competitive market-like arrangements (Le Grand 1991; Laegreid and Mattei 2013; Benish 2018), such as competitive tendering (in which governmental commissioning units serve as consumers of contracted services) and choice-based services (in which service users can directly choose a service provider). As a result, bureaucrats and professionals in public institutions are expected to take on market-oriented roles and to adhere to market-type mechanisms (Pollitt and Bouckaert 2017). Layering and mixing also occur in instances when public accountability norms and mechanisms are extended to private companies (see, e.g., Benish and Levi-Faur 2012; Benish 2014b; Benish and Maron 2016), thus "exporting" the bureau-legal logic of the state to market actors.

Thus, understanding each accountability regime separately is important, but insufficient. Today's reality of accelerated hybridization requires us to understand how accountability regimes—with their inconsistent and, at times, conflicting logics—interact with each other. As Halliday (2004, 89) pointed out more than a decade and a half ago, "It remains substantially unclear how these regimes mingle and compete within the administrative arena and we have much still to learn about the complex relationships between the various accountability regimes." Answering this question remains timely, given the unprecedented levels of complexity created by the coexistence of accountability arrangements (for a detailed analysis see Benish and Mattei 2019). Notably, this is not only a theoretical question; it goes deep into the day-to-day realities of the current privatized and marketized governance of welfare state services. The ability to design and steer such services depend profoundly on our ability to understand how the street-level agents of the welfare state—physicians, teachers, social workers, and so on—react and negotiate the multiple and competing logics under which they operate.

The starting point of examining the interaction between accountability regimes is examining the *compatibility* of their goals, values, and principles (the *content* of accountability) and their steering tools (the *mechanisms* of accountability). Another important consideration is the *relational* aspect of accountability. Accountability is a relational concept (Bovens, Goodin, and Schillemans 2014), and, as such, the level of trust and nature of relations between the parties to accountability may influence both content and mechanisms (Kagan 2010).

Although the dominant narrative in the scholarly literature on hybrid accountability is one of conflict and tension, it seems more sensible conceptually to open the scale and to describe interaction on a continuum of compatibility—from conflict (no compatibility) to tension (low compatibility) to compatibility and mutual reinforcement (high compatibility).

In the sections that follow, I systematically analyze the compatibility of public, market, and professional accountability by assessing the level of compatibility of their content and mechanisms and noting the influence of relational aspects on this compatibility. Ideally, such an examination would include all three regimes simultaneously, but to reduce complexity and allow conceptual modeling, I examine the interactions in dyadic hybrids: public-professional hybrids, public-market hybrids, and professional-market hybrids.

## Public-professional hybrids

Public-professional accountability hybrids, as mentioned above, are not new; professionals were integrated into the operation of social services at the inception of the "provider" welfare state (Dean 2015; Sainsbury 2008). This is why many state-provided social services do not fit the image of Weberian bureaucracies, but are designed as professional institutions, with professionals—doctors, teachers and social workers—playing a central role in translating social rights into particular provisions. Clarke and Newman (1997) call them "bureau-professionals" to convey the hybridity of their organizational sense-making.

The basic interplay in public-professional hybrids is between the bureau-legal logic of the state and the logic of professionalism. In terms of goals, values, and principles, the type of interaction between these accountability regimes— conflict, tension, compatibility, or reinforcement—will depend on the extent to which the content of public policy and individual rights fit the professional standards in the specific field. Compatibility is more likely when public policy relies on professional standards. Under such circumstances, as Evans (2010, 48) notes, "Procedures can be professional tools, embodying good practice, legitimating professional expertise, and promoting professional commitments to the rights of service users." This is illustrated by Binder's (2007) work on federally funded U.S. childcare centers. She describes how early childhood education professionals upheld state rules when they interpreted them as consistent with and reinforcing their professional logic. She shows, for instance, how a center's executive director coupled her practice with the administrative rules, making them "part of her tool kit, or repertoire, for addressing the needs of her young clients" (Binder 2007, 559).

In contrast, when the administrative rules adopt non-need-based goals as central goals of public policy, the potential for tension increases. This is the case, for example, when professionals are required to pursue functions of social control and bureaucratic decision-making. Sainsbury (2008) illustrates the conflict experienced by personal advisers in the UK Pathways to Work program, when they were caught between their professional role as coaches and their role of applying rules of conditionality and invoking sanctions on clients. Such tensions around eligibility and social control functions are relevant to many welfare state services, especially poor-relief programs after the welfare reforms of the last three decades (Paz-Fuchs 2008). Similar tensions are likely to occur when formal administrative procedures try to uphold due process, transparency, or budgetary discipline, as these are sometimes inconsistent with the need-based, informal, and collegial logic of professionalism.

In terms of steering mechanisms, there is clearly an inherent tension between the rule-following logic of public administration and professional judgment. Public accountability mechanisms require "going by the book" (Bardach and Kagan 1982) and treating people according to prescribed standardized categories. In contrast, professional practices require latitude; they are often based on tacit knowledge and on a dynamic process of figuring out the best course of action in situations of uncertainty and unpredictability. While in legal and bureaucratic theory, discretion is often described as "the nemesis of accountability" (Brodkin 2008, 317), professional logic sees discretion as inherent to the ability to respond effectively to situations with high levels of indeterminacy, a characteristic of many social and human services (Evans 2010; Hasenfeld 2010; Evans and Hupe 2020).

The interaction between public and professional accountability regimes is likely to depend on the extent to which administrative rules open a space for professional judgment in decision-making. Instances of explicitly or implicitly delegating decision-making to professionals are not rare, particularly in welfare state services. At times, this is exactly what differentiates sectors or countries (see, e.g., Jewell 2007). For example, physicians are regularly trusted to make decisions on individual eligibility and treatment (Mattei 2016), and apodictic research has shown that, in practice, social codes are full of vague legal terms that are deliberately used to satisfy the purposes of the law (Sainsbury 2008).

This brings us to the relational aspects of accountability. The willingness to rely on professional standards for policy rules and to delegate discretion to professionals will stem from the attitude of account-holders to professionals, particularly their level of trust in them. Low levels of trust will lead to less willingness to delegate rule-making and decision-making to professionals, thereby increasing the tension between public and professional accountability regimes. Low levels of trust may derive, for instance, from higher officials' fear that professionals will "hijack" public policy or use their discretion for opportunistic behaviors that minimize work and maximize the professionals' interests as a group (Brodkin 2008). Citizens may fear discretion as a potential source of administrative absolutism, arbitrariness, and unequal treatment, all of which may endanger their rights (Diller 2000). Such attitudes appear in the transformations in U.S. welfare benefits administration during the 1960s, in which right-wing conservatives feared social workers would be soft on welfare recipients and would use discretion to grant benefits too generously, while left-wing liberals thought the discretion of social workers would be used discriminately to sanction African Americans. The result was a shift from a professional model to a legal model of welfare administration—subordinating welfare officials to detailed rules and strictly enforcing these rules through administrative and legal mechanisms (Diller 2000; Lens 2013).

However, when accountability-holders trust professionals, they will accept, sometimes even prefer, their standards and will allow them to exercise judgment when implementing the rules, thereby making the regimes more likely to be compatible and even to reinforce each other. Evans describes such instances, pointing out that policy-makers and higher officials often assume procedures will not be followed to the letter, and practitioners use their judgement to make the policy work and get the job done. He quotes a message from the chief social services inspector wherein she exhorts practitioners to use their discretion to create "a culture of care, which knows that consistency is important but has to be implemented with intelligence and enterprise, not dogma; a culture of care, which puts an end to checklists that replace thinking and judgment" (Evans 2010, 60). Similarly, Benish, Spiro, and Halevi (2018) present a case of the development of a learning-based approach for regulating social welfare services, in which professional skills, rather than legalistic compliance, was put at the center of the regulation and inspection of at-risk youth homes. Naturally, such attitudes decrease the tension between public and professional accountability regimes and increase their compatibility.

## Public-market hybrids

The hybridization of accountability has rapidly accelerated with the introduction of NPM. These reforms bring the dual logics of managerialism and consumerism into the governance of public service, leading to public-market hybrids. As discussed, managerial and consumerist models of market accountability are related but distinct. Hence, I discuss them separately.

The interaction between managerial and public accountability is about the relations between the bureau-legal logic of the state and the managerial logic of private corporations. In terms of goals, values, and principles, this interaction will depend on the compatibility of the content of the administrative rules with the performance indicators. The basic tension here is between the efficiency values of managerialism and the fairness values associated with the public domain. This tension is demonstrated in Cowan and McDermont's (2006) work on the implementation of UK social housing policy. They show that with the spread of performance-based management, efficiency became the paramount goal. In the case they studied, a small number of performance indicators, particularly the amount of unpaid rent and the number of empty properties, became the over-riding focus of housing organizations. As a result, "the common sense knowledges of front-line staff, to achieve fairness in allocation and tenant satisfaction, lost its value as common sense" (p. 112).

Another common manifestation of this tension is between the public law value of equal treatment and the economic logic of managerialism, with the latter incentivizing staff to focus on the easy-to-serve users to meet their targets more easily and at lesser cost. This is exemplified in practices of "creaming" (i.e., focus-ing on the easy-to-serve) and "parking" (i.e., neglecting the difficult-to-serve), extensively documented in the literature on marketized welfare-to-work services (e.g., Van Berkel, Rik, and Van der Aa 2005; van Berkel et al. 2017). Similar street-level practices were documented in the "old" public administration as cop-ing mechanisms in the face of dwindling resources and as an expression of the value of efficiency in its administrative version. But performance management seems to increase the pressure for such practices (see, e.g., Brodkin 2011). It is reasonable to assume that the trade-off between efficiency and other public val-ues of fairness and equality has generally increased with the advent of contracted-out services, where actors are under pressure to cut costs and maximize profits and when the economic pressure to achieve results gets stronger (for instance, in "no cure, no pay" contracts where meeting performance indicators is the sole criterion for payment).

An important factor in mitigating this basic tension is the extent to which performance indicators can be designed to align providers' incentives with government objectives, thereby overcoming tensions and even reinforcing public values. For example, to mitigate the above-mentioned risks of creaming and unequal access to welfare-to-work services, governments in Germany and in Denmark have opted for a "differential pricing" system, with more money designated to treat the harder-to-serve unemployed (Greer and Doellgast 2017, 150). This is an interesting attempt to solve a problem caused by the method of pay-per-performance by reshaping the way it is used.

Nonetheless, the empirical evidence indicates that the ability to design performance indicators in a way that aligns private and public interest is inher-ently limited in social services because outputs of social policy are multiple and identifying measurable and quantifiable indicators is notoriously difficult and, somewhat paradoxically, often leads to re-bureaucratization (Benish 2010). For instance, in the case of the welfare-to-work services in the UK, the failure to miti-gate creaming and parking merely by re-designing the performance measures led policy-makers to establish rule-based service standards to ensure a minimum level of service to each participant (Greer and Doellgast 2017).

In terms of steering mechanisms, it is important to note that although performance-based management is associated with delegation and decentralization (i.e., *let* managers manage), it is often very hierarchical and centralized (i.e., *make* managers manage) (Christensen and Lægreid 2017). This is why managerial accountability is often described as a variant of bureaucratic accountability, or as a form of modern hierarchical control that preserves the top-down structure of public services by other means. However, performance-based accountability may delegate considerable discretion to street-level actors in how they carry out their tasks (Mulgan 2003). This leverage opens up a space for innovation and efficiency, but such discretion also increases anxieties about the misuse of discretionary powers. Moreover, recent research indicates that performance management using digital measures—a rapidly expanding practice—is experienced by street-level professionals as curtailing their professional autonomy (e.g. Buffat 2013).

Moving to consumerist logic, in terms of goals, values, and principles, the basic interplay stems from the compatibility of public policy and rights with customer preferences and wants. Such tensions between public policy and customer wants may decrease if policy-makers adopt a "hands off" approach and open a space— as part of the policy itself—to allow service users and providers to freely negotiate the details of the service. This is actually a core idea of quasi-markets (Le Grand 1991) and entrepreneurial government (Osborne and Gaebler 1992).

Nonetheless, allowing such autonomy may also allow the importation of market inequalities into public services, undermining equal treatment. Moreover, even under such circumstances, there might be a gap between users' wants and what they actually get because of the competing interest of the service providers to minimize costs. The main mechanism to close this gap is giving consumers the choice of supplier. But the effectiveness of this mechanism depends on the ability of users to become effective judges of the providers' performance and make an informed choice. The literature on choice in social services suggests such ability is often limited—at least for some service users—because of their lack of awareness of their right to choose, along with various educational, economic, cultural, lingual, geographical, and other barriers to exercising their choice (Greve 2011).

As for the relational aspects of accountability, while public accountability tends to portray public officials as "fiduciary trustees" or "knights" of the public interest, under managerial and consumerist logics, *all* providers, public or private, should be regarded as "knaves" (Le Grand 2003). Obviously, differing attitudes reflect different perceptions of trust among account holders and will lead to different approaches to managing relations and allocating discretion to service providers. One approach may use various mechanisms to regain control over providers through both rules and incentives. Another may seek more trusting relations, relying on stewardship relations between the parties (Van Slyke 2006). In fact, Phillips and Smith (2011) find that in many countries, the contracting out of social services has moved to relational contracting arrangements, more similar to the "knights" than the "knaves" approach to street-level actors.

An important factor in accountability relations in public-market hybrids is the conflicting approach of state and market logics to the appropriateness of self-interest. Whereas market logic sees economic self-interest as an acceptable, even desirable, feature of NPM (Osborne and Gaebler 1992), a Weberian perception of public service sees self-interested actions and decisions as inappropriate and sometimes even corrupt. These approaches are so distinct that they challenge the ability to build and maintain trust between parties, particularly when service performance and quality are hard to ascertain, when they include social control functions, and when significant individual and social rights are at stake. The dynamics of declining trust are illustrated in Benish's study (2014a), in which pay-per-performance arrangements based on the reduction of benefits to welfare recipients were publicly perceived as creating "a structural conflict of interest between the economic considerations of the firm and its obligation to work in the interest of the program's participants" (Benish 2014a, 122). In this case, decreased trust instigated a dynamic of re-bureaucratization and the infusion of public law requirements into the relations with private contractors.

## Professional-market hybrids

In professional-market hybrids, the basic interaction is between the logic of professionalism and the managerial and consumerist logics of markets. As in the previous section, I discuss the logics separately in what follows.

In terms of goals, values, and principles, whether managerial and professional accountability work together or result in tension and instability depends on the content of the performance measures and their compatibility with professional standards and practices. The social administration literature usually emphasizes the incompatibility of efficiency-driven performance-based management with care-oriented professional standards (Marston and McDonald 2006). Dias and Maynard-Moody (2007), for example, show that in the context of a local U.S. training program, the performance-based contract design pressured frontline social workers to place clients quickly and cheaply in jobs. This led to what they describe as a "performance paradox": frontline staff wanted to "help people" and to use their professional power to make a difference in their clients' lives. They tried to tailor their services to what they perceived as their clients' needs but were limited by the management's efforts to meet contractual obligations.

This incompatibility can be at least partly explained by the fact that the content of performance measures is often externally imposed on care professionals by inspectors (Power 1997, 51). As Munro (2004, 1082) stresses, significant voices within care professions support the use of performance-based indicators in social care service. For instance, the child indicators movement (see, e.g., Ben Arieh 2007) strongly supports the use of measuring and monitoring outcome indicators as a professional best practice. The important point here is that when performance indicators are designed by and for professionals, they are more likely to be compatible with the professional logic. This emphasizes the importance of *who* determines the performance standards and enforces them.

This is also closely connected to the aspect of the compatibility of steering mechanisms under managerial and professional regimes. By and large, performance-based mechanisms are much more compatible with professional accountability than bureaucratic ones. As Mulgan (2003, 34) points out, "Professionals can be held accountable for results but cannot be tied down by rules and procedures." The mutual ground is that both logics allow high levels of autonomy among the account-givers. Therefore, the potential for compatibility is higher.

As for the interaction between professional and consumerist logics, the compatibility of accountability goals, values, and principles will be influenced by the compatibility between what professionals think clients need and what the clients actually want, given the competitive pressures to recruit and retain customers in choice-based settings. Clients' needs and wants often point in the same direction, but this is not always the case. Lundström and Parding's (2011) study of reform in upper secondary schools in Sweden illustrates "clashing logics and clashing identities" among teachers. The teachers in the study said their pedagogical tasks were competing with new tasks related to market competition, such as marketing the school. They noted that the logic of the market was apparent in efforts to attract students. One teacher commented, "You have to adapt to the teenagers and what they want. Perhaps do a bit of selling as well, like give a subject that you might think doesn't give that much but might attract teenagers. And if you can make them learn other things, it might be worth giving a subject in styling, make-up, spa, or whatever you call it" (Lundström and Parding 2011, 7). Similarly, Cohen, Benish, and Shamriz-Ilouz (2016), in their examination of the practices of social workers in choice-based elderly care services, suggest the social workers' professional logic was filtered by the economic interests of their employers and the consumerist relations were regularly subject to the goal of profit maximizing.

As to the relational aspects, the compatibility of these regimes depends on the willingness of policy-makers to trust professionals to make and implement policy. For example, in the context of the U.S. program of No Child Left Behind (NCLB), Ladd (2012, 14) observes the NCLB has generated a range of undesirable side-effects—including a narrowing of the curriculum and "significant amounts of cheating by teachers due to an extreme pressure to raise student test scores." Thus, it seems that politicians introduce economic incentives because they do not trust professionals, but the dynamics created by these incentives and the entrepreneurial spirit they inspire might, in the longer run, result in the increasing mistrust of service users and undermine the trustworthiness of decision-making.

## Conclusion

The logics of accountability provide a useful prism through which to study accountability in an era of hybridization. Here, I have shed light on hybridity by systematically exploring the compatibility between the content and mechanisms of accountability regimes and the relational aspects that accompany them. The analysis of interaction in terms of level of compatibility—rather than conflict or tension—is more open conceptually. It allows us to identify instances when regimes undermine each other, but also when they are mutually reinforcing, and under what conditions.

This analysis shows that while much of the literature on accountability focuses on the mechanisms of accountability (the *how* question), the compatibility between regimes significantly depends on the content of accountability (the *for what* question). Regimes can be more compatible and even reinforce one another if the content of policy is compatible with the logic of the street-level actors or at least opens up a space for their norms and practices. For instance, policy rules can adopt professional norms and practices or allow professional discretion; performance indicators can be created to uphold public service norms, or policy-makers can make room in choice-based services for providers and consumers to negotiate individualized policies.

The analysis also highlights the importance of the relational posture of the parties. Accountability relations may adopt a range of attitudinal approaches from trust-based, collaborative, and flexible relationships at one end of the spectrum, to mistrustful, adversarial, and rigid relationships at the other end. For instance, in public-market and professional-market hybrids, relationships may follow the mistrustful logic of markets, which assumes the interests of the parties will conflict; alternatively, they may draw on stewardship theory, which is based on shared norms and trust rather than rigid monitoring and threats of punishment (Van Slyke 2006). This analysis reinforces the importance of trust as a central factor in accountability relations in both how the content of accountability is shaped and how it is enforced (Kagan 2010).

The importance of relational aspects and trust requires greater attention to the second-order question on the identity of the parties to the accountability relations. An overarching factor influencing the compatibility of accountability regimes seems to be the proximity of the institutional logics of the account holders to those of the account-givers. As the examples above illustrate, actors take identity and meaning from their institutional logics. Bureaucrats, managers, and social workers will each design and enforce accountability differently. Thus, the closer the institutional logics of account-holders and account-givers, the greater the likelihood that the content of accountability will be compatible, and the account holders will opt for a trust-based and collaborative approach to manage accountability relations.

The conceptual framework developed in this article can help to analyze hybrid structures, and it can also assist in the mission of designing more stable and effective accountability systems. However, since this is still a relatively new field, I have investigated these interactions in broad terms. Future research should go beyond dyadic interactions to allow a nuanced and multilevel understanding of each of these interaction categories, with increased attention to variations in policy fields and sectors. Further research is also needed on how street-level workers react to the web of interactions within which they need to meet multiple accountability commitments, as well as whether some accountability commitments are more prominent in decision-making than others and why (see Cohen, Benish, and Shamriz-Ilouz 2016; Klenk, this volume).

# References

Adler Michel. 2003. A socio-legal approach to administrative justice. *Law & Policy* 25 (4): 323–52.

Bardach, Eygene, and Robert Kagan. 1982. *Going by the book: The problem of regulatory unreasonableness*. Philadelphia, PA: Temple University Press.

Ben-Arieh, Asher. 2007. The child indicators movement: Past, present, and future. *Child Indicators Research* 1 (1): 3–16.

Benish, Avishai. 2018. The privatization of social services in Israel. In *The Privatization of Israel*, 173–200. New York, NY: Palgrave Macmillan.

Benish, Avishai. 2014a. Outsourcing, discretion, and administrative justice: Exploring the acceptability of privatized decision making. *Law & Policy* 36 (2): 113–33.

Benish, Avishai. 2014b. The public accountability of privatized activation–The case of Israel. *Social Policy & Administration* 48 (2): 262–77.

Benish, Avishai. 2010. Re-bureaucratizing welfare administration. *Social Service Review* 84 (1): 77–101.

Benish, Avishai, and David Levi-Faur. 2012. New forms of administrative law in the age of third-party government. *Public Administration* 90 (4): 886–900.

Benish, Avishai, and Paola Mattei. 2020. Accountability and hybridity in welfare governance. *Public Administration* 98 (2): 281–90.

Benish, Avishai, and Asa Maron. 2016. Infusing public law into privatized welfare: Lawyers, economists, and the competing logics of administrative reform. *Law & Society Review* 50 (4): 953–84.

Benish, Avishai, Dana Halevy, and Shimon Spiro. 2018. Regulating social welfare services: Between compliance and learning. *International Journal of Social Welfare* 27 (3): 226–35.

Binder, Amy. 2007. For love and money: Organizations' creative responses to multiple environmental logics. *Theory and Society* 36 (6): 547-571.

Mark Bovens, Robert Goodin, and Thomas Schillemans. 2014. Public accountability. *The Oxford handbook of public accountability* 1:1–20.

Brodkin, Evelyn. 2008. Accountability in street-level organizations. *International Journal of Public Administration* 31 (3): 317–36.

Brodkin, Evelyn. 2011. Policy work: Street-level organizations under new managerialism. *Journal of Public Administration Research and Theory* 21 (2): 253–77.

Buffat, Aurélien. 2013. Street-level bureaucracy and e-government. *Public Management Review* 17 (1): 149–61.

Christensen, Tom, and Per Lægreid, eds. 2017. Accountability relations in unsettled situations. In *The Routledge handbook to accountability and welfare state reforms in Europe*, 194–207. London: Routledge.

Clarke, John, and Janet Newman. 1997. *The managerial state: Power, politics and ideology in the remaking of social welfare*. Thousand Oaks, CA: SAGE Publications.

Cohen, Nissim, Avishai Benish, and Aya Shamriz-Ilouz. 2016. When the clients can choose: Dilemmas of street-level workers in choice-based social services. *Social Service Review* 90 (4): 620–46

Cowan, David, and Morag McDermont. 2006. *Regulating social housing: Governing decline*. London: Routledge Cavendish.

Dean, Hartley. 2015. *Social rights and human welfare*. New York, NY: Routledge.

Dias, Janice Jonshon, and S. Maynard-Moody. 2007. For-profit welfare: Contracts, conflicts, and the performance paradox. *Journal of Public Administration Research and Theory* 17 (2): 189–211.

Diller, Matthew. 2000. The revolution in welfare administration: Rules, discretion, and entrepreneurial government. *New York University Law Review* 75 (5) :1121–1220.

Evans, Tony. 2010. *Professional discretion in welfare services: Beyond street-level bureaucracy*. Farnham, UK: Ashgate.

Evans, Tony, and Peter L. Hupe, eds. 2020. *Discretion and the quest for controlled freedom*. London: Palgrave Macmillan.

Friedson, Eliot. 2001. *Professionalism: The third logic*. Chicago, IL: The University of Chicago Press.

Gilbert, Neil. 2013. Citizenship in the enabling state: The changing balance of rights and obligations. In *Social policy and citizenship: The changing landscape*, eds. Adalbert Evers and Anne-Marie Guillemard, 80–96. New York, NY: Oxford University Press.

Greer, Ian, and Virginia Doellgast. 2017. Marketization, inequality, and institutional change: Toward a new framework for comparative employment relations. *Journal of Industrial Relations* 59 (2): 192–208

Greve, Bent, ed. 2011. *Choice: Challenges and perspectives for the European welfare states*. New York, NY: John Wiley & Sons.

Halliday, Simon. 2004. *Judicial review and compliance with administrative law*. Oxford: Hart Publishing.

Hasenfeld, Yeheskel. 2010. *Human services as complex organizations*. Thousand Oaks, CA: SAGE Publications.

Jantz, Bastian, Tanja Klenk, Flemming Larsen, and Jay Wiggan. 2018. Marketization and varieties of accountability relationships in employment services: Comparing Denmark, Germany, and Great Britain. *Administration & Society* 50 (3): 321–45.

Jewell, Christopher. 2007. *Agents of the welfare state: How caseworkers respond to need in the United States, Germany, and Sweden*. New York, NY: Palgrave Macmillan.

Kagan, Robert. 2010. The organization of administrative justice systems: The role of political distrust. In *Administrative justice in context*, ed. M. Adler. Oxford: Hart Publishing.

Klenk, Tanja. 2020. Views from below: Inspectors' coping with hybrid accountabilities. *The ANNALS of the American Academy of Political and Social Science* (this volume).

Klenk, Tanja, and Nissim Cohen. 2019. Dealing with hybridization in street-level bureaucracy research. In *Research handbook on street-level bureaucracy*. Cheltenham, UK: Edward Elgar Publishing.

Ladd, Hellen F. 2012. Education and poverty: Confronting the evidence. *Journal of Policy Analysis and Management* 31 (2): 203–27.

Lægreid, Per, and Paola Mattei. 2013. Introduction: Reforming the welfare state and the implications for accountability in a comparative perspective. International Review of Administrative Sciences 79 (2): 197–201.

Lahat, Lahat, and Neta Sher-Hadar. 2019. Coping with the implementation challenge: Decision-making strategies and their implications for collaborative governance. In *Collaboration in public service delivery*. Cheltenham, UK: Edward Elgar Publishing.

Le Grand, Julian. 1991. Quasi-markets and social policy. *Economic Journal* 101 (408): 1256–67.

Le Grand, Julian. 2003. *Motivation, agency, and public policy: Of knights and knaves, pawns and queens*. New York, NY: Oxford University Press.

Lens, Vicki. 2013. Redress and accountability in US welfare agencies. In *Work and the Welfare State*, eds. E. Z. Brodkin and G. Marston. Washington, DC: Georgetown University Press.

Levi-Faur, David, and Sharon Gilad. 2004. The rise of the British regulatory state: Transcending the privatization debate. *Comparative Politics* 37 (1): 105–24.

Lundström, Ulf, and Karolina Parding. 2011. Teachers' experiences with school choice: Clashing logics in the Swedish education system. *Education Research International*. DOI: 10.1155/2011/869852.

Marston, Greg, and Catherine McDonald, eds. 2006. *Analysing social policy: A governmental approach*. Cheltenham, UK: Edward Elgar Publishing.

Mashaw, Jerry L. 2006. Accountability and institutional design: Some thoughts on the grammar of governance. Yale Law School, Public Law Working Paper No 116.

Mattei, Paola, ed. 2016. Public accountability and health care governance. *Public management reforms between austerity and democracy*. New York, NY: Palgrave MacMillan.

Mulgan, Richard. 2003. *Holding power to account: accountability in modern democracies*. New York, NY: Springer.

Mulgan, Richard. 2006. Government accountability for outsourced services. *Australian Journal of Public Administration* 65 (2): 48–58.

Munro, Eileen. 2004. The impact of audit on social work practice. *British Journal of Social Work* 34 (8): 1075–1095.

Osborne, David, and Ted Gaebler. 1992. *Reinventing government: How the entrepreneurial spirit is transforming the public sector*. Reading, MA: Addison-Wesley.

Paz-Fuchs, Amir. 2008. *Welfare to work: conditional rights in social policy*. New York, NY: Oxford University Press on Demand.

Phillips, Susan, and Steven Rathgeb Smith, eds. 2011. *Governance and regulation in the third sector: International perspectives*. New York, NY: Routledge.

Pollitt, Christopher, and Geert Bouckaert. 2017. *Public management reform: A comparative analysis-into the age of austerity*. New York, NY: Oxford University Press.

Power, Michael. 1997. *The audit society: Rituals of verification*. New York, NY: Oxford University Press.

Romzek, Barbara S. 2014. Accountable public services. In *The Oxford handbook public accountability*, eds. Mark Bovens, Robert Goodin, and Thomas Schillemans. New York, NY: Oxford University Press.

Romzek, Barbara S., and Jocelyn M. Johnston. 2005. State social services contracting: Exploring the determinants of effective contract accountability. *Public Administration Review* 65 (4): 436–49.

Sainsbury, Roy. 2008. Administrative justice, discretion and the "welfare to work" project. *Journal of Social Welfare and Family Law* 30 (4): 323–38.

Scott, Collin. 2000. Accountability in the regulatory state. *Journal of Law and Society* 27 (1): 38–60.

Skelcher, Chris, and Steven Rathgeb Smith. 2015. Theorizing hybridity: Institutional logics, complex organizations, and actor identities: The case of nonprofits. *Public Administration* 93 (2): 433–48.

Stirton, Lindsay, and Martin Lodge. 2001. Transparency mechanisms: Building publicness into public services. *Journal of Law and Society* 28 (4): 471–89.

Thornton, Patricia, Michael Lounsbury, and William Ocasio, eds. 2012. *The institutional logics perspective: A new approach to culture, structure, and process.* Oxford: Oxford University Press.

Van Berkel, Rik, and Paul Van der Aa. 2005. The marketization of activation services: a modern panacea? Some lessons from the Dutch experience. *Journal of European Social Policy* 15 (4): 329–43.

Van Berkel, Rik, Dorte Caswell, Peter Kupka, and Flemming Larsen, eds. 2017. *Frontline delivery of welfare-to-work policies in Europe: Activating the unemployed.* New York, NY: Taylor & Francis.

Van Slyke, David M. 2006. Agents or stewards: Using theory to understand the government-nonprofit social service contracting relationship. *Journal of Public Administration Research and Theory* 17 (2): 157–87.

Verhoest, Koen, and Paola Mattei. 2010. Welfare governance reforms and effects in the post-golden age. *Public Management Review* 12 (2): 163–71.

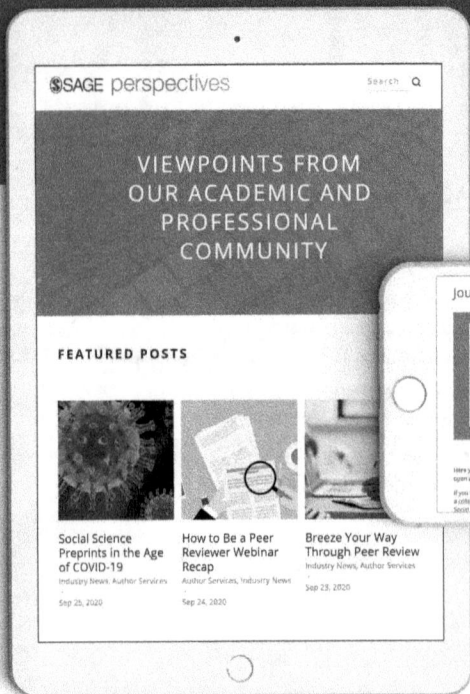

www.ingramcontent.com/pod-product-compliance
Lightning Source LLC
Chambersburg PA
CBHW060311030426
42336CB00011B/994